MOTOCROSS & OFF-ROAD
PERFORMANCE HANDBOOK

ERIC GORR

ACKNOWLEDGMENTS

Thanks to all the people who supported the first edition of this book in 1996, and especially to Lee Klancher at MBI Publishing Company, my editor and the visionary who recognized the need for books like this and the riding techniques book.

For the first two chapters of this book, Dave Antolak of TUF Racing gave me the use of his motorcycle shop, racing team, and mail-order business. That was very helpful for getting photos of used bikes and compiling information on the costs of repairs and on mail-order services. Robert and Matt Davis of Throttle Jockey provided the seat cover and graphics installation demonstration. Denny Calvert supplied his Honda XR and CR for the chapter on converting bikes for off-road racing.

The suspension chapter features advice from several people. George Quay and DJ Korzen of Pro Action provided spring charts, help with the definitions of terms, and the benefit of half a lifetime worth of suspension repair and tuning knowledge. Mark Hammond of MH Racing in England made available his excellent workshop and expertise during the preparation of the shock-rebuilding section. Jeremy Wilkey of MX-Tech gave me help on the tuning tips section.

The top-end chapter features the expertise of many people. Tom Turner of TSR and Curt Leaverton of VP Engineering provided me with PC design programs for two- and four-stroke engines, plus hours of telephone support and engineering consultation. Steve Johnson of Wiseco Piston Co. provided help on top-end engineering projects related to overboring and electroplating of cylinders. Sean Hilbert of

Red Cedar Engineering contributed some material for the piston section and supplied me with one of his excellent crankshaft-rebuilding tools for the crankshaft section. Sean also provided the drawings of the two-stroke engine for the basic two-stroke tuning section.

The lower-end rebuilding chapter features the expertise of these guys: Fred Bramblett and Scott Summers of Summers Racing Concepts for help on the XRs, and Jeff Fredette of Fredette Racing Products for help on the KDX models. The model tuning tips section also includes information gained from a number of people working at bike shops. Those shops and TUF Racing's technicians include Garry Borelli, Eric Bleed and Andy Stacy; Service Honda's Doug and Brad Goines; and MJ Church Racing's Richard Church. On the Internet, special thanks to the guys who helped refine the chapters through constructive criticism: Rich Rohrich, MXTuner, MikeeP., High Lord Gomer, OT and Bob Van Orden of DirtRider.Net.

Veteran photographer Brad Nordloff shot the excellent cover photo of the CR500AF supplied by Service Honda and built by AJ Wagoner. Aaron Vincer of Motorsports Park provided the background scenery. Most of all I'd like to thank my parents. My dad, John, for bringing home mechanical junks for me to disassemble and learn from, and my mom, Carolyn, for teaching me how to use a camera and encouraging me to write.

—Eric Gorr

First published in 2000 by MBI Publishing Company, 729 Prospect Avenue, PO Box 1, Osceola, WI 54020-0001 USA

Edited by Jack Savage
Designed by Tom Heffron
Layout by Jim Snyder

Library of Congress Cataloging-in-Publication Data

Gorr, Eric.
    Motocross & off-road performance handbook/Eric Gorr—2nd ed.
      p. cm. — (CyclePro)
    Rev. ed. of: Motocross and off-road motorcycle performance handbook. c1996.
    Includes index.
    ISBN 0-7603-0660-5 (pbk. : alk. paper)
      1. Trail bikes—Maintenance and repair. 2. Trail bikes—Performance. 3. Motorcycles, Racing—Performance. I. Gorr, Eric, Motocross and off-road motorcycle performance handbook. II. Title. III. Series.
TL441.G67   2000
629.227'5—dc21   00-063831

On the front cover: This 2000 CR500AF is a hybrid built by AJ Waggoner for Service Honda. Available for a mere $8,000, this power junkie special packs the punch of an open-classer into a CR250 aluminum frame. The CR500AF is the weapon of choice for Seth Enslow and Robbie Knievel. *Brad Nordloff*

On the back cover: Left: Bleeding air from your fork oil is key to properly setting the oil level. *Right, top:* Setting valve clearance is one of the tricks YZ400/426 owners have to learn. *Right, bottom:* A little epoxy applied to proper areas of the transfer ports boosts crankcase compression, giving you better low-end power.

Printed in the United States of America

CONTENTS

INTRODUCTION

The better the bike performs, the easier it is to meld with your bike. Whether that means faster lap times or just a better experience on the trail, performance is what this book is all about. By raising your awareness of how to get in touch with your bike's performance, you can learn to fix little problems before they become catastrophic. Learning how your bike works, and gaining a basic understanding of how to tune the engine and suspension to complement your riding demands, will enhance your dirt riding experience. Whether you are flying through the air, climbing an impossible hill, or just exploring the wilderness with your friends, dirt bikes are the most fun when they run right.

With each component of the motorcycle, I used my years of experience as a race mechanic and tuner to show you all the tricks that the shop manual doesn't tell you. I'll show you how to keep your stock bike performing its best, lending inside tips and techniques on everything from exhaust valves and changing fork oil to choosing tires and setting up your suspension. I'll also tell you how to modify your bike and create anything from a grunty torque beast for Supercross or enduro to a top-end monster capable of gobbling straights on motocross or desert courses.

The book is designed for readers with a wide range of mechanical skill levels. Tasks like suspension set-up, jetting, and gearing are important for the rider to understand well, and I cover these things thoroughly. I'll also take you step-by-step through tasks like top-end rebuilding, brake repair, linkage maintenance, and so on. You might find that as you gain confidence and try more, you will grow as a mechanic. The great thing about that is the more you do yourself, the more you have to spend on your bike!

Of course, there are always things that need to be sent out. Porting is a good example of a job best left to the pros (although I'll show you a few tricks if you want to give it a shot). Suspension revalving is another thing the novice tuner is better off avoiding. For this situation, I've provided some links on my Web site for tuners in the United States and Europe.

You'll also benefit from my 25 years of answering questions about dirt bikes. Every day I answer email from my Web site and Internet news groups and forums. For each section of the book, I've chosen the most common questions and compiled them into a list of frequently asked questions (FAQs). When you have a problem, you probably aren't the first one, and the answer may be in the FAQs! I've also built an archive of tech questions and a search engine for sorting through it. That information is posted on my Web site.

You may find it helpful to keep a journal along with this book, to write down questions and file copies of the answers. Recording race day data and suspension settings can also help you get your bike set up properly and, ultimately, get around the track or through the woods faster.

The information presented in this book assumes that you know the limitations of your mechanical abilities. If you lack the specialized knowledge or tools needed to do the job right, then have the sense to trust the work to a qualified technician. Remember that it costs twice as much to fix it the second time!

Thanks for purchasing this revised edition of *Motocross and Off-Road Performance Handbook*. The original PHB was a best seller and won a Bronze Medal for "How-To" books in the International Automotive Awards. Considering how much dirt bikes have evolved over the past five years, I'm pleased to be able to update the book.

Ever since the original book was published in September 1996, I've supported the readers' questions and comments by email, telephone, and participation on Internet news groups like rec.motorcycles.dirt and forums like DirtRider.Net. By answering questions posed by readers, I've been able to refine the old material, build new tuning tips, and gain insight into what readers want from a performance handbook.

For this revised edition, editor Lee Klancher and I have tried to decide what irrelevant material we could cut out to make room for new information. Based on informal surveys, we found that people wanted more of the basic set-up tips, suspension tuning info, and model tuning tips on current bikes.

This is the first motorcycle book to be supported by its own Web site. The Web site provides updates on the book, new products, and a master archive of readers' questions and answers, and links to other dirt biking Web sites.

www.eric-gorr.com

GETTING STARTED

TYPES OF DIRT BIKING

There are several different types of dirt-bike sports, each with bikes designed especially for the demands of the application. Off-road sports include enduro, hare scrambles, cross-country, dual sport, and desert. Motocross related sports also include stadium and freestyle. Some of the more off beat sports include dirt track, grass drag, hillclimb, and trials. Here is a guide to the different types of dirt bikes and some things to consider when looking for used bikes to buy.

Off-Road Bikes

Choosing an off-road bike is greatly dependent on the terrain of your local riding areas as well as the laws regarding off-road use. Recent government legislation restricts the use of two-stroke engines in dirt bikes manufactured after December 31,

1997. That means that on government owned off-road vehicle parks (ORV), you can't buy a license tag (green sticker) for two-stroke dirt bikes of a 1998 model year and newer. You can ride older bikes in those areas as well as four-stroke bikes.

If you're looking for a well-rounded bike that you can ride on the street to the trails, then consider a dual sport bike. Models like the KTM LC, Suzuki DR, Kawasaki KLR, and Honda XRL are street-licensable dirt bikes. These bikes aren't designed for serious off-road use but they can be adapted for competition in enduro, hare scrambles, cross-country, or desert racing.

If you're committed to off-road competition including MX, and not interested in street riding, then consider an enduro bike. Models like the Honda XR, KTM XC, Suzuki DRS, Yamaha WR, and Kawasaki KDX are versatile, strong-built bikes that hold their value better than a modified dual sport bike.

For off beat sports like dirt track, hillclimb, or freestyle you'll need to make varying modifications in order to adapt the bike and conform with the rules of competition. Sports like trials require a very specialized and expensive bike. Most trials clubs have a competition class for dual sport bikes. Overall a dual sport bike is a great way to get into dirt biking and when you get serious about a particular sport, you'll probably want to keep your old dual-sport bike for a spare.

EVALUATING USED DIRT BIKES

Whether you are figuring out what to do to modify your own machine or buying a used bike, the best way to start is to use the following simple tests to evaluate the bike. Here is a list of the major components of a dirt bike, and some tips on evaluating and estimating the cost of repairs. Use chapter six's sections on model-specific tuning tips to help you focus on the characteristic mechanical problems of the model you are looking to buy. Those sections have subsections on flaws, fixes, and best value mods. The section on mods can help you evaluate the aftermarket accessories on the bike. Some aftermarket products really give performance value, but others can actually cause mechanical failures.

Spark Plug

A spark plug is a record of the engine's condition. Large globules of aluminum melted to the plug denote that the piston is disintegrating because of a crankcase air leak. A glazed finish on the plug denotes sand that passed through the air filter and has probably ruined the engine. Heavy carbon build-up denotes a leaking crankshaft seal on the clutch side. A bike with this problem will have white smoke billowing out the exhaust pipe and oil oozing from the exhaust manifold.

Compression Test

The correct way to perform a compression test is to thread the gauge into the spark plug hole, hold the throttle wide open, hold the kill button on, and kick the engine over until the gauge needle peaks. An 80, 125, 200, or 500cc bike should have 150–190 psi. A 250cc bike should have 170–230 psi (these numbers are for sea level). If the compression gauge reading is far below these numbers, the top end will need to be rebuilt. Prices for this vary based on the condition of the cylinder bore. Modern plated cylinders cost $200 to electroplate, while steel-lined cylinders cost $40 to bore. Piston kits and gasket sets range from $50 to $100.

Crankshaft

Remove the flywheel cover and look for rust or corrosion on the flywheel. That indicates that water either entered the side cover or condensation was allowed to occur. Look for an oily residue below the flywheel. This denotes a crankshaft seal leak. A new seal only costs about $5 and can be replaced externally except on KX 80s, 250s, and 500s. On those bikes, the cases must be split, which can be very expensive. To check the main bearings, grasp the flywheel and try to move it back and forth and up and down. If you feel any movement, the engine's lower end needs to be rebuilt. Normal service intervals for lower ends are once per season on 60cc to 125cc engines and every two to three years on 200cc to 500cc engines. That is assuming that the owner serviced the air filter regularly and always mixed oil in the fuel. The average cost to have a motorcycle shop rebuild the lower end is $300–500.

Air Filter

You can tell a lot about how a guy maintains his bike just by looking at the air filter. If he neglects the filter, he probably never works on the rest of the bike. Check the filter for tears that could have allowed dirt to enter the engine.

Frame

Lay the bike on its side and inspect the underside of the frame. Look for smashed

TUF Racing in Illinois is a dirt-bike dealer that offers new and used bikes and parts by mail order.

frame tubes, a cracked shock clevis (common on YZs), and bent link bars. Smashed frame tubes and broken motor mounts look expensive to fix, but a good fabricator can splice in a new tube or weld a mount if you strip the entire frame down. Frame repairs range from $50 to $200. New frames cost from $500 to $800.

Suspension Components

Check the rear shock for oil leaks. If the seal is leaking, then the gas bladder may be punctured. The average cost of rebuilding a shock is $150 for parts and service. Look closely at the shock shaft. If the chrome has peeled, has deep scratches, or is blue from overheating, then the shaft will need to be replaced or re-plated. The average cost of this is $150 more than standard rebuilding.

Hold the front brake and compress the forks. Does oil ooze out of the seals? Are the forks difficult to compress? Check the fork tubes and the aluminum sliders for rock dents. Rock dents in the tubes can be incredibly expensive to repair. Each of the four fork tubes can retail for as much as $300!

Coolant System

Remove the radiator cap and check the fluid level. A low level means the system has a leak. If the color of the coolant is brown, the head gasket may be leaking internally. That means combustion pressure has leaked into the coolant system. The worst-case scenario is when the leak has caused erosion on the top edge of the cylinder. That costs $300 to repair and new cylinders cost from $300 to $850. If the color of the coolant is gray and foaming, that indicates that the water pump seal is blown. The blown seal allows transmission oil to mix with the coolant. Check the radiators for crash damage. Radiators can be welded or sealed with epoxy when minor damage occurs. Check the side of the cylinder head where the head-stay is mounted. Look for white or green residue of leaking coolant. This is common on older CR250s and all KXs. This indicates that the head gasket is leaking externally. Cylinder head surfacing costs about $50 and a gasket or O-ring set is about $25. The common cause of external leaks is excessive forces transferring from the top shock mount through the head stay brackets. Check the

TYPES OF DIRT BIKES

PeeWee 50cc automatic MX

MX bike converted to dirt track

Enduro/Dual-Sport

Desert/Rally

Trials

Side-Hack MX

Mini-MX

rear-suspension linkage on a bike with an external leak, chances are the bearings are seized or worn.

Swingarm and Linkage

Sit on the bike and bounce up and down to compress and rebound the rear suspension. Do you hear a screeching noise? Is the rear suspension seized in an extended or compressed position? This would indicate that the bearings, bushings, and seals need to be replaced because they weren't greased. The cost of this repair could vary greatly. The average cost of just the bearing parts is $125.

Grasp the linkage with your hand and try to move it back and forth to feel for free-play. If the linkage is bent or the bearings have disintegrated and elongated the mounting holes, then the linkage will need to be replaced. The average cost of the linkage is $100 without any bearing parts.

Wheels and Brakes

Put the bike on a stand and grasp each wheel with your hands. Try to move the wheel from side to side with the axle held stationary. If you feel any movement, then the wheel bearings are worn out. This could cost as little as $30 for new bearings, or the hub could be damaged from riding the bike with the bad bearings. Hubs cost about $180 each. Check the surface of the brake discs for deep scratches or signs of overheating. Discs can be resurfaced for as little as $25. Bent front discs on enduro bikes are common. New discs cost about $130. All brake pads have wear-indicator lines scribed into the sides of the pad for quick visual checking. If you can't see the lines, then the pads need to be replaced. Average cost is $30 per set.

Drivetrain

The drivetrain consists of the clutch, transmission, chain, and sprockets. The trans oil can give clues to mechanical problems. Dip a strip of white paper in the trans oil. If the oil sample is gray and bubbly, then the water pump seal is blown, and the coolant has polluted the trans oil. You can confirm this problem by test riding the bike. The clutch action will be prone to slipping when loaded and dragging when engaged.

Take a compression test on every used bike that you're considering for purchase.

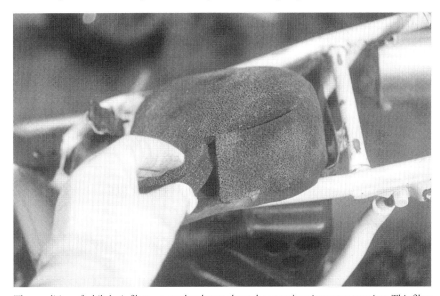

The condition of a bike's air filter can speak volumes about the owner's maintenance practices. This filter is torn, indicating that the engine may have ingested dirt, causing accelerated wear.

The chain and sprockets can be visually checked for wear. The chain can be checked by putting the bike on a stand so you can rotate the wheel and check the chain slack at several different points. If the slack varies greatly, then the chain is worn out. The average cost of replacing the chain and sprockets is $115.

The cost to replace the water pump shaft, seals, and bearings is about $90 and labor is about 1.5 hours.

TIPS ON TEST RIDING

Clutch

Pull in the clutch lever and put the bike in first gear. Rev the engine. Does the bike oroop forward? If oo, thon tho olutoh baolict may need to be replaced. When you rev the engine does the clutch slip? If so, then the plates and springs may need to be replaced. That can cost between $55 and $90. The price of clutch baskets varies from $150 to $350.

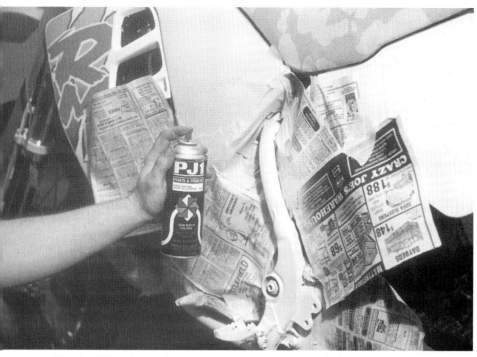

PJ makes OEM color matched spray paint. Cosmetic changes are the best investment when prepping a bike for sale.

Throttle Response

Ride the bike in second gear at 1/4 throttle. Snap open the throttle quickly. Does the bike bog or die completely? If so, then the engine may have a problem as simple as a clogged pilot jet or a major problem such as a crankcase air leak.

Transmission

Ride the bike in third gear. Accelerate while gently applying the rear brake. Does the clutch slip? Does the transmission pop out of gear? Third gear is the most abused gear in the transmission. If the transmission pops out of gear, the shift forks may be bent or the engagement dogs on the gears may be worn. This is a common problem on RM250s and KX500s. Repair costs range from $300 to $550 if a motorcycle shop performs the repairs.

Brakes

Apply the brakes separately. Does the lever or petal pulsate as you apply the brake? This means that the disc is bent or warped and needs to be replaced. Does the front brake have a spongy feeling? If so, then the problem could be as simple as

trapped air in the system or as major as a worn master cylinder. Check the brake line for leakage. Even if the guy cleaned the leak, brake fluid will damage the plastic cover on the brake hose.

Crankshaft

Put the transmission in neutral. Rev the engine and let off the throttle. Does the bike make a loud shuttering vibration? Do you feel the vibration transfer through the foot pegs and handlebars? If so, then the engine's lower end may need to be rebuilt.

Once you've been through the bike, you can calculate how much it will cost to bring the bike back to tip-top condition. At this point, you can decide whether or not it's worth fixing your bike or begin to budget. If you are looking at a used bike, you can determine how much you are willing to pay for the bike (see section on buying a used bike later in this chapter).

WHERE TO SPEND YOUR MONEY

The road to better performance is paved with pitfalls. Simply throwing money at your bike won't make it faster. Even if it does, it might become so hard to ride that you go

slower despite the fact that your bike is faster. The key to performance mods is starting with the biggest problem areas, which may turn out to be swingarm and steering head bearings rather than engine or suspension work. Once you have your bike working the way it should, you can start to intelligently improve the systems that need the most help. In this way, you'll spend less money and get the results you're after.

The place to start is evaluating your bike (this is the same process you go through if you're buying a used bike). Check all the basic systems and figure out what needs help. Then take an inventory of your checkbook, and decide how much more you can spend. Now you can map out a path to better performance.

In order to make your bike perform better, you need a clear understanding of what it's doing well and where it needs help. Certainly, you'll have some basic ideas already: "It needs more low end to get a better drive out of corners," or "It seems to need more top end because I'm getting passed on long straights and uphills." In order to get more specific, though, you should start a log and keep notes on your bike. When you notice a problem, make a note of it. When something is working well, write that down. Keep track of when you service and replace things or if you inspect a component. Use the suspension data log (see chapter three) to track what suspension settings you're using and how the suspension works in different conditions. After a while, you'll find you have a very specific idea of what works and what doesn't on your bike.

Perhaps you've looked over the latest models of dirt bikes and decided that those bikes aren't that much better than the bike you're riding. And maybe you're in the market to upgrade your current bike to be competitive with the new bikes. If you are considering investing in rebuilding services or performance mods, then use this section as a guide to determining a budget and priority list of upgrades. The most important thing to remember is to focus your resources on improving the mechanical condition of your bike before spending your money on the "wants." A new pipe won't make up for the horsepower you lose to a worn top end, and a suspension revaluing can't cure the instability found with shot steering head or swingarm bearings.

BIKE EVALUATION CHART

Use the following chart to make notes as you evaluate a bike, either your own for your modification plan or a bike you are considering buying. Note if each system is OK, and refer to the text for more specific information on each test.

Spark plug condition?

Compression Test:_____psi

Crankshaft (engine revs smoothly?)

    Oil under flywheel cover?

    Main bearings tight?

Air filter condition?

Frame condition

    Frame tubes?

    Motor mounts?

    Shock mount?

    Linkage mount?

Suspension

    Rear shock oil leaks?

    Rear shock shaft OK?

    Front fork seals?

    Front fork tubes?

Coolant system

    Fluid level?

    Fluid clear-green color?

    Radiators straight?

    Radiators leaking?

Swingarm and Linkage

    Suspension compresses
       smoothly and silently?

    Rear linkage tight?

Wheels and Brakes

    Hubs tight?

    Brake discs smooth?

    Brake pads fresh?

Drivetrain

    Transmission oil clean?

    Chain and sprockets fresh?

Test Ride

    Throttle response smooth?

    Transmission OK?

    Brakes smooth and positive?

    Crankshaft balanced?

Approximate Repair Costs

Note: These costs are average for a Japanese full-size bike. You may find you pay a bit more or less for your particular model, especially if you have a European bike (more) or a mini. Still, this should give you a ballpark figure to use when estimating repair costs or evaluating a used bike. Note that the labor is listed in times. Call your local shop to get an hourly rate, and you can figure costs.

Component	Parts	Labor (hours)
Rebuild top end	$100–150	2.0
Rebuild bottom end	100–150	4.0
New exhaust pipe	125–300	0.3
Carburetor rebuild	25–35	0.5
New radiator	80–200	0.8
New chain and sprockets	80–150	1.5
Replace fork seal	20–30	1.0
Install new fork tubes	200–300	1.0
Rear shock rebuild	125–150	2.0
New rear shock	400–650	1.0
Replace brake pads (per caliper)	20–25	0.3
Brake rotors	150	0.6
New hubs	150–300	–
New spoke sets (per wheel)	90	–
Replace and true wheel	–	1.3
New tires	50–100	0.3

Also, you can keep track of questions that arise and forward them to me. This is the first book in off-road motorcycling that offers you a reader service for answering your questions on dirt bike repair and tuning. Refer to the appendix for ways to contact me with your questions.

Aftermarket accessories such as radiator and tank graphics, seat covers, and colored plastic are one of the biggest temptations and they won't do you any good if the engine is ready to fall apart!

In order to evaluate the condition of your bike, you have to be very objective. Most guys tend to deny certain mechanical problems exist because they don't want to deal with fixing the problem. Make a list of the maintenance tasks that you've been avoiding. Then think about the hidden problems that your bike might have. Review the sections of this book that describe how to inspect and evaluate

components such as the crankshaft, transmission, brakes, shock, etc. In the end, your list should be tiered, starting with maintenance tasks, followed by performance mods, and ending with cosmetic changes.

If you are considering some performance mods for your bike, you've got to ask yourself questions about your riding demands. Are you having problems keeping up with lesser-skilled riders because your bike doesn't handle right? If so, then you should browse chapter three—in particular, the section on revalving. That chapter also contains a suspension troubleshooting guide that helps you determine what changes will be needed to the forks and/or shock.

Regarding engine mods, you also have to ask yourself what types of riding demands you have. Consider things like powerband choices, fuel economy, the type of fuel, the altitude where you ride, noise restrictions, and engine longevity. Chapter four contains key information on how changes to engine components affect the powerband. Also, check out the model-specific tuning tips in chapter six for recommendations on the best value mods for your dirt bike.

SHOPPING FOR REBUILDING & TUNING SERVICES

The popularity of mail-order engine rebuilding and tuning services has increased in recent years. Most people who live in rural areas don't have any dirt bike shops near them. Buying by mail order offers them access to experts.

The tasks of rebuilding dirt bike components such as shocks, engines, and forks are fairly complex for the average franchised-dealership mechanic. Sometimes you need to look to specialists. There are companies that specialize in crank rebuilding; porting; cylinder boring, sleeving, and electroplating; suspension; and wheels There are several specialists in each category so you'll have plenty to choose from nationwide. Read on for como tips on evaluating the best specialists to suit your needs and budget.

If you have already read chapter three's section on suspension-component rebuilding, then you know how difficult and tedious suspension servicing can be. The average cost of

Before

After
From Rat to Racer. This 1988 Yamaha YZ250 was bought for $400 and sold for considerably more. Cosmetic changes like new plastic, seat cover, graphics, frame paint, and tires were all that was needed to boost the value of this used dirt bike.

$60 to perform basic service to a set of forks or a shock doesn't seem very expensive. Buyer beware—not all suspension technicians do the same quality work. Technicians aren't regulated by the manufacturers, and it doesn't take a big investment in tools to get started in suspension servicing. As a consequence, the motorcycle industry is glutted with suspension-service companies. How can you choose a suspension technician that you can trust? Here are some tips on screening technicians in order to find the best one to suit your ongoing suspension servicing needs.

Screening Tips for Rebuilding and Tuning Services

1. Make a list of at least five potential shock service companies, preferably a mixture of local and national mail-order companies.
2. Determine what range of services the technicians offer—suspension oil changing, seal and bushing replacement, shaft chroming, and revalving; engine cylinder repair, crank rebuilding, porting, electrical, and carbs.
3. Make a survey list of prices for services and ask what is included. Examples: labor, oil, parts, or cleaning supplies. Inquire about a complete breakdown of the costs. Some companies charge extra for rush service, and some charge excessive shipping and handling fees.
4. Ask about technical support. Some companies provide free support materials in the form of booklets and videos; other companies direct technical phone calls to a toll 900 number. These are things that must be considered when comparing costs for services.
5. Ask about turnaround times on services. Consider the time it takes to ship your package there and back.
6. Ask what information you need to supply with your parts. The most important things are your name, address, city, postal code, telephone number, and the best time to call you.

Additional Information

In order for a technician to do a proper job, he may need information about your riding demands and the condition of your bike. If the suspension is being revalved, copy and complete the suspension data log in this chapter. The more information you can provide to your suspension technician, the better he can tune your suspension components.

Pricing Methods

The last thing you should be concerned with is the price. A reputable technician will charge a fair price for high-quality work. Don't

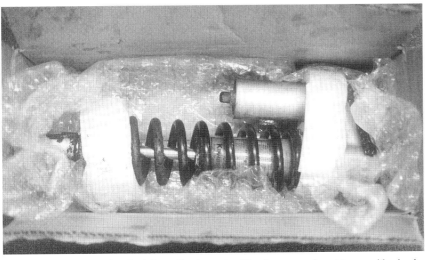

This is the best way to pack a shock for mail-order service. Tape foam around sensitive areas like the clevis and compression adjuster. Bubble wrap or newspaper makes good packing material.

make the mistake of rating technicians by price. Oftentimes, novice technicians will set high prices because it takes them longer to do a job than an expert. Some companies set their prices based on volume. In the motorcycle business there is absolutely no connection between price and quality. Prices for mail-order services vary based on factors such as the average price published in magazines. If a company spends a lot of money on race teams and support programs, their prices are bound to be a little higher.

Packaging Parts
for Mail-Order Service

If you've made the decision to send your engine or suspension components to a mail-order company, then you will need to package the parts carefully. Here is a checklist of how to package your parts for mail-order service:

1. Start by getting a strong cardboard box that is about 1.5 times larger than the part you are sending.
2. Leave the engine or suspension component assembled, especially engine parts. Those parts are heavy, and if they bump up against one another they could get damaged. If you are sending a shock, don't bother removing the shock spring. The difference in shipping weight doesn't reflect much in the shipping price. If the shock has a remote reservoir, don't loosen the banjo bolt that connects the hose to the reservoir.

The suspension technician won't know where to position the hose when he tightens it to complete his work.
3. Center the part in the box and tightly pack crumbled newspaper around the part. Styrofoam peanuts don't offer good impact resistance, and they are difficult to pick out of the part. If you are sending a cylinder, make sure you protect the sleeve that protrudes out of the bottom of the cylinder. I recommend using a four-inch PVC cap fitting to protect the sleeve. Those are available from any hardware store, located in the plumbing department.
4. Put a letter in the box with your name and address information. You will need to include your telephone number and the best time to call, just in case the technician has any specific questions about your parts.
5. Ship the box by UPS and insure the package for the retail value of the parts. Insurance is cheap, at about 30 cents per $100.

Special Packaging
for Engines and Forks

If you are sending a set of forks for service, you will need a special box. A box that is rectangular and 40 inches long. Look to your local auto parts dealers. Ask for a box used to package parts such as mufflers, suspension control arms, and torsion bars. Even if you have to pay $10 for a used box, it's still

worth it if the box prevents the forks from being damaged in transit.

If you are sending an entire engine, put it in a plastic milk crate first, then into a cardboard box. Always drain the engine fluids. It is illegal to knowingly send flammable liquids through the post without the proper labels.

Personal Suspension Tuners

When your suspension is tuned properly, it will make you a more competitive racer and your bike safer to ride. I recommend that you find a suspension technician with whom you can develop a long-term working relationship. Everyone has questions on suspension tuning. Once you develop a rapport with a technician by purchasing his services, you can then ask his advice on tuning. Take care not to abuse this privilege! Suspension tuners spend a lot of time developing their proprietary knowledge without pay. You may think they charge a lot of money for revalving, but consider this: When you call to ask a basic question, he has to stop working to answer your free question.

Most technicians work on commission, so they are only earning money when working, not talking! Try not to waste their time by asking questions that are already answered in this book. Let this book educate you so you can ask important advice from your tuner. To get the most benefit from your tuning questions, keep a logbook of all the current settings. A good tuner will need settings data before he can make an informed suggestion as to how to fix a tuning problem. The best type of information that you can provide to a suspension tuner is a video tape of you riding your bike on the sections of terrain where handling problems occur. Refer to the section on video suspension tuning in chapter three.

BUYING A USED DIRT BIKE

Buying a used dirt bike can be very risky because the most expensive components to repair are the ones that are most difficult to examine. First, use the section earlier in this chapter on evaluating a used bike. It gives you a guide to examining a used dirt bike and estimating the cost of repairs, so you can gain bargaining leverage with the seller.

Too Old to Fix

Question: I have a 1971 Yamaha CT175 with a problem in the engine. When I let off the gas it acts like I just turned the key off. I tried taking spacers out of the oil injector (it fouls plugs bad, too). But it had no effect; it still makes a cloud of blue smoke when I gas it. The engine bogs out when I let off the gas. I have also tried bending the float tab so it won't let so much gas in the float bowl, but it didn't work. Can you help?

Answer: If the engine kills when you let off the throttle, the pilot jet might be clogged. Set the float level back to stock, with the levers parallel to the float-bowl gasket surface. The main bearings are probably worn on your old bike. The oil is coming from the transmission. Disabling the oil pump is a bad idea. That engine needs a pre-mix ratio of at least 30:1 if the oil pump is disabled. Consider finding a newer dirt bike. That bike would cost you a fortune to repair, even if you could get the OEM parts.

My First Dirt Bike

Finally, after years of pain and suffering, I recently found my way to purchase a used bike. It's a 1984 RM250 and it seems to be in pretty good shape (it looks better than a lot of 1990s bikes I saw). Now that I actually have a bike, I have a few questions that I would like to ask you.

Question One: When I rode the bike before I decided to buy it, the bike would cut off if you didn't give it any gas. Granted that it had not been cranked in over a year, but it still would not idle. Otherwise, the bike rode great. The guy I bought the bike from told me about this beforehand. He said that it was just a characteristic of the 1984 RM250. He also said that it was a general trait of a two-stroke engine. I personally have not encountered this problem with any of the other two-stroke bikes I have ridden. Could you please give me some guidance on this? It sounds like it could be the jetting but I am not sure.

Answer: Many dirt bikes have carbs without idle circuits. I don't remember if that carb was like that. Is there a screw mounted horizontally on the left side of the carb? If the jetting is too lean or the carb jets are partially plugged, then that would cause the dying problem when the throttle is closed.

Question Two: The bike has never had a top-end job or had the air filter replaced. How soon should I have these things done?

Answer: As soon as possible! Especially the air filter. You should take apart the air box and seal the flange and box with weather-strip adhesive.

Question Three: The bike also has a very stiff clutch. Is this a characteristic of the 1984 RM250 or can something be done to smooth out the clutch action?

Answer: Try lubricating the cable. Also take apart the clutch and check the condition of the plates. The old oil that was in the bike while it was stored is causing a chemical reaction with the aluminum to form sulfuric acid. The acid may make the clutch plates and inner hub fuse together, making the clutch lever hard to pull in. If you clean the clutch hubs and plates with degreaser, that will probably solve the problem.

Good luck with your new bike and don't hurt yourself working on it!

The hardest thing about packing a set of forks for shipment is finding a box. Any of those packing franchises will have a long rectangular box. Take care to protect the ends of the forks with bubble wrap.

too expensive. In most cases the dealer just wants to get rid of the bikes because they take up space in the service department.

Where to Find Used Dirt Bikes

There are three main places to look for used dirt bikes: motorcycle shops, riding areas, and newspapers. Here is how each rate in time spent versus the value of the deal.

Few franchised dealers take trades on dirt bikes. However there are independent motorcycle shops who service, buy, and sell used dirt bikes. These are good places to buy your first dirt bike from because the shop owner will know some maintenance history on the bike. Another reason is you will need to know people who can answer your questions and supply you with reliable parts and services. Sometimes you can meet other enthusiasts at dirt bike shops and get leads on new places to ride.

Race tracks and riding areas are also good places to find used bikes, especially in the summer. In the heat of the summer, dirt bike riders tend to slack off riding and switch to water sports. Some riders get injured and desperately need to sell their bikes. Others may want to sell their bike in order to buy a

Rats and Race Bikes

Bikes that are trail ridden usually have more time on them than race bikes. Used race bikes purchased from expert riders are normally well maintained and have relatively little running time. Expert riders usually have several sponsors so their bikes may have extra accessories such as suspension or engine modifications, stiffer springs, good tires and brakes, or a special pipe. Don't be afraid of

race bikes, they can be a good bargain.

"Rats" are bikes that have been crashed and abused. Normally they will have loads of serious mechanical problems. If you are mechanically confident, you can do well to repair and resell these bikes. Normally you can buy these types of bikes very cheap. Sometimes franchised motorcycle dealers will have dirt bikes that were abandoned by their owners because the repair estimate was

This mobile workbench started life as a Kawasaki KX250 crate. I added bracing, castor wheels, a vise, bench top, 3-gallon parts washer, toolbox, mini air compressor, power strip, and some parts bins.

new bike when they are released in August. Often times, riders will show their bike at the race track. You can also ask racers if they know of anyone who wants to sell their bike. July and August are the best months to find deals on used bikes from private parties.

The newspapers can be real lame places to look for dirt bikes. In the Chicago area there is a popular consumer newspaper where many people advertise their bikes. This newspaper only charges for the ads if you sell your merchandise. Shopping for bikes in that paper can be frustrating because the advertisers either put a ridiculous asking price on the bike, or they have already sold the bike and are dodging the accounts-payable people from the newspaper. The best newspapers for used bikes in the U.S. and England are *Cycle News* and *Motorcycle News*. Their classified advertisers tend to be serious enthusiasts who price their bikes and parts to sell.

Negotiating a Fair Price for a Dirt Bike

Whenever you check out a used bike, try to contain your enthusiasm so you can look at the bike objectively and see all the hidden things that could cost a lot to repair. Copy and use the Bike Evaluation Chart when you check out a used bike. Also, clip ads from dirt bike magazines that feature discount prices

for OEM parts. That's good information to include with the Bike Evaluation Chart. Another excellent tool for negotiating the price of a used bike is a Blue Book guide. These guides are available from libraries or over the Internet. Although the prices listed for used dirt bikes do not reflect regional market values, they are a good indicator for determining if the seller is way out of line on the price of a bike. Normally the Blue Book value will be lower than the typical price you would be able to pay for a used bike; motorcycle shops use these guides to negotiate trade-in value.

Buyer Beware!

If you are looking for a 1980s-model Japanese or Italian dirt bike, consider that the price of OEM Japanese parts increases over time, and because of the acquisition of Husqvarna by Cagiva, some parts for those bikes aren't even available anymore.

Motorcycle are built with parts from several small sub-contractors and assembled by a motorcycle manufacturer. The manufacturers try to order all the parts for the bikes and parts stock, up front. If the manufacturer runs out of stock, they have to order a new batch of parts from the sub-contractor. Each sub-contractor has a minimum order for a parts run, so individual parts orders may accumulate for months before they are fulfilled.

Small parts runs mean that the individual part's price will be higher. Generally speaking, parts for older bikes are more expensive than parts for new bikes. Example: A cylinder for a 1986 CR250 is over $100 more expensive than a 1996 cylinder.

When Cagiva bought-out Husqvarna in the early 1980s, the OEM-parts-manufacturing network of sub-contractors had to be revised. All the blueprints and specs on the parts had to go through a bidding system in Italy before the contracts could be awarded to the small manufacturing firms. There are some models of Huskys that you can't even get parts for. For replacement parts, you would have to look to salvage companies. If you have one of these bikes sitting in a shed broken-down and waiting for a part, then your bike is worth more in pieces than together.

SELECTING THE RIGHT TOOLS

If you've made the commitment to spend more time working on your bike, you will need the right tools and workbench set up. This section is a guide to the different types of tools needed to maintain a dirt bike and rebuild the engine or the suspension components. Having the right tools can make a tough job less frustrating and save you money in labor.

Tool Lists

Here are lists of tools for different types of maintenance applications. You could spend a fortune on good tools or buy a bunch of cheap tools that wear out fast. Then, there is the rip-off factor to consider. If you have expensive tools, people will borrow them and conveniently forget to return them.

I believe in buying cheap tools for the items such as T-handles, wrenches, and screwdrivers. Craftsman (Sears) makes good-quality tools for a low price and you can get free replacements if the tools break. Harbor Freight company sells T-handle sets for under $10. Eventually, the socket corners will become rounded but overall they are a good bargain.

Light Maintenance

There are only about five different sizes of bolts on Japanese dirt bikes, so you don't

Race Tech makes the most complete line of suspension specialty tools.

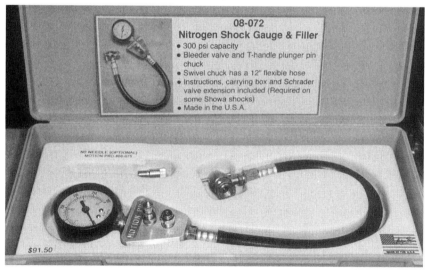

Motion Pro makes excellent gauges and testers like nitrogen charging regulators, compression testers, and pressure testers.

32mms; and Allen sockets in sizes of 2.5, 4, 5, 6, 8, and 10mms
2. Combination wrenches in sizes of 22, 24, 27, and 32mms
3. Needle-nose and channel lock pliers, side cutters, chain clamp, and tweezers
4. Hand-powered, electric, or pneumatic impact driver
5. Torque wrench, 3/8-inch
6. Ball-peen hammer
7. Rat-tail, big flat fine and triangular files; set of needle files; and a thread file
8. Large and small diameter round punches and a 1/4-inch-wide flat chisel
9. Parts washer
10. Miscellaneous tools: flywheel puller, chain breaker, magnet, flashlight, and propane torch

Engine Rebuilding

These are the tools you will need to rebuild a two-stroke engine. Include the tools from the light- and intensive-maintenance lists. You may also need some special tools that are brand and model specific, such as case splitters, flywheel pullers, or blind-side bearing removers.
1. Bearing and seal driver set
2. V-block and dial indicator
3. Machinist's square
4. Crankcase-splitting tool
5. Stud remover
6. Flywheel puller
7. Dial caliper
8. 10-ton Press

Suspension Rebuilding

These are the tools you will need to rebuild Showa and Kayaba forks and shocks:
1. Scribe set
2. Oil level setting tool
3. Nitrogen tank
4. Pressure regulator
5. Bladder cap remover
6. Allen socket, 14mm
7. Vise
8. Cartridge wrenches
9. Seal drivers
10. Bleeder rods
11. Digital caliper

Some excellent sources for special tools include Motion Pro, Race Tech, and White Brothers.

need a lot of tools to do light maintenance. Here is a list of the basic tools that you need in your tool collection:
1. Special wrenches: spark plug, spoke, rear-axle, and carb main jet wrenches
2. Combination wrenches in sizes of 8–19mms
3. T-handles in sizes of 8–14mms
4. Screwdrivers: one wide and one narrow flat-blade (10 and 3mms wide) and a #2 and a #3 Phillips driver
5. Allen-wrench combination set (2.5, 4, 5, and 6mms)

6. Miscellaneous tools: feeler gauge, air-pressure gauge, measuring tape, cable-lubing tool, chain brush, pliers, and plastic mallet

Intensive Maintenance

These are the tools you will need to do intensive maintenance on Japanese dirt bikes. Include all the tools listed in the light-maintenance list plus the following:
1. 3/8-inch ratchet wrench and sockets in six-point shallow socket sizes of 8, 10, 12, 14, 17, 19, 22, 24, 27, 30, and

HOW TO BUILD A MOBILE WORKBENCH

It's difficult to work on your bike when you don't have the tools. Reserving a small place in your garage, shed, or basement is too permanent for most people. What you need is a mobile workbench that you can move around to whatever place suits you best. On sunny days you don't want to be stuck in a dingy basement working on your bike, and what do you do when you go to the races? Move all your tools around like a gypsy? Here is an inexpensive solution to the problem of organizing your tools and workshop.

Think about the things you need for a workshop. You need a solid bench, a vise, a parts washer, and a safe place to store your tools and parts. I designed a mobile workbench that I could use in my shop or put into my van for use at the races. I started with a steel motorcycle crate that I picked from the garbage at a local motorcycle shop. These types of crates are ideal because they are fastened together with bolts and are very sturdy. Next, I bolted wheels to the bottom so I could pack a lot of weight in it and still move it around easily.

Then I increased the rigidity and made it more secure by bolting sides and a bench top to the crate. I bought a stainless steel sink from a building supply store so I could rebuild engines or suspension components in it without making a mess. Then I positioned a large vise over the sink so I could hold the engine or suspension in place while I worked on it. The next thing I needed was a parts washer. I mounted a three-gallon mini parts washer (Harbor Freight or Enco) under one basin of the sink. Once you clean parts you need to blow them dry with air, so I bought a 1/2-horsepower electric compressor and linked it to a five-gallon air tank for storage. This little unit makes enough pressure and has enough volume to pop the bead on tires. There was so much space left in the motorcycle crate that I added storage shelves and bins, and still had enough room to mount a toolbox. Because I had some expensive tools housed in the crate, I made it secure by adding flip up sides with hasps so I could fit a lock. The sides of my mobile workbench were so large and blank that I just had to fill them up with stickers from my friends' businesses.

This is a view of the immaculate workshop training facility of American Honda. Honda Pro Mechanics attend a weeklong course covering every aspect of maintenance of the CR line of dirt bikes. Retired factory race tuners teach the course.

So there you have it! Next time you are scrounging through your messy garage looking for a 10mm T-handle, or you just had your toolbox stolen from a race track, think about this simple inexpensive mobile workbench.

ENVIRONMENTALLY FRIENDLY CLEANING

Cleaning is a part of dirt biking. Having the right kit can make it easy to maintain your bike. Choosing the right chemicals and cleaning methods can be environmentally conscious and safer for your health. Many of the maintenance tasks that you'll need to perform on your bike revolve around a parts washer. You'll use it to do preliminary cleaning like degreasing. You can buy the components of the parts washer, the tank and the chemicals, but the disposal of the chemicals can be the expensive part. Companies like Safety Kleen offer rental on parts washers, a variety of different chemicals, and the disposal service. Their services are fair, about $80 for solvent and the disposal. That's about the same amount that it would cost you to either buy the solvent or dispose of it legally.

The cleaning chemicals used in parts washers are either mineral spirits solvents or alkaline detergents. Some areas of the country prohibit mineral spirit solvents because of air pollution or flammable considerations. The alkaline detergents are advertised as biodegradable, but don't be fooled into thinking that you can just pour it down the drain when its spent. As soon as you clean an oily part in it, it's contaminated and fits into a different waste category. The alkaline detergents tend to be harsher than mineral spirit solvents on unprotected skin. In fact, some solvents have lanolin, a skin moisturizer, mixed in with them. Solvents are also graded in flash points. Generally speaking the higher the flash point the better the cleaning action. Most local fire departments have the right to inspect your parts washer and specify what type of chemicals you use, the flash point temperature, and the type of fusible link fitted to the tank's lid. Fusible links are used on all dedicated parts washers. They are built into the hinge of the lid and will melt if the solvent catches fire, closing the lid and smothering the fire.

Gloves should always be used when cleaning parts in solvents or detergents. You don't have to wear big clumsy gloves anymore; the latest thing is nitrile gloves. They fit like a second set of skin. Over the years my skin has become hypersensitive to solvents and detergents, yet the tactile nitrile gloves keep me from breaking out in a rash.

BASIC MAINTENANCE

The best way to extract maximum performance from your bike is to maintain it well. It's just that simple. Maintenance is generally economical and doesn't require a ton of time. It can, however, make the difference between the front and back of the pack or a great ride and being left stranded in the woods.

This chapter covers the myriad maintenance tasks that you will need to perform to your bike on a frequent basis. In addition to explaining simple maintenance tasks and enabling you to diagnose and repair common problems, this section is packed with tips and techniques not found in factory service manuals or even the off-road magazines. At the end of nearly every section there is a subsection titled "Frequently Asked Questions." These FAQs will help you expand your mechanical experience by learning from others.

DIRT BIKE CLEANING TECHNIQUES

Cleaning a bike is just blasting the hell out of it with a power washer, right? Not quite. Actually, cleaning a dirt bike takes a lot of care because you can do more damage by cleaning it than by leaving it a muddy mess. Dirt bikes trap dirt and water. Compulsive cleaners tend to chase dirt with the power washer and can sometimes force dirt and water into areas where it can damage expensive engine components. When washing a bike, a bucket of water and a wise selection of brushes are just as effective as a power washer. If you routinely use a power washer, deflect the dirt away from the bike rather than forcing it into crevices.

Here is a step-by-step guide to cleaning a dirt bike:
1. Start by scraping off the big clods of mud under the fenders, on the tires, and around the engine.
2. Remove the seat, air filter, and chain. Stuff a rag in the intake air boot or buy a Twin Air filter cover and fasten it in place. Cap the end of the silencer with a rubber plug to prevent water from entering the pipe.
3. Use a strong degreaser like Formula 409 on the oily areas of the bike like the swingarm and crankcases.
4. Don't spray the brakes, fork and shock seals, electrical connections, chain, or the seat with detergent—strong detergents are alkaline and work similar to acids in the way they corrode certain materials. For example, alkalines can break down the bonding agent in the brake pads causing them to disintegrate quicker. The electrical connections can corrode and cause greater resistance and an increase in voltage which may contribute to the premature failure of these expensive parts.

Pressure washers are either electric or gas powered and are available from hardware stores. Remove the seat, side panels, and radiator scoops to gain access to areas where dirt can accumulate.

5. Clean the outside of the seat with a brush and be careful about soaking it—the seat foam can absorb water like a sponge. The water will cause the seat foam to break down and lose its cushion effect.

After you clean the bike you should spray certain parts with some chemicals. Remove the magneto cover and spray the flywheel and coils with non-chlorinated brake cleaner. Spray the disc brake rotors too. This will remove the dirt and water. Spray steel parts with WD40 or LPS to displace the water. Spray the tires and plastic parts with silicone, which will protects from drying out and cracking. The silicone also covers any scratches in the plastic, renewing its look, and reducing the chance of dirt sticking to the plastic, making it easier to clean the bike after your next ride.

The chain requires special maintenance similar to servicing air filters. Soak the chain in a container with a mild solvent, then scrub it with a nylon brush to remove dirt and debris. Let the chain drip dry and lubricate it. The latest product in chain lubrication is chain wax. It doesn't attract dirt or sling off and make everything around the chain oily and attractive to dirt.

To help prevent mud from sticking to the fenders, consider SRC Fender Skins. This product is a synthetic fabric that works like a sock to provide a flexible layer to the fenders, thereby preventing mud from sticking to the plastic.

AIR INTAKE SYSTEM

The air intake system comprises the air box, boot, air filter, and box drain. A cheap piece of foam and a thin barrier of oil—the filter—is all that protects the expensive engine parts from disintegrating into a pile of melted metal, so if you don't learn the basic maintenance practices for air filters fast, you won't be riding for very long! I remember when I was a service manager at a motorcycle dealership, and a guy brought in his kid's bike. The bike was only two weeks old, yet the engine seized because dirt had passed through the filter. This man was outraged and argued that his car went 30,000 miles before it needed a new air filter. Air filter maintenance doesn't seem obvious until your engine chokes to a grinding halt, but by then it's about $500 too late!

Twin Air makes covers for the air boot so you can wash the dirt from inside the air box.

Clean and Inspect

Every time you clean a filter you need to check the seams for tears. Some filters are sewn together, and others are bonded together with adhesives Filters don't last forever. Over time the seams will split. Professional racing teams only use a filter for a moto. That may be extreme, but the point is to replace the filter after about 20 cleanings.

The best way to clean a filter is with detergent and water. I recommend mixing equal parts of water and Simple Green, a biodegradable detergent made by Gunk that is sold at most hardware and auto parts stores. Let the filter soak for five minutes and then work it with your hands. If you have

Specialty cleaners and lubricants are needed for operating and maintaining dirt bikes.

Store extra filters in a plastic bag. That way you won't have to clean the filter at the races.

Seal the air boot to air box junctions with weather-strip adhesive.

sensitive skin, wear a pair of rubber gloves to protect your hands. Squeeze and expand the filter several times until all the particles of dirt have come off the filter. Rinse the filter with running water. Dry the filter by squeezing it and allowing it to air dry. The remaining moisture will be displaced when you oil the filter. There are filter oils that are biodegradable. The protection is better than pre-mix oil but not as good as Twin-Air or Maxima air filter oil.

Oil and Grease

The filter must have a special oil for the foam, and grease for the mounting surface. Filter oil is blended with chemicals that keep the oil diluted so it pours and spreads throughout the filter. These chemicals evaporate quickly in the open air, allowing the filter oil to become very tacky. Don't be tempted to use substitutes for filter oil. Filter oil is available from most motorcycle shops. Apply the oil evenly and sparingly across both the inner and outer surfaces of the filter, and squeeze the filter several times, adding oil periodically until the filter foam is lightly saturated with oil.

Apply a thin layer of grease to the flange-mounting surface to help prevent leakage at the mounting surface. I recommend Bel Ray waterproof grease.

Making It Easy

Nobody likes to clean and oil air filters, but there are a couple of things you can do to make air filter maintenance easier. If you can extend the time between cleaning and do three filters at one time, you'll save yourself time, so I recommend that you buy two spare filters. Apply oil to the filters and store them in Zip-Lock plastic bags. Then, if you have to service the filter at the race track or riding area, you don't have to clean it, just replace it with one of the pre-oiled spares. Disposable rubber gloves (thin nitrile) are useful for keeping the goo off your hands when changing filters between motos. The gloves come in boxes, typically of 100 for about $15.00. You can find nitrile gloves at cleaning supply, industrial, and hardware stores.

Filter covers can extend the service interval of air filters. There are two types of filter covers: cloth sock covers for the filter and plastic lid covers for the top of the air box. These things shield the filter from dust and mud. Some people think that the plastic air-box covers choke off the air flow to the air box and hinder performance. That's not true; the covers are designed to reduce intake noise. When you remove the cover, the bike makes more noise, and you think it has more power. Leave the plastic cover on the air box. It will save you from cleaning the filter so often.

The Air Box and Boot

It's easy to overlook the air boot and box when you don't even want to clean the filter, but consider this: A small leak at the air boot or box flange can allow dirt to bypass the filter and go directly into the engine. Here are some tips to consider when servicing the filter:

1. After you remove the filter, look into the air boot from the filter side. Look for dirt that indicates a leak. Sometimes, the chain roller will wear through the boot, or sticks and rocks could puncture it.
2. Never aim the power-washing wand directly at the boot-to-box flange. There is sealant at that junction, but the high-pressure detergent can easily penetrate the flange and blow out the sealant. It is advisable to power-wash the air box from the top. Twin-Air makes special air-boot covers so you can block off the boot and wash the box. This serves to flush the drain located on the bottom of the box.
3. Seal the flange-to-box junction with weather-strip adhesive only. Never use silicone sealer because it is fuel soluble.
4. When washing the bike, remove the seat and the air filter. Install a Twin-Air filter cap. That will enable you to seal off the carb from water and wash the dirt out of the air box and flush out the drain pipe.

SPARK PLUG BASICS

Spark plugs must operate within a fairly narrow temperature range. At idle, a spark plug must run as hot as possible so it doesn't cold foul, which occurs at about 800 degrees Fahrenheit. At full throttle, a spark plug must dissipate the heat quickly so it doesn't exceed 1,800 degrees Fahrenheit, where pre-ignition occurs. Consequently, many riders often curse spark plugs as they sit stranded on the side of a trail, trying to clean the oily goo off the plug. This section will tell you how a plug problem can be a sign of a more serious mechanical problem.

Common Problems

Modern dirt bikes have come a long ways from the days when a pocketful of spark plugs was necessary for even a short ride. Some bikes even had two plugs in the head so you could switch when one fouled! Today, if your bike is tuned properly, a spark plug can last an entire season. Even so, two-stroke engines do occasionally foul plugs. If you do have chronic troubles, here are a few places to look.

Cold Fouling

Question: I trail ride a 250cc dirt bike. My bike fouls a spark plug on every trail ride. The carb is a Keihin and I have adjusted the choke knob so the engine idles. What could be wrong with my bike?

Answer: The Keihin PJ model carbs, commonly used on Honda CRs, use those adjustable choke systems to aid starting and warm-up in cold temperatures. You should not use the choke knob to set the engine idle. That knob controls the flow of raw fuel into the carb's venturi. If you raise the knob by turning it counterclockwise, that richens the fuel-air mixture, causing the spark plug temperature to fall and cold foul the plug.

Ground Arm Melts

Question: My bike has a strange problem. It frequently melts the ground electrode of the spark plug. The engine is running great right before it shuts off. Do you think my ignition is too hot? I put an aftermarket booster wire on the ignition coil that produces 150,000 volts.

Answer: You say that the engine runs great, which tells me that the carb jetting may be slightly lean. That would raise the spark plug temperature, causing the ground arm to melt off. Check the old plug. Look at the stub of the ground arm. Is the stub end rounded, as if it had melted? You may be using a spark plug with a funky ground arm design that can't take the heat and pressure that a modern two-stroke engine produces.

Regarding the question of the hot spark, the amount of voltage needed to jump the spark plug's gap is proportionate to the pressure in the cylinder and the size of the gap. Electricity will jump the gap with the minimum required voltage. When an aftermarket company claims that their product produces so much voltage, that means their product is capable of producing that amount of voltage, if needed to cause the spark to jump the gap. Aftermarket voltage boosters don't deliver high voltage to the plug on each engine revolution, so you don't have to worry about the spark being "too hot."

Engine Loads Up and Wet-Fouls Plug

Question: I have a problem with my 1995 YZ250. Every time I start it up after it has sat for a while it will load up and bog, causing the spark plug to wet foul. And this is before I even move! Once I put a new plug in it and get it started, I have to hold the throttle open to clean it out so it won't load up. Once I have cleaned it out, it runs like a top. Still, this will make it very hard to get it running properly at a race, especially on the starting line. I've checked the carb jets and have the recommended 48 pilot and the stock main jet. I have everything to spec, and I have the mixture at 40:1 with Yamalube. My uncle said it's the pilot, but I'm not sure. I have a lot of plugs in three different heat ranges and they all have fouled out at least once. I think it's in the carb, but I need an expert like you to give me some advice.

Answer: Do you ever leave the fuel valve on? It sounds as if fuel is getting into the crankcases. That's why the plug fouls only when you start it. Check the fuel tank's valve by turning it off, unplugging the hose from the carb, and routing the hose to drain into a catch-tank. Check it after 10 hours to see if there is any fuel leakage. If there is fuel, then you need to replace the fuel valve.

Cold Fouling

This occurs when the bike and engine are still cool. On the extreme, cold fouling occurs when the plug's electrode temperature falls below 800 degrees Fahrenheit. At this point, carbon deposits accumulate on the insulator (the ceramic part of the spark plug that holds the center wire). The voltage will travel the path of least resistance. Deposits such as these are a path for the voltage to follow to ground rather than arcing across to the plug's electrode. Keep in mind that it is more difficult to fire a spark plug under compression pressure than at atmospheric pressure. Just because a plug fires in the open air, doesn't mean it will work inside the engine.

Melted Plug

When you find a plug that has been melted or is coated with globules of melted metal, something is seriously wrong. Combustion preignition occurs when the spark plug or anything in the combustion chamber reaches a temperature over 1,800 degrees Fahrenheit. At this point, the hot-spot could ignite unburned mixture gases before the spark occurs. Hot-spots can be caused by everything from too-lean jetting, air leaks, lack of cooling, lack of lubrication, or a sharp burr in the head.

Heat Ranges

The length of the insulator nose largely determines a plug's heat range of operating temperatures. Colder range plugs have a short heat flow path, which results in a rapid rate of heat transfer. The shorter insulator has a smaller surface area for absorbing combustion heat. Conversely, hotter range plug designs have a longer insulator nose and greater surface area to absorb the heat from combustion. It is most important to install a spark plug of the heat range specified by the manufacturer, as a starting point. When tuning racing engines, it is not uncommon to go up or down three heat ranges of plugs to optimize performance. For example, when your jetting is slightly rich but not enough to require a jet change, you could select a plug one range hotter to achieve the target exhaust-gas temperature. Each step in heat range will effect a 50 degree Fahrenheit change in the exhaust-gas temperature.

Examining the spark plug can tell a lot about the condition of the engine. This plug has tiny beads of a gray colored material, aluminum. This engine overheated, causing the piston to melt and disintegrate, transferring metal to the spark plug.

MAINTENANCE INTERVAL CHART

The following are recommended intervals for maintaining different components of your bike. Keep in mind that these are averages; if you are riding in extremely dusty, muddy, or wet conditions, times will be shorter.

| | Riding Hours | | | | |
Component	2	5	10	20	50
Chain	C&I	—	—	—	R
Air filter	C&I	—	—	R	—
Brake pads	C&I	—	—	R	—
Cables	C&I	—	L	—	—
Brake fluid	—	—	R	—	—
Radiator coolant	—	R	—	—	—
Transmission oil	R	—	—	—	—
Top end	—	C&I	RB	—	—
Reed valve	—	C&I	—	—	—
Air boot	—	C&I	—	—	—
Magneto	—	C&I	—	—	—
Crank seals	—	—	—	R	—
Clutch plates	—	—	R	—	—
Bottom end	—	—	—	C&I	—
Shock fluid	—	—	C&I	RF	—
Fork fluid	—	—	—	RF	—
Wheel bearings	—	C&I	R	—	—
Spokes	—	—	C&I	—	—
Steering head bearings	—	—	L	—	—
Swingarm & linkage bearings	L	RB	—	—	—

Key: Clean & Inspect (C&I), Replace Fluid (RF), Lubricate (L), Rebuild (RB), Replace (R)

TYPES OF SPARK PLUGS

Fine-Wire Plugs

Fine-wire electrodes provide easier starts and reduced cold fouling, partly because they require slightly less voltage to fire the plug, compared to standard-size-electrode center wire. This is because the fine wires are made of precious-metal alloy that is an excellent conductor of voltage. Fine-wire spark plugs produce a more direct and confined spark that is better for igniting the air-fuel mixture.

Projected-Insulator Plugs

Projected insulator refers to the extension of the insulator beyond the end of the shell. This design can only be used if there is sufficient clearance to the piston crown at top dead center (TDC). The advantage of this design is that it benefits from the cooling effect of the incoming fuel charge at high rpm, which provides some pre-ignition protection. At low rpm when cold fouling occurs, the insulator is more exposed to combustion. This helps to burn off deposits on the insulator that can cause cold fouling. Projected-insulator plugs can be used on any 200cc to 500cc dirt bike. These types of plugs cannot be used on 125cc engines with shallow-domed combustion chambers or ones with flattop pistons. These engines do not have enough clearance between the piston and head, and the piston would contact the plug.

Resistor Plugs

Non-resistor spark plugs give off excessive electromagnetic interference (EMI). This can interfere with radio communications. That is the primary reason why the manufacturers recommend resistor spark plugs. In North America, engine manufacturers must install resistor plugs in new engines because many people in rural areas depend on CB radios for their communication needs. In Canada, it's actually a law that you must use resistor plugs in your off-road vehicle.

The resistor in the plug demands higher voltage to jump the gap. On older bikes, where components of the ignition system are deteriorating, resistor plugs might foul more often than non-resistor plugs or run rough because the ignition system cannot produce enough voltage to jump the gap. I don't recommend using resistor plugs because they are overpriced and offer no advantage in performance.

Spark Plugs with Gimmicks

There are many different types of plugs on the market featuring every possible gimmick. Some manufacturers make ridiculous claims for their plugs, such as resistance to fouling, more power, or better fuel economy. There is an old saying, "Paper accepts all ink in advertising and litigation." That is certainly true with spark plug ads. The sad truth is that if an engine isn't tuned properly, an expensive plug will foul just as fast as a cheap plug. The best spark plug design is one with a precious-metal electrode and ground arm, shaped to a fine point, and core sealing ring that resists high pressure. Unfortunately, no such plug exists. However, there are plugs with precious-metal electrodes and excellent core designs. Forget about the funky ground-arm shapes because the spark is going to jump from the electrode to the ground arm at the point of least resistance, so these specialized ground-arm shapes with multiple points offer no real advantage. Worse, the shapes of some ground arms can actually make them susceptible to breaking off. A really good design for a ground arm is the 45-degree. This ground arm doesn't have a bend in the middle so it's not susceptible to breaking due to the pressure conditions in the combustion chamber. Nippon Denso sells these plugs for the most reasonable price, about $5.00. Forget the gimmicks and spend your money testing three or more different heat ranges until you find the plug that best suits your riding demands.

THROTTLE MAINTENANCE

It's the feeling all dirt riders dread! A total loss of control! Your throttle is stuck at the worst possible time. The engine is revving so high that the kill switch is ineffective and you have to pull the carb's choke just to stop the engine!

Many top riders are cautious about their throttles. Factory mechanics routinely disassemble and clean throttles between races, and sometimes between motos if the conditions are muddy. Use the following tips on how to clean a throttle and identify trouble signs.

Basic Cleaning and Inspection

After removing the throttle's rubber dust cover and plastic housing, examine the throttle pulley and cable for frays in the cable or dirt in the pulley. Examine the plastic guide for cracks, which can cause the cable to fray or catch on a tree branch, pulling the throttle wide open. If this happens to your cable, don't try to fix it with tape, just replace it with an OEM part.

The throttle pulley is made of nylon and doesn't require lube, but the cable does. Use

The throttle tube traps dirt and that can lead to binding of the tube on the bar. Use brake cleaner to spray out the inside of the tube.

a cable lubing tool to force chain lube down the throttle cable. Remove the carburetor slide and stuff a rag into the top of the carburetor to prevent any dirt from entering the carburetor. Make sure you disconnect the cable from the carburetor slide first, otherwise you will force dirt and lube from the cable down into the slide, and that can cause the throttle to stick open.

Clean the throttle grip and pulley with brake cleaner. Lube the grip and bar with penetrating oil, unless the throttle contains one of the new Teflon throttle tubes, which are self-lubing.

Inspecting the Slide and Carb

Check the corners of Keihin PWK carbs for dents or deep wear marks. Newer-model slides are chrome plated, older models are a dull gray color. The gray PWK slides tend to wear at the corners and can cock and jam in the carb's slide bore when the throttle is turned wide open. This is a common problem on older KX 250s and 500s. Replace the gray slides with chrome plated ones when they get worn. The chrome slides are the standard OEM part for 1993-and-later KXs and are available from accessory companies such as Moose Off-Road, Carbs Parts Warehouse, and Sudco in America.

Replacing the Throttle Grip

The stock throttle grips on modern off-road bikes are molded to the throttle tube. If you damage the grip and need to replace it, it's a very tedious job to remove the old grip. Here are some tips on removing and replacing the grip:

1. Use a pocketknife to strip off the grip.
2. Use a file, a wire wheel, or a lathe to remove the plastic splines and the remains of the rubber grip.
3. Apply a thin coating of grip cement to the throttle tube and slide the new grip onto the tube and let it dry for 24 hours.
4. As an extra safety precaution, wrap the grip with 0.020-inch or 0.5mm stainless steel safety wire. Wrap the grip at two equidistant points and twist the wire end and clip it with 1/4 inch remaining. Position the wire end so it faces on the lower palm side of the grip. This way it won't stick to the rider's glove.

This is a cable-lubing tool. It clamps around the cable and enables a plastic tube from an aerosol can to be attached so the lubricant can be sprayed down the cable.

Both Factory Concepts and Works Connection make aluminum throttle tubes. These tubes are less sensitive to damage during crashes and are easier to change the grip on.

Throttle Tubes

Stock throttle tubes are made of plastic and aftermarket tubes are made of aluminum. The aluminum tubes offer advantages of being less likely to crack in a crash and also easier to change the grip.

Fixing Sticky Throttles

You should have a factory-trained technician disassemble and clean the carb, throttle grip, slide, and cable. If the cable is dry or rusted, replace it with an OEM part. Sometimes, the slide will have dirt wedged between it and the carb. The dirt indicates that the air filter was leaking. Sometimes the slide is worn and scratched so bad that it needs to be replaced in order to fix the problem. If there is any dirt in your carb, carefully inspect the air filter for tears at the seams. Also check the air boot that links the air box and carb.

Sometimes the air boots will leak at the bolted flange that fastens the boot to the air box. Honda makes a special sealer for the boot flange. Automotive weather-strip adhesive works well, too. Never use silicone products to seal any parts in the intake system of a motorcycle because silicone deteriorates when exposed to fuel vapor.

CHAIN & SPROCKET MAINTENANCE

The condition of the drive train is the one thing that has a significant effect on both the handling and the engine performance of a dirt bike. The simple chain-and-sprocket drive train is still the most efficient way to transfer power from the engine to the rear wheel, especially on a motor vehicle with 12 inches of travel. The forces transferred through the chain and into the suspension can have a positive effect on handling. During acceleration, the chain forces push the rear wheel into the ground. That's why when you land from a jump with the throttle on, the rear suspension has more resistance to bottoming. Pro racers depend on the chain forces when pre-jumping and landing. If the chain is too tight, too loose, or the wheel is not aligned in the swingarm, a good rider will notice the difference. When the chain and sprockets get packed with mud or corroded from lack of lubrication, they can generate a significant amount of friction to load the engine. A poor set of chain and sprockets could absorb as much as 5 horsepower from the average 250cc dirt bike. Learning the basics of drive train maintenance can improve your riding performance because you'll be able to use the chain forces to your advantage.

Clean and Lube

After each ride, spray the chain and sprockets with degreaser, rinse the chain with water while scrubbing it with a wire brush, and then spray the chain with a water-displacement chemical such as WD40 or LPS. When you scrub the chain and sprockets, make sure you remove the dirt and oil deposits that become embedded near the teeth of the sprockets. If you don't clean off this debris, the sprocket will wear faster.

The ideal chain lube is a spray lube with a chemical that penetrates the chain's links

O-Ring Chain Care

Question: What is the best way to clean and lube an O-ring chain? Should I use detergent when I power-wash the chain? Is there a special chain lube I should use?

Answer: Lightly power-wash the chain with water only, while periodically brushing it with a soft wire brush. Then, spray it with some type of water-displacing chemical such as WD40 or LPS.

Sprockets or Gears?

Question: Currently I desert-race a 1992 CR500, which I believe, is still competitive with the latest models. I've made some obvious mods to make the bike more competitive, things like an aftermarket exhaust system, fork springs, and shock revalving. Now I'm interested in changing the power delivery with changes in gearing or the tranny, if necessary. The A-Loop wide-ratio tranny kit is kind of expensive. Do you think I can make the changes I need by the final-drive sprockets alone?

Answer: Changing the trans gear ratios is much more effective than changing the final-drive ratio through different sprocket combinations. I've used gears from A-Loop on motocross bikes and enduro bikes. To determine if wider gears will complement your riding style, you need to analyze your riding demands. Normally, I install just fifth-gear sets for guys who only use top gear for wide-open running. The transition from stock fourth to wide fifth is big, and you can only do it on flat ground with a minimum load. Other riders, 250 motocross experts for example, like to change third and fourth only because the tracks require you to carry one gear longer. In your situation, I recommend splitting the crankcases and examining the transmission gears, shafts, and shift forks. An engine with four riding seasons should at least need new crankcase main and transmission bearings. The A-Loop gears are about the same price as replacement Honda parts, so if the old gears are worn, you might as well replace them with wide-ratio A-Loop gears.

Master Link Problems

Question: Every few times I ride my 1989 KD80X, my master link will pop off. I don't mean pop I mean break apart and *fly* off. I have tried tightening and loosening the chain tension, but nothing works. It is getting very costly having to buy new master links so often (three times a month). It's also hard work pushing my bike home when even my spare link breaks.

Answer: The most basic problem could be that the master-link clip isn't positioned correctly. Make sure that the open side of the clip faces opposite of the direction of rotation. The next thing to check is the wheel alignment in the swingarm. There are marks on the swingarm at the rear axle, but those marks could be inaccurate, so use a tape measure to check the distance between the rear axle and the swingarm pivot. Adjust the wheel to the same distance on both sides of the swingarm. The proper chain free-play is 3/4 inch when the swingarm is parallel to the ground. Also, if the swingarm and wheel bearings are worn, the wheel could twist out of alignment when you accelerate. Check the swingarm or wheel by trying to move the components back and forth, with the bike on a stand. There shouldn't be any movement in the swingarm or wheel. If there is, then the bearings need to be replaced.

but doesn't fly off or attract dirt, and there are many different types of chain lube that fit this ideal, to varying degrees—oil, moly, lithe grease, and even chain wax. However, each is designed for a specific use. Chain lube made from moly is good for street bikes because it doesn't make a mess, but it offers little resistance to water. Spray-lithe grease lasts a

long time and offers protection against water damage, so it is good for enduro and trail riding. Chain wax was designed for motocross race bikes that are serviced every moto or practice session. Chain wax is a light coating that seals the link and doesn't fly off or attract dirt. This type of lube is easily stripped off when the bike is power-washed.

|

A busted chain will turn your legs into the drive train!

The front chain guide was removed from this bike. When the chain derailed it broke a hole in the crankcases.

Tips on Chain Adjusting

The two most important things to know about chain adjusting are to maintain alignment of the sprockets and to correctly set the chain free-play when the swingarm is parallel to the ground.

There are a few ways to set the sprockets in alignment—by adjusting the axle to stamped marks or using an alignment gauge. All dirt bikes have marks stamped in the swingarm at the axle mounts. The chain ad-

justers have marks denoting the center of the rear axle. Normally, you would use the marks to keep the rear wheel centered in the swingarm while adjusting the chain's free-play. However, production frames are robot-welded, and there are slight tolerance differences that can put the stamped marks out of alignment. That's why race mechanics prefer to use an alignment gauge, which fits into the centers of the rear axle and swingarm pivot bolt. Race Tools in New York makes a simple alignment bar that fits all dirt bikes. You just fit it in the centers of the axle and pivot while you adjust the wheel position for the proper chain free-play.

No matter how much travel a dirt bike has, the ideal chain free-play is 1/2 inch or 13mm, measured when the swingarm is parallel to the ground. At that point, the rear axle is at the farthest point from the swingarm pivot. The chain free-play will be at its minimum, and it should never be less than 1/2 inch or 13mm.

Just because the wheel is aligned when the bike is still doesn't mean it will stay in alignment when the bike is accelerated up a bumpy hill. Whenever you set the chain free-play, try to wiggle the rear wheel and the swingarm. If any of the bearings are worn, the drive train can run out of alignment, causing a big power drain.

Types of Chains

There are two types of chain, conventional and O-ring. Conventional chains use steel pins with some type of press-fit soft-metal bushing to form each link. These chains use a mechanical seal to protect the link. Mechanical seal means that there is minimal clearance between the rollers and links. O-ring chains use the O-ring to seal lubrication in the link, and dirt and water out. O-ring chains are more durable, more expensive, and heavier. These chains are great for long-distance off-road riding because the chain doesn't require as much maintenance as a conventional chain.

Some chains are advertised as having the ability to resist stretching, but this claim is misleading. No chain really stretches because metal doesn't stretch and stay at a larger size. When you turn the bike's rear wheel and the chain has points where the

This rear sprocket is worn out. Notice how the teeth are shaped in the direction of rotation.

free-play varies, it's due to chain wear not stretch. It's normal for a chain to wear at different rates at different points. The variance of the wear is greatly dependent on sprocket alignment and the chain's free-play.

Checking a Chain for Wear

There are a few different ways to determine if a chain needs to be replaced. Examine the chain for kinks—points where the link and roller have seized, preventing them from freely rotating—and replace the chain if kinks are found. Then, with the chain installed, cleaned, lubed, and adjusted, rotate the wheel and check the chain's free-play at different points. If the chain needs to be adjusted frequently and has many points where the free-play varies, then the chain needs to be replaced. Normally, the sprockets wear twice as fast as the chain, but replace the chain, too, when the sprockets are worn enough to need replacement. If you install a new chain on worn sprockets, the chain will wear prematurely.

Master Links

There are two types of master links, slip-fit and press-fit, but both use a clip. Conventional chains use slip-fit links, and O-ring chains use press-fit links. The clips should be positioned so the opening faces opposite the direction of rotation. Press-fit links can be installed by pressing against the link with the end of a hammer handle and pressing the link plate on by placing an 8mm socket over the link pins and tapping on the socket with another hammer. Tap on the socket alternately until the link-plate is pressed-on so far that the entire clip notch is exposed.

Types of Sprockets

Sprockets or chain rings come in many different colors, patterns, tooth designs, materials, and sizes. Patterns and colors don't mean anything, but some sprocket designs can be problematic, especially those that have grooves that allow dirt to flow into the chain. Well-designed sprockets have relief grooves positioned around the circumference of the sprocket, allowing the dirt to be channeled away from the chain. Tallon Engineering's Radialite design is a good example

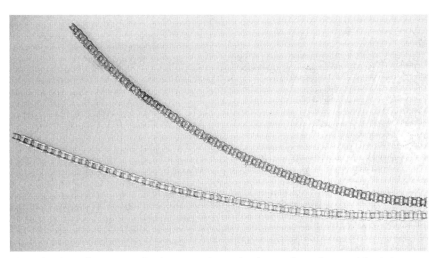

This is the chain whip test. Lay the chain out and try to bend it in a shape of a curve. The chain on top is worn and the one on the bottom is new. The chain shouldn't curve more than 8 inches at the ends.

This is a Radial Lite sprocket.

of the proper type of channel groove. Sprockets are made of either steel or aluminum. Steel is a better material for longevity, but aluminum is lighter and more expensive. The individual teeth of the sprocket tend to wear in the pattern of a wave. When the profiles of the front and rear sides of the teeth look different, the sprocket is worn out. Once the teeth wear so far, they allow the chain links to skip over the top of them. Don't let your sprocket get worn so far that the chain skips. If the chain derails while you're riding it, you could get injured!

TIPS FOR CHANGING THE SPROCKETS

Countershaft Sprocket

There are two different types of front-sprocket retaining methods, bolt/nut and circlip. Circlip retainers can be easily removed with circlip pliers, available at any hardware store. The bolt/nut retainers are often over-tightened so that special tools and knowledge are needed to remove and tighten them, but the job is much easier if the chain is left in place while the bolt/nut is loosened. The

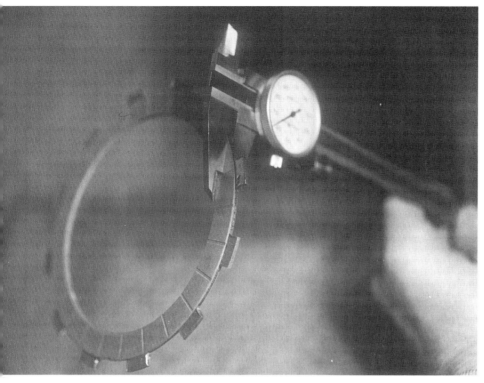

Looking at the depth of the serration can be a good visual method for inspecting the fiber plates. You can also measure the thickness of the plates with a caliper.

Match the front and rear sprocket size to determine the final drive ratio. The formula is to divide the number of teeth of the rear sprocket by the number of teeth of the front sprocket.

	12	13	14
49	4.08	3.76	3.50
50	4.16	3.84	3.57
51	4.25	3.92	3.64
52	4.33	4.00	3.71
53	4.41	4.07	3.78

COOLING SYSTEMS

A dirt bike's cooling system is such a compromise of design. Because of the emphasis on low weight and compactness, motorcycle designers are forced to fit aluminum radiators to one small area at the front of the motorcycle chassis, an area that is constantly hammered with sticks, stones, and crashing. At the 1990 500cc USGP, Rodney Smith collided with another rider. The other bike nailed Rodney's KX500 and crushed three channels of one radiator. I was working as Smith's mechanic, and we had to repair the bike before the next practice session. I applied epoxy to the damaged area of the radiator, and it held for the entire race!

average torque setting for the front sprocket is 24 foot-pounds. If you don't have an electric or pneumatic impact wrench to remove the sprocket's retaining bolt/nut, you'll need to prevent the sprocket from turning so you can loosen the retainer with a hand wrench. The best way to do this is to apply the rear brake so that the chain will prevent the sprocket from turning—assuming, of course, that you did not remove the chain first. Never wedge anything between the chain and sprocket while removing or tightening the front sprocket bolt/nut because the wedge can come out and injure you or damage the chain and sprocket.

Once you remove the sprocket, I recommend that you clean the inside and outside of the countershaft bushing, which is the spacer that fits between the bearing and the sprocket on the countershaft. The bushing is sealed on the outer edge by the countershaft seal that fits into the crankcase and by an O-ring on the inside. After cleaning, apply a dab of Bel Ray waterproof grease to the inner and outer faces of the bushing to help keep out water and dirt.

Rear Sprocket

Rear sprockets are bolted to the wheel hub. Normally, a tapered-head bolt with a flanged nut is used to fasten the sprocket to the hub. Sprocket bolts tend to loosen up. That makes mechanics over-tighten them, causing the Allen hex head or the nut to strip. Avoid these problems by using blue Loctite on the threads of the bolts. Always use a six-point box wrench on the sprocket nuts, and tighten the bolts in an alternating diagonal pattern.

Gearing Tips

You'll have to change gearing to suit different tracks. Tracks with steep hills, many tight turns, and long whoop sections will require higher final-drive ratios. Fast tracks require a lower ratio. A simple rule of thumb: For more top speed, switch to a countershaft sprocket with one more tooth than stock; for quicker acceleration, switch to a rear sprocket with two more teeth than stock. Use this gearing chart to find the difference between different combinations of sprockets for your model bike.

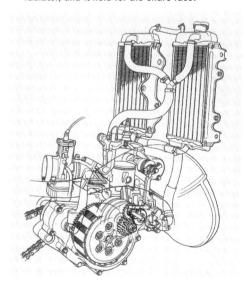

This drawing shows the complex path that the radiator follows. The coolant flowing from the radiator, up through the cases, cylinder and head, then to the top of the radiators where it exchanges heat into the cores to be cooled by air pressure channeled from the scoops and louvers.
Drawing courtesy of Yamaha International

Here are some tips on how to maintain a cooling system for maximum performance, and how to do emergency repairs to a punctured radiator.

Soft Tools

There are several excellent products that are invaluable to have on hand when you need to repair your coolant system. Duro Master Mend epoxy can be used to make temporary repairs to the outside of the radiator. Alumaseal can be used to make temporary repairs to the inside of the coolant system, and it works great for chronic head-gasket leaks. Radiator cleaner should be used to flush out the coolant system on a yearly basis because corrosion, debris, and waste products from combustion gases leaking into the coolant system can accumulate in the tiny channels of the radiator and reduce the cooling efficiency.

Enginekool, Moose Juice, or Spectro coolant products transfer more BTUs of heat to the radiator than an equal mix of water and antifreeze. These products are available from most auto parts stores. Moose Juice is available from Moose Racing or your local dirt bike shop.

Basic Cleaning and Inspection

A dirt bike's cooling system should be flushed and changed once a year. Before you drain the cooling system, add four ounces of an aluminum radiator flushing fluid. Several companies make these products, and they are available from any auto parts store. Run the engine for about 10 minutes and then drain the cooling system. Take care when disposing of the old coolant. Some states have severe EPA regulations regarding the disposal of used coolant. Call your local auto repair garage and ask if they have a recycling drum for used coolant. Now there are non-toxic coolants available. These types of coolant additives are biodegradable.

Remove the water pump cover and check for corrosion and debris. Check the water pump's bearings by grasping the water impeller with your fingers and trying to move it up and down. If you feel any movement, then the water pump bearings and seals need to be replaced. If you see oil leaking into the water pump housing, it may be a sign that the

Coolant Clinkers

Question: I removed the water pump cover on my bike and was shocked to find these white and green clinkers (deposits). I use a popular brand of antifreeze and tap water. What did I do wrong and how can I flush the system of these clinkers?

Answer: There are only three brands of coolant additives that prevent the magnesium water pump covers from corroding: Moose Juice, Spectro Coolant, and Peak. Use one of these. Also, you should only use steam-distilled water, which you can buy at the grocery store. Regarding flushing agents, auto parts stores sell several different brands; just make sure the flushing agent is formulated for use in aluminum radiators and engine blocks.

Coolant Blows Out of Vent Tube

Question: The other day I was riding my bike and when I stopped I noticed steam rising from the front of the engine. Then I looked at the clear hose on the top of the radiator just under the cap. There was foaming green stuff flowing out of that clear hose. It does it when I ride on sand whooped tracks. What's happening to my engine?

Answer: That clear hose that is mounted under the radiator cap is a pressure-release tube. When the temperature of the coolant gets too high, the pressure actuates a spring-loaded valve in the radiator cap, so the coolant can flow out and reduce the pressure in the radiator. The temperature rises on sand-whoops sections and causes the problem for two reasons:

1. The terrain puts a greater load on the engine and that makes it run hotter. Try pushing your bike through sand whoops and see how hard it is!
2. There is a greater load on the rear shock. The top shock mount is fastened to the frame tube near the cylinder-head brackets. When bikes get older, the frames deflect under hard bumps, such as sand whoops. This makes the head brackets move and twist the cylinder head, allowing a bit of combustion pressure to leak past the head gasket or O-rings and into the cooling system. That pops the radiator cap and blows the coolant out the vent hose. When it really gets bad, the cylinder head must be machined on a lathe to make the head flat to factory specifications. You can check the head by looking for black marks on the sealing surface. Also look for tears in the gaskets and O-rings.

Gray Bubbly Transmission Oil

Question: My KX60 has a little window mounted in the right side cover. I poured brown oil in the transmission, and after a couple of rides, the oil changed to a gray, bubbly color. Now the engine is overheating easily. Could these problems be related?

Answer: This is a common problem on older water-cooled dirt bikes. There is a rubber seal between the water pump and the transmission. When the seal wears out, coolant leaks into the trans, causing the oil to turn that bubbly, gray color. When any volume of coolant is lost from the system, the engine overheats easily. Replace the bearing and seals for the water pump, and that will fix the problem.

seals and bearings are worn too. Sometimes, the bearings will be so worn that they cut a groove in the water pump shaft. In most cases, when the water pump seals and bearings are worn, so is the shaft. It's best to replace these parts as a set because they aren't that expensive. The water pump is gear-driven by the crankshaft. Some bikes use gears made of plastic, but other bikes use metal gears. Metal gears are more durable but are very noisy. Plastic gears are vulnerable to melting,

especially when the gearbox oil is low and at very high temperatures.

Filling and Bleeding Tips

Some bikes have bolts located on top of the cylinder head or water spigot that are used for bleeding trapped air in the coolant system. If the air isn't bled from the system, the air pocket will prevent the coolant from circulating and the temperature will rise until the radiator cap releases. The proper way to

Removing the water-pump cover enables inspection of the impeller and the deposits in the ports. A radiator flushing liquid helps break up the deposits so they can be flushed out. Some impellers are made of plastic and are prone to melting if the engine is overheated.

These are some of the soft tools you should have in your workshop.

With the right-side engine cover removed, you can check the condition of the water-pump drive gear and the bearings. Try to wiggle the gear. If you feel excessive movement replace the shaft, bearings, and seals. Some water-pump gears are made of plastic and are prone to melting on bikes where the clutch is fanned constantly.

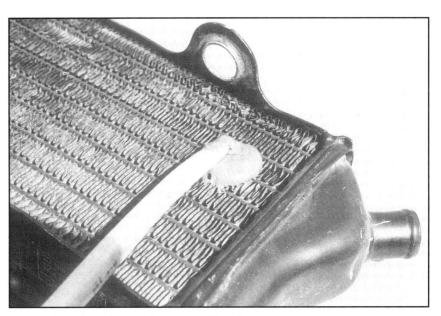

Epoxy can be used to make external repairs to seal the radiator cores.

bleed the trapped air is to fill the system to the top of the radiator, leave the cap off, and then loosen the bolt until coolant streams out. Then top off the radiator, install the cap, and run the engine for 10 minutes before checking the coolant level. CAUTION: Let the engine cool down before releasing the radia-tor cap; otherwise, the hot coolant could rush out and burn your hand.

Damage Control

The radiators of dirt bikes seem to mysteriously attract rocks and branches. Crashing a bike can damage radiators too. Radiators and exhaust pipes are like bumpers for dirt bikes, so chances are you will have to perform emergency repairs on your bike's cooling system. It may be at a race, on the trail, or in the wilderness several miles from any roads. Every trail rider should carry epoxy in his tool bag.

Any type of quick-setting epoxy works great for radiator repairs. Epoxy isn't an adhesive, in that it isn't sticky. Epoxy bonds when it can wrap around the edges of surfaces. It's easy to get epoxy to bond on a radiator because there are so many edges on the cores and the surrounding fins, but the area affected must be cleaned before the epoxy is applied. Quick-setting epoxies need

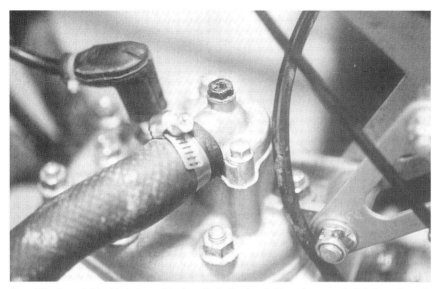

Some bikes have air-bleed bolts located in the cylinder head to facilitate the removal of air from the cooling system. Once the radiator is topped with coolant, loosen the bolt until coolant flows out. Then top off the radiator with coolant.

TROUBLESHOOTING TIPS

Use this guide of common symptoms and problems to aid in the troubleshooting of coolant systems.

Symptom: Coolant flows out of the overflow tubes.

Problem: Leaking head gasket, trapped air in system, or stripped water pump gear.

Symptom: Engine overheats quickly.

Problem: Coolant is low or radiator is clogged.

Symptom: Grinding noise from right side of the engine increases with rpm.

Problem: Water pump bearings and seals are worn.

Symptom: Clutch slipping, water in transmission oil.

Problem: Water pump bearings and seals are worn.

Symptom: Coolant leaks from rear of cylinder head.

Problem: Chronic head gasket leaks are usually due to frame problems.

only about 30 minutes' drying time when air temperatures are over 75 degrees Fahrenheit, longer in colder weather.

Epoxy radiator repairs should be regarded only as temporary fixes. When you get your bike home, replace the damaged radiator or

have it heli-arc welded by one of the many companies who specialize in radiator repair, such as Carpinello's in New York, Myler's in Utah, and Fontana Radiator Works in California.

Protection for Radiators

Radiators can be protected on the front and on the sides. Aluminum bars are used to protect the sides of the radiator from damage if the bike is dropped on its side. Screens are used in place of the plastic louvers in front, to protect the radiator cores from being punctured by tree branches, but this protection comes at a cost because the cooling system will not work as efficiently when the louvers are removed and replaced with screens. The louvers serve to collect and channel air at high velocity into the cores. DeVol Racing makes guards for radiators, and they may have models to fit your machine.

CLUTCH REPAIR

A motorcycle's clutch has a significant effect on power delivery and handling. If the clutch doesn't engage and disengage smoothly, the bike's rear wheel could break loose and compromise traction or, worse, cause the rider to crash.

Does your bike lurch when you fan the clutch? Do the clutch plates break or burn out fast? Does the clutch make a grinding

Clutch Slips and Drags

Question: My bike's clutch has the strangest problem. The clutch slips and drags. I've tried adjusting the cable several different ways and it has no dramatic effect. The bike is five years old. Could that have something to do with this problem?

Answer: The problem is either the outer pressure plate or the clutch basket. The pressure plate could be worn too thin. That will affect the clutch-lever free-play and the dragging problem. The clutch basket can cause the same problems because the drive plates (fiber) wear grooves in the clutch basket. The grooves prevent the plates from shifting position when the clutch is disengaged. Conversely, the grooves prevent the plates from moving closer together and providing the necessary friction. Another obscure problem could be that you're using aftermarket clutch plates. It's possible that the driven plates (steel) are thinner than the original plates. In that case you could just add one more fiber plate positioned next to the pressure plate. Using an extra fiber plate is also a "shade-tree mechanic's" cure for compensating for a worn pressure plate.

Clutch Nut Gets Loose

Question: My bike has a recurring problem. The center nut that holds the clutch on to the transmission main shaft gets loose and nearly falls off! What do I have to do to keep this nut tight? Does anyone make Nylok nuts large enough to fix this problem?

Answer: Most modern dirt bikes use a nut and a tab washer to secure the clutch. The washer has two tabs, one to align with the inner clutch hub and one that bends over one flat side of the nut. If you torque the nut to the manufacturer's specification and use a new tab washer, the nut will stay tight. However, if the problem continues, then check the engine's main bearings and the bearings that support the transmission shafts. Worn bearings could be the source of excessive vibration, which would cause the clutch nut to unthread.

The driven plates can be de-glazed and checked for flatness by rubbing them on sandpaper on a flat surface. Check the plates for sanding marks that indicate that the plate is warped. Replace the plates when they become warped or too thin.

It's possible to polish the inner clutch hub when chatter marks form, but when the chatter marks form on the outer clutch basket, you have to replace it when the marks get 1mm deep.

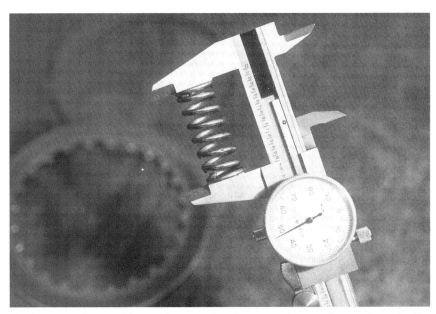

Clutch springs sack out and become shorter. Replace them every other time that you change the fiber plates. Worn springs make the clutch plates slip.

Drilling holes in the inner hub enables oil to flow through the plates. Drill one or two holes in each spline.

noise when the engine is idling in neutral? This section will give you insight into the problems that affect clutches, and some tips on how to permanently fix clutch problems.

Common Clutch Problems

Too many riders replace their clutch plates before they are worn out. They don't measure the plate thickness, plate warpage, or the spring free length. One guy called me on the telephone, complaining that he had spent over $600 in clutch plates in one riding season. He said his bike burned up clutch plates on every ride. I asked him to send me the entire clutch and all the old plates and springs. The problem was that the springs were sacked-out and didn't exert adequate spring tension on the plates. That allowed the plates to slip, causing them to burn. All of his clutch plates were the standard thickness and none of the plates were warped. The plates all had a minor surface-glazing problem. That

was easily fixed using medium-grit sandpaper. The average cost of replacing a set of clutch plates is about $90, which brings up the moral of this story: Spend some time looking for the cause of a clutch problem rather than just throwing money at it.

Measuring Tools

There are three inexpensive tools that you need to perform basic measuring of clutch parts. A flat surface, such as a piece of glass or preferably a thick piece of steel, will give you a surface to check plate

After baskets require RED Loctite on the Allen bolts to fasten the gear.

Installing an aftermarket clutch basket like one from Hinson Racing is easy. Use a drill press to drill out the rivets, then the gear can be removed.

warpage and de-glaze the plates. A feeler gauge will enable you to measure the plate warpage. A dial caliper will enable you to measure the free length of the clutch springs and the plate thickness. Dial calipers are available from Sears, auto parts stores, or Enco.

How to Measure the Parts

Before you attempt to measure the clutch parts, you will need the manufacturers recommended dimensions for the parts. The factory service manual lists this information, or you can call your local motorcycle dealer. The dimensions for parts such as the clutch-plate thickness or the spring free length will be listed as standard and minimum. The standard dimension refers to the dimension of a new part, while the minimum dimension refers to the worn-out dimension of the part.

Measuring the Plates

Clutch plates wear thinner with use and can warp if they become overheated. Use the caliper to measure the thickness of the face of the plates. If the plate thickness is within spec, then place it on a flat surface such as glass or steel. Press the plate down evenly and try to insert a 0.020-inch feeler gauge between the plate and the flat surface. If the feeler gauge can be inserted under the plate, then the plate is warped and cannot be repaired.

Measuring the Springs

Clutch springs sack out with use, meaning that they become shorter in length. Measuring the free length of the spring is the best way to determine if the springs should be replaced. Use the caliper to measure the free length of the spring and compare the dimension to the minimum-length spec listed by the manufacturer. Sacked-out clutch springs will cause the plates to become glazed and the clutch to slip.

Troubleshooting Clutch Problems

The previous section covered basic clutch service, but what happens when you have a serious clutch problem such as a grinding noise or a combination of both dragging and slipping. This section provides some insight into troubleshooting common and serious clutch problems.

Grinding Noises

Warm up your engine, put the transmission in neutral, and turn the throttle so the engine runs steadily, just over idle. Pull the clutch lever in slightly. Check for a significant reduction in vibration and the grinding noise. If the noise is reduced, then the needle bearing and bushing that fit between the clutch basket and main transmission shaft are slightly worn. This is very common on KX250s, but it isn't a serious problem. There is no way to measure the needle bearing, but the service manual will list a dimension for the bushing diameter. Always replace the needle bearing and bushing as a set.

If the grinding noise isn't affected by engaging the clutch, then the problem may be more serious. Check the bolt that retains the primary gear to the crankshaft and the nut

This is a typical clutch from an auto 50cc bike. The centrifugal force of the spinning shoes overcomes the spring tension, allowing the shoes to contact the outer hub and transfer through the drive train. Stiffer springs raise the engagement rpm of the clutch. The pads on the shoes eventually wear out. Removing the master links easily changes them.

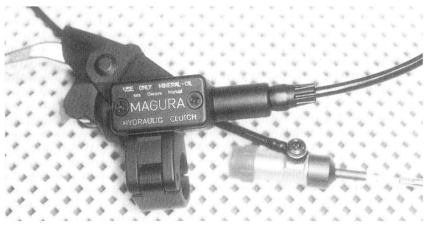

This is an aftermarket hydraulic clutch lever kit made by Magura.

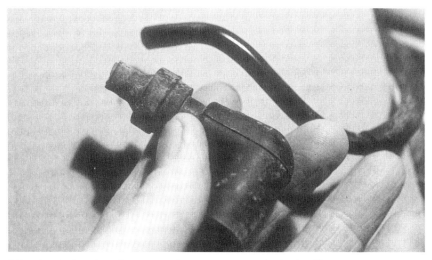

A frayed spark plug wire or loose cap are the most common spark related problems.

that retains the clutch hub. If the nut and bolt are tight, then the crankshaft main bearings may be worn out. In 1991 and 1992, Suzuki RM125s and 250s had a characteristic problem with bad primary-gear bolts. Suzuki has corrected the problem, and the new bolts are available from any Suzuki dealer. There is no implied warranty from Suzuki, but I suggest replacing the bolt just for safety's sake.

Dragging or Lurching Problems

These problems are primarily caused by deep notch marks that form in the clutch basket and inner hub. The notch marks are the result of wear caused by the splined teeth of the clutch plates. Eventually, the notch marks become so deep that the plates just stick in one place and resist engaging or disengaging. If the notch marks are less than 0.020 inch deep, then it's possible to draw-file down the high spots of the notches. Be careful, though, because if you file too much aluminum from the clutch basket or inner hub, then the clutch will be prone to dragging. A common symptom of dragging is the bike creeping forward when you put it in gear.

Before you attempt to draw-file the notches from your clutch basket, you must check the basket for hairline fractures at the base of each of the fingers. If you find any cracks, replace the basket. If the fingers break off, the debris will cause catastrophic engine damage. If you draw-file a basket with fracture cracks, it will fail much faster! Late-model KX125s (pre-1993) and 1992 RM250s have characteristic problems with clutch baskets. The manufacturers have re-designed the clutch baskets, and they are available from your local dealer.

Draw-filing refers to a filing method whereby you stroke the file in one direction, evenly, along the length of a surface. This will enable you to file down only the high spots of the notches equally. You will need two types of files, a flat file for the clutch basket and a triangulated file for the inner hub. You'll also need a file-card to clean the aluminum debris from the file; otherwise, the file grooves will become clogged with aluminum and prevent the file from cutting.

Aftermarket Clutch Baskets

There are two aftermarket manufacturers offering replacement clutch baskets. Hinson Racing () machines baskets from billet aluminum then applies a surface engineered coating of hard anodizing with Teflon impregnation. This makes the surface splines hard and slippery to resist forming chatter marks. LA Sleeve distributes a billet basket manufactured in England. The LA Sleeve kits are less expensive but are not coated. Both kits require you to swap the primary gear. That sounds difficult but it isn't. Basically you use a 13/64-inch drill bit to bore-out the stock rivets that retain the primary gear. The aftermarket clutches use tapered panhead Allen screws to retain the gear. The Hinson product comes with new rubber dampers. Always use Red Loctite on the threads of the bolts for the gear, and tighten them with a hand-impact driver.

ELECTRICAL & IGNITION SYSTEM

Electrical systems fail for the stupidest reasons. Water, heat, and vibration are the three main causes of electrical component failure. Simple preventative maintenance can save you hundreds of dollars in electrical parts. Simple tasks such as cleaning the dirt and condensation from the flywheel and stator to prevent corrosion, applying dielectric grease to the connectors, and periodically checking the spark plug cap for tightness may save you from pushing your bike rather than riding it. This section will show you how to care for your motorcycle's electrical system and what can go wrong if you neglect a problem. It also provides a troubleshooting guide for detecting fluke electrical problems.

Ignition System

Modern ignition systems are designed with specific timing curves. The typical Japanese ignition system fires at about 6 degrees before top dead center (BTDC) at idle, then advances to 20 degrees BTDC at the rpm of peak torque. At high rpm, the timing changes back to the retarded position of 6 BTDC. This serves to reduce the heat in the cylinder and shift it into the pipe, to prevent the engine from overheating and seizing. The "black box" or "igniter" controls the timing curve. That is the small plastic box located under the fuel tank on most dirt bikes.

Stator Plates

Question: My YZ125 has become increasingly harder to start over the last two months. The bike is three years old and I haven't had any problems with the bike's electrical system. Is there any component that steadily wears out?

Answer: All Kawasakis and Yamahas have Mitsubishi stator plates. The coils on Mitsubishi stators have poor insulating characteristics, causing the coil windings to break down over time. Your bike's stator coils are probably breaking down. If you do an ohm test you might find that the ohms values are lower than the manufacturer's specification range (10 percent variance). The Mitsubishi stator plate is rebuildable. Ricky Stator in Santee, California, offers a service of wet wrapping for better insulation properties. This service sells for about half the cost of a new stator plate.

Points Ignition Timing

Question: My son has an XR75. I don't have much experience working on motorcycles, but I'm mechanically inclined. I need to know the procedure for setting the ignition timing. Can you give me some tips?

Answer: The Honda XR75 has the old-style points ignition. On this points ignition system you should set the points gap to 0.014 inch. The ignition timing will be close enough as long as the point's shoe isn't worn too far. Replace the points and condenser as a set, after approximately 100 engine running hours. Remember to coat the points lobe with a thin film of grease to prevent the points shoe from wearing out prematurely.

Factory Ignitions

Question: I sneaked into the pits at the Red Bud motocross National last summer to check out the factory bikes. I noticed a factory mechanic flipping some switches mounted near the igniter black box of the bike. When I asked the mechanic what he was doing, he noticed that I didn't have a pit pass and he chased me out. What do you think the mechanic was doing with those electrical switches?

Answer: Many of the factory bikes use the latest type of digital igniter boxes. These igniter boxes house the circuitry that makes it possible to switch to one of eight different ignition-timing curves. There is a dip switch module mounted away from the igniter box, in a safe place such as under the fuel tank. The factory tuners adjust the dip switches to change to an ignition-timing curve that best suits the track conditions. In Japan, factory test riders have been using a two-position switch mounted to the handlebars. The rider can switch the timing curve from one that suits Supercross tracks to one that works best on fast outdoor tracks. That gives riders the ability to change the timing for different sections of the track—slow whoops sections and fast straights. Now don't go bothering those hard-working factory mechanics anymore.

Condensation Corrosion Under Magneto Cover

Question: I routinely inspect the magneto cover on my bike, for water and dirt. Can't the manufacturers make a cover that seals properly so I don't have to clean the magneto so often?

Answer: Most European bikes have aluminum magneto covers with a waterproof O-ring seal and vent tube to reduce condensation. My suggestion is to buy an aftermarket aluminum magneto cover, add a 1/4-inch hose fitting, and route the hose up under the fuel tank to the ignition-coil cavity. That way there is little chance of water getting into the hose and flowing down to the magneto, yet the vent hose will allow the condensation and heat to escape from the magneto. Then, you can spend more time riding your bike instead of working on it!

The black box has either analog or digital circuitry. Analog circuitry uses a series of zenier diodes to trigger the spark based on the amount of voltage generated by the rotor magnets and stator coils. Analog black boxes produce and are vulnerable to heat. Digital ignition systems use chips that sense rpm and adjust the ignition timing to suit. It isn't possible for us to change the timing curves of digital or analog black boxes, but it is possi-

Applying di-electric grease to the wire fittings will prevent corrosion and water penetration.

The stator coils are prone to corrosion. You need to polish the corrosion off with sandpaper.

and dirt to enter the magneto and cause corrosion. If you want to protect the magneto on your Japanese dirt bike, I suggest installing a Boyesen Factory Racing side cover.

To clean the magneto properly, you'll need a flywheel puller (K&N and Motion Pro sell flywheel pullers for under $20). First you remove the flywheel nut and thread the puller into the flywheel, in the counterclockwise direction. Most flywheel pullers use left-hand threads on the main bolt that threads onto the flywheel. The center bolt is right-hand thread. This bolt pushes up against the crankshaft end, forcing the flywheel off the crankshaft's tapered end. It's best to apply a dab of grease to the crankshaft end so the puller's bolt doesn't damage the end of the crankshaft.

With the stator plate removed from the engine, you can use fine-grit sandpaper to remove the corrosion from the coil pick-ups. Clean the stator plate coils with brake cleaner. Check the coils for dark spots that would indicate a shorted wire and a heat build-up.

How to Adjust the Ignition Timing

Rotating the stator plate relative to the crankcases changes the timing. Most manufacturers stamp the stator plate with three marks, near the plate's mounting holes. The center mark is the standard timing. If you loosen the plate's mounting bolts and rotate the stator plate clockwise to the flywheel's rotation, that will advance the ignition timing. If you rotate the stator plate counterclockwise to the flywheel's rotation, that will retard the ignition timing. Never rotate the stator plate more than 0.028 inch or 0.7mms past the original standard timing mark. Kawasaki and Yamaha stator plates are marked. Honda stators have a sheet-metal plate riveted to one of the mount holes. This plate insures that the stator can only be installed in one position. If you want to adjust the ignition timing on a Honda CR, you'll have to file the sheet metal plate with a 1/4-inch rat-tail file.

Diagnosing Electrical Problems

The Kill Switch

A faulty kill switch is the most common electrical problem. The kill button can be easily checked with either a simple continuity

ble to change ignition timing by adjusting the position of the stator plate.

Basic Ignition System Maintenance

Apply Dielectric Grease to Connectors

Auto parts stores sell dielectric grease. If you apply it to the wire connectors, they will never corrode. Clean the connectors with brake or contact cleaner, let the connectors dry, then apply a light coating of the grease. Wipe the plastic covers of the connectors to seal out water. Take care to route the wires and

connectors clear of the exhaust system and away from the rider's boots. Electrical tape can be used to route the wires, but zip ties should not be used because the wires can get pinched or severed and can then ground to the frame.

Cleaning and Checking the Magneto

The magneto of a dirt bike consists of the stator plate for mounting the generator and signal coils and the flywheel rotor that houses the magnets. Japanese dirt bikes have plastic magneto covers that are flexible and prone to leaking. That can allow water

light or a multi-meter. Link the two test leads between the two wires from the kill switch. When the switch is depressed, the circuit will be continuous. Neither wire should ever be grounded to the handlebar.

Spark Plug Caps

Spark plug caps can break loose from the coil wire after repeated removal of the cap. Most caps thread into the wire. Whenever you re-install a cap, first cut 1/4 inch from the end of the wire. This will insure that the cap threads are biting into fresh wire. The only company that sells an aftermarket wire and cap is Nology. It's a high quality item that requires you to thread-on and glue the wire into the coil. Spark plugs can also be faulty. Refer to the section on spark plugs for more information.

Wire Connections

Poor wire connections or faulty ground eyelets are also a common cause of electrical problems. Check the wires from the magneto for burn marks or cuts. Often, the wires will be routed too close to the pipe and melt. Flying rocks can also hit the wire,

You'll need a flywheel puller tool to remove the flywheel. If the flywheel puller doesn't work on the first try, then use a propane torch to heat the area around the shaft and spray it with penetrating oil.

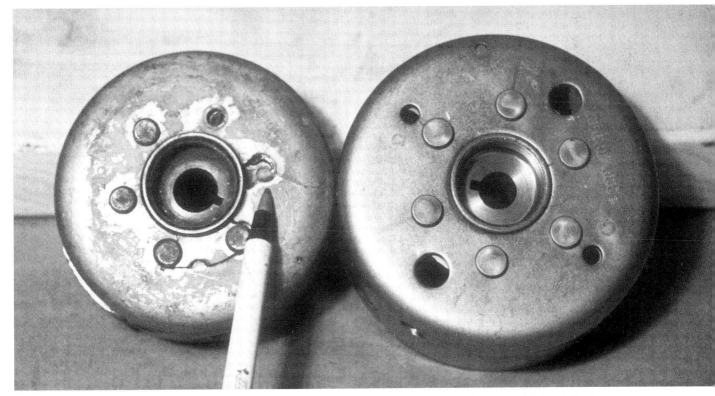

Check the rivets on the outside of the flywheel for cracks. This problem cannot be repaired and is usually caused by worn crankshaft main bearings.

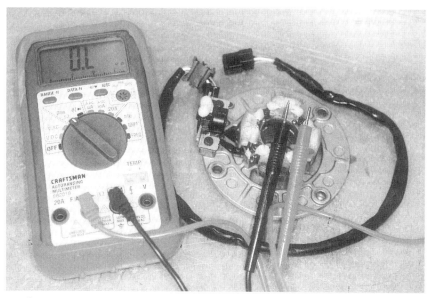

A multimeter is required for testing electrical components. Ohm resistance is the most common test. Look to your factory service manual for exact specs on electrical testing.

This is a PVL aftermarket ignition. It features an internal flywheel with less inertia than a standard external flywheel.

coil. The generating coil is also known as a primary coil, and the signal coil is also known as a pick-up coil. The generating coil produces the primary AC voltage, and the signal coil is the trigger that releases the voltage to the igniter/black box. The additional coils mounted to the stator plate are charging coils for some type of lighting system. Some manufacturers put all the coils under the flywheel rotor, and some mount the signal coil outside of the flywheel.

The individual coils of the magneto can be tested two ways, for resistance (ohms) and AC voltage output. The resistance is measured with an ohmmeter. The manufacturers publish resistance-testing specs in their factory service manuals. They specify what two wires to connect to the ohmmeter and what the ohms spec should be. The output of the generating coil can be tested with a multi-meter set to AC volts. At the average kick-starting speed (spark plug removed) the AC voltage output of the generating coil should be at least 45 volts.

Igniter Box

The igniter or black box contains sensitive electronic circuitry that controls the ignition timing in accordance with changes in engine rpm. All sorts of things can cause a black box to fail, and it is very difficult to test them for anything but complete failure. The main causes of black-box failure are heat and vibration. The electronic circuitry is encased in an epoxy material to insulate the components from the heat and vibration of the motorcycle.

Black boxes are usually mounted in areas of free airflow, such as the frame neck, under the tank, or under the seat. Sometimes water gets into the black box or the epoxy cracks and causes damage to the circuitry. There are some simple ways to test a black box for complete failure, using an ohmmeter. The manufacturers publish wire connection and ohms specs for their black boxes.

The black box can also be tested dynamically with an inductive pick-up timing light (plastic body). Remove the magneto cover, start the engine, and point the timing light at the flywheel. Look for timing marks to appear at one side of the flywheel, and focus the strobe light at that area. You should see "T" and "F" and "|" marks. The

causing it to break or fray. If the wire connectors aren't insulated properly, they could short out from moisture or corrode. Clean the connectors with contact cleaner and apply a thin coating of dielectric grease to protect the connectors from corrosion. Check the ground wires too. They are colored solid black or have a white stripe. These wires

have eyelets that fasten to bolts such as those on the coil or black-box mounts.

Magneto

The magneto consists of a flywheel with magnets (rotor), and a stator plate with a few types of coils mounted to it. The two basic coils are the generating coil and the signal

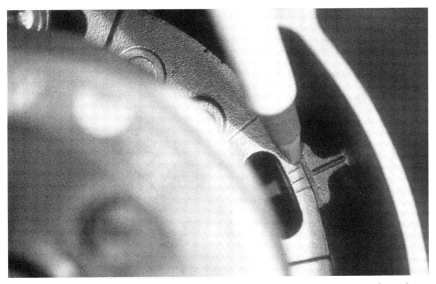

Most stator plates are staked with alignment marks that indicate standard, full advance, and retard timing marks. Retarding the timing helps overrev and advancing it gives the power band mid-range hit.

There are a few companies making aftermarket ignition black boxes. This Fire Power box is popular in Europe with riders looking for more top end overrev.

"T" means TDC (top dead center), the "F" means fire at low and high rpm, and the "|" line means full advance. The "F" mark should line up with a fixed point on the crankcase at idle. When the engine is revved to mid throttle, the timing mark will advance to the "|" line. When the engine is revved higher the timing mark will jump back to the "F" mark. If the spark is occurring after TDC, the engine may idle rough. If the ignition timing doesn't go to the"F" mark at high rpm, then the piston may seize from too much cylinder pressure and heat.

FITTING ALUMINUM HANDLEBARS

There is nothing worse than the sinking feeling you get when you land from a big downhill jump and the bars fall to the tank, preventing you from steering. This section provides tips on how to custom-fit aluminum handlebars and keep them tight in the clamps. First, determine the optimum width of the handlebars, based on your body positioning and riding needs. For example, if you are a tall guy with wide shoulders, you will leave your bars at the maximum width, but if

TROUBLESHOOTING CHART

Problem: The engine is hard to start and dies periodically.

Solution: Unplug the kill switch; if it cures the problem then replace the switch with an OEM part.

Problem: The engine coughs under hard midrange acceleration and misfires at high rpm.

Solution: The stator coils are probably deteriorating. Use a multi-meter on the ohm setting to check the coils. Ohm specs for the coils are listed in the service manual. Sometimes the coils become corroded from condensation and just need to be cleaned. Stator coils are rebuildable for about $125.

Problem: The engine runs fine on flat ground but misfires when riding over a series of whoops or braking bumps.

Solution: Check the top coil mounted under the fuel tank. Make sure the ground wire, coil mounts, and spark plug cap are tight and clean. There is also a slim possibility that the black box is faulty. These units are potted with epoxy to hold the fragile circuits from breaking apart. Sometimes the epoxy material breaks down, allowing the circuits to vibrate and short-out when you ride over rough terrain. Unfortunately, there is no reliable way to test an intermittently faulty black box, but an ohm test can determine if the unit has completely failed. See your factory service manual for testing procedures.

Problem: The engine overheats, the pipe turns blue in color, and the piston is melting in the front center of the dome.

Solution: The ignition timing is too far advanced at the stator plate or the black box is faulty and doesn't retard the ignition timing curve at high rpm. This is simple to check with the aid of an inductive pick-up timing light. See your local franchised dealer and a service technician can run a test for you.

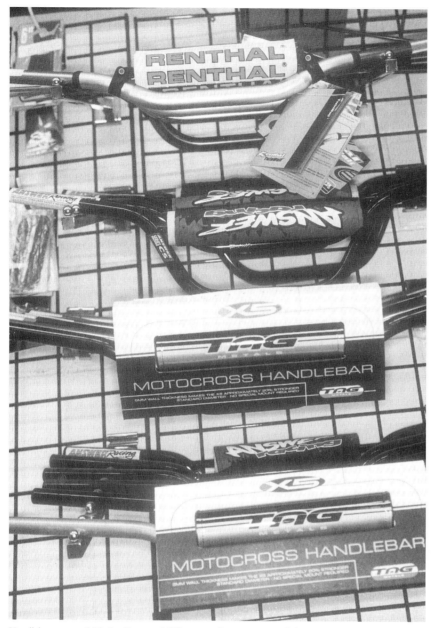

Handlebars are available in all sorts of different configurations. Handlebars are rated for rise height and sweep back distance. ATV handlebars have a much greater rise height and are better suited to extremely tall dirt bikers.

you ride enduros through tight woods sections, then you will need to cut the bars down so the bike fits between trees.

Cutting and Polishing

In general, cut the bars to a width that matches the width of your shoulders. You may want the bar a bit wider or narrower than this to suit your personal taste and riding conditions. Motocross riders tend to use wider bars for a bit more leverage, and en-

duro riders tend to cut them narrower (down to about 28 inches) for maneuvering through tight trees.

Measure and mark the area of the bar that you need to cut, and wrap a piece of black tape around the bar. This will help guide your hacksaw and enable a smooth, straight cut. After cutting the bar with a hacksaw, wrap a piece of medium-grit emery cloth around the rough-sawed edge and polish it smooth. This must be done because the

rough edge of the saw cut will gouge the inside of the rubber grip or plastic throttle grip, and may cause the throttle to stick wide open! Remember to install the end-plug in the bar after you have finished sawing and polishing. Some aluminum handlebars do not have diamond-shaped knurling for the handlebar clamps. It may be difficult to keep these bars tight, especially if the clamp and bar surfaces have deformities. It may be necessary to lap these surfaces together to increase the clamping surface area.

Lapping and Fitting the Bars and Clamps

Factory mechanics in Europe recommend using medium-grit valve-lapping compound ($3 at auto parts stores) to lap the surfaces of the bars and clamps so the clamps can get a tighter grip on the bars. To begin the process, apply the compound between the handlebar and clamps. Then snug the clamps down and rotate the handlebars back and forth. This procedure polishes the high spots off the surfaces of the bar and clamp and effectively increases the clamping surface area. After lapping, the handlebars will stay tight in the clamps, eliminating any chance of slipping. This method of clamp-to-bar lapping is also recommended for the cross-bar clamps. Normally they have a locking agent applied to the clamp from the manufacturer, but a couple of hard landings cause the locking agent to break bond with the bar. The lapping method is a reliable way to keep the cross-bar tight.

Race Tools in New York has developed an excellent method for matching the triple clamps to the handlebars. They recommend using a 7/8-inch reamer to line-bore true the top clamp and handlebar clamps. The amount of material removed varies from bike to bike. The handlebar clamps should also be draw-filed flat. Race Tools recommends using one-piece bar clamps for extra rigidity.

Handlebar Tightening Warnings

Pay attention to the manufacturer's recommendation on how to tighten your handlebar clamps, and to what torque specification. Some handlebar clamps are designed for equal-distance gaps on each side of the bar and some are designed for zero

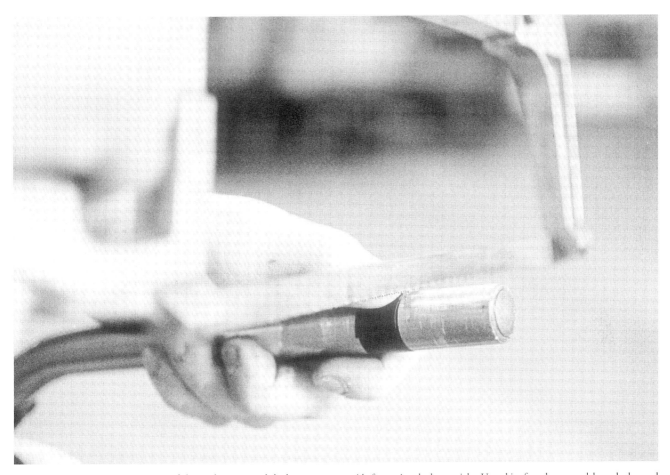

To change the bar width, wrap a piece of electrical tape around the bar to use as a guide for sawing the bar straight. Use a bit of sandpaper to deburr the bar end after sawing is complete.

gap on one side. For example, Honda stamps one side of the clamp with a dot mark. That indicates that the dot should face the front of the bike and that clamp bolt should be tightened until the clamp has zero gap. This is a common clamping system used on late-model Japanese motorcycles. Honda uses this system on all the front-end clamps from the handlebars to the controls and the front-axle clamp. Some other manufacturers use arrows to denote directions of forward or up. If you are ever unsure of which direction a clamp should face, refer to your factory service manual or call your local franchised motorcycle dealer.

Vibration in Handlebars

If vibration in the handlebars is making your hands go numb, then you may want to consider some options. You can fill the inside of the bars with a liquid silicone rubber to isolate vibration. Products such as these

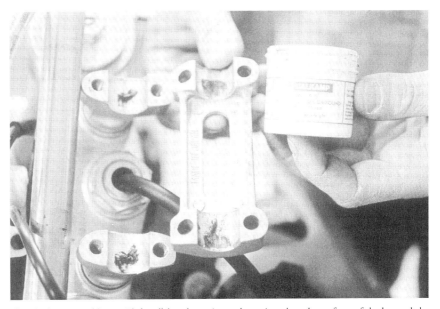

If you're having problems with handlebars loosening and rotating, then the surfaces of the bar and the clamps need to be mated for maximum clamping area. You can do this by rubbing a dab of valve grinding compound between the handlebars and the clamps, then rotate the bars back and forth several times. Take care to clean off the compound's entire residue since it is oil based.

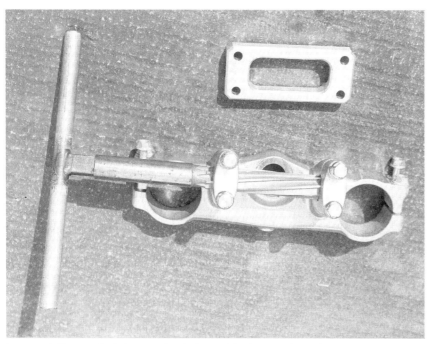

Pros use a different method of insuring that the bars and the clamp are aligned for maximum contact area. This is a reamer, a precision tool that removes metal. Single bar clamps are also good for tight clamping.

GRAPHICS FAQs

Stained Fuel Tank

Question: My bike has a white fuel tank. It is stained with fuel residue that has turned the white plastic brown in color. I want to cover the stains with rad and tank stickers. How should I prep the tank before I install the stickers?

Answer: You will never get the brown stains off the tank. However you can prep the tank surface for installation of the stickers. Wet-sand the tank with 320-grit wet/dry sandpaper and Soft Scrub brand kitchen tile cleaner. Rinse the tank, being careful not to allow any water to enter the tank. Then use a clean cloth and acetone to wipe the surface area where the sticker will bond to the tank. Acetone seals the pores in the surface of the tank and removes the soap film.

Fix Peeled Stickers?

Question: The edges of the rad stickers on my bike are peeling off. What can I do to re-bond the sticker?

Answer: I suggest using a razor knife to trim the part of the sticker that has peeled off. There is no aftermarket adhesive that will bond to the stickers.

are sold at home improvement stores under the category of bath-tub sealer. The sealer comes in a foot-long tube and requires a caulking gun to pump the silicone into the handlebars.

There is also a product designed for handlebars called the Bar-Snake. It is a solid piece of rubber that can be threaded through the bars. Another option is to use a tapered-wall-tubing bar without a cross bar. On some models you can adapt top triple clamps that use the rubber mounted bar clamps. Clamping methods such as these tend to get damaged easily in a crash but offer a lot of protection from vibration.

Notes on Tapered-Wall-Tubing Bars

Aftermarket handlebars like the Answer Pro-Taper and the Magura Bulge Bar are tapered-wall-tubing bars designed for a bit of flex. Handlebars such as these do not use cross bars. The extra flex is intended to absorb some of the vibration or shock of impacts transferred up the forks. These types of handlebars may require different top clamps and handlebar clamps. Check with the manufacturer as to the availability of clamping kits for your model bike before purchasing these products.

FITTING RADIATOR GUARD AND TANK STICKERS

Are you a little nervous about trying to apply those expensive radiator and tank stickers to your bike? Here are some tips on how to reduce the chances of misaligning the stickers, making bubbles, or having them peel off the first time you ride your bike. Robert and Matt Davis of Throttle Jockey provide us with a demonstration on how to apply stickers and staple seat covers.

Clean and Prep

If the plastic panels are scratched, you should consider replacing them. If your bike has an exposed fuel tank and it is deeply scratched, you can repair it by sanding down the scratches with 220-grit sandpaper. Clean all the plastic parts with contact or brake cleaner and wipe dry with a clean cloth. When applying stickers to an exposed fuel tank, it's best to drain the fuel first because the fuel vapors seep through the plastic and deteriorate the adhesive.

Some sticker manufacturers include an acetone-soaked swatch so you can clean the outside of the plastic. The acetone actually dissolves the substrate of the plastic, sealing it from leaking fuel vapors while the stickers are applied.

Keep It Straight!

The best way to keep the stickers straight while applying them is to remove a small section of the backing paper and align the covered part of the sticker on the plastic. Then press down the exposed part of the sticker. Now carefully peel off the backing while pressing down the sticker. This will insure that no air bubbles get trapped between the sticker and the plastic. If some air bubbles get trapped under the sticker, you can remove them by popping them with a pin and pressing out the air. Popping the bubble results in a slight distortion in the sticker but nothing compared to what would happen if you tried to press the air bubble across the sticker to bleed it out at the edge.

A completely different technique for installing rad and tank stickers is to coat the plastic with a light film of water and dishwashing liquid. Then remove the backing from the entire sticker. Now apply the sticker to the plastic and slide it into position. You'll need a plastic scraper to force out all the water and air bubbles.

Care for New Stickers

Stickers will eventually start to peel at the edges. Here are some tips on reducing the wear and tear on stickers. Don't pressure-wash the stickers directly at the edges. Also, be careful not to use harsh detergents meant for use on stripping grease from metal parts. These detergents will deteriorate the adhesives in the stickers. The best way to clean the stickers is with a sponge and water. If the edges of the sticker start peeling, use a razor knife to remove the peeled part of the sticker.

FITTING SEAT COVERS & FOAM

Have you ever spent $50 on a seat cover and botched the installation, leaving it look like the ruffled trousers of a wobbly old man?

There are two different opinions on how seat covers should be installed. Some people believe you should install a new seat cover over the top of an old cover. That may work on a cheap seat cover, but not on one that is designed to fit properly. One important thing to consider when installing a new cover is the

foam. Seat foam deteriorates when you power-wash the seat with detergent. When you strip off the old cover, you may find pieces of foam have crumbled off. This is an indication that the foam is gone bad and that the foam must be replaced, too.

Aftermarket Seat Foam

There are many different types of seat foams available from aftermarket companies. You have the option of stiffer foam in two degrees, or foam of different heights both shorter and taller than stock. Before you

buy a new seat cover and foam, consider your height, weight, and riding style. A very tall, heavy rider will need the tallest, stiffest foam possible. Stiffer foam will make the seat seem taller.

MXA specializes in making tall, stiff foam for riders over 74 inches in height. MXA foam is stiffer than stock foam and is more resilient over time. They have two different foam heights to choose from. The taller foam will help, but extremely tall riders might also find that higher Tecnosel foam is very stiff and is designed for riders who stand often

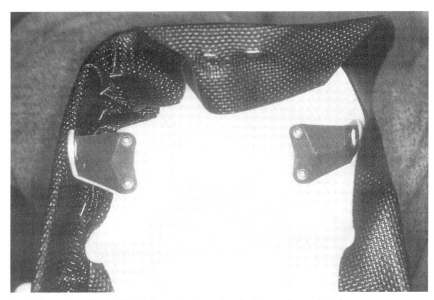
Install the staples at least 1/2 inch from the edge so they don't protrude out the sides.

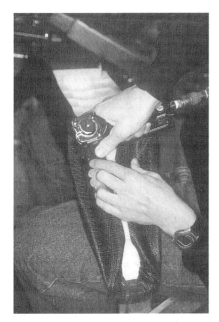
Use a pneumatic staple gun to secure the seat cover.

Clean the plastic with some type of lacquer thinner.

Before you remove the sticker backing, line it up on the plastic part to get some visual reference marks.

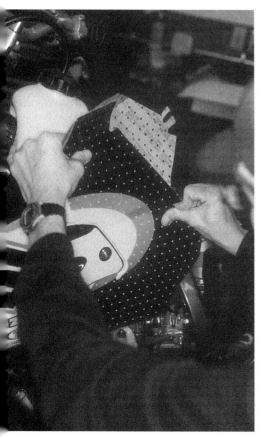

Peel one edge of the backing and start with one corner and work your way across.

and use their inner thigh muscles to grip the seat and turn the bike. That is why Tecnosel seat covers have the grip material up on the top front edges. Riders who sit down all the time (enduro or hare scrambles riders in particular) may experience lower back pain because Tecnosel foam is not designed to absorb impacts. Conversely, soft, worn-out foam can have the same effect on your back.

If you are not a tall rider and want to lower the stock seat foam, you may want to trim the foam. This will enable the rider to rest his foot flat on the ground when coming to a stop or waiting at the starting line. Trimming the foam lower is accomplished with a "hot-wire." Most upholstery shops can handle this task. Then, you will need to stretch the seat cover tighter and reposition it on the seat base.

Fitting the Seat Cover

You will need some tools to fit a seat cover right. You need a staple remover, a razor knife, and a staple gun. A pneumatic staple gun is best because it requires significant force to inject the staple into the plastic seat base. If you try to do it with a hand-squeeze stapler it will be difficult to get the staple to bite into the base while keeping the cover taut. If the staple

doesn't seat into the base, the cover will just tear apart and the staples will fall out. If you doubt your abilities, take the seat and cover to an upholstery shop and make a copy of this section on seat-cover installation tips to guide the person doing the work.

1. Remove the old seat cover by extracting the old staples with a hooked staple remover. You can also use a flat-blade screwdriver and side-cutter pliers.
2. Hook the seat cover to the front of the seat and pull it tight at the back. Remove all the wrinkles along the length of the seat before you staple it.
3. Start stapling the seat at the back. Just put four staples in to begin.
4. The next point to staple the seat is at the front corners. Pull the cover tight and put two staples on each side.
5. Now take a razor knife and cut the cover to accommodate the seat mounting tabs. Just cut two vertical lines on each side of the tabs. Pull the cover tight on each side equally and put a staple on each side of the tabs. Take care in aligning the seat equally on each side. Now that the cover is set into position you can staple it every 1/2 inch around the perimeter.

RACE DAY PREPARATION

Every time I go to the races, I see racers fumbling around with their bikes for hours between motos; later, they push their bikes back from the second moto because their bike broke down for some silly reason. It only takes about 20 minutes to thoroughly inspect and service a bike between motos. Servicing a bike can give a rider confidence and peace of mind. It's also a great way to channel "nervous energy." Many talented professional riders share some of the maintenance duties with their mechanics as a way of preparing for the next moto. Paul Cooper cleans his throttle, Jeff Stanton adjusts his bars and levers, and Danny "Magoo" Chandler used to change his own tires just to psyche out other racers. Too many riders and mechanics are unorganized when performing between-moto maintenance. This section is a guide to help you become more organized and build your mechanical confidence.

RACE DAY LOG

In order to improve your bike, you need to know what it is doing. Although the seat of your pants will give you some general impressions, a race log is the hot ticket to pinpointing areas that are lacking performance. Ideally, fill out a race log for each race of the season. This will give you baseline settings for the track and an excellent picture of how your bike is working in different conditions.

General Data
Date:
Location:
Air Temperature:
Humidity:
Elevation:
Terrain & conditions:

Suspension Fork
Spring rate:
Oil level:
Compression (clicks out):
Rebound damping:
Fork tube height in triple clamp:

Shock
Spring rate:
Low-speed compression (clicks out):
High-speed compression (clicks out):
Rebound damping: (clicks out):
Shock sag:
Shock preload:

Chassis
Front tire:
Front tire pressure:
Inner tube or bib mousse:
Rear tire:
Rear tire pressure:
Front brake pad brand and type:
Rear brake pad brand and type:
Accessories (handguards, skid plate, etc.):

Engine
Fuel type:
Premix oil brand and ratio:
Main jet:
Needle jet:
Pilot jet:
Clip position: (from top):
Air screw (turns out):

Comments
What obstacles or parts of the track did the suspension work well on:

Where did the suspension perform poorly and what was happening:

Where did the engine work perfectly:

Where did the engine work poorly and what were the problems:

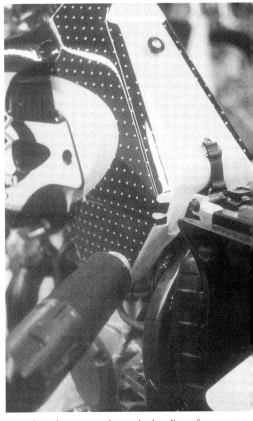

Use a hair dryer to accelerate the bonding of the adhesive.

Start During the Race

A good mechanic prepares during the race for the tasks he will need to do between motos. For example, if the rider gets involved in a crash but continues the race, the mechanic will think of what parts were damaged in the crash. If the mechanic hears that the engine is detonating at the end of a long straight he'll know that he must increase the carb's main jet size between motos. If the first race starts muddy but the sun begins to shine and the wind starts blowing, he'll know that in the next moto the track will dry out. This will require him to change the suspension settings and perhaps even the tires in order for his rider to have a competitive advantage in the next race. Here is a checklist for moto maintenance, listed by priority order.

Washing the Bike

This seems like a very simple thing, but washing a bike incorrectly can cause more damage than racing. Start by scraping the majority of the mud from the bike. This will reduce the amount of water needed to wash the bike and keep your pit area clean. Remove the seat and air filter then cap the silencer end and the air boot. Seat foam manufacturers warn not to power-wash seats because the foam acts like a sponge to absorb water

(added weight) and the water and detergent can break down the seat foam to make it "mushy." Never point the power-washing wand directly at rubber seals (forks, shock, sprocket, wheel bearings). Never spray detergent on the brake pads or disc in order to clean them. The detergent bonds to the disc

and glazes the first time you use the brakes, rendering the pads useless. The best way to wash the bike between races is with a stiff brush, sponge, and a bucket of water.

At the 1993 USGP, a factory mechanic criticized my bike for not being perfectly clean. He spent a lot of time making his bikes perfectly clean, but that reduced the amount of time he could spend doing maintenance. This mechanic was later made famous for forgetting to put gas in his bike, costing his rider valuable points at a national championship race. However, the bike was clean when the rider pushed it back to the pits!

After you wash the bike you need to do some things immediately. Drain the carb's float bowl just in case water seeped past the air-filter cover. Dry the air box and boot with a towel. Grease the air-filter flange and install a clean filter to prevent anything from accidentally falling into the exposed air boot. Finally, use a wire brush on the chain and spray it with chain lube to prevent it from corroding.

For race days when the dust and water are minimal, you can use a thin disposable

The happy mechanic always remembers to top the tank before sending his rider out on the track!

The starting line of a minibike race can be nerve-racking for kids, mainly because parents get a little too excited. A good mechanic is quiet and supportive.

sock over the filter. Rather than changing your filter between motos, you can simply pull off the sock and have a clean filter. Some systems allow you to pull off the sock without even removing your seat. Several companies sell them in America and Europe.

Fuel Precautions

If you use petroleum or synthetic pre-mix oil, you should immediately top off the tank with fuel-oil mix after washing the bike so you don't forget. If you use a castor-based pre-mix oil, then you should dump the fuel from the previous moto and mix your fresh batch of fuel just prior to staging. Castor-based oils separate quickly from fuel and that can cause either spark plug fouling or piston seizures. On very hot days, place a wet white towel over the fuel tank so the sun doesn't heat the fuel. Cool fuel gives a definite advantage on the start of a race.

Quick Check

Grab a set of T-handles and check all the bolts on the bike. This will force you to look over the entire bike, enabling you to find problems such as worn, bent, or broken parts. Check the brake pads at the wear-indicator lines scribed on the sides of the pads after every moto because mud races can wear out a set of pads in one moto. Check the chain adjustment. Look for oil leaks at the suspension components. Adjust the clutch cable if the lever has too much free-play.

Wheels and Tires

Check the tire pressure and make corrections based on track conditions. Here are some basic guidelines. Muddy conditions: front 8 psi, rear 6 psi. Dry conditions: front 14 psi, rear 12 psi. Always use heavy-duty inner tubes because they allow you to run lower tire pressure without the threat of a puncture.

If you can't afford a new rear tire for every moto, use a hacksaw to cut the rounded edge from the knobs. Don't ignore the braking edge of the knobs (backside) because it's just as important to stop as to go. There are some good tools available for the purpose of restoring the edges on the knobs between motos.

The best way to tighten the spokes is to start at the valve stem and tighten every third spoke 1/8 turn. When you get to the stem again, start with the next spoke and repeat the procedure. Once you have tightened three spokes from the stem you will have tightened every spoke equally. Check the spokes for loose ones, then tighten them to the same tension as all the others. Don't use the "tap the spoke and listen to the pitch of the sound method." It doesn't work! You have to develop a sense of feel for spoke tension. If the spoke is too tight, you'll hear stress-relief sounds.

Involve the Rider

I make it a practice to always involve the rider in the final sequence of between-moto maintenance. Have the rider sit on the bike and check the rear spring sag, handlebar and lever positions, brake- and clutch-lever adjustments.

Ask him how the bike worked in the race and if there is anything he wants you to check or change. This is mainly done for psychological reasons. You are showing the rider that you care about what he thinks and proving to him that the bike is in great working order. This will give him confidence and also prevent him from making up some bogus mechanical problem as a reason for quitting during the next moto.

The Rider-Mechanic Relationship

I place a lot of emphasis on being willing to do whatever it takes to give the rider an advantage. I've been able to get better-than-normal results out of riders just by being an emphatic listener between motos. I like to finish the bike maintenance as quickly as possible so I can talk to the rider and help him prepare for the next moto by doing things together, such as walking the track, watching the start of other races, observing how the track develops. Your mutual respect and confidence can help your rider boost his results in a race. The simple truth is, a good mechanic has to be able to respond to the rider's needs in an organized manner.

Always bring a spare spark plug to the starting line to avoid the last second push-start. Oh well, at least dad is getting a workout!

Pro rider Tom Hoffmaster uses a POWER START timer. The electronic device straps to the front fender and features a clock and LED lights. When used in combination with beacons positioned on sections of the track, the rider can gain instant feedback on his riding techniques.

Chapter 3

HOW TO CONVERT YOUR MX OR DUAL-SPORT BIKE FOR OFF-ROAD RIDING

This Honda XR650L street bike has been modified for off-road with a set of knobby tires, stiffer springs and revalving by MX Tech, a larger fuel tank, White Bros. Pipe, and a set of guards for the engine and discs.

Off-road riding consists of everything from enduro, cross-country, hare scrambles, desert, and rally. This versatile form of motorcycle riding usually requires some modifications in the typical MX or dual-sport (street and trail) bike.

In the early 1970s, street legal dual-sport bikes were entry-level bikes for many motorcyclists. These bikes were far from off-road worthy and required modifications, such as bigger front wheels, gearing changes, knobby tires, plastic fenders, serrated footpegs, and wider handlebars in order to handle any serious off-road duty. These bikes were also heavy and required stripping-down the nonessential street kit—gauges, turn signals, horns, reflectors, and mirrors.

Modern dual-sport bikes come with most of the basics, but they too still need modifications based on the degree of challenge presented by the terrain you plan to ride on.

Late-model MX bikes often need to be de-tuned and built stronger in order to handle the long rides off-road. Components like crash guards, narrower handlebars, bigger fuel tanks, and spark arrestor tailpipes are some of the basic parts needed to make your MX bike off-road reliable. Depending

The Honda CR500 was converted to a street legal bike with products from E-Line and Baja Designs. Baja makes lighting kits that include switches, wiring harnesses, and battery kits.

on how serious you are, more complex changes may need to be made to the engine and suspension.

BASIC CHANGES

Dual-Sport Bikes

It's important to remove unnecessary parts from your bike to save weight and keep protrusions from injuring you in a crash. Remove the passenger pegs and brackets, chain guard, luggage rack, reflectors, and electrical switches. These original parts are expensive to replace and you might as well pack them in a safe place to maintain the resale price of your dual-sport bike. Exchange the bulky mirrors, turn signals, and taillight for parts designed for off-road use. Companies like Acerbis, Moose, and UFO make miniature mirrors, turn signals, and taillights that are rubber mounted to reduce the chance of damage if you fall.

Dual-Sport Tires and Wheels

Selecting tires requires careful consideration. If you ride on roads to get to areas where the terrain is hard packed and dry, consider the DOT knobbies. You'll get better traction than with a full knobby tire. If you ride strictly off-road and you're looking for maximum traction, use the chapter on tires to select the right tire for your needs. Don't ignore the inside of the tire! Most dual-sport bikes aren't equipped with rim locks to prevent the tire from rotating on the rim. You'll need to fit one rim lock to the front wheel and two rim locks to the rear wheel. Regarding inner tubes, heavy-duty tubes are a must. If you ride on terrain with sharp rocks then you might consider fitting mousse in place of the inner tubes. Mousse is heavier and affects the wheel balance, so it's not suitable for prolonged periods of high-speed street riding, but you'll never get a flat while riding off-road.

Some dual-sport bikes have steel rims as standard equipment. Steel rims bend easily when hitting rocks or big jumps. There are three aftermarket manufacturers of strong alloy rims, Tallon, Excell, and Sun. Companies like Tallon in England make complete wheels designed for heavy-duty off-road use.

Lighting Kits

A street legal dirt bike must have a 12-volt battery in order to provide lights when the engine is shut off. Several battery manufacturers make units that can survive being tipped upside-down in a crash and the constant vibration that occurs while riding off-road.

If you just want to fit lights to your MX bike to make it enduro legal, all you need is a functional head and taillight, and a mirror. Companies like Acerbis and UFO make headlight number plates, and taillights built into

This is Rodney Smith's Team Suzuki/FMF GNCC race bike. Most GNCC bikes start as MX models with modifications to make them more reliable and hold more fuel. The engine and suspension components are modified for a wider range of conditions.

a rear fender. These lights can be powered two different ways, either by 12V DC or AC volts. The 12V DC set-up requires a nicad battery, a simple switch, and a wiring harness connecting the head and taillights. This is a total loss charging system. The battery is only good for about one hour, then it has to be recharged.

An AC lighting system involves the use of generating coils mounted near the flywheel magnets, a voltage limiter, a switch, and a wiring harness. There are two types of kits available for most late-model MX bikes. One set-up is a simple coil that bolts on to the stator plate, the other is a more powerful system for greater headlight wattage. One company that distributes the high wattage system is CRE. The kit has an alloy side cover with a ring of several coils positioned around the outside of the flywheel magnets.

The simple lighting coil kits sell for about $80 and the deluxe kits sell for over $300.

Companies like Moose and Pro Racing sell the less expensive bolt-on coils along with other kits like wiring harnesses, voltage limiters, and switches.

Fuel Tanks

The typical range of an MX bike's fuel tank is about 30 minutes. If you intend to ride long distances you may want to consider getting a larger fuel tank. Aftermarket companies like Acerbis and Clarke make fuel tanks with capacities of 3.5 gallons or more. You can also buy smaller auxiliary fuel tanks that clamp to the cross bar or fit in place of the front number plate.

Damage Control

If Murphy had a law for off-road riding it would be that you will hit things, fall down, and break a component of your bike that makes it necessary for you to push it for several miles over harsh terrain. Zen law infers that if you spend the money on protection, then you'll never need it.

Whether you ride converting a dual-sport or MX bike for serious off-road use, you'll need to give it a shield of armor. Starting with the top of the bike and working down, the handlebars and controls are the most important area to concentrate on because that's where your hands are! There are

stronger handlebars available, with tapered wall tubing or stronger cross braces. The standard width of an off-road handlebar is 28 inches. The Answer Pro-Taper and Magura Bulge-Bar are made of tapered alloy tubing that allows a certain amount of flex to prevent permanent bending upon impact. These bars also absorb some of the vibration transferred through the forks and into the bars.

If you use a traditional handlebar you might consider filling the inside of the bar with an energy absorbing rubber. A popular product is a "Bar Snake." It's a rubber rod that can be inserted through the handlebar, to help absorb vibration.

Fastening guards to the ends of the handlebars is very important because they protect your hands from getting hit by tree branches and flying rocks. Hand guards come in a variety of designs. The two main types are aluminum flat-stock and injection-molded plastic. Fredette Racing, Moose, and Summers Racing Components make the aluminum hand guards. The Summers guard features bushings at the mounts to enable a bit of movement. The plastic type guards are made by Acerbis and UFO. These guards are very lightweight and feature shrouds that give added protection against rock roost.

Moving down to the radiators, companies like Devol Racing and Works Connection make aluminum guards that reduce the chance of the radiators being crushed in a fall. Devol also makes a guard for the front of the radiator to prevent branches from poking holes in the radiator, however this type of guard replaces the standard louver and reduces the cooling efficiency of the radiator.

The exhaust pipe of most two-stroke dirt bikes is prone to being damaged by rocks, ruts, trees, and even from casing the bike in deep whoops. There are a couple of different types of guards that are effective against flying debris but don't really offer any great protection during crashes. The second skin type aluminum and composite pipe guards also have an added feature of insulating the pipe from big changes in temperature that could affect the tuning. There are a few new pipes on the market designed with protection in mind. The Extreme aluminum pipe and the FMF Burley pipe are made of thick-gauge material. The Extreme pipe is made of aluminum for light weight and the FMF is made of steel. Considering the replacement cost of a pipe, weight isn't that big of an issue. The advantage of steel pipes is that it is easier to remove the dents from the pipe using heat and pressure type tools.

On the bottom of the bike there are some key areas that need added protection. The frame tubes, crankcases, engine side covers, brake and shift levers all need protection against rocks and trees. Guards for the bottom of the engine range from lightweight to heavy- duty. The lightweight guards designed for MX are usually made of either aluminum or carbon fiber, and are designed to streamline the bottom of the engine and make the bike less prone to grounding out on the peaks of jumps. The heavy-duty guards are huge aluminum pans that cover the bottom frame rails and extend up on the edges to protect the side covers. These guards are designed for use in conditions where there are a lot of big rocks and fallen trees. IMS

E-Line makes high wattage generators that include a side cover with a series of coils positioned around the flywheel.

The stock plastic disc guards won't withstand impacts from rocks or logs. Use an aluminum guard to protect the disc from damage.

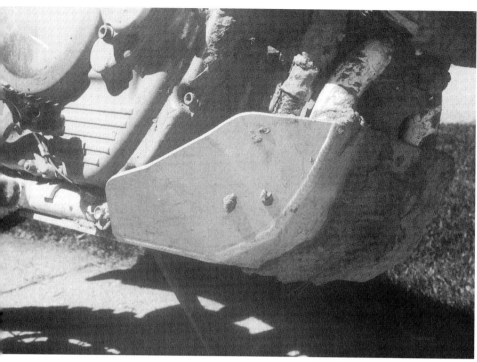

This is an IMS brand skid plate. It covers the frame and engine and is popular in off-road racing where boulders are encountered.

specializes in these types of guards because they serve the desert racing market.

If you are a handy fabricator you might want to make your own skid plate. If your bike has a steel frame, get a sheet of 1/8th inch mild steel and cut it to encompass the outer frame tubes and the bracket for the shock linkage. For more information, see the chapter on frame maintenance.

Another popular form of guard is the Works Connection side cover guards. These guards fasten to the engine mounting bolts and protect the side covers as well as the foot levers. Another common way to protect the foot levers from being torn loose by ruts and trees is to use a steel cable connected to the front edge of the levers and attached to the frame. You can buy the raw materials at the hardware store or buy the cable guards from companies like Moose, White Bros., WER, and Works Connection.

Waterproofing

There are two major areas of a dirt bike that need to be waterproofed, the electrical system, and the air and fuel intakes. An extreme off-road adventure might require that you submerge the bike up to the tailpipe in a river.

Starting with the electrical system, there are two materials needed for sealing wire connections, di-electric grease and electrical tape. Di-electric grease seals out water and prevents corrosion and enables a good electrical connection. Electrical tape can be wrapped around connectors to give added protection against moisture.

The intake system needs attention in these key points: the inlet and bottom drain of the air box, and the carb vents. Most dual-sport bikes have constricted air boxes and the drainpipes are usually routed to a one-way check valve chamber that allows outward flow only. MX bikes use a short rubber tube with slots that restrict airflow and enable free fluid flow out the bottom of the air box. The Honda XR250 uses an excellent check valve that can be adapted to the air box of most dirt bikes. The key is to enable outward flow in case water runs down the fuel tank or from the sides and seeps into the air box. If the air box has seams on the sides then you need to seal them with weather-strip adhesive.

All carbs use vent tubes to allow air to flow in and apply atmospheric pressure to the fuel floats. The vent tubes also enable fuel to flow out of the carb when the bike is tipped over. Normally the vent tubes exit from the bottom of the carb; that makes them vulnerable to drawing in water when crossing a stream. The best way to waterproof the carb's vent system is to buy 5 feet of 1/8th inch inner diameter tubing and replace the original vent tubes. Route the new vent tubes up into the top of the air box. That way if the bike falls over the fuel will spill into the air box where it can be safely collected by the bottom drain valve.

ENGINE MODIFICATIONS

Dual-Sport Bikes

Street bikes are normally plugged-up to meet noise and emission standards. There are baffles in the exhaust pipe, louvers and shrouds around the air box, and the carbs are jetted lean. It's not a simple matter of removing the obstructions to flow; the carb jetting may need to be compensated richer in order to get any power gains. Some aftermarket companies sell tailpipes and jetting kits as a set. These items will yield the biggest performance gains for the money, plus the aftermarket tailpipes are usually lighter in weight.

Changing the gearing usually requires a complete set of sprockets and chain. Get an O-ring chain for less maintenance. Expect to set the final drive at about 4 to 1. That equates to a 12-tooth sprocket on the engine and a 48-tooth sprocket on the rear wheel.

MX Bikes

Dirt bikes need to be de-tuned for off-road riding. Most MX bikes have high compression ratios that require expensive fuel. Also, the powerbands are designed for aggressive high rpm racing. Off-road riding conditions vary in terrain and available traction. It's also implied that there is a lot more slow-speed riding. This requires a powerband that is centered in the low- to mid-range rpm. In the case of an MX bike, de-tuning means that the powerband is shifted down the rpm range and the compression ratio is lowered to reduce the hit in the powerband to make the bike more controllable when riding over rocks and tree roots. A typical list of engine modifications for a two-stroke engine would include cylinder head modification to reduce the compression ratio, switching to dual-stage or thinner single-stage reeds, a fly-wheel weight, steel clutch plates, a spark arrestor tailpipe, and advancing the ignition timing. For more specifics on changing the engine's powerband for more low end, check out the chapter on two-stroke tuning.

The transmissions on MX bikes have closely spaced gear ratios, thereby limiting the bike's top speed. It is possible to install wide ratio gear sets for the two top gears. Companies like A-Loop and IMS sell kits for popular 250 and 500cc MX bikes.

The carburetion on MX bikes needs some attention too. Because most trail riding is done at low throttle openings, it's important to fine tune the jetting of the pilot/slow jet, air screw, throttle slide, and jet needle. Sometimes you need to jet leaner or use a hotter spark plug just to prevent wet-fouling while riding on and off the throttle through tight trails. Most MX bikes have carbs that aren't designed to idle. The Kehin PJ and Mikuni TM carbs don't have an idle circuit. Instead these carbs bleed raw fuel through the choke system or the needle jet. This just makes the spark plug wet-foul quicker. A good choice for an aftermarket carb is the Kehin PWK Air-Strike. It has an efficient idle circuit and two airfoils positioned in the air inlet of the carb to boost the velocity and direct the flow for quicker throttle response.

SUSPENSION MODIFICATIONS

Dual-Sport Bikes

Street bikes are usually sprung too soft for off-road riding. The heavy weight of the bike requires much stiffer springs than normally used on an MX bike. Modifying the suspension components of a dual-sport bike isn't as easy as just changing the springs. The valving must be changed to suit the harsh conditions and the stiffer springs. An increase in damping on the compression and rebound circuits is needed. Some of the shocks on dual-sport bikes are sealed units and cannot even be serviced, let alone revalved.

MX Bikes

Dirt bikes are designed with suspension valving that works best on the high end of the damping scale—meaning big jumps

Works Connection makes these lightweight radiator guards. They help prevent the radiator from being crushed when the bike is laid down. Radiators are expensive!

and square-edged bumps. That usually requires a sacrifice in damping performance for other riding conditions. You may read motorcycle magazine articles that refer to the "mid-stroke harshness" of a bike's forks or shock. That term best describes how an MX bike handles when you don't ride it hard enough! For riding off-road, you may want suspension that rides plush because you will spend more time sitting on the seat than standing in an aggressive position. You may also want the suspension to be sprung softer so you can easily shift the bike's weight and carry the front end over small obstacles. Softer springs enable the bike to sag more, which makes it easier to handle tight turns without the front end pushing to the outside of the turn.

SUSPENSION & CHASSIS

stand. Measure the rear from the axle to the base of the back of the seat. Measure the front from the axle to the triple clamp. Be sure to measure from the same point each time.

Use a metric tape measure and record the extended lengths of the front and rear ends. A metric tape measure is ideal because millimeters are small increments and you won't have to deal with subtracting fractions of an inch, as you would with an American tape measure.

2. Set the sag after practice and refuel the bike with the normal amount of fuel that you race with. If it's a mud race, don't scrape the mud off the bike.

3. The rider should be fully dressed in his racing clothing.

4. The rider should get on the bike and bounce up and down while the mechanic pushes the bike. This will help work out the stiction from the suspension so you can get an accurate measurement. Coast the bike to a stop; tapping the brake will shift the bike's weight and give you a false measurement.

5. The rider should sit in his normal racing position and someone should hold the bike vertical. The bike should be on flat ground for best accuracy. The mechanic should measure the compressed distance on the rear suspension at the same two points where he measured the extended distance.

6. Increase or decrease shock-spring preload to set the rear sag at 90–105mm.

7. Measure the front-fork sag the same way, and if necessary, adjust the sag to 35–50mm with 5–15mm of fork-spring preload (measured internally).

8. Finally, measure the unladen sag of the rear shock. Be sure to measure this AFTER you have the sag adjusted with the

Your bike's handling is critical to your riding experience. If your bike handles badly, it destroys your confidence and can make your body ache for days after riding. The information presented in the later part of this chapter is targeted to the needs of veteran riders and race mechanics who want to gain control over their suspension servicing and revalving needs. Novice riders and mechanics can benefit from this information, too, because it will make them a more informed consumer when shopping for suspension tuning services.

BASELINE SETTINGS

Every day I see people sending out their suspension for expensive revalving before they ever attempt to adjust and record the baseline settings—settings such as the front and rear spring sag, the compression and rebound clickers, the fork-tube overlap, or even the tire pressure. In many cases, the suspension components only need to be rebuilt and sprung correctly for the rider's weight and riding demands.

Measuring Sag

The rear sag should be measured and set before measuring the front sag. If the rear sag is too little and is corrected, more weight will then be placed on the front end and it will sag more than normal. Here are some guidelines for measuring the sag:

1. First measure the distance of the front and rear ends while fully extended on a bike

rider aboard. Let the bike sink under its own weight and measure the sag. It should sag 15–25mm if the spring rate is correct. If the sag is less than 15mm, then the spring is too soft for your weight. If the sag is greater than 25mm, then the spring is too stiff for your weight. It sounds backwards but think of it like this: If the sag is too little, then you had to preload the spring too much in order to get it to have the correct race sag for your weight.

Determining Spring Rates

Measuring the unladen sag of the rear shock, after you have set the race sag, is a good guide for the rear spring rate. The front is more difficult. You need to measure the fork sag and then compare the internal fork-spring preload. Expert riders may choose stiffer forks springs than the sag and preload indicates because they use the front brake hard and transfer more weight to the front end. One of the main causes of head shake is too soft of a fork spring rate or too low of an oil level in the forks.

Damping Circuits and Adjusters

The suspension circuits of the forks and shock are the HSC (high-speed compression), HSR (high-speed rebound), LSC (low-speed compression), and LSR (low-speed rebound). The compression adjuster for the shock is located on the reservoir, and the rebound adjuster is on the clevis (bottom shock mount). The compression adjuster for the forks is located on the bottom of the forks, and the rebound adjuster is located on the fork cap. Not all forks have rebound adjusters. Kayaba first used rebound adjusters on production cartridge forks in 1989.

LSR and LSC Circuits

The low-speed circuits work in two common track sections: braking for tight turns and accelerating on a straight with far-spaced, shallow whoops. All Japanese dirt bikes have suspension adjusting screws that affect the low-speed circuits only. Turning the adjusting screws clockwise will increase the damping and slow/stiffen the low-speed circuit. Turning the screws counterclockwise will decrease and speed-up/soften the low-speed circuit.

To get valid sag measurements, roll the bike and bounce up and down until the bike settles with the rider's weight.

With the bike held upright on flat ground, the rider sits in his race position. The mechanic measures the sag.

The front sag should be checked once the rear is adjusted. The normal fork sag range is between 35 to 50mm.

This is an example of a self-check, performed after practice on a muddy track. Mud can collect on the bike and cause the suspension to sag too much.

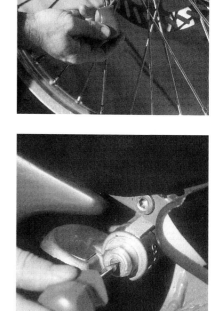

Top and above: Check the fork and shock compression and rebound clickers and record the settings in a log book.

SPRING WEIGHT/RIDER WEIGHT CHART

This chart will give you a starting point when trying to determine the proper spring rate for your weight.

	Shock-SpringRate (kg)		Fork-SpringRate (kg)	
	125cc	250cc	125cc	250cc
Rider Weight (lb)				
130-140	4.6	4.8	0.36	0.38
140–150	4.6	4.8	0.36	0.38
150–160	4.8	5.0	0.38	0.39
160–170	5.0	5.2	0.39	0.40
170–180	5.2	5.4	0.40	0.41
180-190	5.4	5.6	0.41	0.42
190-200	5.6	5.8	0.42	0.43
200-210	5.8	6.0	0.43	0.43
210-220	6.0	6.3	0.43	0.44
220-230	6.3	6.7	0.44	0.45

HSC and HSR Circuits

The high-speed circuits work in two common track sections: landing from big jumps and accelerating on a straight with tightly spaced, sharp-edged whoops. In 1996, Honda was the first to introduce HSC adjusters on the rear shock of the CR models. The adjuster has an inner screw for the LSC circuit and an outer ring for the HSC circuit. This adjuster can only make a slight difference in the high-speed damping.

White Power shock and fork adjusters are high-speed-only adjusters.

Basic Torque Settings

There are some basic torque settings that have a dramatic effect on the handling of a bike. The torque settings of the rear end are covered later in this chapter so we'll focus on the front end. The critical torque settings on the front end include the steering head, triple clamps, and axle clamps.

Modern dirt bikes have tapered steering head bearings that require a balance to torque. Too much torque makes it difficult to steer. Too little torque allows the forks to rock fore and aft during braking or when hitting

bumps. Improper torque on the bearings can also contribute to premature wear.

A generic way to adjust the steering head tension goes like this:

1. Put the bike on a stand and elevate the front wheel.
2. Loosen the top clamp bolts and the large center nut of the steering stem's bolt.
3. Use a steel punch and hammer to tighten the spanner nut located just below the top clamp. Turn the spanner nut 1/8 of a turn at a time and check the steering

SUSPENSION DATA LOG

Make some spare copies of this data log and record all of the pertinent data about your suspension, ideally at every track. This information is also vital for having work done on your suspension.

Personal Data

Rider's weight (with gear): _____(lbs.)

Height _____

Skill Level _____

Type of riding
(circle those you do regularly)

motocross   enduro   DTX   Supercross

desert   hill-climb   dual sport

Terrain Data
(circle conditions you encounter frequently)

Soil content: sand   mud   rocks   tree roots

                loam   hard clay

Elevation: big hills   off-camber   many jumps   sand

                whoops   square-edged bumps

Motorcycle Data

Brand _____ Model _____ Year _____

Fork Data

Spring rate _____ kg

Spring sag _____ mm

Unladen sag _____ mm

Spring pre-load _____ mm

Fork tube overlap _____ mm

Steering head tension set? _____

Compression adjuster: _____ clicks out

Rebound adjuster _____ clicks out/number

Maintenance history of the forks, including any crash damage

_____

_____

_____

_____

_____

_____

_____

Handling problems with the front end, including terrain condition and riding circumstances

_____

_____

_____

_____

_____

_____

_____

_____

Shock Data

Spring rate _____ kg

Spring sag _____ mm

Unladen sag _____ mm

Oil brand and weight _____

Compression adjuster _____ clicks out

Rebound adjuster _____ clicks out

Maintenance history of the shock, including frequency of link lubrication and bearing replacement

_____

_____

_____

_____

_____

_____

_____

_____

_____

_____

_____

_____

_____

Handling problems with the rear end, including terrain condition and riding circumstances

_____

_____

_____

_____

_____

_____

_____

_____

_____

_____

Tire Data

Front Brand _____

Model _____

Pressure _____ psi

Rear Brand _____

Model _____

Pressure_____ psi

This is the linkage fork designed by Ribi and used by Roger DeCoster. It uses a rising rate linkage and a shock absorber.

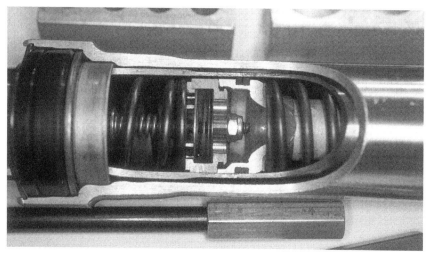

This is a cutaway of a Race Tech Emulator valve for an early model non-cartridge fork.

tension by turning the handlebars. Remember that when you tighten the large center nut on the steering stem that the steering tension will increase.

Steering tension is largely based on rider preference. Some mechanics use the flop test. They turn the handlebars slightly off center and the front-end flops to the steering stop. Keep in mind that the steering tension will decrease with use and require periodic maintenance. When a bike is new the tension changes quickly because the bearings and races are still in the process of seating on the frame and steering stem.

Triple Clamp and Front Axle Clamp Torque Settings

The clamp bolts must be loosened and re-tightened periodically to reduce the stress on the fork's internals, and to realign the forks in the triple clamps. If the clamp bolts are too tight the forks will be constricted causing binding in the fork travel. Another important aspect of the triple clamps is the fork tube overlap. Measure the overlap distance of the tubes and make sure they are equal. Then torque the clamp bolts to the specification listed in your bike's service manual.

Front axle clamps on telescopic forks are very critical to a fork's performance. If the fork tubes are not running parallel from top to bottom then the forks will have excessive stiction which will cause binding and premature wear of the bushings. This is a generic procedure for insuring that the fork tubes are parallel before you tighten the axle clamps.

1. Place the bike on a stand and elevate the front wheel.
2. Torque the axle to factory specs, but leave the fork to axle clamps loose.
3. Spin the front wheel with your hand and quickly grab the front brake. Repeat this procedure at least three times. This will help align the forks parallel.
4. Make sure the arrows on the axle clamps are pointing up then tighten the top bolts first until the clamp bottoms out. Now torque the bottom bolts to factory torque specs.

Suspension Data Log

You should keep a log of suspension adjustments and settings to help you in tuning. The log should track the following data for the fork: oil level, spring rate, spring preload, oil weight, fork-tube overlap, compression-adjuster setting, rebound-adjuster setting, tire type, and tire pressure. Keep similar logs for the shock, with the following data: spring rate, spring sag, oil weight, compression-adjuster setting, rebound-adjuster setting, tire type, and tire pressure. You'll find a handy blank data log in this chapter in the section on video suspension tuning.

Final Tips on Basic Tuning

Remember to do the tasks that are listed earlier in this section in order for the best results. Record the race sag and adjuster positions in a race logbook. Check the sag every four races because shock springs loosen up and break in. Fork springs tend to sack out within about one season. Try setting your race sag first and install the correct springs for your weight and riding demands before you spend $600 on revalving.

This is a WER steering damper. These devices are popular in off-road applications because the forks can be revalved for slow-speed trail riding and the steering damper prevents head shaking at high speeds.

CARTRIDGE FORK SERVICE & TUNING

More likely than not, your bike uses cartridge forks. They were introduced in 1986 on Kawasakis, and were used by most bikes in 1987.

In this section I'll show you some tips for getting better performance out of any cartridge type fork. Some tips involve just replacing worn bushings, while other tips are difficult to perform and require specialized knowledge and tools. Some parts of the cartridge are easily damaged and expensive to replace. Before you attempt any servicing of your bike's cartridge forks, purchase the factory service manual for details on assembly and tightening torque specs.

How a Cartridge Fork Works

The cartridge is basically two tubes with damping valves. The tubes slide together. The large tube is the damper rod, and it houses the compression valves. The small tube is the piston rod, and it houses the rebound valves. Cartridge forks rely on several plastic and metallic bushings to keep the telescopic rods from binding as they slide back and forth.

Cartridge fork valving consists of thin washers and cylindrical pistons with tiny bleed passages and slightly larger ports for the fluid to flow through. Damping is accomplished by restricting the fluid flow. An inherent problem with cartridge forks is that the debris from the bushings gets trapped between the valve washers and in the piston, thereby ruining the damping effect. This is the main reason why cartridge forks need to be cleaned and have the oil changed so often (every 10–15 hours of riding). The twin tube design features improvements to extend the service time between cartridge servicing, and improve the high-speed tuning (resistance to hard bottoming).

Evolution of the Cartridge Fork

Twin-tube forks were a big deal when they appeared on the RMs in 1994, but the technology had been around since 1975. It developed when front fork travel went from 6 to 12 inches in 1975. Factory teams were scrambling to find forks that were soft enough for slow-speed, bumpy, off-camber turns yet

This is a close-up view of a damper rod and a holding tool for a cartridge fork. Holding tools are required to prevent the damper rod from spinning when threading the base bolt.

CARTRIDGE FORK FAQs

Forks Rebound Fast

Question: The forks on my 1990 KX250 rebound very fast. When I hit bumps, they rebound so fast that my arms are getting pumped up. Also there is a clanking noise when the forks top out. I tried turning the rebound screws for more damping, but that made no difference. Could these problems be related? What do I have to do to fix these problems?

Answer: This is a common problem on Kayaba forks. The bushings that support and seal the piston rod and damper rod are worn. The worn bushings allow oil to bypass the rebound piston, causing a loss of damping. There is one bushing in each fork leg. It is located under the head cap of the damper rod. The head cap is threaded to the damper rod with normal right-hand threads. This is a difficult service job because the cartridge has to be removed from the forks and disassembled, and this disassembly requires special tools. Replacement bushings can be purchased from aftermarket companies such as Pro-Action, White Bros., and Race Tech.

Yamaha WR250 Headshake

Question: I have a WR250 and I love this bike. I do all sorts of riding with it, everything from technical woods riding to riding wide open down fire roads. The bike has a slight handling problem, headshake. The headshake occurs when I decelerate from top speed. The bike develops the headshake at a certain speed. My question is, can I do anything to eliminate this problem without affecting the bike's slow-speed handling characteristics?

Answer: Every dirt bike has a vehicle speed where headshake occurs. Enduro bikes are designed for slow-speed technical riding. The suspension components are valved to be responsive to tree roots, rocks, and muddy off-camber turns. If you revalve the suspension to handle high-speed headshake, then the bike won't handle well in slow-speed riding situations. The best compromise is to install a steering damper. Steering dampers can be tuned to absorb headshake at high speed, and also slow-speed deflections of the forks caused by rocks and ruts.

1990 CR250 Forks Clogged

Question: Every time I disassemble and clean the forks on my CR250, the base valve is clogged with gray metal debris. If I spend the money to hard-anodize the forks, will that reduce the debris that clogs the base-valve?

Answer: The source of the metal debris that clogs the base valve will surprise you. The debris isn't from the inside of the aluminum slider, it originates from the springs and the preload cones. The preload cones fit between the fork cap and the springs. The stock Showa cone is made of steel, which wears on the spring. The coating on Japanese fork springs flakes off through use and vibration.

The best fix is to install Eibach springs and Pro-Action preload cones. Eibach springs don't flake, and the Pro-Action cones are made of aluminum. You can find these parts at most shops, through mail order companies, or from Pro-Action.

What Are Anti-Bottoming Devices?

Question: I've seen products advertised as anti-bottoming devices for the forks. How do these devices work, and what rider types would it benefit the most?

Answer: The anti-bottoming devices for cartridge forks consist of an angled cone and a cup. These products replace the stock hydraulic bottoming cone and cup. The aftermarket products have more progressive angles machined into the cone and cup that soften the impact of the fork bottoming. These products require that you disassemble the cartridge, which requires special tools. This product is best for heavy or very aggressive riders who are still experiencing fork bottoming even after installing stiffer fork springs.

Front Wheel Plows and Climbs Out of Ruts

Question: I ride some real fast rutted trails down here in Texas. My bike has some strange handling problems. It's all in the forks; the front end plows to the outside of tight turns, and when I'm riding a rut the front wheel tries to climb out of the rut. I bought the bike used from a guy who weighs 40 pounds more than me. I think maybe he installed fork springs best suited to his weight. How can I determine if I should spend $60 on new springs?

Answer: If your bike's front wheel plows to the outside of turns and tries to climb out of ruts, then the front forks are either too stiff from the spring rate or the damping. To determine if the fork springs are too stiff for your riding weight, first set the rear sag to 100mms or 4 inches. Then measure the front fork sag just as you would the rear, with the bike fueled and all of your riding weight on the bike. Measure the forks extended and then sagged. They should sag 30–55mm or 1.25–2.25 inches. If they sag less, you probably need lighter springs.

Also, compression and rebound adjusters that are set too stiff/slow might also cause or contribute to the problem. Turn the adjusters in until they stop; then turn them out (counterclockwise) to 12 clicks compression, 10 clicks rebound. That is a good baseline setting for most cartridge forks. Then check the tire pressure. Average front tire pressure for different conditions is 10 psi for mud and 14 psi for dry conditions.

You may want to experiment with the fork-tube-to-top-clamp overlap. The standard settings range from flush (0mm) to 10mm. The more overlap, the tighter the bike will turn—but some high-speed stability will be sacrificed.

Rebound Adjusters Won't Stop

Question: I rebuilt my RMX250 forks for the first time, and now one of the rebound adjusters won't thread down to the zero position; it just keeps turning. What did I do wrong and how can I fix it? I hope I didn't mess the forks up.

Answer: Don't ride your bike until you fix this problem! It is likely that the piston rod was not threaded completely into the fork cap before the jam nut was tightened, so the rebound adjuster screw has nothing to stop against. If the jam nut loosens, the piston rod will unthread from the cap and the loose parts will flop around inside the fork tube causing major internal damage. Fix this problem a soon as possible! If you don't trust your mechanical abilities, trust the work to a qualified suspension technician.

Chronic Fork-Seal Leaks

Question: I'm having problems with leaky fork seals on my bike. I even bought the seals that claim to be leak-resistant. That didn't make any difference. What could I be doing wrong?

Answer: Check the fork tube for scratches or rust marks. There must be some imperfections in the tubes for it to leak after changing the seals and bushings. Also make sure you don't overfill the fork tubes with oil. Check the factory service manual for recommendations on oil volume. If the tubes are scratched, try polishing out the scratches with 400-grit wet/dry sanding paper.

Here is a tip to use when installing new seals: Place a plastic bag over the end of the fork tube so the seal doesn't get scratched during installation.

Air-Bleeding Forks

Question: I want to know why forks pump up with air and the proper way to bleed out the air when the forks are hot.

Answer: Forks draw in air when they rebound because the fork tube is misaligned with the slider and the air seeps past the wipers, seals, and bushings. The proper way to bleed the forks is to fully extend the forks (put the bike on a stand) and bleed the air from the Schraeder valves located on the fork caps. Many people make the mistake of bleeding the air pressure while sitting on the bike. That is bad because the forks are compressed, so the trapped air space is reduced. Trapped air space acts as an anti-bottoming device when landing from big jumps.

Forks Getting Softer

Question: I have been racing intermediate motocross for two years on my 1993 KX250. The problem has been a steady decline in the fork's performance. I have the oil changed every 5 or 6 races; they check the seals, and everything is great. But I have been riding faster all the time, and I have noticed that I am bottoming more and more. I raised the oil level to almost maximum spec. The compression adjuster is at full click, but the forks aren't working as they should. The bike still handles fairly well, except for the bottoming. How can I fix my forks?

Answer: The steady decline in your fork's performance is probably due to two factors: the fork springs are sacked out or the bushings are worn. First, check the free length of the springs and compare that to the spec listed in your Kawasaki service manual. If the springs are too short, replace them, and that should go a long way toward solving your problem. Take care when selecting a new set of fork springs. Make sure you choose a spring rate that complements your riding demands and geared weight.

Then, have a suspension technician check the bushings because if the bushings are worn, the oil will bypass the compression piston and valves, thereby reducing the damping effect. Regarding the clicker position, the fork clickers on your model only affect the low-speed damping. The suspension is in the high-speed damping mode when you land your bike from big jumps. Raising the oil level will affect the hydraulic bottoming resistance and will also make the damping more harsh in the mid-stroke of the fork travel.

Bottom of Forks Leaking Oil

Question: I have a 1989 KX80 and I recently replaced the fork seals because they were leaking. The forks are filled with 140mms of fork oil in each fork. It worked fine for a while, but recently the forks started leaking oil out of the bottoms. I tried tightening the Allenhead bolt on the bottoms of the forks, but it would not tighten because something inside the fork turned also. Please help me!

Answer: Don't ride the bike until this problem is fixed! The bolts that hold the forks together are unthreading. There are special copper washers under the heads of the bolts. You need to replace those and tighten the bottom bolts with the aid of a special tool that holds the damping rods. The bottom bolt threads into the damper rod. The top of the damper rod has a fitting that couples with the holding tool, enabling you to hold the damper rod and torque the bolt. The tool is available at any Kawasaki dealer. Most Kawasaki service departments will charge you about $35 to replace the copper washers and torque the bolts that hold the forks together. You will still have to install the springs, oil, and caps on the forks. Figure about $80 if you have a shop do all the work.

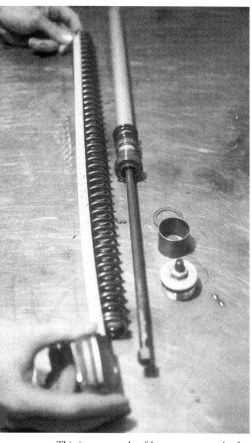

This is an example of how to measure the free length of the fork spring. Springs sack out over time and use. Pro riders replace their springs every four races.

The damper rod head is staked into place so it can never unthread. This is an example of how the stake mark is drilled in order to facilitate unthreading of the damper head.

Under the damper rod head is a bushing that supports and seals the rebound rod. If it wears out the rebound damping will become softer/faster.

stiff enough for hard landings from big jumps. Yamaha turned to a partnership with Steve Simons to try and make the long-travel suspension work. This alliance signaled the start of the best innovations in front forks.

In 1977, Yamaha adapted the accumulator from their monoshock to each fork cap on the front forks of the YZ250. Basically it consisted of a cylindrical chamber with a free-floating piston that separated two nitrogen gas-charged, spring-backed chambers. These accumulators worked as a pneumatic high-speed compression damping control. Modern cartridge forks use hydraulic damping controls (pistons and washers). Yamaha was bold to include this innovation on production bikes, but it was doomed to suffer the same fate as the Yamaha B.A.S.S system for rear shocks from the mid-1980s. The average mechanic had no tuning or service information so they weren't maintained properly.

In 1978, Steve Simons invented and patented a hydraulic bottoming cone and cup design that is used in all Kayaba cartridge forks. In the mid-1990s, companies started selling aftermarket bottoming cones for cartridge forks. These products were based on the original Simons design but were slightly different than OEM parts. The forks still have a hydraulic lock but it occurs more progressively than the stock part.

Terry Davis' Two-Stage Reservoir product was popular with desert riders in the early 1980s. It was designed for non-cartridge forks. It was a hydraulic/pneumatic version of Yamaha's accumulator fork cap. The main difference was that Terry Davis' design linked the fork tubes together with balance tubes and connected them to one giant aluminum-finned reservoir. It looked like you were riding with a beer-keg clamped to your cross bar. Despite the horrendous looks, it worked great if you had the patience to tune it.

This technology was used on Honda factory bikes in 1989 and nearly appeared on the 1990 CR250. These 1989 Showa factory forks were actually more advanced than the 1994 RM fork! Instead of using a floating piston and a spring, this design used a nitrogen-charged gas bladder (same as a rear shock). The gas pressure was increased if more resistance to bottoming was needed. These forks were the factory riders' favorite for Supercross because they were specially developed for front wheel landings. This fork design was scheduled for the 1990 CR250, but Honda switched at the last moment because they didn't feel the average guy could service these forks, and was more likely to ruin something. They were right. Better to have bad damping than no damping.

1994 Twin-Tube Showa RM Forks

In 1994, one of the Japanese manufacturers finally had the bullocks to select the

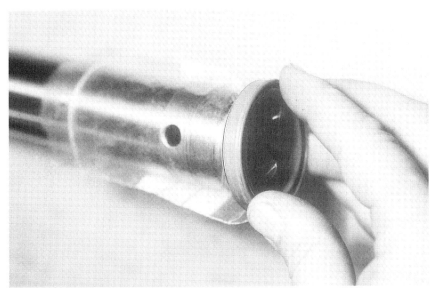

To prevent the seal from being damaged, wrap a plastic bag over the end of the fork tube.

This is a seal driver. There are several different types for conventional and upside-down forks.

Showa forks. The fork cap houses the compression valve at the top of a semi-sealed cartridge, so debris can't clog the valve. The fork cap also houses a free-floating piston-backed spring. The spring is used only during very high compression and full bottoming of the forks. This system offers track-side quick change capability of the compression-damping circuit; that is, once somebody figures out how to revalve and spring these forks for different types of riders.

1995

This was the year for aftermarket fork innovations. Bottoming cones became the rage. Products such as these replace the stock OEM hydraulic bottoming cones that fit on the piston rod of cartridge forks. The aftermarket cones are longer that the OEM cones and have more progressive angles that enable the forks to hydraulic lock at an earlier point in the travel. Another innovative product was designed by Terry Davis of Terry Products. The Double-Pumper kit also enables the cartridge to be replenished with oil during a series of high-speed compression impacts.

1996

This was the year that signaled the return of conventional cartridge forks that featured innovations similar to the Double Pumper. Two of these fork designs were the RM Suzuki Showa and the WP fork made in Holland.

FMF licensed a patent from a European inventor that returns the forks and shock to the sag point of the suspension. The sag point for the shock is about 95mm and 55mm for the forks. The device is basically a spring-backed cartridge that enables a tuner to adjust the point to where the suspension components top-out in travel. This eliminates some inherent problems associated with rear-end kicking during braking or head-shaking of the forks. Apparently a rider must adjust his pre-jumping skills because the suspension won't top-out completely. Ohlins experimented with a similar device in the early 1990s, but abandoned it.

2000

Kawasaki picked up on an idea that Honda abandoned in 1990, adding a rubber bladder to the forks to provide a pressurized air space. In Europe, Sylvain Geboers' Corona Suzuki racing team used remote reservoirs with nitrogen-pressurized floating pistons. Perhaps we'll see this innovation on future models of Suzuki RM models.

Special Tools
for Servicing the Cartridge

It takes more special tools to service cartridge forks than to rebuild the motorcycle's engine. The basic tools include a damper rod holder, a bleeder rod, and a seal driver. Race Tools is the only company that

sells suspension rebuilding tools, besides the Japanese motorcycle manufacturers. In addition, a tape measure can be used to set and measure the oil level, but a suction-type level-setting tool is more convenient.

Damper rod holding tools are used to prevent the rod from spinning when the base-valve bolt is unthreaded. These holding tools are not universal in size and flange shape because the flange shape on top of the damper rod is different from brand and model.

Bleeder-rod tools thread on to the top of the piston rod. During the final air-bleeding procedure, it's necessary to stroke the piston rod through its travel in order to facilitate bleeding of the cartridge. Four different sizes of bleeder rods are made to service cartridge forks made 1986–96.

Seal drivers are metal slugs machined to fit the outer diameter of the fork tube. There are two types of seal drivers—solid and split. Split drivers are needed for upside down forks because those types of fork tubes

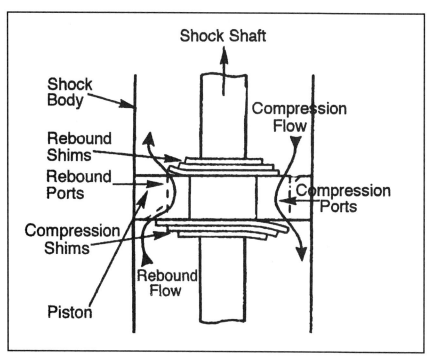

This illustration shows how the shim stack (or leaf stack) affects oil flow. By altering the size and number of shims, a suspension tuner can tailor dampening to specific needs.

The preliminary air bleeding technique involves capping the end of the fork tube and compressing the fork to force oil through the cartridge by building air pressure. This technique is for cartridge forks, not twin tube forks.

have axle clamps. Conventional cartridge forks can use solid seal drivers because the driver is installed from the top of the tube.

Servicing twin-tube forks does not require a holding tool or a bleeder rod; you will need two special wrenches; one for the fork cap and the other to hold the damping rod. However you still need a seal driver to install the fork seals.

There are also some general tools that you'll need, including a vise with soft jaws, an assortment of large-diameter six-point sockets, a plastic mallet, a flat-blade screwdriver, an oil pan, and cleaning solvents.

If you are interested in revalving the fork valves, then you'll need some very special tools—such as digital calipers for measuring the shims and drivers to remove the peened tab on the bottoming cone. The bottoming cone is located in the middle of the piston rod. By removing the bottoming cone, you can separate the piston rod from the damper rod.

Changing Fork Oil

I strongly recommend that you completely disassemble and clean your cartridge forks every 20 riding hours. However, if you are sure that the forks are in good condition

and you just want to change the oil, here is a simple method.

1. Remove the forks from the bike.
2. Unscrew the jam nut on the fork cap.
3. Unscrew the fork cap.
4. Remove the plastic spacer.
5. Slide out the spring.
6. Turn the fork upside down and drain the oil from the forks.
7. Stroke the piston rod to pump the oil out of the cartridge while draining the forks.
8. Add about 4 ounces of fork oil to each tube and use it to flush out the tubes.
9. After you have drained out the flushing oil, follow the procedure listed later in this section for filling the oil and bleeding air from the cartridge.
10. Reassemble the forks and put them back on your bike, being careful to torque the pinch bolts to recommended settings.

Disassembling Forks

Simply changing the oil is fine for periodic maintenance, but if your forks haven't been serviced in a season or more, you'll have to disassemble and clean the cartridge. Cartridge forks are especially susceptible to dirty oil, as gook tends to accumulate around

the cartridge and the fork loses damping.

1. Remove your forks and drain the oil (see above).
2. Take the nut off the very bottom of the fork, either with an air impact wrench or by holding the damper rod in place with a damper rod holding tool (available at your dealer or from Race Tech).
3. Pull the cartridge out of the bottom of the fork.
4. Lay out all the parts and clean thoroughly with contact cleaner (note that at this point, the fork tube can be pulled from the fork slider to replace fork seals, etc.).
5. Replace any worn seals or bushings (see below).
6. Install the cartridge.
7. Tighten the nut on the bottom of the fork, using the special tool or an air impact wrench (be VERY careful with the impact

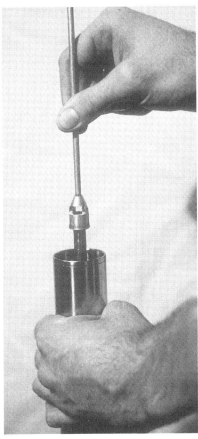

The secondary air bleeding technique involves the use of a bleeder rod that threads to the rebound rod. Stroking the bleeder rod through its full travel helps force out the trapped air.

wrench; you can blow the O-ring off of the cartridge and lose all damping).

8. Install the spring and spacer.

9. Follow the procedure listed later in this section for filling the forks with oil and bleeding air from the cartridge.

10. Reassemble the forks and put them back on your bike, being careful to torque the pinch bolts to recommended settings.

Replacing Bushings

The seals, wipers, and bushings should be replaced at least once a year. If you are looking for the highest level of performance, replace the bushing that fits in the head of the damper rod and supports the piston rod. The standard bushing has excess clearance that can cause the piston rod to go off-center and produce more stiction in the forks. After you have spent the time to polish the bearing sur-

An oil level setting gauge insures that the oil level is the same in both fork tubes.

faces of the damper and piston rods, then replace the standard bushing with an accessory bushing that has tighter clearances and a low coefficient of friction. Enzo Racing in America offers a racing bushing for Kayaba forks.

When your forks lose rebound damping, the main cause is worn piston rod bushings. When these bushings are worn out, they allow the cartridge fluid to bypass the bushing and piston rod, thereby losing the damping effect. If your bike's cartridge forks make a clunking sound when they extend, the piston-rod bushing is worn out.

The piston rod bushing can be replaced by unthreading the head from the damper rod, where the bushing is housed. This procedure is done by heating the steel head to break the bond of the locking agent on the threads. Then, use a chain-clamp wrench to grasp the steel head and unthread it from the aluminum damper rod. After the bushing is replaced, the threads of the damper rod and head must be carefully cleaned and a permanent locking agent applied. Then, tighten them with the chain-clamp-wrench. Warning: This procedure is very difficult and should only be entrusted to a professional suspension technician. The

Teflon bushings support the fork tube to the slider. You can tell when they are worn because there will be discoloration on the load-bearing surface. These bushings are easy to replace and should be changed once a year. The slider bushing (large-diameter bushing) falls out when you separate the two tubes. The fork-tube bushing (small diameter) is under spring tension, so it must be removed by using a straight-blade screwdriver to spread the bushing at the side slit and slide it off the end of the fork tube. When you install the large-diameter bushings, take care to seat them properly in the slider before trying to install the fork seals. You do not need to use any special oil or grease on these bushings because they are Teflon-coated.

Replacing Fork Seals

Once you have the forks disassembled and the fork slider and tube separated (see previous section), the fork seals can be removed. When installing the new seals, you must be very careful not to tear them when sliding them over the fork tube. Some grease and a plastic bag are key to getting your new seals installed without tearing.

1. Apply Teflon grease to the wiper and seal.

2. Place a plastic bag over the end of the fork tube.

3. Slide the seal over the plastic bag and onto the fork tube. The plastic bag covers the bushing grooves and prevents the seal from tearing as it slides over the sharp edges of the bushing grooves.

Now, you can reassemble your forks and be confident that your new seals will hold.

Filling with Oil and Bleeding Air from the Cartridge

Here are some tips for filling Showa or Kayaba cartridge forks with oil and bleeding out the air.

1. During the initial filling and bleeding sequence, compress the fork tube and fill the fork to within 2 inches of the top.

2. Extend the fork, cap your hand over the end of the tube, and compress the fork. You'll feel air pressure building up under your hand. That is good because the oil is under pressure and that will help force tiny air bubbles through the shims of the compression valve and also displace the

air that gets trapped between the fork tube and slider. Repeat this procedure at least four times, adding oil each time.

3. Use a stroker rod to grasp the piston rod, and stroke the rod up and down until the tension through the stroke is equal. Equal tension is an indication that the air is bled from the cartridge.

4. To set the oil level, remove the spring and compress the fork. Use a thin ruler (preferably metric) to measure the distance between the top of the tube and the top of the oil. An oil level setting tool (or a large syringe with a bit of hose attached) is the quickest way to set your oil level. Also, make sure there is an excess amount of oil in the fork so the oil level setting tool can suck out oil to set the proper level.

5. The oil level should be set with the spring removed and the fork tube bottomed. Kawasaki recommends setting the oil level 10mm higher than the spec because that will compensate for the small amount of air trapped between the slider and tube. That bit of air works its way out when the bike is ridden.

Twin-Tube Maintenance and Tuning

The twin-tube cartridge forks are essentially a cartridge in which the oil doesn't re-circulate into the outer tubes. The twin-tube fork doesn't require as much maintenance because the internal cartridge is sealed from the outer tubes, and the sliding interface between the two outer forks' tubes is the source of the metallic contamination that ruins the performance of a cartridge fork. Twin-tube forks also don't require special tools to service the cartridge. Some companies like Motion Pro make dedicated wrench sets for the top cap and the cartridge rod; you can use standard wrenches to do the same job. This is a generic procedure for servicing a twin-tube fork.

1. Loosen the fork cap with a six-point box wrench (usually 50 millimeters). It's best to hold the fork tube in the bike's triple clamp; just be sure to loosen the top clamp bolts. If the forks are separate from the bike, you can use soft jaws in a vise; just take care not to clamp the vise so tight that you crush the fork tube.

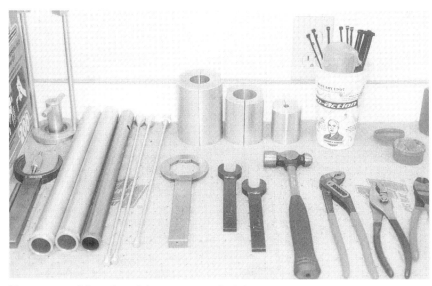

These are some of the tools needed to repair twin tube forks.

These two wrenches are essential. The large wrench is for the fork cap and the small shouldered wrench is for the bottom of the cartridge. Race Tech sells these tools.

2. Loosen the bolt at the bottom of the fork until it separates from the bottom fork tube.

3. Depress the fork cap until the cartridge rod extends out the bottom of the fork far enough to expose the wrench flats. Use an open-end wrench to hold the cartridge rod and unthread the bottom bolt completely. Take care when removing the bolt because the telescopic rebound adjuster tube will fall out of the bottom of the cartridge.

4. Remove the cartridge from the fork tubes by pulling it out from the top.

5. Use a straight bladed screwdriver to remove the wiper, then remove the circlip that retains the fork seal.

6. Use a propane torch to heat the area around the seal so as to break the bond of the bushing.

7. Grasp the fork tubes with both hands and yank them apart rapidly several times until the tubes separate.

8. Carefully inspect the bushings, inside and outside, to look for wear marks. Normally you should replace the bushings and seals every time you change the

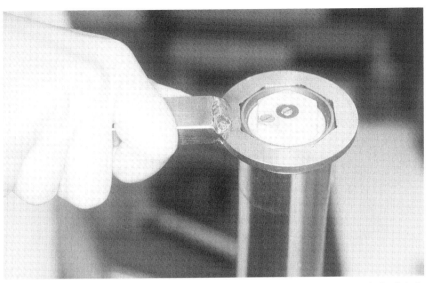

Start by removing the fork cap. Don't squeeze the tube in a vise; try to loosen the cap with the forks in the triple clamps, or by holding the tube with a strap wrench.

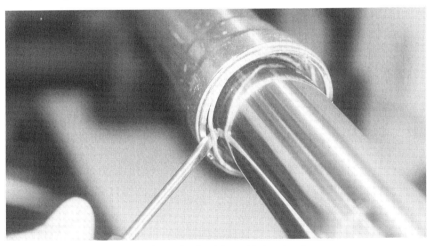

The fork tubes are held together with a circlip that is located below the wiper.

Extend the cartridge out the bottom of the forks and use the small shouldered wrench to hold it while you loosen the base bolt with a six-point socket.

fork oil, or about every 50 riding hours. That will insure that the expensive aluminum fork slider doesn't wear out prematurely. Installing new bushings and seals is the same for normal cartridge forks. See the photos for examples.

9. Disassemble the compression valve and clean any debris from the piston ports and between the shims by spraying brake cleaner on the parts.

10. To assemble the forks, start by filling the inside of the cartridge to the level specified by the manufacturer. Usually that is a ledge where the compression valve fits.

11. Bleed the cartridge of air in the normal way by slowly stroking the cartridge rod through its full travel. Do this until the rod moves smoothly. Smooth travel indicates that the air is bled to the top of the cartridge.

12. Now put the cartridge in the top of the forks, insert the telescopic rebound rod, and tighten the bottom bolt.

13. Fill the outer tubes with a measured volume of oil based on the manufacturer's specification.

14. Thread in the top cap and compression valve.

Basic Fork Revalving

The latest design rage for cartridge forks is to increase the diameter of the compression and rebound pistons, and separate the compression valving into low, medium, and high-speed damping modes. For our tuning tips discussion we refer to the two states of compression valving as Passive (slow speed) and Active (high speed). The following models use this new design: all 1996 and later models of 125cc and 250cc Japanese MX bikes. Expect other models of forks to evolve to this type of design in the near future.

Circulating Controversy

The main difference between the popular models of cartridge forks is the circulation path of the oil. Twin-tube forks are non-circulating whereas most other cartridge forks are circulating. Twin-tube forks use the oil in a sealed cartridge. The theory is that the main sources of contamination in a fork are the wear between the spring, interface of the fork tube and slider, and the bushings. The metallic debris generated from these moving parts contaminates the oil and forms deposits in critical areas like the pistons and valve stacks. Aftermarket tuning companies like Pro-Circuit offer services to convert circulating cartridge forks to non-circulating types. They don't convert it to a twin-tube fork, but a hybrid design.

Other tuners like Terry Davis of Terry-Cable manufacture aftermarket fork kits that increase circulation in non-twin tube forks. The theory is that in desert racing the vehicle speeds are so fast that when you ride over a section of washboard terrain, the cartridge doesn't have the ability to replenish with oil. The oil is pumped into the outer tubes and the damping fails because of air lock. Generally

To disassemble the cartridge, clamp the wrench flats of the upper part of the cartridge in a vise with soft jaws.

speaking the Pro-Circuit modification is intended for stadium motocross and the Terry-Cable kit is designed for desert racing.

Passive and Active Valving

On a modern cartridge fork, the rebound piston controls the active rebound and compression damping. The adjusting screw controls the passive damping. Different types of pistons and shim valves can separate the compression damping. The compression valve and adjusting screw are mounted on one end of the forks, usually at the top of the forks on twin tube forks, or to the bottom of re-circulating cartridge forks. The rebound adjuster is mounted in the bottom of the forks on twin tube forks and to the fork caps on re-circulating forks. It doubles as the bolt that fastens the cartridge tube to the lower fork leg, thereby holding the forks together.

The compression valve is mounted in a column of fluid (fork oil) inside the cartridge. The type of damping that the compression valve absorbs is passive in nature, because the valve doesn't move through the oil. The oil is forced through the compression valve by the displacement action of the moving rebound piston.

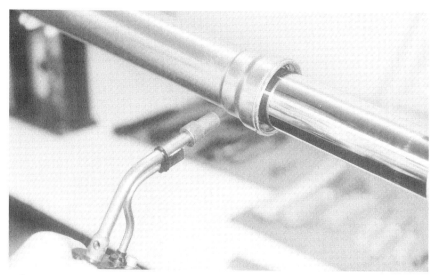

Before attempting to separate the tubes, use a propane torch to heat the area where the bushings fit. This will reduce the chafing between the bushings.

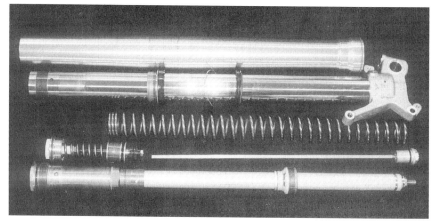

This is a disassembled twin tube cartridge fork. From top down and left to right: fork slider, fork tube, spring, fork cap with compression valve, telescopic rebound rod and base bolt rebound adjuster, and main cartridge.

The backside of the rebound piston and a set of valve shims control the active damping of compression. When the forks compress, the piston rod and rebound piston accelerate through the column of fluid inside the cartridge. The rebound piston has bi-directional ports to allow oil to flow through to a set of valve shims. The active valve shims are located on the top side of the rebound piston. These shims have a huge effect on the mid-stroke and high-speed damping of the fork. In order to modify the active valving, you have to disassemble the cartridge, including removing the head from the damper rod. That is a difficult procedure and should be entrusted only to a professional suspension technician.

Problems that Mimic Poor Tuning

Mechanical problems, such as worn parts, can cause your forks to act as if they are poorly tuned when they are not. Before you spend a lot of money on revalving or other fork tuning, make sure there is not a mechanical cause for your fork's problems. The following is a list of potential trouble spots to check on your forks:

1. Oil breakdown can make the damping seem too fast or soft, especially when the fork oil gets hot. Debris can also accumulate in the valving to hinder the damping. Fix by cleaning the forks and changing the fork oil.

2. Blown oil seals cause a lack of damping and a number of other catastrophic

Shock Rebound Adjuster Seized

Question: I have a 1989 CR250, and the rear shock's rebound adjuster is seized. I can't turn it with a screwdriver. What's wrong?

Answer: The problem you describe is common for Showa shocks on 1986–89 CR250s and CR500s. The rebound adjuster consists of a fine-threaded screw and a ramp-shaped nut. Condensation causes the fine threads to become corroded, and the corrosion keeps the adjuster screw from turning. It is possible to remove the rebound adjuster cartridge and clean the threads of the screw so the adjuster works; this task requires that you discharge the nitrogen gas pressure from the shock's bladder. If you do not have the special tools or knowledge required to service suspension components, then don't try to repair the adjuster. Instead, trust the job to a professional suspension technician.

Rebound Damping

Question: Your writings on suspension revalving mention high- and low-speed rebound damping. You say that it works similar to high- and low-speed compression damping. Is this right? The rebound circuit doesn't take spike hits; the maximum return rate should be pretty predictable. It's with the wheel returning with no load. With any load on the wheel, it will return more slowly. Does the shim stack for the rebound circuit on most rear shocks have a high-speed and low-speed stack separated by a transition shim, as is the compression stack?

Answer: Some rear shocks have a transition shim separating high- and low-speed shim stacks—commonly used on heavy bikes that have to be sprung stiffly. The purpose of the rebound circuit is to damp the release of the spring's stored energy and slow the return speed of the shock shaft. When the shock is bottomed, the stored energy of the spring will be at its maximum, so more damping is needed when the bottomed shock starts to extend than when it is fully extended. The rebound damping must be closely matched to the stored energy of the spring. When suspension tuners install stiffer-rate shock springs, they typically need to revalve the rebound circuit for more damping.

Rear Suspension Kicks

Question: I have a 1993 YZ250 with stock suspension. I don't race, just ride at my local track. I have tried all the recommended settings for the suspension and none have worked. These are the settings that have worked the best—Shock: R-5, C-18; Fork: R-5, C-10. I am 5 feet, 9 inches tall and weigh 160 pounds. Sag is set at 95mms. Oil height for the forks is 110mms. The bike has stock spring rates. My problem is that the rear is kicking back at me. It seems to be kicking out to my left. All my suspension parts are in great shape, with no slack. This seems to happen only off of big jumps. The suspension feels pretty good on the rest of the track. Also, when I land from the big jumps my suspension springs up too quick, lifting me off of my footpegs. If I change my shock rebound to 4, it seems to hang-up too much on jumps. All my settings are out from all the way in. I have watched the other bikes on the track land off of the same jumps and their suspension does not bounce near as much as mine. We seem to be going about the same speed (third gear) and landing in the same place. Do you have any suggestions besides getting the suspension professionally rebuilt? I'm trying to get by without spending a whole lot of money.

Answer: When you bottom the bike and compress the shock spring, there is a considerable amount of stored energy in the spring. The rebound circuit absorbs part of that energy. Your shock is rebounding too fast, causing the sprung mass of the bike to accelerate rapidly and the rear tire to lose traction and slide the rear end sideways. When a bike kicks, that is another indication that the rebound damping is too fast/soft. Has the oil ever been changed in the rear shock? The oil could be broken down, causing the too-fast rebound problem. That is the first thing you should do. If you don't have the knowledge or tools to rebuild the shock, trust your shock to a suspension technician. The rear-spring-sag spec of 95mms is contributing to the problem. After the shock is rebuilt, set the rear spring sag to 100mms, and check the bike's unladen sag. It should be 17–25mms. Start with the basics of rebuilding the shock. I understand that you are on a budget, but there is no free way to fix this problem. Consider this: If you let that shock run too long with poor-quality oil, the shock body could wear out. Then that $50 oil change will seem minuscule in comparison to a $600 shock.

problems such as worn bushings. Replace the seals.

3. Worn rebound piston rings. Most bikes use a plastic seamless band for a rebound piston ring. If your forks seem to rebound too quickly, the oil may be bypassing the rebound piston and shim valving. Unfortunately this seal band cannot be replaced; you must buy the entire piston-rod assembly.

4. Sacked fork springs. Fork springs become shorter in length with use, which can cause headshake or wobbling at high speed. Plan on replacing fork springs every season. Check to make sure they are even in length as a set.

5. Dented aluminum sliders. The sliders are made from thin-walled aluminum tubing, so the rocky roost from other bikes can easily cause dents in the sliders. These dents can cause the forks to bind, making the fork damping harsh. Replace the sliders when they get dented, and install plastic rock guards to prevent rock dents.

6. Worn bushing for the piston rod to damper rod. This bushing is located in the head of the damper rod and it supports the piston rod. If your forks appear to have lost rebound damping, this bushing is probably worn and must be replaced.

Tuning with Oil Viscosity

There are two ways to rate suspension fluids, the Society of Automotive Engineers (SAE) weight and the viscosity index number. The SAE determines the weight number with a standard test that measures oil flow through a fixed orifice at a certain temperature in a 30-minute period. The viscosity

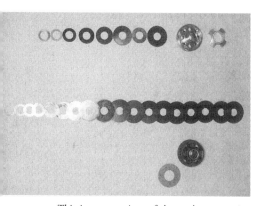

This is a comparison of the stock compression valve assembly and a Pro Action replacement valve. The Pro Action system uses a two-stage shim stack rather than the traditional single tapered shim stack.

On Japanese shocks the cover for the seal pack is wedged into place. Remove it with a punch and hammer by tapping on the indentations machined in opposing sides of the cap.

index number is a measurement of the oil's flow rate through a fixed orifice, over a specific temperature range in a set time period. The fluid velocities through the tiny steel shim valving and pistons of the cartridge forks are much greater than in the old-style forks, which used drilled jet passages.

Be sure to use a cartridge fork oil when you replace the oil, and the weight is in reality not that important. Cartridge fork oil is available from about 2 1/2 to 7 weight, and any of those work well. In general, with higher weight oil, you'll get an incremental increase in compression and rebound damping. In reality, most riders wouldn't be able to notice these differences.

In general, raise the oil level when you're bottoming hard. Increased oil will help the last third of the stroke only.

Fork Oil Breakdown

The fork oil breaks down when its additives are depleted and it is contaminated with aluminum and bronze debris. The additives that enable the oil to have a low flow resistance are polymer particles, and they eventually accumulate as a varnish-like coating on the inside of the fork tubes. Consequently, the oil in new-style cartridge forks should be changed every 15 or 20 rides to maintain the best performance.

The main source of debris in the oil is spring flaking. Only Eibach aftermarket springs are coated with a flexible polymer that resists flaking. The aluminum damper rods and sliders, along with the plastic and bronze high-wear bearing parts, also slowly break down during use and contaminate the oil. Further debris is produced when steel preload rubs against the springs. Pro-Action sells aluminum preload cones of an updated design for the early 1990s Japanese dirt bikes. These cones greatly reduce the amount of debris produced by the cones rubbing on the springs.

Fork Spring Preload Tuning

Before you try to measure and set the preload, measure the length of both springs and compare the measurements to the manufacturer's spec for minimum length. If the springs are too short, it means they are sacked out and need to be replaced. When you purchase new springs, make sure you get the proper spring rate for your bike and rider weight. The Japanese manufacturers have recommendations listed in the service manual for the best spring rate based on rider weight. If you are an expert rider and use the front brake hard or ride on tracks with big jumps, you should select the next stiffer spring rate from the one recommended in the service manual.

Here is how to measure and set the spring preload. Disassemble the fork. Let the fork tube bottom and extend the piston rod. Slide the spring over the piston rod. With the rod extended, measure the distance between the end of the spring and the point where the spring retaining collet clips into the rod. That gives you the preload measurement. Normally the preload should be 5–15mm. The only way for you to vary the preload is to adjust the jam nut height on the piston rod to set the correct preload.

White Power and Ohlins fork springs are available in a wide variety of spring rates, and are the proper length to replace extra-long Japanese springs that have too much preload. True-Tech sells aftermarket fork caps for 1990s models of Japanese dirt bikes.

These fork caps feature an adjusting screw to vary the spring preload. This is an excellent product, but they require frequent maintenance. If you purchase a set of these fork caps, be sure to pick up a spare set of seals for the caps.

REAR SHOCK SERVICING

This section is a general overview for single-shock servicing. I'll show you what things you can clean and inspect yourself and how a professional service technician would service a shock. This section is also intended to give a thorough understanding of how suspension works and tell you all the things they leave out of the service manual. I want you to become a more informed consumer by learning when to have your shock serviced and how to shop for suspension services.

Total shock service with cleaning and oil changing should be performed every 15–20 riding hours. Servicing suspension components is a specialized task that requires knowledge, experience, and access to special tools and replacement parts. If you lack any of these important things, don't attempt to

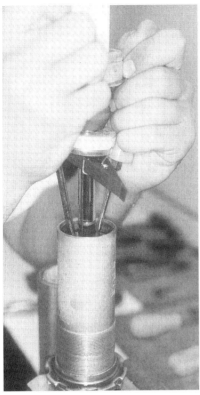

Use a clothespin to hold the cap out of your way and use two punches to depress the seal pack so you can remove the circlip.

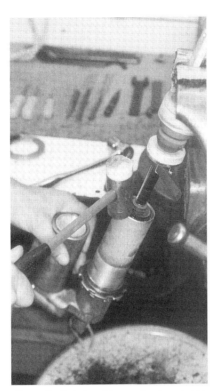

Clamp the clevis in soft jaws and a vise to hold it while you gently tap on the shock body with a plastic mallet to separate the body from the shaft assembly.

Ohlins shocks use a different way of retaining the shaft assembly. A threaded cap bolt is used to secure the shock together. Ohlins shocks require a set of expensive, special tools in order to service the shock.

service your suspension components yourself. Trust revalving to a suspension technician.

Also, you should regularly clean, inspect, and grease your rear linkage. See the "Servicing Rear Suspension Linkage" section later in this chapter for more details.

Your bike's shock is constantly subjected to internal and external torture. Inside the shock, the bronze piston ring scrapes up against the hard-anodized aluminum shock body walls in oil that reaches temperatures of 450 degrees Fahrenheit. The bronze and aluminum particles quickly contaminate the small volume of shock oil, causing the oil to break down.

To make matters worse, the shock is also constantly subjected to external torture. The outside of the shock is constantly subjected to dirt particles being rammed into the shock seal by the foam bumper and the high-strength detergents from the spray of a pressure washer.

Common Problems

The external elements cause the wiper and seal to fail. Small quantities of oil flow past the seal and you hardly notice until most of the oil is lost and the shock shaft turns blue from overheating. It's easy to forget about the shock because it's bolted into the center of the bike, but it's hard to forget about the replacement cost of a shock if it fails!

Basic Cleaning

This procedure should be performed every five riding hours:

1. Power-wash the shock. You want the dirt off the outside of the shock before you do the detail cleaning. Take care not to spray directly at the shock seal. Also, be sure to spray clean the fine threads on the shock body.
2. Spray penetrating oil on the threads and wait 15 minutes before you try to unthread the spring retaining nut. Unthread the nut so you can remove the spring collet and the spring so you can remove the seal cap. There are two types of spring collets. One has an open slot and the other is a solid

disc with a circlip. The circlip must be removed before you can remove the spring.
3. Use a plastic mallet and punch to rock the seal cap back and forth until the cap pops loose from the shock body. Notice how much dirt and debris is under the seal cap, jammed up against the seal wiper. It's very important to carefully clean under the foam bumper and the seal cap with detergent and water.
4. Check the seal wiper for oil seepage. Seepage indicates that the seal is worn and needs to be replaced.
5. Check the shock shaft for deep scratches and a blue color. The blue indicates that the shock was severely overheated, probably from the loss of oil at the seal. The shaft can be replated or replaced if it is discolored or deeply scored.
6. Your factory service manual lists a minimum

Late-model Showa shocks use additional stake marks to prevent the compression bolt from unthreading. These stake marks must be drilled before attempting to remove the compression bolt. Otherwise the fine threads on the bolt will be stripped, as it is unthreaded.

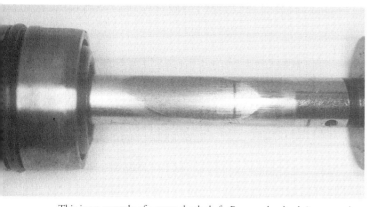

This is an example of a worn shock shaft. Because the shock is mounted on an angle, one side of the shaft will wear out quicker. If the shaft isn't bent, then it can be rechromed.

Japanese shocks have a standardized method for retaining the parts on the shaft. A nut is threaded onto the shaft and then peened over. In order to do any service tasks to the shaft, like seal changes or revalving, the nut must be removed. The easiest way is to grind the nut on a 45-degree angle until the peened edge is gone. Then the nut can be unthreaded. A bench grinder and a steady hand are needed to do this task.

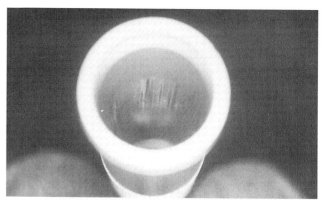

This is an example of a worn shock body. Notice the deep vertical scour marks? A dial bore-measuring gauge will reveal that the body is worn too much at that spot. Sometimes the body can be reconditioned with nickel electroplating. Hard anodizing treatments are ineffective at repairing shock bodies because the material cannot be applied thick enough.

free-length for the shock spring. Measure it to make sure it hasn't sacked out.

7. Remove the seals from the top shock mount and clean the dirt and old grease from the seals and spherical bearing. The bearing doesn't require lube but you should pack the seals with grease to prevent dirt and water from reaching the bearing.

8. Check the lower shock-mount clevis for cracks at the bolt hole. Cracks are common on YZ shocks because the bottom shock mount protrudes below the frame tubes.

Shock Disassembly

The following is a typical disassembly procedure that a professional service technician would follow when servicing a shock:

1. Depressurize the gas bladder, noting any oil mist escaping with the gas, which would indicate a perforated bladder that needs to be replaced.

2. Remove the compression adjuster bolt and let the oil drain. Take care when unthreading the compression bolt. Examine the first threads for three deep peen marks. You may need to drill the centers of the peen marks or the threads could be damaged.

3. Use a bladder-cap-removing T-handle to depress the bladder cap enough to remove the circlip. Now, the bladder cap can be removed.

4. Remove the shock shaft by popping up the seal cap, depressing the seal-pack assembly with two drift rods, and removing the circlip that holds the seal pack in place. Use a scraper to remove the burr left by the circlip because this burr could prevent the seal pack from lifting out of the shock body. Remove the shaft assembly from the shock body.

5. Clean all the shock parts thoroughly in mineral spirits solvent, but never in fuel. Fuels are explosive and will damage the rubber seal and foam bumper.

6. Smart technicians measure the inside

bore of the shock body for excessive out-of-round wear. Although the shock bodies are hard anodized, they can still wear out and let oil bypass the piston and shim valves, thereby reducing the damping effect. Those shock bodies wear out in a few seasons of riding. Some manufacturers don't offer the bodies through spare parts, but there is a way to repair worn-out shock bodies. The body is rebuilt by honing it straight and electroplating it with nickel silicon carbide then diamond honed to size. The service costs about $125.

7. Other high-wear parts of the shock include the seal pack and piston ring. The seal pack has a bushing built into the inside of it, along with the seal and wiper. When the wiper fails, the seal and bushing wear out fast. They should be replaced as a set. Average replacement cost of a seal pack is $50. The best way to install the seal packs on the shock shaft without damaging the seal is to wrap a piece of Teflon tape over the end of the shaft threads. Piston rings are made of either bronze or plastic. The bronze ones wear fast and should be replaced every time you have the oil changed.

8. Check the shock shaft for deep scratches, straightness, and bluing. If the shaft is bent, blued, or deeply scratched, repair or replace it. European manufacturers offer replacement shafts, but some Japanese manufacturers don't offer any replacement parts for their shocks. Luckily, some companies offer rechroming and polishing services for shock shafts. The best method of shaft plating is titanium-nitrate. The material is gold in color and is very hard and resistant to chipping from rock roost.

Assembling the Shock and Bleeding Air

While reassembling the shock, it is critical for good damping performance that you make sure that no air is trapped in the shock. If air is trapped in the shock, the oil will become aerated and break down faster. Also, the air travels through the piston and shim valves, reducing the damping effect. That can be dan-

Good suspension service shops will measure the spring to make sure that it isn't sacked out and that the rate is correct for your geared weight and riding style. This is a digital spring tester made by Longacre Automotive.

gerous because the shock will rebound faster and cause the rear end of the bike to kick. The following is a general procedure that technicians use when reassembling shocks:

1. Pour shock oil into a cup and set the compression adjuster bolt and the piston side of the shock shaft assembly in the oil for at least 30 minutes before assembling the shock. This will reduce the chances of air becoming trapped between the tiny shim-valve washers.

2. Now pour some oil into both the shock

This is what the shaft assembly looks like when it is disassembled. The washers (shims) on the right side control the compression damping and the ones on the left control the rebound damping. Starting from the top, the larger diameter shims control the low-speed damping. The small shims in the middle of the shim stack are called transition shims. The diameter and thickness of these shims is critical because the low-speed shims flex over the transition shim to contact the high-speed shims. Suspension tuners experiment with an infinite combination of these shims. Companies like Race Tech make replacement shims and pistons and provide a chart of shim combinations for different riding needs. However no one publishes revalving specs for any bike.

This is a close-up view of a Showa rebound adjuster. A fine threaded screw runs through a wedge shaped piece that contacts a telescopic rod that runs through the shock shaft to a tapered needle that controls an orifice near the piston. Occasionally water will corrode the adjuster requiring it to be disassembled and cleaned. This is a common problem on late-1980s Honda CR250 and 500s.

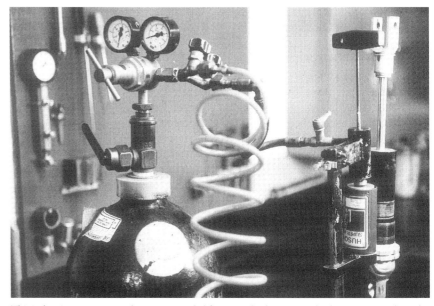

This is the nitrogen pressure-charging rig needed for a WP shock. Japanese shocks are easier to charge because they use a simple Schraeder valve. Motion Pro makes an excellent tool, which combines a regulator and a pressure gauge. Nitrogen tanks are available from welding supply stores. A small tank is all you need to charge shocks and tires.

Some shocks like Ohlins and mid-1980s Kayaba use a floating piston in the reservoir rather than a rubber bladder. These types of shocks require precise positioning of the piston during assembly, using a special tool. They also use a pressure valve that requires a needle similar to the type used to fill a football.

body and reservoir, and install the compression bolt. Clamp the top shock mount in a vise, and pour shock oil in both the reservoir and shaft sides of the shock body.

3. Pour oil to within 1/2 inch of the top of the reservoir. Apply Denicol or Noleen seal grease to the top edge of the bladder. Install the bladder and its retaining circlip.

4. Pressurize the bladder with 10 psi of nitrogen gas. This will make the bladder inflate to full size and force oil through the reservoir, past the compression bolt, and into the shaft side of the shock body. This also helps to force tiny air bubbles out of the shock. Let the air flow up out of the shock for at least 30 minutes.

5. Pour oil to within 1 inch of the top of the shock body and install the shaft assembly. It will be difficult to depress the seal pack in order to install the circlip because you are compressing the inflated bladder. The shock is now overfilled with oil. This is done to facilitate the final air-bleeding procedure.

6. Some shocks, such as those built by Kayaba, have a 5mm Allen bolt on the top shock mount of the body that is used for bleeding air from the shock. Others, such as older Showa shocks, do not. These

shocks must be bled though the compression adjuster bolt. Take care when removing the compression adjuster bolt. You must use a tiny drill bit to drill down the center of the three center-punch points, where the threads of the shock body and the compression adjuster are threaded together. Drill into center-punch points about 0.030 inch—just enough to drill through the points. The compression adjuster can then be unthreaded without the threat of damaging the fine threads. In either case, position the top shock mount in the vise so the bleeder bolt or the compression adjuster is at the highest point. This will insure that no air enters into the shock during the final bleeding procedure.

7. Compress and extend the shock shaft several times so the trapped air congregates at the highest point on the shock, near the bleeder bolt. Lightly tap on the shock body and reservoir with a hammer. This will help tiny air bubbles to break loose from the sides of the body. If you feel any tight and loose spots during the shaft's travel, then there must be a lot of air trapped in the shock and you must start completely over.

8. If the shaft travels smoothly, then you can

extend the shaft and slowly remove the bleeder bolt. The excess oil and air will flow out of the shock.

9. Set the bladder pressure to the factory-recommended spec. Normally that is 150 psi of nitrogen. Never use air to pressurize the bladder.

Installation Tips

Check the shock linkage and steering-head bearings for wear and grease. Also, be sure to reset the race sag on the back end. On full-size bikes, the rear race sag should be 90–105mms with unladen sag of 17–25 mm. Always check race sag with your full riding gear on, the fuel tank at race volume, and your feet on the pegs! If you go to a mud race set the rear race sag after the bike gets muddy in practice. You'll be surprised how much it varies from when the bike is clean.

Servicing Rear Suspension Linkage

Remove the link bolt that fastens the linkage to the swingarm and elevate the rear

This is a disassembled view of a Fox air shock. Popular in the late 1970s, these shocks are making a comeback in twin-shock and vintage racing classes. Fox still makes parts for them and Pro Action offers a rebuilding service.

Placing the bike on a stand, removing the linkage bolts, and elevating the rear wheel helps you gain access to the linkage bearings.

A brush used for soldering is a handy tool for dabbing grease in the needle bearings.

wheel with the 10-inch block. This allows greater access to the shock bolt and other link pivot bolts. Take care when removing the links because some bikes use thin shim washers between the linkages. The linkage consists of two main parts, the frame-mounted link arms and the swingarm-mounted link bar.

Remove the rubber seals from the ends of the pivot bushings. Push the bushings halfway out and use degreaser and a shop towel to remove the old grease and dirt build-up. If the needle bearings are dry or corroded, then the seals are leaking, so the bearings and seals should be replaced. If the bearings still have grease on them, then use a small brush to apply new grease to the bearings. Take care not to displace any of the needle bearings because they don't have a race-cage to hold them in place. Repeat this procedure to the bearings on the other side of the linkage.

If you have to change the bearings from the linkage or swingarm, check for a retaining circlip before attempting to hammer out the bearings.

To grease the swingarm pivots, you'll have to remove the swingarm pivot bolt. You may have to remove the brake pedal to remove the pivot bolt, and you should grease the brake pivot too. Remove the chain or you won't be able to extend the swingarm back far enough to reach the pivot bearings. The pivot bolt may be difficult to remove, so use a brass drift rod and a hammer to drive the bolt out. The brass rod is softer than the pivot bolt and won't damage the threads. If the bolt is still very difficult to remove, then loosen the engine mounting bolts. Clean and grease the bearings and bushings the same way as you did the linkage parts.

If your linkage bearings are corroded badly you'll need to replace the bearings, seals, and bushings as a set. The least expensive alternative to buying all the individual OEM parts is to buy a complete kit from Pivot Works. They package all the parts you'll need to rebuild the linkage and swingarm. Prices of the kits range from $75-$100.

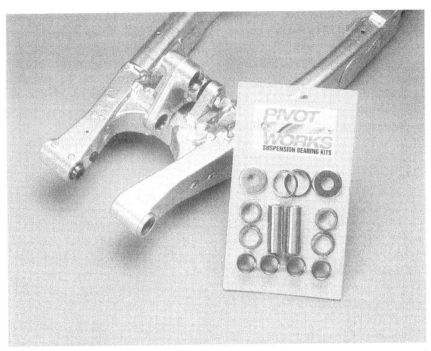

PIVOT WORKS (www.pivotworks.com) makes inexpensive aftermarket kits to rebuild the swingarm and linkage of dirt bikes.

The final task in servicing the linkage is to torque the bolts to factory recommended torque specs.

VIDEO SUSPENSION TUNING

Suspension tuning can be a mystery for both the rider and the mechanic. As a rider on race day, you go out for your practice session and your suspension nearly kills you! You come back to the pits and your mechanic asks you if the high-speed rebound feels too fast? You haven't got a clue because for the last 20 minutes you tried to keep your motorcycle on two wheels! After riding and tuning motorcycles for years, I still cannot diagnose suspension problems by riding or watching the bike on a race track.

The best suspension tuners in the world have a well-developed sense of high-speed vision. They can watch a bike and rider on various sections of the track to determine how well the four different suspension circuits are working. Some suspension tuners are starting to encourage riders to make video samples for review.

You can acquire that same sense of high-speed vision with the help of a video camera. After video-taping the rider attacking various sections of the track, you can replay the tape one frame at a time and see exactly how the four different suspension circuits damp the impacts of jumps, whoops, and other track irregularities.

This section tells you how to use videotape to tune your suspension. First, I'll explain the four suspension circuits and the track sections that help isolate each circuit. At the end of this section is a troubleshooting chart that will help you to identify problems with each circuit. A suspension-data log sheet is also provided so you can record all the pertinent information on your bike and have the data reviewed by a suspension-tuning expert. The data log will help you to develop a mental framework for setting up your suspension properly. Finally, I will explain what changes suspension tuners make during revalving. A warning though: Do not try to revalve your own suspension! One small mistake can put you over the bars! First, set up your suspension with the proper springs, settings, oil heights, and so on. If you still need revalving performed, at least

When video taping a rider, stand back far enough to keep the rider in the viewfinder. You want to be able to video the bike in full frame while it's landing over a jump or riding through whoops. That way when you replay the video in slow motion, you'll be able to concentrate on the shock or fork action.

Making leaps like this means putting a lot of trust in your suspension. In this chapter you'll learn about suspension tuning with video feedback. *Jim Simpson*

Donny Schmit on a tabletop jump.

then you will know exactly what your suspension needs. Too many people have their suspension parts revalved without first trying to set up the bike properly.

Tuning with the Damping Circuits

As previously mentioned, the four suspension circuits of the forks and shock are the high-speed compression (HSC), high-speed rebound (HSR), low-speed compression (LSC), and low-speed rebound (LSR). Your main objective in video suspension tuning is to make video samples of the rider on sections of the track that best isolate two of these circuits at a time. Before you start riding and taping, change the suspension fluids, grease the linkage, and have the proper spring rates and sag settings on the shock and forks.

Low-Speed Compression (LSC) & Low-Speed Rebound (LSR) Tuning

The low-speed circuits work in two common track sections, braking for tight turns and accelerating on a straight with far-spaced, shallow whoops. When taping a rider, be sure to have the whole bike and part of the ground in the film frame. Stand far enough back from the track section and pan with the rider for at least 25 yards. Replay the tape one frame at a time and pay attention to how the wheel follows the ground as the bike hits the bumps. The wheel shouldn't compress quickly or rebound abruptly. All Japanese dirt bikes have suspension adjusting screws that affect the low-speed circuits

Former world champion Pedro Tragter hammers through the whoops. In this photo he hits a big square edged bump and the front end is packing under compression and not yet touching the ground. The rear wheel is completely bottomed out showing that the rear shock's high-speed compression damping is adequate to handle these types of bumps.

only. Turning the adjusting screws clockwise will increase the damping and slow/stiffen the low-speed circuit. Turning the screws counterclockwise will decrease damping and speed-up/soften the low-speed circuit.

High-Speed Compression (HSC) & High-Speed Rebound (HSR) Tuning

The high-speed circuits work in two common track sections, landing from big jumps and accelerating on a straight with tightly spaced, sharp-edged whoops. Video a rider as he lands from a big jump, and for about 15 yards after he lands. That is important because there are usually many small bumps in the landing path after a big jump. Replay the tape one frame at a time and watch to see how equally both the front and rear suspension compress and rebound. If the rear shock rebounds too fast, the rear end may spring up so fast that it loads the forks. If both ends rebound too fast, the whole bike may spring up off the ground. That can be hazardous if there is a turn after the jump.

When taping in whoop sections, try to pan the rider in as much of the section as

This rider, in the same whoops section as the rider before, has some serious handling problems. The high-speed rebound is too soft and the springs are too stiff. The rider has lost control because the bike isn't flying straight, so even if the tires were contacting the ground it probably wouldn't track right.

This rider's bike is sprung too soft and the suspension fluid is probably trashed. The rider was off the gas, landing uphill at slow speed. The bike shouldn't bottom-out like this! If the rider landed on rocks they could've punched a hole in the crankcases or broken the shock linkage.

possible. Watch how the suspension reacts to the sharp-edged whoops at speed. The rear wheel shouldn't pack-up. Packing is caused when the HSC and HSR are too slow to react to the terrain. The wheel will stay compressed as it hits the next whoop. Eventually the rider loses control and must slow down. Taping in whoops also helps the rider; if the bike is reacting properly, he may gain enough confidence to go faster through the section.

If the video tape indicates that you need to change the high-speed circuits, you must take the suspension to an expert in revalving because there are no external adjustments that you can make to the high-speed circuits.

Suspension Revalving

How Damping Works

Suspension fluid (oil) flows through the ports of the piston and up against the shims. The shims pose a resistance to the oil flow, which provides a damping effect. The damping effect is directly related to the diameter and the thickness of the shim. The shims act as a series of tiny springs, flexing to increase the flow area for the oil. The greater the flow area, the greater the oil flow and less the damping effect. The first shims that the oil encounters are the ones that affect the low-speed damping. These shims are large in diameter and thin in thickness. The oil deflects these shims easily because of their large surface area and the relatively thin steel poses low spring tension.

The shim stack, or valving, is arranged in a taper shape. The large-diameter low-speed shims are positioned closest to the piston and the small-diameter high-speed shims are positioned farthest away from the piston. The low-, mid-, and high-speed circuit shims are separated by transition shims. Think of the valve stack as gears in a transmission, and the transition shims as shift forks. The more tapered the valve stacks, and the thinner the transition shim, the plusher the suspension becomes in its handling. Less plush suspension is typically too stiff to absorb the small bumps on acceleration, and too soft for square-edged bumps at speed. Much of the problem has to do with a mismatch between the piston's port arrangement and the overall valve stack.

Why Revalve?

The term *revalving* is often tossed around in the dirt bike magazines, but have you ever wondered what suspension tuners do to revalve a set of forks or a shock? The answer ranges from not much to a whole lot. Some unscrupulous tuners just power wash the outside of the components, turn the clickers, and charge you a lot of money. Other tuners replace the pistons and valve stacks, carefully crafting the arrangement of the valve shims to suit your riding demands and compensate for the idiosyncrasies of your model bike. Tuners need information about you and the way you ride in order to revalve your suspension. If they don't give you a survey form to complete or interview you, then be suspicious about the work they are asking to be paid to perform!

Revalving can be defined as the removal, reposition, or replacement of shims in the valve stacks of the compression and rebound pistons of a cartridge fork or rear shock. Revalving should be performed when you've exhausted the basics, such as setting the sag and making sure your bike has the right springs and the forks and shock have fresh oil, seals, and bushings. Only then can you make a determination whether your bike needs revalving in order to make it handle better. The main reasons why you need good handling suspension on a dirt bike are:

1. To keep the wheels in contact with the ground to provide traction and drive for the rear wheel and steering for the front wheel.
2. To minimize the impacts and vibration on the motorcycle.
3. To minimize the stress loads on the rider and prevent fatigue and injuries.

The rear wheel must stay in contact with the ground in order to provide driving force. The front wheel needs to stay in contact with the ground in order to provide steering control. Impacts on the motorcycle

This photo of a rider accelerating out of a turn highlights the force lines. As the rear wheel spins it drives into the ground, the resultant force travels up the swingarm and into the frame, causing the front end to lift into a wheelie.

Pro-Action has franchised service dealers all over the world. They drive mobile workshops to the race tracks and can help you with any kind of handling problem.

can cause all sorts of problems like loose bolts, foaming of the fuel in the carb's float bowl, long-term damage to the bearings that support the suspension components, and long-term damage to the electrical components. A poor-handling bike also causes chronic problems for the rider—forearm

pump-up is probably the most common. Long-term damage to the rider's neck and spine may take years to manifest, but some people might immediately feel pain. Having a professional suspension tuner revalve your suspension might seem expensive (average cost of total rework with parts is

This is a DeVol link, an aftermarket accessory for late-model Japanese motorcycles. The eccentric hex-mounting lug enables tuners to change the rising rate of the linkage system. Symbols like + and - denote a steeper rising rate and a shallow rising rate respectively.

This is a raw machining of a piston. The oval holes are compression ports and the round holes are rebound ports. From this stage the piston will be finish machined and polished.

This is a layout of a rear shock piston and valve stack. The left side is the single stage rebound stack and the right side is a two-stage compression stack.

$600) but what price do you put on pain?

The main things that a suspension system is affected by are:

1. Changes in the sprung mass from moving up and down.
2. Changes in motion like acceleration, braking, and turning.

The sprung mass of a moving dirt bike can be hard to define because the entire motorcycle leaves the ground! Technically the sprung mass includes everything except the wheels, swingarm, lower fork tubes, and the rear shock. Those parts are considered unsprung mass. Because dirt bikes are capable of jumping, gravity and the weight of the rider affect the sprung mass. The movement of a motorcycle's suspension going up is termed rebound and the movement down is compression.

Changes in the motion of a motorcycle can cause it to roll, pitch, yaw, or any combination thereof. When a motorcycle accelerates the bike pitches backward. The driving chain forces try to wrap the swingarm underneath the bike. Of course that cannot happen because the shock is a finite length and connects the swingarm to the frame, but it causes a transfer of force. The rear wheel pushes down into the ground, transferring force up the swingarm and causing the front end to lift. The natural tendency of the rear wheel is to hop because the damping isn't enough to compensate for the spring force.

When a motorcycle brakes for a turn the bike pitches forward, shifting the weight to the front. The rear end tends to kick because of the torque reaction of the brake caliper on the swingarm and the weight shift.

When a motorcycle turns it rolls, pitches, and yaws at the apex of the turn. A complicated motion! The front end is forced to either compress or change the fork angle or extend and plow out of the turn. Meanwhile the rear end tries to make a radial motion without losing traction and spinning out.

Internal and External Adjustments

Suspension dampers can be adjusted two ways, internally and externally. External adjustments are limited to the riding circumstances and the adjustment range on the compression and rebound clickers. Internal adjustments are virtually unlimited because it encompasses revalving and re-porting of the damper piston and valve shim stack.

The external adjusters, low-speed compression and rebound, can only affect minor changes in handling. Typical low-speed compression or rebound riding situations might include far-spaced shallow whoops, tabletop jumps, braking, and accelerating around tight turns. All compression and rebound clicker adjusters are marked S and H, meaning soft and hard. That can also be interpreted as soft fast and hard stiff.

The focus of a professional suspension tuner's work revolves around internal adjustments. When a suspension component is revalved, it is also rebuilt, meaning that the bushings and seals are checked for replacement and the oil is changed. Revalving is the discipline of repositioning, removing, or replacing valve shims in such an order as to affect a change in the damper's performance.

Aftermarket Piston Kits

The latest trend is to combine a piston design with a valve shim pack to affect a greater change. There are two main types of piston/shim systems. The manufacturers are Race Tech (Gold Valve) and Pro-Action (3-Stage Incremental). The main difference between the two is the port design of the piston. The Race Tech set-up relies on a high-flow piston with a large series of shims that can be rearranged in set patterns to adapt to the needs of a set number of rider profiles. The Pro-Action set-up relies on a piston with smaller ports and a multi-stage shim arrangement that separates the circuits of passive and active to give the damper a wider tuning range. The piston works at the edge of the spectrum and provides a hydraulic lock capability during riding situations where all the suspension travel is used quickly.

From a marketing standpoint, the Race Tech Gold Valve is simple and can be installed by inexperienced technicians. The support provided by Race Tech is excellent. The kits come with detailed instructions as well as training seminars geared towards amateur race tuners and home-based mechanics. A video is optional.

The Pro-Action 3-Stage Incremental valve isn't available over the counter. It can only be installed by a Pro-Action franchise because the valving must be set-up for the individual, and they offer a wider variety of valving patterns to suit virtually any rider profile. The Pro-Action approach also relies on matching the proper spring to the valving. Pro-Action's set-up is more expensive than a typical revalving job, but it's more comprehensive and produces a truly custom set-up.

How Incremental Valving Works

The rear shock valve stack is comprised of a series of steel washers with a variety of outer diameters and thicknesses, mounted on two sides of a piston. This is called a bi-directional valve. One side handles the compression damping and the other handles the rebound damping. The valve shim stacks have different arrangement patterns because the compression stack aids the spring and the rebound stack controls the stored energy release of the spring. With regard to the sizes of the shims, the larger the diameter and the thinner the thickness, the more easily the shim will bend and increase oil flow through the piston. The faster the oil flow the less the damping.

Stock Japanese dampers use high-flow pistons with a complicated series of shims that aren't very sensitive at slow shaft speeds. The shims don't open at slow shaft speeds and mostly the clickers control the damping. However, that can cause some potential handling problems when accelerating out of turns. The bike is riding at a point on the rear spring where the clickers don't provide enough damping and the piston valving isn't in the response range, so the bike chatters. The Pro-Action incremental valving concept separates the three main damping phases of low, mid, and high. They do this by using a special piston and a valve stack with transition shims to separate the three circuits. The incremental valve stack is more sensitive at low shaft speeds so the clickers don't have to carry the damping load. The mid-speed valve helps make the transition from low- to high-speed damping modes to give a plush ride, especially under an acceleration load. The piston has smaller ports, which provide a hydraulic lock effect at high shaft speeds. That reduces the load on the nitrogen charged gas bladder and the elastomer foam bumper.

On the front forks, design has evolved faster than for rear shocks because riding

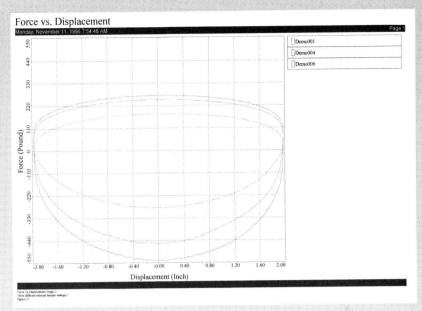

This is a plot of three distinctly different damping patterns from a Roehrig shock dyno. The three circular patterns give a measurement of the force from the rebound and compression circuits. The innermost patterns show very little damping. The next two patterns have thicker valve shims which increases the damping force. These patterns coincide with the demands of the rider. Beginning riders need less damping than pro riders, more like the inner pattern.

Fritz Huebner is a bit big for his CR250 and he doesn't like to sacrifice the handling by riding a 500cc bike. He made some changes to his bike to better suit his stature. The front and rear suspensions were sprung stiffer and revalved.

techniques have changed over the years. Riders tend to do more front-end landings, so the manufacturers have concentrated on cartridge fork design. Modern forks contain a bi-directional valve on the rebound rod and a mono-directional valve for the passive compression. Pro-Action is the only company that uses a two-stage passive compression circuit with a low-flow piston that handles a greater share of the active compression damping. In

Fritz installed the highest rise Pro-Taper handlebars, wide setback foot pegs, and an extra tall seat.

some cases they even remove the active valve stack from the rebound rod.

The Shock Dyno

A shock dyno is a computer-controlled electro-hydraulic machine that simulates and measures the damping characteristics of dampers (rear shock or front fork). A shock dyno is comprised of an electric motor, a hydraulic ram, a mounting guide, and a load cell (pressure transducer). A shock dyno quantifies how much resistance (force in pounds) the damper produces at different shaft speeds (velocity in inches/second) and stroke lengths (displacement/travel in inches).

The load cell is connected to a PC program that plots the damping of the compression and rebound over a range of shaft speeds. The two basic types of graphic plots that a shock dyno provides are force vs. velocity and force vs. displacement. There is an optimum profile for these plots, so a suspension technician can use the results of the plots to see if there is an obvious problem with a shock or fork. The force vs. displacement plots can show how smoothly valve shims are opening, if there is air trapped in the shock, the condition of the seals and bushings, and the condition of the oil with regards to fading over time. The shock dyno can also test the condition of the adjusters, the gas bladder, and the bearing on the top mount. In autosports, it's routine to test shocks before and after servic-

ing. It enables the professional suspension technician to test and verify his work.

Suspension Tuning for Uniquely Sized People

The one thing that most frustrates me about dirt bikes is that they're all the same size. Riders are made in all different sizes, but dirt bikes are made for skinny guys who are 5 feet 10 inches tall. Over the years my Web site has received questions from every shape of dirt biker imaginable. These questions can be divided into two categories: too big, or not tall enough to touch the ground. Here are some set-up tips from some experimentation on real dirt bikers.

Shortening Suspension for Rider Comfort

Ever wonder why dirt bikes are built with 12 inches of travel when 4 inches of it is sag? Why don't the manufacturers offer a kit to give a bike 8 good inches of travel? Perhaps they will after they read this book! Suspension tuners can modify forks and shocks for shortened lengths. With FMF's contractive suspension, for example, springs were fitted to the rebound side of the shock shaft or fork damper rods. When the bike topped out its suspension it would rely on the springs to contract to the point where the bike normally sags (8 inches). The magazine tested some prototype bikes and raved about the handling through turns but criticized the bike for its vulnerability at getting grounded in deep

ruts. Jeremy Wilkey of MX-Tech (, a suspension tuner located near Chicago, handles all sorts of suspension tuning but specializes in shortening suspensions for DTX (dirt track) or other off-road applications.

A suspension component can be shortened a few different ways, and many factors have to be considered when performing such modifications. When you change one suspension component it affects several other things. For a rear shock, a spacer can be turned on a lathe to fit between the rebound stop washer and the seal pack. A 1-inch long spacer will shorten the rear travel by 4 inches because of the linkage system. Most shocks have enough threads on the shock body to accommodate adjustment of the spring. If they don't, then the spring must be shortened. When a spring is shortened it becomes effectively stiffer. When the spring is stiffer the rebound damping must be increased to compensate for the additional potential stored energy of the stiffer spring.

Generally speaking, if you are a heavy person, shortening the travel will adjust the spring to your weight but the shock will still need to be revalved. If you are a lightweight person you may need to switch to a progressive shock spring. Obviously, by changing the ride height of the bike the rising rate of the linkage system is going to be narrowed. One product that is available to adjust the linkage ratio is the Devol Link. The mounts of this product are fitted with adjustable lugs. For modifications to the front forks, it may be possible to just shorten the spring and place the cut-off section of spring on the rebound rod in place of the top-out spring. I did that on my XR600 to make contractive suspension.

Some types of cartridge forks don't have the space for a spring, but a plastic or elastomer foam rubber spacer can be made to shorten the fork travel. As with the rear shock, the spring rate is the biggest factor. You don't have to shorten the front travel as much as the rear because you can still adjust the forks at the triple clamps. Normally a bike with shortened travel will be better suited for low-speed riding. Consideration will need to be given when jumping or riding through deep ruts because the lowered ground clearance will make the bike more prone to grounding-out.

Suspension Tuning for Big Guys

Big guys face the same problems as the vertically challenged—dirt bikes just aren't designed for them. Adjustments big guys make on their bikes include revalving the suspension and installing a stiffer set of springs. Tall guys have the added problem of leverage. When they stand up and lean forward or backward they can easily change the pitch of the bike and drastically affect the handling. That's why stiff springs are important. Taller guys often customize dirt bikes by creating a taller seat using special seat foam and covers, using ATV handlebars with a high rise, forward off-set handlebar clamps, extended shift and brake levers, and wider footpegs. These mods are done to adjust the ergonomics of the bike but may compromise the handling.

The Engineering and Mathematical Aspects of Suspension Tuning

Engineering students and suspension tuners email all the time with questions about other books on suspension engineering. The two best books that I've found focus on the shock absorber and roadracing motorcycles. Of course the material can be applied to any type of suspension engineering. My favorite motorcycle-engineering book is *The Racing Motorcycle* by John Bradley, which is available from Motorbooks (800-826-6600) for $65.00. (In England this book is available

Rich Rohrich wanted his bike lowered to the usable range of the suspension (8 inches of travel). Besides inserting spacers on the suspension shafts, the springs had to be shortened, making them stiffer. That compensated for Rich's geared weight of 240 pounds. The bike holds a tight line and gives up nothing on the jumps.

from the author at Broadland Publications (01904 414763).) The Society of Automotive Engineers publishes an excellent book on shocks, *The Shock Absorber Handbook* by John Dixon, which sells for $55.00 from the SAE (724-776-4970). Both of these books contain material geared towards university level engineering studies and contain a wide range of mathematical formulas, and an understanding of algebra is required.

Quick Link Lubing

Follow these steps to quickly lubricate the rear suspension link:

1. Place the bike on a stand and remove the linkage pivot bolt that goes through the swingarm.
2. Elevate the rear wheel with a 6-inch-tall block.
3. Unbolt the link stay bars from the frame.
4. Clean the old grease and dirt from the seals and bearings with a rag and regrease the bearings with wheel-bearing grease.
5. Reinstall the parts and torque the linkage pivots to factory specs.

This is a view of a rear shock shaft assembly. The white plastic spacer is installed to limit the shock travel. The spacer is inserted between the seal block and the stop washer. Figure on lowering the bike's rear end 3 inches for every inch of spacer in the shock.

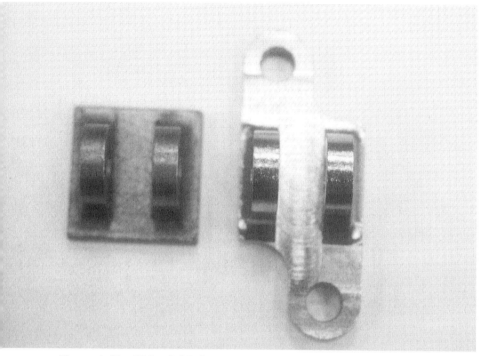

These are the Terry-Kit brand of KX foot peg mounts. These items are welded in place of the original mounts.

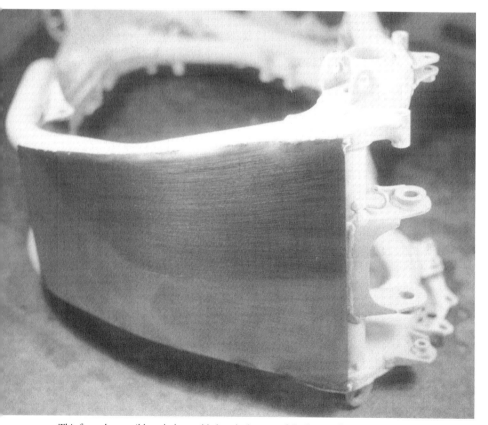

This frame has a mild steel plate welded to the bottom of the frame. This technique adds life to a nearly worn out frame.

FRAME CARE

Most people think of frames as the thing that all the rest of the motorcycle parts bolt to. That is true in a sense, but a frame can be a tunable component of the suspension system. The stiffness of the frame is one thing that distinguishes a new bike from an old bike. A stiff frame gives you confidence when you ride, the confidence of knowing that you can bottom the bike from jumps or stuff it into a berm without losing control.

Let's think about what makes a frame feel worn out and twitchy. The front forks, shock linkage, and swingarm are fastened to the frame with large bolts that pivot on bearings. When the bolts loosen up, the bearings lose the side tension needed to keep the components in alignment. If the bearings are worn on the linkage, dangerous side forces will be applied to the shock as it compresses, increasing rear stiction, causing a handling problem or, worse, a bent shock shaft. Also, the tapered roller bearings that support the triple-clamp assembly loosen up over time, and too little tension will allow the fork assembly to rock back and forth when the bike hits bumps and when braking for turns. Slop in the steering-head bearings is the major reason for side-to-side shaking of the front end.

This section is a guide to inspecting and protecting a frame and its attached components. I'll give you tips on how to care for the bearings and tension pivot bolts, and I'll show you how the factory race teams gusset frames for greater strength.

Inspecting the Frame

Most dirt bike frames are made of mild steel with only 2 percent chrome-moly. Metal fatigue can occur when the engine-mount bolts or pivot bolts get loose. Excessive vibration from the engine and flex forces from the swingarm and steering head can cause frame cracks. Check for frame cracks where the neck is welded to the top and down tubes. Also check the engine-mount sleeve flanges that are welded on each side of the tube because cracks can form around the circumference of the tube. This is a common failure on early-model KX perimeter frames. Some bikes have thin plates for engine mounts. The manufacturer doesn't weld along the entire seam of the plate and frame tube; they only spot-weld the plate at key places. Look for cracks on the spot welds. The frame can crack at both the motor mounts and the top shock mounting plate. Also, if the bottom frame tubes aren't covered with a skid plate, they may be susceptible to water corrosion, so inspect the bottom of the frame, too.

Frames will become sprung with use, the most common evidence of which is a "spreading" apart at the engine cradle. That is why you will often hear a cracking noise and see gaps open up between the mounts and the engine when you loosen the engine mounts.

Tightening Pivot Bolts

The torque on the pivot bolts is critical because if it is too high, the swingarm and

This is a view of the neck of the frame. Japanese frames are spot-welded. Pros have their frames completely welded along all the seams and mount plates. It's a lot of work but worth it to have a stiff frame.

The area where the bottom frame tubes butt to the linkage bracket is an ideal place for a gusset plate to strengthen this critical area of the frame.

SUSPENSION TROUBLE-SHOOTING CHART

Legend: C cause, E effect, P problem, A action suggested, LSC low-speed compression, LSR low-speed rebound, HSC high-speed compression, HSR high-speed rebound.

Front Forks Cause and Effect

C) Springs too soft.
E) Front end dives when braking for turns. Tendency to understeer.

C) Springs too stiff.
E) Front end washes out of turns. Tendency to oversteer.

C) LSC too soft.
E) Braking bumps transfer impacts through handlebars
  and into rider's arms.

C) LSC too stiff.
E) Front wheel deflects over braking bumps.

C) Mid-speed compression too soft.
E) Forks feel like they dive too much when hitting the face of a jump.
  Bike pitches forward and tries to endo.

C) Mid-speed compression too stiff.
E) Forks feel like they hydraulic-lock when hitting the face of a jump.
  Compression forces transfer to the rear and pitch bike backwards.

C) HSC too soft.
E) Forks bottom out hard over easy jumps.

C) HSC too stiff.
E) Forks lock halfway down when landing from jumps.

C) LSR too soft.
E) Forks extend too fast when exiting from turns,
  driving rider to outside of turn.

C) LSR too stiff.
E) Forks don't extend fast enough on braking bumps causing the front
  wheel to skip over bumps.

C) HSR too soft.
E) Forks rebound fast causing rider to get arm pump, forks may make
  clunking noise on top-out.

C) HSR too stiff.
E) Forks rebound slow, front ride height pitched too far forward.

Front Forks Problem, Cause, and Action Suggestions

P) Front end bottoms after big jumps.
C) Fork springs too soft, fork oil level too low, HSC damping too soft.
A) Install stiffer springs, raise fork oil level 10mm, revalve HSC for
  more damping.

P) Forks make clunking sound on bottoming.
C) Fork oil level too low, bottoming cone needs more aggressive angle
  or length.
A) Raise oil level, install aftermarket bottoming cone
  (Magnum DeVol).

P) Forks make clunking sound when topping out.
C) Forks rebound too fast.
A) Check bushing in the top of damper rod head, check top-out spring
  or stop.

P) Forks shutter when riding downhill over bumps.
C) Fork tubes unbalanced, spring rate, oil level, height in triple
  clamps or torque.
A) Service forks, check spring lengths, carefully set axle clamp, and
  triple clamp torque.

P) Headshaking occurs on deceleration.
C) Front tire pressure too low or sidewalls are shot, fork springs too
  soft, or not enough preload, fork oil level too low, natural steering geometry phenomenon.
A) Increase tire pressure to 15 psi, check for cracks in tire's sidewall,
  change to stiffer springs or add preload spacers, raise fork oil
  level 5mm, install a steering damper.

P) Forks dive during braking.
C) Fork springs too soft or worn out, fork oil level too low, fork oil con-
  taminated, compression valve stuck open from trapped debris,
  damper bushing worn out, too soft LSC.
A) Replace fork springs with the correct rate, service forks, turn in
  LSC adjuster 3 clicks.

P) Front end climbs out of ruts.
C) LSC too stiff, springs have too much preload.
A) Turn compression clicker out (S) 3 clicks, set spring preload to 5-
  10mm.

P) Front end washes out in turns.
C) Fork springs too stiff, LSC too stiff, fork tubes not enough overlap.
A) Install softer springs, turn out compression adjuster 3 clicks, in-
  crease fork tube overlap 5mm.

P) Front end understeers in turns.
C) Fork tube to clamp overlap too great, fork springs too soft, LSC
  too soft.
A) Reduce fork tube overlap, install stiffer springs, turn in
  compression adjuster 3 clicks.

SUSPENSION TROUBLE-SHOOTING CHART

P) Forks compress with inconsistent feel.
C) Fork clamps at axle out of alignment, lower triple clamp bolts too tight.
A) Realign front axle clamps, loosen and retorque triple clamp bolts.

P) Forks lock when riding up the face of a steep jump at speed or when landing into the face of a jump.
C) Mid-speed valves are too stiff.
A) Revalve midvalve for softer damping.

P) Fork sag reduced after riding in hot weather.
C) Fork bushings worn allowing aeration and pressure build-up in forks, fork oil contaminated.
A) Service forks, let forks cool down fully extend and bleed off air pressure through fork caps.

P) Front end rattles and shakes fore and aft when riding or braking over bumps.
C) Steering head bearings loose or worn.
A) Check steering head bearings and preload torque.

P) Front end self-centers and steering feels notchy.
C) Steering head bearings worn.
A) Replace steering head bearings and races.

P) Race sag more than 2 inches.
C) Fork springs worn out or too soft of a spring rate.
A) Install stiffer springs.

P) Fork seals are chronic leakers.
C) Fork tubes scratched, bushings worn out, seals not installed properly.
A) Check tube for scratches, replace bushings seals and wipers, wrap a plastic bag around seals on installation and use Teflon grease on the seals and wipers.

Rear Shock Cause and Effect
C) Spring too soft.
E) Rear end bottoms easily.

C) Spring too stiff.
E) Rear end rides harsh, bike pitches forward, rear end pogos after landing from jumps.

C) LSC too soft.
E) Rear end chatters during acceleration from turns.

C) LSC too stiff.
E) Rear end packs when braking for turns or when riding through whoops.

C) Mid-speed compression too soft.
E) Rear end doesn't absorb square-edged bumps, rear end sinks quickly through midstroke.

C) Mid-speed compression too stiff.
E) Rear end kicks after small bumps at speed, rear doesn't compress on jump face causing front end pitching in midair.

C) HSC too soft.
E) Rear end bottoms easily.

C) HSC too stiff.
E) Rear end never bottoms even on big jumps.

C) LSR too soft.
E) Rear end extends quickly over braking bumps, rear braking is affected because the wheel loses contact with the ground.

C) LSR too stiff.
E) Rear end packs on braking bumps.

C) HSR too soft.
E) Rear end doesn't extend fast enough to absorb the next bump, rear end packs.

C) HSR too stiff
E) Rear end retracts quickly causing the rear wheel to lift off the ground and lose traction.

Rear Shock Problem, Cause, and Action Suggestions
P) Bike has too much sag.
C) Spring needs more preload.
A) Tighten the spanner ring on the shock to reduce sag, tighten jam nut.

P) Bike has too little sag.
C) Spring needs less preload.
A) Loosen the spanner ring on the shock to increase sag, tighten jam nut.
P) Bike has too much unladen sag when the race sag is correct.
C) Spring rate is too stiff for the rider's weight.
A) Install the next lower rate spring.

P) Bike has too little unladen sag when the race sag is correct.
C) Spring rate is too soft for the rider's weight.
A) Install the next higher rate spring.

P) Rear end kicks over braking bumps.
C) LSR is too soft/fast.
A) Turn in the LSR adjuster 3 clicks.

SUSPENSION TROUBLE-SHOOTING CHART

P) Rear end chatters under acceleration out of turns.
C) LSC too soft.
A) Turn in LSC adjuster 3 clicks.

P) Rear end packs while riding over whoops.
C) LSC too stiff, LSR too soft.
A) Turn out LSC adjuster 2 clicks, turn in LSR adjuster 2 clicks.

P) Rear end pogos when hitting small square-edged bumps, or swings from side to side through whoops.
C) Mid-speed rebound valving too soft/fast.
A) Revalve shock or increase rear sag and turn in LSR adjuster 3 clicks.

P) Rear end bottoms out hard when landing from big jumps.
C) HSC too soft.
A) Reduce rear sag, increase gas pressure 25 psi, or revalve shock.

P) Rear end hardly compresses when landing from big jumps.
C) HSC too stiff.
A) Revalve forks.

P) Damping performance becomes noticeably softer after riding for 20 minutes.
C) Oil is contaminated.
A) Service shock.

P) Rear end wants to swing around when cornering.
C) Wheel alignment incorrect, rear axle loose.
A) Check wheel alignment.

P) Bike pitches back as if in a wheelie.
C) Spring bias incorrect.
A) Check front vs. rear spring sag, reduce rear sag.

P) Bike pitches forward as if in an endo.
C) Spring bias incorrect.
A) Check front vs. rear sag, increase rear sag, increase fork spring preload.

P) No unladen sag after shock gets hot.
C) Air trapped in shock, gas bladder punctured.
A) Service shock and check bladder.

P) Shock leaks oil.
C) Seal pack worn, shaft's chrome worn down, shaft scratched.
A) Rebuild shock and examine shaft for wear.

---

linkage will bind. If the torque is too low, the swingarm and linkage will twist when the suspension is bottomed, making the bike handle twitchy. See your service manual for correct torque figures.

Shimming the mounts is as important as tightening the bolts to the proper torque. As mentioned earlier, frames become sprung with use, which results in gaps between the mounts and the engine, swingarm, or top shock mounting plate that bolts to the mounts. If you tighten the bolts on perimeter frames without shimming these gaps, you put the frame under considerable stress, and the stress may cause the frame to crack faster than normal. Kawasaki makes thin engine-mount shims (8mm and 10mm inside diameter) that can be inserted between the engine and frame to take up the excess clearance and reduce the stress on the frame. These shims fit the motor mounts of any Japanese dirt bike.

SUSPENSION TERMINOLOGY

Have you ever read a magazine test on a new bike and been confused by the words used to describe the bike's handling? The reason for this is that suspension terminology is a mixture of engineering terms and slang words. Read this section before you read any of the sections on suspension servicing.

Angular Motions

Pitch—A motion fore or aft, when the front end dives or when the rear end squats.

Roll—A motion where the motorcycle leans left or right from straight-up riding.

Yaw—A motion that veers left or right from the motorcycle's heading angle.

General Terms

Anti-Squat Ratio—A formula that calculates the relation between the drive sprocket, rear-tire contact patch, swingarm pivot height, and the chain force lines to determine the rear suspension's resistance to squatting under acceleration.

Arm pump—When the muscles in a rider's forearms tense up to the point that hand-grip is weakened or uncontrollable. This can be caused by forks that are transferring the impacts to the wheel to the rider's arms rather than absorbing the bumps.

Axle—The axis about which a wheel spins.

Base valve—The compression piston and valving that fits onto the compression-bolt assembly.

Bladder—A closed-end, thick rubber, cylindrical-shaped piece that contains the nitrogen gas in a rear shock. The bladder works like an extra cushion on HSC.

Bottoming—A riding situation in which all the suspension travel is used.

Bumper—A tapered, dense foam piece that fits on the shock shaft and provides last-ditch resistance to bottoming.

Bushing—A bronze or plastic ring used as a load-bearing surface in forks or shocks.

Center of gravity/mass center—The center point of the motorcycle's mass, normally located somewhere behind the cylinder and below the carburetor of a dirt bike.

Chassis—The frame, swingarm, suspension, and wheels of a motorcycle.

Clevis—A fork-shaped piece of aluminum used as the bottom mount for most shocks.

Clickers—The knobs or screws that control the LSC and LSR circuits of the forks or shock. Also aerial maneuvers.

Clickers—The screws or knobs used to fine-tune the low-speed damping on forks or shocks.

Compression damping—The damping circuit that absorbs the energy of compression forces on the damper.

Compression-bolt assembly—A large-diameter bolt that houses LSC adjusting screw and the compression-valve assembly.

Counter steering—When the rider applies steering pressure in the opposite direction of the turn.

Damper assembly—The parts of a shock comprised of the clevis, shaft, bumper, piston, and shims.

Damper rod—The large-diameter aluminum tube in the lower leg of telescopic forks.

Damper speed—The relative speed at which the moving end of a damper compresses or rebounds. The two different speeds are high and low.

Damper—A fluid chamber with a means of regulating the fluid flow to restrain the speed of the moving end of the damper during the compression or rebound strokes. A set of forks and a rear shock are considered dampers.

Damping circuits—There are normally four damping circuits that affect the damper's speed: both a low-speed compression (LSC), high-speed compression (HSC), low-speed rebound (LSR), and high-speed rebound (HSR).

Damping—The process of absorbing the energy of impacts transmitted through the forks or rear shock on the compression stroke, and the process of absorbing the energy of the spring on the rebound stroke.

Flicking—The action of putting the bike into a full-lean position quickly.

Front-end diving—This is what happens when the front forks compress quickly. It usually occurs when braking for turns.

Handling—The quality of response from the chassis of a motorcycle while riding through a variety of obstacles such as turns, jumps, hills, whoops, and bumps.

Harshness—An undesirable quality of the damping that results in sharp shocks being transferred through the suspension to the chassis.

Headshake—The high-speed oscillation of the forks when braking for a bend at the end of a fast straightaway. Every motorcycle has a certain frequency band in which its front end oscillates. This frequency can be tuned to a higher vehicle speed with a sacrifice in the bike's ability to turn.

High side—What happens when a bike falls to the outside of a turn.

Hopping—When the tire bounces up off the ground due to a reaction from a bump.

HSC—The high-speed compression circuit is affected most when riding fast over square-edged bumps.

HSR—The high-speed rebound circuit is affected in the same riding circumstances as HSC.

Kicking—Describes both "pogoing" and "packing."

Low siding—What happens when a motorcycle falls to the inside of a turn.

LSC—The low-speed compression circuit is affected most when riding through turns.

LSR—The low-speed rebound circuit is affected in the same riding circumstances as LSC.

Mid-turn wobble—When the bike wobbles or weaves near the apex of a turn.

Nitrogen—An inert gas used to pressurize the bladder or reservoir of shocks.

Packing—When the rear shock is compressed by the wheel hitting one bump and cannot rebound quickly enough to absorb the impact of the second or third bump.

Piston ring—A ring that fits around the piston and prevents oil from bypassing the piston and shims.

Piston rod—A small-diameter steel rod that fits into the upper legs of cartridge forks. It fastens to the fork cap on one end and holds the rebound piston and shims on the other end.

Piston—A cylindrical piece of steel with several ports arranged around the periphery so as to direct oil towards the face of shocks.

Pivot—A fixed point about which a lever rotates. Examples: swingarm or suspension linkage.

Pogoing—When the rear shock rebounds so quickly that the rear wheel leaves the ground.

Preload—Preload is applied to the fork and shock springs to bring the bike to the proper ride height or race-sag dimension. The preload can be biased to change the bike's steering geometry. For example, high preload/less sag in the front forks will make the steering heavy/slow and more stable at high speed.

Race sag—The number of millimeters that the forks or shock sag with the rider on the bike in full riding gear. This is essential to proper suspension tuning but is often overlooked or adjusted incorrectly.

Rake—The angle between the steering axis and a vertical line.

Rear-end squatting—When you accelerate the motorcycle, the chain forces push down on the rear wheel, and the resultant forces are transferred up the swingarm into the main frame, causing a lifting force that extends the front end, causing a weight shift backwards.

Rebound damping—The damping circuit that restrains the release of the stored energy in the compressed spring to reduce the rebounding speed of the damper.

Reservoir—A cylindrical device that contains oil and nitrogen gas.

Revalving—Altering the compression and rebound shims in order to fine-tune damping characteristics.

Seal—A rubber or plastic cylindrical piece that prevents oil from being lost from the damper.

Shaft—The chrome-plated rod on the rear shock that has a clevis on one end and the piston and shims fastened to the other end.

Shim—A circular flat washer of thin steel, used to exert resistance on the oil flow through a piston. A series of shims (valve stack or valving) with varying outer diameters and thicknesses arranged in sequence to provide a damping affect.

Shock body—The aluminum cylinder that contains the damper assembly.

Shock dyno—A machine that cycles a shock absorber at different damper speeds and measures the resistance posed by the four damping circuits.

Shock fade—When the shock oil becomes so hot that the damping effect is reduced, so the shock compresses easily and rebounds quickly.

Speed wobble—When a motorcycle wavers back and forth rapidly at high speeds.

Spiking—How the forks work when the damping is too stiff/slow. This is also associated with arm pump.

Spring—A steel wire that is wound into a coil shape and tempered to provide resistance to compression forces and store energy for expansion to the extended position.

Steering angle—The angle of the handlebars as you rotate them left or right about the steering axis.

Steering axis—The axis about which the forks rotate.

Stiction—A combination of the words "static" and "friction." This word is used to describe the drag exerted on the moving damper parts by the stationary parts such as the bushings, seals, and wipers. Low stiction is desirable because it results in more responsive suspension.

Stiff/slow or soft/fast—Describes the damping characteristics of the forks or shock. With regard to the clickers, these words refer to the direction of rotation that you will turn the clickers in order to improve the damping. Turning the clickers clockwise will make the damping stiff/slow. Turning the clickers counterclockwise will make the damping soft/fast.

Swapping—When the rear end of the bike skips from side to side very quickly.

Swingarm angle—The angle of rotational motion about the swingarm pivot axis.

Swingarm pivot axis—The point where the swingarm mounts to the frame and about which the swingarm rotates.

Swingarm—The rear fork that connects the rear wheel to the frame.

Tank slapper—When the forks rotate from stop to stop rapidly and your arms and body slap back and forth against the motorcycle's gas tank.

Trail—On the front end, the horizontal distance between the point where the steering axis reaches the road surface and the center of the front tire's contact patch. Generally, forks with offset axles have more trail than forks with straight-through axles.

Transition shims—These are shims with very small outer diameters that are used to separate the normal shims of the low- and high-speed valve stacks.

Transmittability—This term refers to the suspension oil's ability to transmit shock loads. As the oil's temperature rises, the transmittability falls. For example, with every increase in temperature of 18 degrees Fahrenheit, the transmittability of the oil falls 50 percent.

Trapped air space—The height of the air space that forms in the top of the fork tube between the fork cap and the oil.

Triple-clamp assembly—Includes the steering stem, bottom clamp, and top clamp. The triple-clamp assembly connects the forks to the frame.

Unladen sag—The number of millimeters that the bike sags under its own weight without a rider.

Unsprung/sprung weight—The unsprung weight of the motorcycle comprises many parts such as the wheels, brakes, swingarm and suspension linkage, and the lower front fork legs, the weight of which does not bear down on the fork and shock springs. The sprung weight is all the parts of the motorcycle that are supported by the suspension.

Valves—Refers to a series of shims either for the compression or the rebound damping.

Viscosity index—The flow rate characteristic of the oil over a range of temperatures. The VI rating of an oil is directly linked to the oil's transmittability. Cartridge-fork oil has a VI number of 115. Shock oil normally has a much higher average operating temperature so its VI number is 300.

Viscosity—A rating system for oils that measures the oil's flow rate through a fixed orifice at a certain temperature. Also known as the oil's weight, as in 30-weight oil.

Washout—A term used to describe what happens when the bike's tires lose traction and slide to the outside of a turn, causing the bike and rider to fall to the inside of a turn.

Weight bias—Also called weight distribution. The amount of weight on each wheel of the motorcycle.

Wheelbase—The distance between the front and rear axle centers.

Wheelie—A motorcycle in motion with the front wheel off the ground.

CARBURETOR TUNING

Carburetor tuning has the greatest effect on engine performance. When a motorcycle manufacturer builds a bike, they usually install jets in the carb that are too rich. The manufacturers sell the same model worldwide, so they couldn't afford to install different jets in the carb to suit all the different climates and types of fuel. In addition to the climate and fuel, the manufacturer would also have to consider many other factors, such as the terrain and type of riding. And then there is the most important jetting consideration, the rider.

When I worked as a mechanic, I was in charge of jetting the bike over the course of the day. During morning practice sessions, the track was usually muddy and the air temperature was at its lowest point. I had to jet the bike rich for practice because the air density was greater and the mud put more of a load on the engine. Then I had to watch the rider and the bike perform on different sections of the track. I would go to the ob-

stacle on the track that presented the greatest load on the bike, typically an uphill straight section. I'd listen to my engine and watch the rider. I'd listen for pinging or knocking noises or excessive smoke from the pipe. I would watch to see if the rider had to fan the clutch a lot and how my bike pulled in comparison to others. Getting feedback from the rider is difficult because they are concentrating on riding not the bike's performance. At a pro national there is one practice session, followed by a series of qualifiers and eventually two race motos. The time spacing of the riding sessions over the course of the day was such that I had to compensate the jetting two or three times. Otherwise, the bike would either seize from being too lean in the morning or run too rich for the second moto.

Race mechanics have different techniques for carb jetting. These techniques range from asking other mechanics what jets they are running to using precise measuring gauges to monitor the engine performance.

These are the three models of Mikuni carbs. Starting from the left, the earliest model is the round slide. A big clunky carb with a huge amount of jets available especially needles. Next came the first flat slide model, the TMX. This carb had a higher peak flow rate. The latest model Mikuni carb is the TM. It's smaller and easier to work on, but has fixed parts like the air and needle jet.

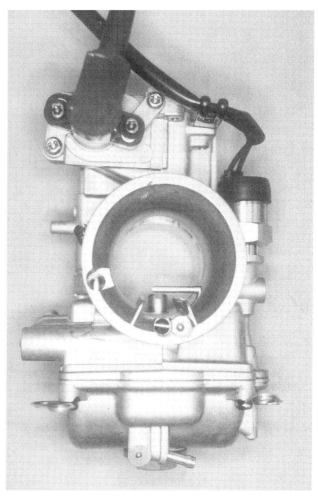

These are the two models of Kehin carbs. On the left is the PJ model. It's a simple carb with an oval shaped slide, fixed needle jet, and a choke system that doubles as the idle circuit. The carb on the right is the electronic PWK model. The PWK has a crescent-shaped slide with a separate idle circuit. This model carb features all the latest innovations. The Air-Strike model featured a set of airfoils cast into the air bell to direct and boost the air velocity. Later models featured electronics like a solenoid pump that siphons fuel from the float bowl and sprays it into the air stream during midrange rpm.

In motocross races, where most of the riders are of equal skill levels, a holeshot in the start can mean the difference between a place on the podium and 30 minutes of roost in your face! The difference in horsepower between the bike that gets the holeshot and the bike that brings up the back of the pack may only be a few ponies! The race mechanic can give his rider an awesome advantage if he carefully monitors the carb jetting.

This section will give you insight into the carb tuning process, from diagnosing mechanical problems that mimic poor jetting to tuning tools such as gauges. It will also give you tips on a jetting method that I've developed called the "ride-and-feel" method, which I consider to be the best

method It's a technique that I teach to all the riders I've worked with. You don't need any fancy tools, just the ability to make observations while you ride.

THE DIFFERENCES BETWEEN TWO-STROKE & FOUR-STROKE CARBS

The difference in fuel delivery between two-stroke and four-stroke engines is intake velocity. Two-stroke engines have lower velocity, so the needle jet has a half-moon shaped hood protruding into the venturi to produce a low pressure area that aids in drawing the fuel up through the needle jet. Four-stroke carbs need to atomize the fuel more than a

two-stroke carb because so much of the fuel shears along the intake port and separates from the mixture stream. Four-stroke carbs have more jets and finer adjustment screws, plus they usually are equipped with an accelerator pump. A typical state-of-the-art four-stroke carb is the Keihin CR.

The latest trend in two-stroke carbs features a pump that sprays fuel into the venturi from 1/4 to 3/4 throttle. In the past, carb manufacturers made jet needles that attempted to compensate for the natural lean condition of the mid-range, but compromised the jetting at full throttle. The auxiliary pumps are powered by electricity supplied by the alternator (about 5 watts) and controlled by either a throttle position or an rpm sensor.

This is the needle jet stack of a Kehin PWK carb. Some hop-up shops over-bore these carbs and that requires the stack to be removed. Sometimes the star bolts that retain the stack can vibrate loose. The double O-rings aren't sold separately.

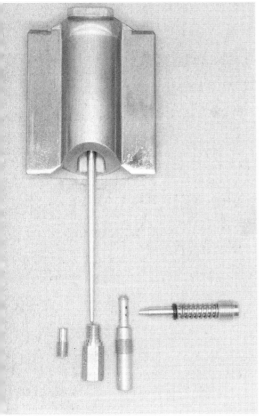

These are the jets of a PWK. The slide and needle, air-screw, and the three fuel jets: L) power jet, C) main jet, R) slow jet.

IDENTIFICATION GUIDE TO POPULAR CARB TYPES

On two-stroke engines, several different model carbs have been used over the years, but there are basically two big carb manufacturers. Either Keihin or Mikuni, two popular brands of Japanese carbs, are used on nearly every dirt bike.

Keihin has several different models. The most popular are the PJ, PWK, and PWM. The PJ is used on Honda CR125, 250, and 500 models 1985-1997. The slide is oval shaped and there are no additional pumps; it's just a simple carb. In fact it's so simple that the choke and idle screw share the same jet. The PWK was the next step up from the PJ. The PWK has a crescent shaped slide and a separate idle circuit from the choke. The PWK is used on Kawasaki KX125, 250, and 500 models 1990-97. The latest version of the PWK features a pump to supply extra fuel in the midrange. The PWM is similar to the older PWK (no pump) and the overall length is shorter.

Mikuni has several different model carbs too. The original model VM has a round slide. There are many different parts available including needle jets of different diameters and jet needles with different taper angles and diameters. The next model is the TMX, which became available in 1987. It is a flat-slide carb, which offers a greater peak flow rate. The TMX has been revised several times, becoming smaller with fewer parts. The TMS carb introduced in 1992 has no main or pilot jet. The slide and jet needle handle all the jetting. That carb worked great on 250cc bikes but never became popular. The PM is the latest Mikuni model. It features an oval crescent shaped slide and a very short body. That carb comes standard on Yamaha YZ125 and 250 1998 and newer models.

CARBURETOR PARTS & FUNCTION

A carburetor is a device that enables fuel to mix with air in a precise ratio while being throttled over a wide range. Jets are calibrated orifices that take the form of parts such as pilot/slow jets, pilot air screw, throttle valve/slide, jet needle, needle jet/spray-bar, air jet, and main jet. Fuel jets have matching air jets, and these jets are available in many sizes to fine-tune the air-fuel mixture to the optimum ratio for a two-stroke engine, which is 12.5:1.

Fuel Jets, Air Jets, and Throttle Positions

Three circuits control the air: the air-screw, the throttle slide, and the air jet. Four circuits control the fuel: the pilot/slow jet, the spray-bar/needle jet, the jet needle, and the main jet. The different air and fuel circuits affect the carb jetting for the different throttle-opening positions, as follows:

Closed to 1/8 throttle—air-screw and p lot/slow jet

1/8 to 1/4 throttle—air-screw, pilot/slow jet, and throttle slide

1/4 to 1/2 throttle—throttle slide and jet needle

1/2 to full open—jet needle, spray-bar/needle jet, main jet, and air jet

(Note: On many modern carbs the spray-bar/needle jet and air jets are fixed-diameter passages in the carburetor body and cannot be altered.)

BASIC CARB SERVICE

Nobody likes to fiddle with a carb if they don't have to. Wedged in between the engine and frame with tubes, cables, and wires sprouting out like spaghetti, carbs are a pain to work on. Carbs require cleaning just like anything else, and some careful observations can save you big money in the long run.

Start by washing the bike, especially around the bottom of the carb where roost from the tires and oil from the chain accumulate. Take care when removing the carb; it's easy to damage the cable. It's better to remove the sub-frame so as to enable unrestricted access to the carb. This will also make it easier to route the vent hoses in their proper positions.

When you remove the carb look at the vent hoses. Are they melted from heat or clogged with mud? If so, that can cause a vapor-locking problem in the float bowl and make the engine bog.

Remove the top of the carb and disconnect the cable from the slide. Is the cable frayed or kinked? Is the rubber dust cover missing? If so, then replace the cable. Now remove the float bowl, jet baffle (white plastic shroud around main jet), float and fuel inlet needle, and the air-screw. Shake the floats and listen for fluid that may have seeped inside. If so, replace the floats; otherwise the engine might suffer from constant fuel flooding. Check the fuel inlet needle. It has a Viton rubber tip and occasionally fuel additives and dirt damage the tip. Also check the spring-loaded plunger on the opposite end of the tip. If the spring doesn't push the plunger all the way out then replace it.

Check the air-screw—there should be a spring and O-ring on the end of the needle. The spring provides tension to keep the air-screw from vibrating outward and the O-ring seals out dirt and water from entering the pilot circuit. Next check the bell mouth of the carb. Look for the two holes at the bottom of the bell mouth. The one in the center is the air passage for the needle jet and the other hole offset from center is the air passage for the pilot circuit. It's typical for those passages to get clogged with dirt and air filter

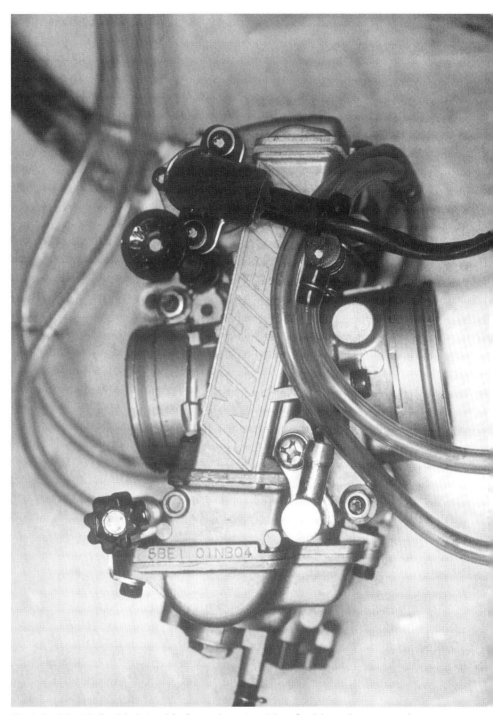

This is the Kehin CR flat slide designed for four-stroke engines. It has a flat slide, accelerator pump, throttle position sensor with solenoid pump, and a lot of jets!

oil. That would cause the engine to run rough because, without a steady stream of air to mix with and atomize the fuel, raw fuel droplets make the jetting seem rich.

Once the carb is stripped down (pilot/slow and main jet still in place), you can

flush the passages. Get an aerosol can of brake or carb cleaner from an auto parts store. Make sure you get the type with the small-diameter plastic tube that attaches to the spray tip. Direct the tip into the air-screw passage. When you spray the cleaner you

This is a view of the bottom side of a Kehin CR carb. With the float bowl removed you can see the three jets in the middle: L) power jet, C) main jet, R) slow jet. The screw in the top center is the low-speed fuel mixture adjuster. With the float bowl installed you can see how the mixture screw is exposed for easy adjustment with this handy Motion Pro knurled screwdriver.

should see it flow out the pilot/slow jet and the air passage in the bell mouth. Next spray through the pilot/slow jet; look for flow through a tiny passage located between the venturi and the intake spigot. Spraying cleaner through these passages insures that the low-speed air and fuel circuits are open and free flowing.

The last area to flush with the carb cleaner is the slide bore and slide. Dirt tends to trap there, causing the mating surfaces to develop scratches that could cause the throttle to stick!

Just a small amount of water and dirt can get trapped in the tiny passages of the carb and cause havoc with jetting or even engine damage. How often should you service the carb? When it gets dirty! For example, if you ride in muddy, wet conditions you should at least check the vent hose. If the riding conditions are dusty and your air filter is covered with dirt, then it's a good idea to do a basic carb servicing.

MECHANICAL PROBLEMS

The process of jetting—changing air or fuel jets in order to fine-tune engine performance—is very simple. Jetting becomes complicated because mechanical problems sometimes mimic improper jetting. This causes you to waste time and money trying to correct the problem with expensive carburetor jets.

Before you ever attempt to jet a carb, make sure the engine doesn't have any of the problems in the following list. If you are in the process of jetting a carb and you are stumped with a chronic problem, use this section as a guide to enlightenment!

Crankcase air leaks—Air leaks can occur at the cylinder base, reed valve, or the magneto seal. Air leaks make the throttle response sluggish and may produce a pinging sound. That sound occurs when the air-fuel mixture is too lean.

Crankcase oil leaks—The right-side crankcase seal is submerged in the transmission oil. When this seal becomes worn out, oil can leak into the crankcase. The oil is transferred up to the combustion chamber and burned with the air-fuel mixture. The oil causes the spark plug to carbon-foul. This mechanical problem makes the jetting seem to be too rich.

Coolant-system leaks—Coolant system leaks commonly occur at the cylinder-head gasket. When the coolant leaks into the combustion chamber, it pollutes the air-fuel mixture and causes a misfire or popping sound at the exhaust pipe. Check the engine's coolant level frequently. Hondas and Kawasakis have characteristic coolant leaks because they use steel head gaskets. Yamahas and Suzukis use O-rings to seal the head and cylinder. Coolant-system leaks lower the engine's peak horse-

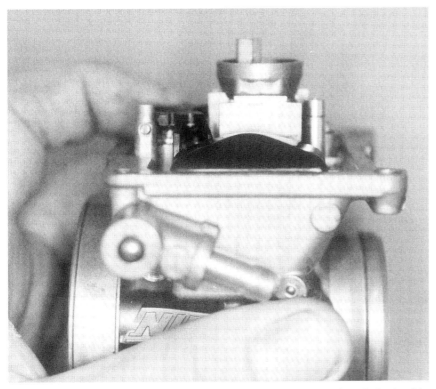

This is the generic way to set the float level as demonstrated on a Kehin carb. Adjust the height of the floats with your index finger. Make sure that the fuel inlet needle's plunger is extended with the needle tip seated. Now sight the side of the floats; the centerline of the floats should be parallel with the float bowl's gasket surface.

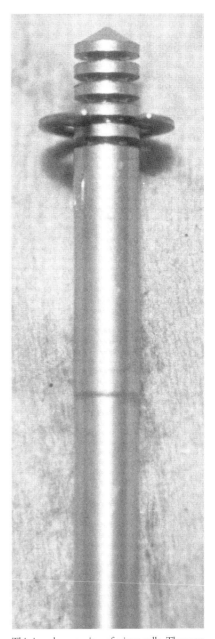

This is a close-up view of a jet needle. There are five clip notches. The lowest notch is the richest setting and the top notch is the leanest setting. If you have to adjust the needle clip position to either extreme position, that is an indication that you need to install a needle that is either one step richer or leaner.

power. It makes the engine run as if the air-fuel mixture is too rich.

Carbon-seized exhaust valves—The exhaust valves sometimes become carbon-seized in the full-open position. This mechanical problem can make the engine run flat at low rpm and make the slow-speed jetting seem lean. The carbon can be removed from the exhaust valves with oven cleaner. Clean the exhaust valves whenever you replace the piston and rings.

Blown silencer—When the fiberglass packing material blows out of the silencer, excess turbulence forms in the silencer and the turbulence causes a restriction in the exhaust system. This restriction makes the engine run flat at high rpm.

Broken reed-valve petals—The petals of the reed-valve can crack or shatter when the engine is revved too high. This mechanical problem makes the engine difficult to start and can also result in a loss of torque. Expert riders should switch to carbon fiber reed petals be-cause they resist breaking at high rpm. Novice riders should use dual-stage fiberglass reeds (Aktive or Boyesen). These types of reed petals provide an increase in torque.

Weak spark—When the ignition coils deteriorate, the engine performance will become erratic. Normally, the engine will develop a high-rpm misfire problem. Check the condition of the coils with a multimeter.

Clogged carburetor vent hoses—When the carburetor vent hoses get clogged with dirt or pinched closed, the jetting will seem to be too lean, so the engine will run sluggish. Always check the condition of your carburetor vent hoses. Make sure there is no mud in the hoses and that the hoses are not pinched between the suspension linkage.

Carburetor float level—When the float level is too low, the jetting will seem to be too lean, so the engine performance will be sluggish. When the float level is too high, the jetting will seem to be too rich.

Worn carburetor fuel-inlet needle—When the fuel-inlet needle wears out, excess fuel enters the float bowl and travels up the slow jet and into the engine. This makes the carb jetting seem to be too rich. Replace the fuel-inlet needle and seat every two years.

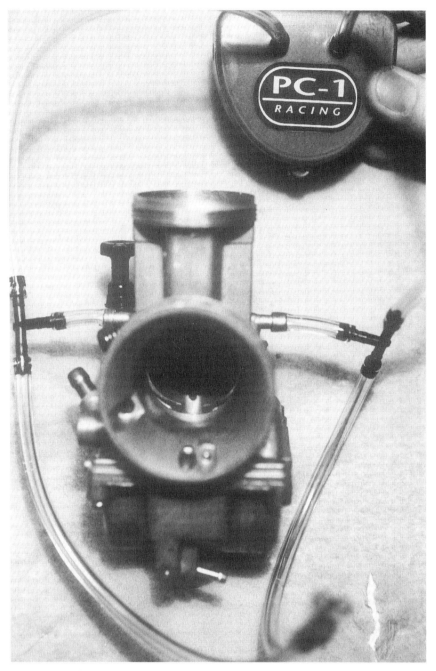

PC-1 makes an aftermarket kit to fit T-vents to older model carbs. The T-vent set up provides an alternative set of vent tubes for the carb's float bowl just in case the tubes that exit out the bottom of the bike get clogged with mud. Clogged vent tubes cause vapor lock which makes the engine bog. The PC-1 kit includes a fuel collector that fits inside the air box.

Jetting Shouldn't Be Scary!

Jetting is the process of making adjustments to the air and fuel jet sizes in order to fine tune the carburetion to suit the load demands on the engine and make the power delivery consistent and optimum. Too much anxiety is placed on jetting. Most people want to just call me on the phone and ask what jets they should put in their carb. That's an impossible question to answer accurately. Any quoted jetting in this book is just a baseline.

The big dirt bike magazines attempt to answer just to increase readership. People get confused because they read jetting specs in a magazine, put those jets in their bike, and seize the engine. Most magazines don't list parameters for their jetting specs. For example: a brand-new bike running VP C-12 fuel with Silkolene oil mixed at 30:1 and a NGK 8 spark plug, ridden by a really slow, lard-ass editor twisting the throttle on a hard-packed track.

Some part numbers and jet sizes are given in the Tuning Tips section for models that definitely need certain jets in order to get the bike near the baseline. There is an old saying that says you can fish for a man and feed him for a day or teach him to fish and enable him to feed himself for life. Jetting isn't all that different—here is a quick lesson on how to jet your dirt bike.

The Ride and Feel Method

The most basic method of determining correct carburetor jetting is "ride and feel." This method requires you to determine if the carburetor tuning is too rich or too lean by the sound and feel of the engine. The first step is to mark the throttle body in 1/4-throttle increments, from closed to full open. Then, this method requires that you ride the motorcycle on a flat, circular course. To check the carb jetting for throttle positions up to 1/2 throttle, ride the motorcycle in second or third gear. Roll on the throttle slowly from 1/4 to 1/2 open. If the engine is slow to respond and bogs (engine makes a *booooowah* sound) then the carb jetting is too lean. You can verify lean jetting by engaging the carb's choke to the halfway position. This will make the air-fuel mixture richer and the engine should respond better. If the carb jetting is too rich, then the engine will make a crackling sound; the exhaust smoke will be excessive and the engine will run as if the choke is engaged. Careful engagement of the choke can help you determine if the jetting is rich or lean. Another important tip is to just change the jets one increment at a time, either rich or lean, until the engine runs better. Most people are afraid to change a jet because they think that the engine will be in danger of seizing. Believe me, one jet size won't make your engine seize, but it could be the difference between running bad and running acceptable.

These reed petals are cracked. This can cause back-flow through the reed valve and that makes the engine hard to start and prone to popping at high rpm.

To check the jetting for throttle positions from 1/2 to full open, ride the motorcycle in third and fourth gear. (You may need to increase the diameter of the circular riding course for riding in the higher gears.) Check the jetting in the same manner as listed above. The carb jets that affect the jetting from 1/2 to full throttle are the jet-needle, main jet, power jet (electronic carbs) and the air jet (on four-strokes).

If you want to take this technique out to the race track, you can test the pilot/slow jet when accelerating out of tight hairpin turns, the needle clip position on sweeper turns and short straights, and test the main jet on the big uphill or long straits. Of course be careful if you try to use the choke technique because you could lose control when riding one handed.

Jetting for Riding Techniques

Certain types of riders require jetting to complement their technique. For example, beginner minibike riders will need slightly richer jetting on the pilot/slow jet and the needle clip position to mellow the powerband and make it easier to ride. Conversely, desert

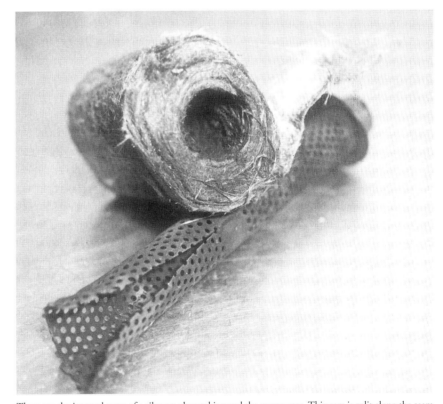

These are the internal parts of a silencer, the packing and the screen core. This core is split along the seam from vibration due to a lack of packing. This packing material is blown-out. This problem causes excessive turbulence in the silencer and reduces the peak flow, causing the engine to run flat at high rpm.

racers who hold the throttle wide open for long periods of time need rich main jets to compensate for the high load.

The Weather Makes the Biggest Difference!

The weather can have a profound effect on the carb jetting because of the changes in air density. When the air density increases, you will need to richen the air-fuel mixture to compensate. When the air density decreases, you will need lean-out the air-fuel mixture leaner to compensate. Use the following as a guide to correcting your jetting when the weather changes:

Air temperature—When the air temperature increases, the air density becomes lower. This will make the air-fuel mixture richer. You must select jet sizes with a lower number to compensate for the lower air density. When the barometric pressure decreases, the opposite effect occurs.

Humidity—When the percentage of humidity in the air increases, the engine draws in a lower percentage of oxygen during each revolution because the water molecules (humidity) take the place of oxygen molecules in a given volume of air. High humidity will make the air-fuel mixture richer, so you should change to smaller jets.

Altitude—In general, the higher the altitude the lower the air density. When riding at race tracks that are at high altitude, you should change to smaller jets and increase the engine's compression ratio to compensate for the lower air density.

Track Conditions and Load

The conditions of the terrain and the soil have a great effect on jetting because of the load on the engine. Obstacles like big hills, sand, and mud place a greater load on the engine, requiring more fuel and typically richer jetting. In motocross, track conditions tend to change over the course of the day. In the morning the air temperature is often cooler and the soil wetter, requiring richer jetting. In the afternoon, when the temperature rises and the track dries out, leaner jetting is needed in order to keep the engine running at peak performance.

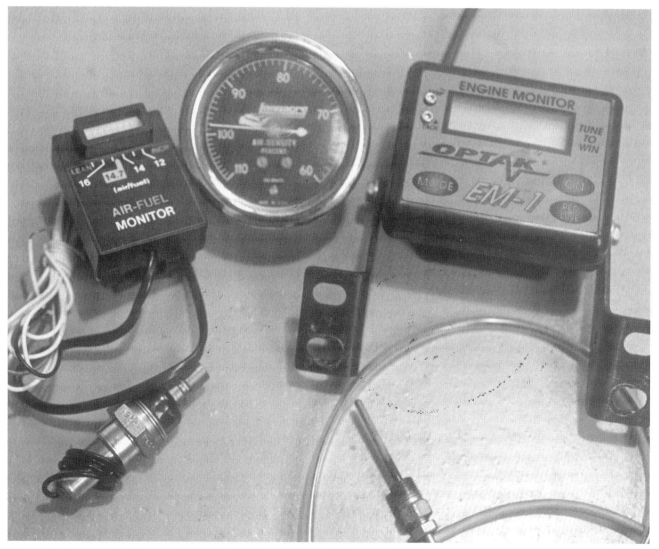

These are the three types of tuning gauges. Starting from the left, oxygen sensor, RAD gauge, and EGT.

Other changes for mud and sand riding might include changing to a lower final-drive ratio (rear sprocket with more teeth) to reduce the load on the engine and help prevent it from overheating. Advancing the ignition timing will make the engine more responsive at low to middle rpm.

FUEL & OIL MIXTURE RATIOS

When we talk about the "fuel" in the air-fuel mixture for a two-stroke engine, we are really talking about a mixture of fuel and oil. If you richen the pre-mix ratio (20:1 as opposed to 30:1) there is more oil and less fuel in the same volume of liquid, which effectively leans the air-fuel ratio. And this fact gives the clever tuner one more tool to use when the correct jet is not available or when none of the standard jets are exactly right. You can richen the jetting by slightly reducing the pre-mix ratio (less oil). You can lean the jetting by increasing the pre-mix ratio (more oil). The best part is that changes in the pre-mix ratio affect the jetting over the entire throttle-opening range, but the changes in ratio must be small to prevent excess wear from lack of lubricating oil or fouled plugs from too much oil.

Pre-mix oils are formulated for a fairly narrow range of pre-mix ratios. You should examine the oil bottle for the oil manufacturer's suggestion on the pre-mix ratio. All production two-stroke dirt bikes have a sticker on the rear fender suggesting that you set the pre-mix ratio to 20:1. That sticker is put there for legal purposes. Always refer to the oil manufacturer's suggestion on pre-mix ratios. In general, small-displacement engines require a richer pre-mix ratio than do large-displacement engines because smaller engines have a higher peak rpm than larger engines. The higher the engine revs, the more lubrication it requires.

Tuning Gauges

There are three types of gauges that professional tuners use to aid carb jetting:

1. Relative-air-density (RAD) gauge
2. Air-fuel (AF) ratio meter
3. Exhaust-gas-temperature (EGT) gauge

The following is a description of how each gauge functions and their advantages.

Too Old to Fix

Question: I have a 1971 Yamaha CT175 with a problem in the engine. When I let off the gas it acts like I just turned the key off. I tried taking spacers out of the oil injector (it fouls plugs bad, too). But it had no effect; it still makes a cloud of blue smoke when I gas it. The engine bogs out when I let off the gas. I have also tried bending the float tab so it won't let so much gas in the float bowl, but it didn't work. Can you help?

Answer: If the engine kills when you let off the throttle, the pilot jet might be clogged. Set the float level back to stock, with the levers parallel to the float-bowl gasket surface. The main bearings are probably worn on your old bike. The oil is coming from the transmission. Disabling the oil pump is a bad idea. That engine needs a pre-mix ratio of at least 30:1 if the oil pump is disabled. Consider finding a newer dirt bike. That bike would cost you a fortune to repair, even if you could get the OEM parts.

Fuel Additives

Question: I've seen some press releases lately on products that are race gas concentrates. Are these products worth the money? What type of fuel do I mix them with? I can buy a no-name race gas at a local station for $2.50 a gallon. In the wintertime this station sells kerosene from the same pump; does that present a problem?

Answer: Reputable companies such as Powermist and Klotz sell a 5-gallon concentrate that mixes with super unleaded premium pump gas to make a total of 20 gallons of safe race gas. Safe meaning that the octane rating is at least 102, and the volatility rating is low. That means you don't have to worry about your engine detonating, causing catastrophic engine damage. Regarding the cheap race gas from the part-time kerosene pump, I've done some random testing and found that type of fuel to contain a high percentage of gasohol, which can be dangerous to run in your engine. This fuel will damage the crankshaft seals, it separates easily from the oil, and demands that you run much-richer jets. The Powermist and Klotz products are a bargain, and they are available by mail.

Hot and Hard to Start

Question: My 1988 RM250 is so hard to start when it is hot that I have to push start it. The bike also fouls plugs. I don't understand it, I use the choke each time to start it. Should I crack the throttle a few times before I try to start it, just to get some gas in the engine?

Answer: Most 250s have a strong fuel signal. In other words they spew up raw gas just when you open the throttle during kick starting. None of the two-stroke dirt bikes have accelerator pumps, so cracking the throttle a few times without the engine turning over won't accomplish anything. However when the engine is cold and you open the throttle with the choke on, it will cancel the effect of the choke and make the engine harder to start. The best procedure for warm-starting a dirt bike is to leave the choke off, hold the throttle wide open, and kick-start it. Also, try installing a spark plug with a hotter heat range. That will prevent the plug from cold fouling.

Too Noisy for Neighbors

Question: My brother and I are taking a lot of flak from our neighbors. We ride on our own property with our 1988 CR and KX 80s. The neighbors complain that our bikes are too loud. Our friend has an XR100, can we make our bikes as quiet as his just by using aluminum silencers? Aren't aluminum silencers quieter than the stock steel silencers?

Answer: You're right that the steel silencers are louder, but the main reason is that you cannot re-pack them with good silencer packing material such as Silent Sport. Those stock silencers are non-rebuildable. My suggestion is to get an FMF silencer and a Sparky. The Sparky is a clamp-on attachment to the end of the silencer that will really quiet the bike down (90 decibels). It may be louder than your friend's XR100, but two-stroke engines produce different pressure waves than four-stroke engines and they are inherently louder. The Sparky can be quickly clamped on for trail riding in your neighborhood and removed for racing use. The best part is that your bikes will make more power because there will be less turbulence in the new packed silencers than in those worn out steel silencers.

YZ490 Runs Erratic

Question: I trail ride an old Yamaha YZ490. The bike has been very reliable for me but lately it has started to run erratic. This is the jetting I'm using: 35 pilot, needle in the middle, and a 420 main jet. The bike has also become difficult to start. It backfires constantly, causing my knee to slam into the handlebars. I'm starting to think that my bike is possessed!

Answer: Chill out biking brother, your 490 is just a piece of metal, not a character from an *Exorcist* movie! I noticed that you haven't changed the slide. Yamaha's *Wrench Report* bulletins suggest that changing to a leaner slide and a richer needle jet can make your bike accelerate smoother off the bottom, with less chance of pinging in the midrange. I've found this jetting to work best for eliminating the pinging and the erratic running: 45 pilot, 3.5 slide, Q-8 needle jet, stock needle in the second position, 440 main, NGK BP6ES spark plug, and a pre-mix ratio of 60:1 with Yamalube R. Be advised that the Woodruff key that aligns the flywheel to the crankshaft tends to shear when the bike backfires or kicks back during starting, which allows the flywheel to shift position and effectively change the ignition timing. Your timing could be way off right now and that could be causing the majority of your problems. Remove the flywheel and examine the Woodruff key; it should have sharp edges. If the edge on one side of the key is rounded, then the flywheel has probably shifted. Replace the key and tighten the flywheel nut to factory torque specs.

Poor Throttle Response

Question: My dirt bike has a low-speed bogging problem when I accelerate. When I shut the throttle, the engine is still revving! I have to hit the brakes with the bike in gear just to slow down the engine. Do you think there is a problem in the carb?

Answer: Stop riding your bike until you get this problem fixed—the engine has a serious problem that makes it dangerous to ride. The problems you describe could be caused by the following:

1. The pilot jet may be clogged. (That jet controls low-speed fuel flow in the carb.)
2. The carb's float level may be too low, thereby restricting the fuel flow to the float bowl.
3. The magneto-side crankcase seal may be leaking. If this seal leaks, fresh air will be drawn into the crankcases, causing a too-lean condition and an increase in combustion temperature.

XR Sticking Throttle

Question: The throttle on my XR350 sticks in the wide-open position. I don't feel any resistance in the throttle grip when I turn it closed. Does that mean that the problem is in the carb and not the throttle?

Answer: Have a factory-trained Honda technician disassemble and clean the carb, throttle grip, slide, and cable. If the cable is dry or rusted, replace it with a Honda part. Sometimes the slide will have dirt wedged between it and the carb. The dirt indicates that the air filter has leaked. Sometimes, the slide is worn and scratched so badly that it needs to be replaced. If there is any dirt in your carb, carefully inspect the air filter for tears at the seams. Also, check the air boot that links the air box and carb. Sometimes the air boots will leak at the bolted flange that fastens the air boot to the air box. Honda makes a special sealer for the boot flange, but automotive weather-strip adhesive works well, too. Never use silicone products to seal any parts in the intake system of a motorcycle. Silicone deteriorates when exposed to fuel vapor.

RAD gauge—This is the best gauge for dirt bikes because of the convenience. The gauge is no good unless you get the jetting perfect once. The RAD gauge provides you with an indication of how much the air density changes, helping you compensate for the effects of changes in the air temperature, altitude, and barometric pressure. The gauge is calibrated in percentage points. Once you set the jetting with the ride and feel method, you can set the calibration screw on the gauge so the needle is pointing to 100 percent. When the air density changes, the RAD gauge will show the relative percent of change. Using a calculator you can multiply the percentage change shown on the RAD gauge by the jet size and determine the corrected jet size for the air density. The pilot/slow and main jet have number sizes that correlate with the RAD gauge, but the needle clip position can only be estimated. Normally for every two main jet increments, the needle clip must be adjusted one notch.

AF ratio meter—The AF meter measures the percentage of oxygen in the exhaust gases, and displays the approximate air-fuel ratio of the carb. The gauge displays AF ratios from 10 to 16:1 The optimum AF ratio for a two-stroke engine is 12:1. The AF gauge utilizes a lambda sensor that is inserted into the center of the exhaust stream, approximately 6 inches from the piston in the header pipe of a four-stroke and in the baffle cone of a two-stroke engine. A permanent female pipe fitting (1/4-inch) must be welded to the side of the exhaust pipe in order to fasten the sensor. The weld-on fitting set-up is also used on the temperature gauges, and the fitting can be plugged with a 1/4-inch male pipe fitting when the gauge is not in use. This gauge is ideal for four-stroke engines.

EGT gauge—The EGT gauge measures the temperature of the gases in the exhaust pipe by means of a temperature probe fastened into the exhaust pipe,

6 inches from the piston. This type of gauge enables you to tune the carb jetting and the pipe together, taking advantage of the fact that exhaust pipes are designed with a precise temperature in mind.

An exhaust pipe is designed to return a compression wave to the combustion chamber just before the exhaust port closes. Most pipes are designed for a peak temperature of 1,200 degrees Fahrenheit. Most dirt bikes are jetted too rich, which prevents the exhaust gases from reaching their design temperature, so power output suffers. Sometimes just leaning the main jet and the needle-clip position makes a dramatic difference.

Digitron is the most popular brand of EGT gauge. It measures both EGT and rpm. This gauge is designed for go-kart racing so it's not suited for wet weather conditions. It is designed to mount on the handlebars. That way the rider can focus in on it. Once you have performed the baseline jetting, send the rider out on the bike with the EGT. The rider observes the EGT to give you feedback on the necessary jetting changes. Once the jetting is dialed, we use the tachometer to check the peak rpm of the engine on the longest straight of the race track. For example, if the peak rpm exceeds the point of the engine's power-peak rpm, then change the rear sprocket to a higher final-drive ratio (rear sprocket with fewer teeth) until the rpm drops into the target range. An EGT gauge is ideal for dirt track bikes and go-karts, where peak rpm temperature is critical.

Leaky Fuel Valve

Question: I have a problem with my 1995 YZ250. Every time I start it up after it has sat for a while, it will load up and bog, causing the spark plug to wet-foul. And this is before I even move! Once I put a new plug in it and get it started, I have to hold the throttle open to clean it out so it won't load up. Once I have cleaned it out, it runs like a top. Still, this will make it very hard to get it running properly at a race—especially on the starting line. I've checked the carb jets and have the recommended 48 pilot and the stock main jet. I have everything to spec, and I have the mixture at 40:1 with Yamalube. My uncle said it's the pilot, but I'm not sure. I have a lot of plugs in three different heat ranges, and they all have fouled out at least once. I think it's in the carb, but I need an expert like you to give me some advice

Answer: Do you ever leave the fuel valve on? It sounds as if fuel is getting into the crankcases. That's why the plug fouls only when you start it. Check the fuel tank's valve by turning it off, unplugging the hose from the carb, and routing the hose to drain into a catch-tank. Check it after 10 hours to see if there is any fuel leakage. If there is fuel, then you need to replace the fuel valve.

Flooded When Dropped

Question: I have a DR350 that runs fine as long as you don't dump it over. When you do, it floods and refuses to clean out. I have to keep the bike rolling to keep it running. This can continue all the way home. I checked the float level and the overflow vents and found no problems. Are these CV carbs junk or what?

Answer: Actually CV carbs are the most responsive type of carb. If certain air and fuel passages get clogged, that could make them run funky. I had a similar problem on my DR. I found tiny droplets of water became wedged in the air-bleed passages of the needle jet. That's all I can think of, good luck.

Black Smoke

Question: I have two Honda XR100s, a 1981 and 1982, both junkers but good for the kids. Both have the same problem—rough low-speed running from idle through 1/4 throttle, with black smoke (small amount). Both have strong acceleration to wide open throttle.

Bike specs:
1. Good compression
2. New points
3. Timed by strobe
4. New timing chains
5. New slow jets (factory spec)
6. Float valves look OK and stop fuel flow at spec dimension
7. Air and fuel jet orifices cleaned (compressed air flows through)
8. Pilot screws look OK, but are there seat problems?
9. Altitude is 700 feet
10. Air filters are kept clean and oiled with SAE 90 weight, then wrung out

Both carbs need to have the throttle stop screws run almost all the way in to idle per specs, at 1,300–1,400 rpm. I was told by one Honda dealer that these bikes are over-carbureted; how can this be?

Answer: The black smoke is raw fuel that passed through the combustion chamber and into the exhaust pipe. This rich condition is probably caused by too much oil on the air filter. Try cleaning the filter and oiling it with an aerosol spray air-filter oil, rather than the 90-weight motor oil. Spray a light coating on the outside of a clean, dry filter, and that will be enough oil to hold back the dirt particles. Those little bikes don't produce enough air flow to suck dirt particles through a foam filter.

TWO-STROKE TOP-END REBUILDING

Top-end rebuilding is the most frequent and costly service routine on two-stroke dirt bikes. Every year, dirt-bike riders waste loads of money on top-end parts that didn't need to be replaced, or make costly mistakes while performing repairs. This section will give you the dos and don'ts to easy top-end rebuilding, plus some tips that aren't printed in your factory service manual.

BEFORE YOU START

Thoroughly wash your bike because dirt stuck to the underside of the top frame tube could break loose when servicing and fall into the engine! Use a stiff plastic brush and hot soapy water to clean off the grit and grime around the base of the cylinder, on the carburetor and intake boot, and especially underneath the top frame rail. Degreaser can be used on metal surfaces, but take care not to leave it on rubber or gasket surfaces.

Tools

You'll need at least some 3/8-inch-drive metric sockets and box wrenches (open-end wrenches will round off the edges on the cylinder or head nuts, and shouldn't be used for top-end rebuilding), a needle-nose pliers for removing circlips, and a gasket tool to scrape the old gaskets away. For soft tools, get some shop towels, aerosol oven cleaner, a Scotch-Brite pad, a locking agent such as Loctite, a gasket scraper, a brush, and a bucket of soapy water. For measuring, you'll need a compression tester, a feeler gauge, and a digital vernier caliper.

Compression Testing

A compression tester is a useful diagnostic tool, readily available from Sears or auto parts stores. Buy the threaded type and make sure the kit comes with an adapter that matches the spark plug threads of your engine. Performing a compression test is simple. Start by removing the spark plug, thread in the adapter, and hold the throttle wide open and the kill button in the off position. This will prevent any spark and enable the engine to draw in maximum airflow. Then kick-start the engine several times until the needle on the pressure gauge peaks. The pressure reading depends on two main factors: the compression ratio, and the altitude at which the engine is being tested.

The compression ratio will also depend on whether the engine is equipped with exhaust valves and their condition. When the exhaust valves are in the closed position the compression ratio will be greater than if the valves are carbon-seized in the open position. The difference may yield a pressure reading 25 psi.

The quality of compression testers varies greatly. The main thing that a compression tester can identify is a change in condition. Whenever you rebuild the top end, take a compression pressure reading and

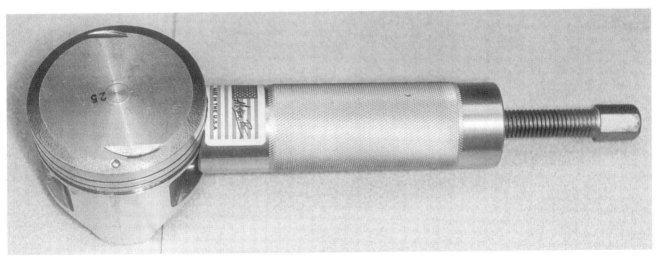

Handy tools for top-end rebuilding. The piston pin extractor saves you from hammering on the rod to remove the piston. The crankcase leak down tester is available from Motion Pro and helps you test the condition of the crank seals.

mark it down. When the pressure changes by as much as 20 percent, check the condition of the piston and rings. Pistons usually last twice as long as rings.

Crankcase Pressure Testing

The crankcase of a two-stroke engine is sealed from the transmission. It's important that the two crankshaft seals are in optimum condition. One side of the crankshaft uses a dry seal and the other a wet seal. The dry seal runs on the magneto side and the wet seal runs in oil on the tranny side. When the dry seal wears, the crankcase sucks in hot air, causing the mixture to run lean and overheat the engine. When the wet seal wears, the crankcase sucks in tranny oil, causing the engine to run rich and eventually wet-foul the spark plug.

A crankcase pressure test involves the use of a vacuum pump with spark plug adapter, and rubber plugs to block off the intake and exhaust manifolds of the cylinder. The piston must be positioned at BDC to allow the transfer ports to be wide open linking the bore and the crankcase. The hand-pump produces vacuum pressure up to a standard setting of 5 psi. The normal bleed-down pressure loss is 1 psi per minute. Cylinders with complicated exhaust valve systems can be difficult to block-off air leaks, and harder to test. Crankcase pressure testing kits are available from Motion Pro.

If I suspect that an engine has an air leak in the crankcases, I do a visual test.

Never use a chisel to raise the cylinder. Instead use a plastic mallet to rock it up evenly. Otherwise damage to the cylinder gasket surface might cause it to leak.

Start by power washing the engine clean. Then remove the magneto cover. Spray the magneto clean with an aerosol can of brake cleaner. Make sure to use a non-chlorinated type of cleaner (green colored can). Now spray baby powder to all the suspect areas of the engine. Spray the powder on the crankcase around the magneto, at the crankcase seam line, the cylinder base, and the reed valve. Run the engine for a while; the white baby powder will highlight any fluid or air leaks on the engine. The baby powder test is much better than the alternative test of blowing raw propane gas at different areas of a running engine and listening for a change in the idle rpm. That is dangerous because it involves flammable gas and a hot engine with random electrical shorts.

107

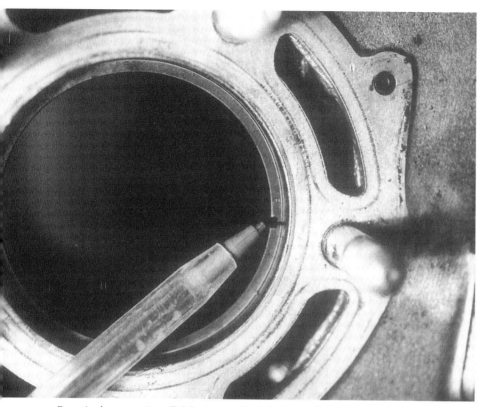

Every ring has an opening called the ring gap. Check the ring gap by inserting it into the bore about 5mm from the top of the cylinder.

Measure the ring gap with a feeler gauge. Normal measurement range is .012-.025 inches.

MAINTENENCE & INSPECTION

A thorough top-end rebuild requires removing the reed valve, cylinder head, and cylinder. You should tear down your top end periodically and inspect the reed valve, cylinder head, cylinder, piston, and so on. Use the following chart to determine when you should tear down your bike:

Displacement:	Tear down after:
80cc	5 hours
125cc	10 hours
250cc	20 hours
500cc	40 hours

Note that air-cooled bikes should be inspected more frequently. Also, you may want to inspect more often if you are riding in fine sand or lots of mud. When you tear down the engine, inspect each system and look for the following trouble signs.

Reed Valve

Check the reed petals for open gaps between the sealing surfaces. In time, the reed petals lose their spring tension, and the back-flow can cause a flat-spot in the throttle response. Stock nylon reeds tend to split at the edges on bikes that are constantly over-revved. Expert riders find that carbon fiber reeds last much longer.

Cylinder Head

Check the head at the edge of the chamber for erosion marks—a sign that the head gasket was leaking. If the head or top edge of the cylinder is eroded, it must be turned on a lathe to be resurfaced.

Cylinder

All cylinder bases use aligning dowel pins around two of the cylinder base studs. These pins are made of steel, and after heavy power washing, they get corroded. That makes it difficult to remove the cylinder from the crankcases. Never use a pry bar! That will damage the cylinder. Instead use a plastic mallet to hit upward on the sides of the cylinder at a 45-degree angle. Alternate from left to right sides so the cylinder lifts up evenly. After you remove the cylinder, stuff a shop towel into the open crankcases to prevent debris from entering the engine.

Cylinder Types

There are two types of cylinder bores used on dirt bikes: steel or cast-iron sleeves, or those with plating on the aluminum. Most dirt bikes made after 1989 have plated cylinders. You can check a cylinder with a magnet. If it sticks to the bore then it is a sleeve. If it doesn't stick then it is plated. There are three types of plated cylinders: Kawasaki Electrofusion, hard-chrome, and nickel silicon carbide.

There are several variations of the nickel silicon carbide process but the most common trade name is Nikasil. The nickel-based processes have many advantages over hard-chrome, Electrofusion, and sleeving. Nickel attracts oil and is an excellent carrier material for silicon carbide particles, a wear resistant material that carries the load of the piston. This material is electro-plated right onto the aluminum cylinder for the optimum thermal efficiency. Nickel can be honed with diamond stones that leave distinctive peak-and-valley scratches in the cylinder wall which retain oil and provide a certain bearing ratio between the running surfaces of the bore. It's possible to rebuild a plated cylinder by fitting it with a sleeve. However you can expect to pay more for bore maintenance over the life of the bike, and lose thermal efficiency and horsepower. Plated cylinders are harder and last longer than sleeved cylinders.

Kawasaki cylinders with the original Electrofusion coating or hard-chromed cylinders can be repaired with nickel plating or sleeving. Steel or cast-iron sleeves cannot be nickel plated unless they are separated from the aluminum cylinder because the pretreatment for the plating would disintegrate the aluminum. There are four companies that replate cylinders in the United States. The average price to replate a cylinder is about $200.

THE PISTON

Some unfortunate guys do more damage replacing the piston than the actual wear on the piston! Remove the circlips with a small needle-nose pliers and throw them away. It is a common mistake to reuse circlips, but the cheap spring-steel wire clips

Thin Sleeve Causing Seizures

Question: My 1987 CR125 has chronic piston seizure problems. The cylinder is bored 1mm oversize. The lower end was rebuilt, so I know it doesn't have a crankcase air leak. What could the problem be?

Answer: The original cylinder for your model bike had a very thin steel sleeve. Honda only offers one oversize piston. When the sleeve is overbored too far, the sleeve cannot transfer out heat into the water jacket efficiently. The heat builds up over the exhaust port, and the piston melts. You have two repair options: buy a new cylinder or install a new thicker sleeve in the old cylinder. Wiseco offers thick sleeves and forged piston kits.

Honda CR250 1988–91 HPP Problems

Question: My 1990 Honda CR250 is making me wacky. I tried to check the exhaust valve system, and I don't think it works properly. I removed the left-side valve cover from the cylinder, revved the engine and the valves hardly moved. They don't open fully when the engine is revved, and they don't close completely either. What is the most common cause of this problem and how can I fix it myself?

Answer: The problem is that the HPP mechanism isn't fully engaged, and the valves are just moving from the exhaust-gas pressure. The most common problem with the 1988–91 CR250 HPP systems is the improper engagement of the governor control and the spindle rod that actuates the HPP valves. The following procedure may cure the problem. Remove the top right valve cover on the cylinder and the round-slotted access cover located under the water pump on the right-side engine cover. Insert an 8mm T-handle through the access hole and onto the detent bolt that locks the governor control to the cam spindle, and turn the bolt 1/4 turn counterclockwise. Now, the bolt has disengaged the HPP system. Insert a straight-blade screwdriver into the slot in the top of the right-side pinion shaft (from the top right side of cylinder). Turn the pinion shaft counterclockwise 1/8 turn, and then turn the detent bolt (located under the right-side engine cover) 1/4 turn clockwise. It is important to release the spring tension from the pinion shafts in the cylinder to engage the detent bolt. This procedure also enables the HPP mechanism to be engaged without any chance of damage occurring to the fragile cam spindle.

Top-End Big Bore

Question: I have an old cylinder for my 250. The bore was ruined when the head gasket leaked, and there is severe erosion on the top edge of the cylinder. I read your article on top-end rebuilding and had an idea and a related question. I compete in amateur enduro events and the rules state that the displacement of bikes competing in the open class must be a minimum of 251cc. My question is, can I salvage this old junk cylinder by overboring the cylinder to fit a Wiseco piston kit and have the bore replated? If yes, will my bike be legal for the open class?

Answer: There are a number of companies offering cylinder repair services and replating. The way to fix the erosion problem is to heli-arc weld aluminum over the erosion and then re-face and bore the cylinder. Wiseco and L.A. Sleeve make oversize piston kits and gaskets for most Japanese dirt bikes. The common overbore displacement sizes for 250s are 265, 285, and 310cc. After the cylinder is replated, the exhaust valves and the cylinder head must be matched to the larger bore size. This involves special metal machining and should be trusted to a qualified tuner or machinist. This type of mod will enable you to race your 250 in the open class.

Kawasaki Air/Oil Leaks

Question: My son and I are just getting started in dirt-biking. Over the winter I bought him a 1989 KX80 as a basket case. We are learning about dirt bike repairs by rebuilding this bike.

(continued on page 110)

It's a lot like model building, only the parts are old and greasy! We inspected the crankcases and noticed that there was some oil leaking from the three oval-shaped plugs that are spaced an equal distance around the main bearings. How can we repair this problem without buying new crankcases?

Answer: Every Kawasaki dealer's service department has a *Team Green* book with tips on how to repair common problems. Ask your dealer's service manager for a copy of the *Team Green* bulletin. It has photos and drawings of how to apply the epoxy over the crankcase plugs.

Top-End Seized After Rebuild

Question: I trail ride a 1989 YZ250. Last winter, I rebuilt the top end after reading your article in *Dirt Rider*. The bore was so worn that I had to skip to a 1mm-oversize piston kit, just so the bore job would clean up a severely worn spot below the intake port. After I rebuilt the top end, I cycled the engine by letting it idle for three 15-minute sessions with adequate cool-down periods in between. When I first rode the bike, I heard some detonation noises but didn't think it was a serious problem, until it seized. What could be wrong?

Answer: Your problem is simple. When a cylinder is overbored, the displacement is increased and that boosts the compression ratio. Whenever a cylinder is overbored more than 0.010 inches (0.25mms), the cylinder-head diameter must be enlarged to the new bore size. Otherwise, the piston could contact the head or the edge of the head surface that extends into the bore could cause a hot-spot and pre-ignition. Also, the cylinder head's squish band must be narrowed by enlarging the combustion-chamber bowl. This also serves to increase the head's volume, thereby lowering the compression ratio. This work must be performed on a lathe by a qualified tuner or machinist. Average cost of this service is $50.

Base Gasket Seeping

Question: I recently rebuilt the top end on my 1991 CR250. I was being as careful as I could be while taking the cylinder off, but the dowels were fused in pretty good and I had to pry it. Needless to say, I gouged the case a bit. I smoothed it out with sandpaper and reassembled the engine. The bike runs great, but a little oil seeps out of the cylinder-to-case mating surface. I assume this is transmission oil? Would it be OK to use something like a thin layer of Permatex Blue or Yamabond here? Would this make it even more difficult to remove the cylinder in the future? Should I just let it alone? The best price I could find on a new left-side case was $215 and I'm sure it would be a lot of work and a lot of replacing gaskets along the way. Am I out of luck?

Answer: Air leaks can be very dangerous because the engine could rev independent of the throttle. An inexpensive way to fix your bike's problem is to draw-file the cylinder base and the crankcases. Then apply a thin coating of Yamabond or any other brand of non-drying sealer to both sides of the base gasket. The best technique for removing cylinders is to tap up on each side of the cylinder with a lead-shot plastic mallet. Remember to put a dab of grease on the cylinder-base dowel pins.

Frequency of Top-End Rebuilding?

Question: I have a 1990 RT180, and I don't think the rings or piston have been replaced. I don't know if the top end has ever been rebuilt because I bought the bike used. How long do piston and rings usually last on a two-stroke engine like mine? How often should the piston and rings be replaced, and should I replace them now?

Answer: Replace the piston and rings before they wear out. The time scale varies between models, usage, and preventive maintenance. The only way to determine the condition of your bike's top end is to disassemble the top end and measure the piston diameter and the ring end gap. Compare the measurement to the maximum wear specs published in the service manual.

will fatigue and break if you install them for a second time.

After removing the circlips, you have to remove the piston pin. Never use a hammer and punch to remove the pin. That will damage the connecting rod and needle bearings. Instead, use one of the pin-extractor tools available from your local franchised motorcycle shop. You can also grasp the piston with one hand and use a 3/8-inch socket extension to push the pin out with your other hand.

Too many people replace their pistons too often. The exact service interval for your bike depends on how hard the bike was run, for how many hours, the quality of the lubrication, and the amount of dirt or other debris in the intake air. Bikes that are run hard with dirty air filters may wear out pistons in only 6 hours, while bikes that are ridden easy with clean filters and adequate fuel octane may last 60 hours.

Measuring the Piston

The best thing to do is measure the piston with a caliper. Digital calipers cost about $100 at industrial tool companies such as Enco or Harbor Freight. A digital caliper is easy to use and gives accurate measurements on the piston diameter and cylinder bore. Measure the widths of the piston (front to back) just above the intake cutaway because this is the widest point of the piston. Check the maximum wear specs in your service manual. Check the piston for detonation marks in the crown, cracks in the skirt, or seizure marks. Look at the underside of the piston crown for a large black spot. The spot is burnt oil deposits that adhered to the piston because the piston crown temperature was too hot. This is an indication that the carb's main jet needs to be richer.

Letter Designations on Cylinders and Pistons

The Japanese manufacturers use a letter designation system for plated cylinders. They intend for you to order replacement pistons based on the letter designation printed or stamped on the cylinder. In mass production you can't guarantee that all parts will be exactly the same size—tool bits become dull, temperatures of machine tools change through production runs, and machine operators have inconsistent performance. The

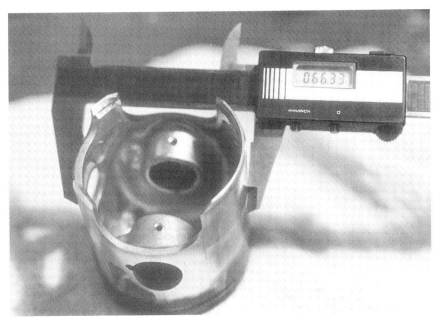

The piston must be measured at the bottom from front to back. That is the biggest point. Pistons are cam ground and tapered specially for engine running conditions. An inexpensive digital caliper is good enough to get an accurate measurement of the piston.

Pro-X piston kits come in increments of .001 inch, for most modern Japanese dirt bikes.

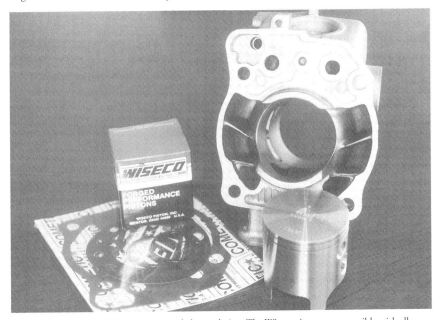

Wiseco pistons are ideal for overboring and electroplating. The Wiseco rings are compatible with all types of nickel coatings.

Japanese manufacturers have between two to four different sized pistons and cylinders, normally labeled A, B, C, and D. The size variance is based on an acceptable level of qual ity. If they only had one size, the piston to cylinder wall clearance would vary between .001 to .006 inches. In the standard Japanese alpha labeling system, "A" denotes the smallest bore or piston size and every letter after that is slightly larger, usually in increments of .0015 inches. The danger is that if you try to put a D piston in an A cylinder, the piston to cylinder wall clearance will be so tight that a seizure might occur.

Pro-X Oversize Piston Kits

Pro-X is a marketing company that sells the surplus pistons from the Japanese company ART, which makes all the cast pistons for the Japanese motorcycle manufacturers. These pistons are the same quality as the OEM pistons, and they are available in sizes larger than the alpha pistons available from franchised dealers. Also the Pro-X pistons are usually priced lower than the OEM pistons. If the cylinder bore is slightly worn (up to .005 inches) with only a small area of bare aluminum exposed, you can install a Pro-X oversize piston. The Pro-X pistons are graded oversize in smaller increments than Wiseco pistons, but a wider range than the OEM pistons. For example, Wiseco sizes are .010 inches and Pro-X is .001 inches increments. Before attempting to order a Pro-X piston, you must measure the cylinder's bore at the smallest point and allow .002 inches clearance between the piston and cylinder.

Measuring the Ring Gap

The best way to know if the rings are worn is to measure the ring end gap. Put the ring in the cylinder and use the piston to push it down about 1/2 inch from the top, evenly spaced. Now use a feeler gauge to measure the width of the ring gap. Normally, the maximum gap is 0.018–0.025 inch.

An aluminum oxide ball-hone is a good tool to deglaze the cylinder bore. Ball hones are available from auto parts stores.

The circlips have an opening. The opening should be positioned away from the clearance notch at either the 6 or 12 o'clock position. Circlips fall out for two primary reasons: bad installation, or a worn out connecting rod bearing.

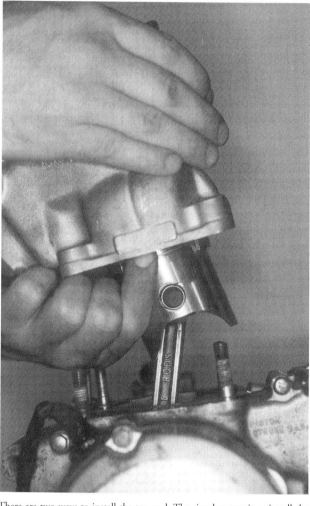

There are two ways to install the top end. The simplest way is to install the piston assembly into the cylinder, then lower the piston and cylinder onto the connecting rod to pin it. Never twist the cylinder or rings when sliding the cylinder and piston together. The ring ends can get trapped in ports and be prone to cracking.

CYLINDER & EXHAUST VALVE CLEANING

Does your cylinder have burnt-on mud on the outside, heavy brown oil glazing on the cylinder bore, or gooey oil on the exhaust valves? If so, here is a tip for cleaning those parts without flammable cleaners. Go to the grocery store and get a can of aerosol oven cleaner. This stuff is great for cleaning the carbon from the exhaust valves without completely disassembling them. CAUTION: Oven cleaner attacks aluminum, so don't leave it on the cylinder for more than 20 minutes. Oven cleaner can be used on both steel and plated bores.

The oven cleaner will help loosen the oil glazing on the cylinder walls. Then, you can use a Scotch-Brite pad to hone the cylinder walls in a crisscross pattern. Wear rubber gloves when you use oven cleaner and flush the cylinder afterwards with soapy water. This will neutralize the acid in the oven cleaner and break the molecular bond of the oil, so the debris can be rinsed away. Sleeved (especially Kawasaki cylinder bores) are vulnerable to corrosion after cleaning. Spray some penetrating oil on the cylinder bore to prevent it from rusting.

Caution: Certain types of cylinders corrode quickly after the cleaning process, so spray the bore area with penetrating oil to displace the water.

Honing the Cylinder Bore

Many people have emailed me with questions regarding honing cylinder bores. If you want to buy a hone to deglaze bores or polish off small scratches, then a ball hone is the best choice. Ball hones are manufactured by Brush Research in Los Angeles, under the brand name Flex-Hone. These hones are available under different labels and they are most easily available from auto parts stores. Buy a size that is 10 percent smaller than the actual bore size. These hones are available in several different materials and grits, but the profile that bests suits both steel and plated cylinders is aluminum oxide 240 grit.

A ball hone cannot remove material from the cylinder bore, especially on the hard nickel-plated bores. However a ball hone can polish down the peaks of the original hone scratches and increase the bearing ratio. In other words, the piston will be touching a greater percentage of the bore. Sometimes that makes the piston wear quicker, but if you have to ball hone the bore to remove scratches, it's a compromise. The one type of hone that you should never use on a two-stroke cylinder is a spring-loaded finger hone. The sharp edges of the stone will snag the port edges and most likely damage the hone and the cylinder.

Top-End Assembly

1. Install one of the circlips in the piston with the opening facing away in the 6 or 12 o'clock position.
2. Grease the cylinder-base alignment pins.
3. Set the exhaust valves in the closed position.
4. On cylinders with reed valves, leave the intake port open because you will need to reach in through the port to push the piston-ring ends back in place.
5. The best way to slip the piston into the bottom of the cylinder is to rotate the rings toward one side of the locating pins and squeeze the rings with your middle finger and thumb. That will leave your other hand free to position the cylinder.
6. There are two methods used to assemble the top end. The first method is to attach the piston to the connecting rod and lower the cylinder onto the piston assembly. The second method is to install the piston assembly into the cylinder and lower the cylinder and piston onto the connecting rod. The second method is easier but involves pinning the piston and installing one circlip with a minimum amount of free space.
7. Take care to align the exhaust valve control mechanism as the cylinder is bolted to the crankcases.

Gasket Hygiene

The oven cleaner you used to clean the cylinders will help loosen the old gasket material so you can remove it. Carefully scrape the gasket off with a gasket scraper. Never use a flat screwdriver to remove the old

There are two types of head gaskets, O-rings and stamped steel. The steel gaskets work better when coated with a copper-based gasket sealer.

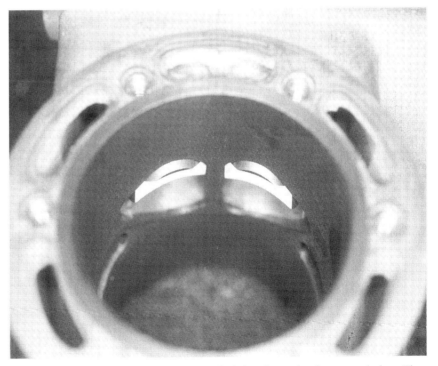
Whenever the cylinder is overbored, you need to check the exhaust valve clearance to the bore. These valves protrude too far into the bore and need to be ground for a piston clearance of 1mm.

gaskets because the aluminum surfaces of the head, cylinder, and crankcases are easily gouged. If these surfaces are gouged on your engine, they should be draw-filed flat to prevent air or coolant leaks.

Never reuse paper gaskets; always replace them with new a gasket, and spray sealer on the paper gaskets so they will seal better and will be easier to remove the next time around. The new-style steel gaskets can be cleaned and reused a few times, but you'll need to spray the gasket with a sealer such as Permatex Spray-A-Gasket or copper-coat.

Keep a Logbook

Keep a logbook that tracks the number of riding days and the periodic maintenance. From reviewing the log, you will learn how often you need to service the top end if you record the measurements of the ring gap and the piston diameter. A logbook also gives you greater leverage when you try to sell your used bike for a premium price.

BIG BORE KITS

One of the best ways to increase horsepower is to increase displacement by overboring the cylinder. This can be ideal for play or Vet Class riders, where the increased displacement won't be illegal for your race class. When done right, a big bore kit can give you more power everywhere rather than an increase in only the top or the bottom of the powerband. Such increases are typically more usable and give you more power where you need it.

Piston manufacturers such as Wiseco make oversize piston kits for popular model bikes. These kits boost the displacement of the cylinder to the limit of a racing class or to a larger displacement class, for example: 80cc to 100cc, 125cc to 145cc, 250cc to 265cc or 300cc, and 495cc to 550cc.

The AMA has a limit of overboring any cylinder used in amateur modified classes. The limit is 2mm. Wiseco makes a line of Pro-Lite pistons for this purpose. Normally no head modifications are needed, but cylinders with exhaust valves that operate close to the cylinder bore will need to be trimmed for clearance. Cylinders that use steel head gaskets will require oversize gaskets. Cometic makes 2mm oversize and big bore gasket kits. The process of overboring and electroplating a cylinder can be a cost-effective way to save a cylinder that suffered a top-end failure and scored the cylinder wall.

Riders competing in the AMA veteran class can ride a bike with any displacement. Riders competing in hare scrambles and enduro can race the 200cc class with a 125

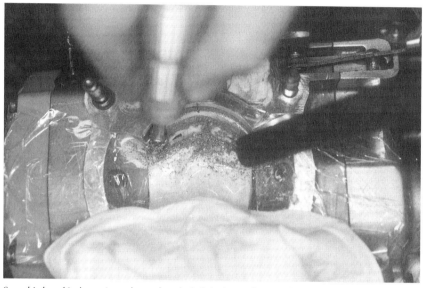

Some big bore kits have pistons larger than the hole in the crankcases. Clearance grinding is required and can be performed with careful taping and the aid of a vacuum cleaner.

A centrifugal governor mechanism converts rotary motion from the crankshaft and turns it into linear motion to vary the exhaust port's effective stroke matched to rpm. The four steel balls travel in channels on a ramp. The higher the rpm the farther the balls travel up the ramp overcoming the force of the spring.

converted to any displacement. AMA motocross and enduro racers can make the 250cc bikes legal for open class by increasing the displacement a minimum of 15 percent (to 286cc). Wiseco makes 74mm piston kits to convert the popular 250s to 300cc. Be careful if you decide to go with a big bore kit, though. If the overbore is not performed properly, it can result in the wrong kind of power or, at worst, a ruined cylinder. When you change the displacement of the cylinder,

there are so many factors to consider, such as port time-area, compression ratio, exhaust valves, carb jetting, silencer, and ignition timing. Here is an explanation of what you need to do when planning to overbore a cylinder.

Also, you should at least consult with an expert before tackling a big bore kit. To get the most from an overbored engine, you need to make sure the carburetion, exhaust, porting, and timing are all adjusted to suit the larger bore.

Port time-area

The term *port time-area* refers to the size and flow range of the intake and exhaust ports, relative to rpm. The ports enter the cylinder bore at angles. When the cylinder is overbored the transfer ports become lower and wider. The same thing happens to the exhaust port. This effectively retards the port timing and reduces the total degrees of duration. When the displacement of the engine increases, so does the demand for more port time-area.

If you just overbored and plated a cylinder, it would have much more low-end power than stock but the top-end power would suffer. Normally tuners have to adjust the ports to suit the demands of the larger engine displacement. The proper dimensions for the ports can be calculated using a computer program from Two-Stroke Racing (TSR). The program "PORTTIME" enables tuners with limited math skills to run strings of formulas for determining the optimum dimensions of the ports. Generally speaking, if the ports in the overbored cylinder were raised to the same heights as the stock cylinder, that would make the port timing sufficient to run with stock or aftermarket exhaust systems.

Cylinder Head

After overboring the cylinder, the head's dimensions must be changed to suit the larger piston. First, the head's bore must be enlarged to the finished bore size. Then, the squish-band deck height must be set to the proper installed

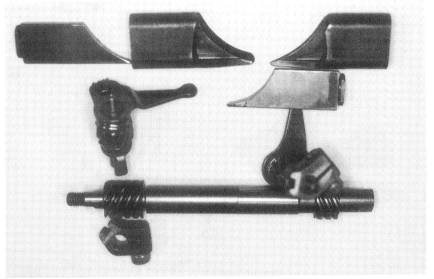

This is a layout of the CR125 HPP 1990-99. Rectangular guides position the exhaust valves that slide in and out to vary the exhaust port. If the clips come off the ends of the valves, the valve could fall into the bore and hit the piston.

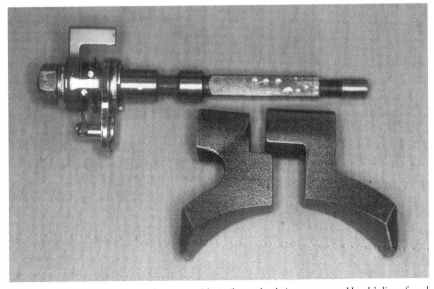

This is the CR125 2000 exhaust valve system. It's similar to the design proven on Honda's line of road racers and two-stroke crotch rockets in Japan. Two main valves are actuated from a single pivot to accurately vary the exhaust port's width and effective stroke.

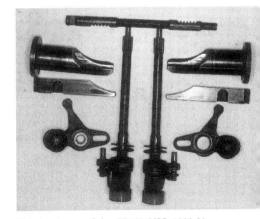

This is a layout of the CR250 HPP 1988-91. This system used a complicated linkage of rack and pinions to control the rectangular valves of the left and right exhaust ports. The cylinder and crankcase actuating joint had to be engaged simultaneously with controls on the cylinder.

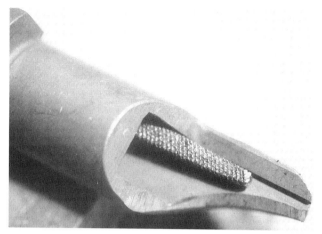

The early-model CR250 exhaust valves had square edged corners that need to be cleaned of carbon. A needle file works good at squaring the corner of the valve guide.

This is the correct position of the HPP pinion shafts, when the cylinder is seated on the cases correctly.

squish clearance. The larger bore size will increase the squish turbulence, so the head's squish band may have to be narrowed. The volume of the head must be increased to suit the change in cylinder displacement. Otherwise, the engine will run flat at high rpm or ping in the midrange from detonation.

Exhaust Valves

When the bore size is increased, the exhaust valve-to-piston clearance must be checked and adjusted. This pertains to the types of exhaust valves that operate within close proximity of the piston. If the exhaust valves aren't modified, the piston could strike the valves and cause serious engine damage. The normal clearance between the exhaust valves and the piston should be at least .030 inches or .75mm.

Carburetor

The larger the ratio between the piston's diameter and the carb's size, the higher the intake velocity. Overbored cylinders produce higher intake velocity which draws more fuel through the carb. Of course a larger engine will need more fuel. Normally when you overbore an engine 15-20 percent, the slow jet will need to be richened and the main jet will need to be leaned. Start with the stock jetting and make adjustments after you ride the bike.

Ignition Timing

The ignition timing has a minimal effect on the powerband. Retarding the timing has

This is the later-model CR250 1992-2000. Unlike earlier models there is no manual engagement bolt. However there is still an actuating rod in the cases and cylinder, that must align properly.

the effect of reducing the hit of the powerband in the midrange and extending the top end over rev. "Overrev" is a slang term that describes the useable length of the powerband at high rpm.

The scientific reason for the shift of the powerband to extremely high rpm is that the temperature in the pipe increases with the retarded timing, and that enables the pipe's tuned length to be more synchronous with the piston speed and port timing of the cylinder.

Advancing the timing has the effect of increasing the midrange hit of the powerband, but makes the power flatten out at high rpm. The reason is that the relatively long spark lead time allows for a greater pressure rise in the cylinder before the piston reaches TDC. This produces more torque in the midrange but the high pressure contributes to pumping losses at extremely high rpm.

Pipe and Silencer

Because only the bore size is changed, you won't need a longer pipe—only one with a larger center section. FMF's line of Fatty pipes work great on engines that have been overbored.

Head Gasket

The head gasket will need to have the bore diameter increased to the dimension of the new piston. If the head gasket overlaps into the cylinder bore more than 1mm on each side, it could contact the piston or be susceptible to pressure blowouts.

10 Tips for Rebuilding a Two-Stroke Top End

1. Before you disassemble your engine, wash the engine and the rest of the vehicle to reduce the risk of dirt and debris falling into the engine. Once you remove the cylinder, stuff a clean rag down into the crankcases.

2. The cylinder and head use alignment pins to hold them straight in position from the crankcases on up. The pins make it difficult to remove the cylinder from the cases and the head from the cylinder. Sometimes the steel alignment pins corrode into the aluminum engine components. Try spraying penetrating oil down the mounting studs before

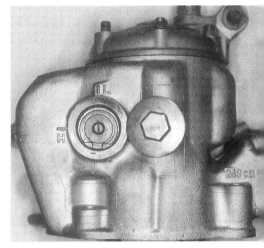

You can quickly check the operation of the HPP system of a late model CR250 (1992-2000). Remove the 17mm cap bolt from the left side of the cylinder. The L and H marks stamped on the cylinder indicate the low and high rpm positions of the valves. The line carved in the center rod is the left HPP valve. You can run the engine with this cover removed to check the valves, but don't let it get exposed to dirt.

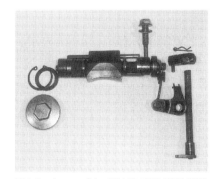

This is a layout of the CR250 1992-2000 HPP system. The center valve pivots from one end and a rod through the front center of the valve links the two subexhaust valves. The stop bolt in the top right can be carefully filed to allow the valves to close a few degrees, giving a boost in low-end power.

This is a view of the forked actuating rod from the bottom of the cylinder. Notice that it is cracked. That happened because the cylinder was tightened down with the actuating rods out of alignment. This part needs to be replaced.

This is a common problem for all KX and KDX models that use aluminum drum valves. The gear teeth tend to shear when the valves get carbon seized.

attempting to remove the cylinder and head. Never use a flat-blade screwdriver, chisel, or metal hammer to remove the cylinder. Instead use this technique; buy a lead-shot plastic mallet and swing it at a 45-degree angle upwards against the sides of the cylinder. Alternate from left to right, hitting the sides of the cylinder to separate it from the cases evenly. Clean the steel alignment pins with steel wool and penetrating oil. Examine the pins closely. If they are deformed in shape, they won't allow the engine parts to bolt together tightly. This can cause a dangerous air leak or a coolant leak. The pins are cheap at about $2 each. Replace them if they're rusty or deformed.

3. Never reuse old gaskets. Remove them with a razor blade or gasket scraper. Don't use a drill-driven steel wool type pad to remove old gaskets because they can remove aluminum from the cylinder and head. That will cause a gasket to leak.

4. Always check the ring end gap on a new ring by placing it in the cylinder between the head gasket surface and the exhaust port. The gap should be between .012 to .024 inches.

5. Always install the circlips with the opening facing straight up or down; that way inertia will hold it tight into the clip groove. Place one clip in the groove before installing the piston on the connecting rod. It's easier to install a clip with the piston in your hand rather than on the rod. There is also less chance that you'll drop the circlip in the crankcases.

6. Always install the rings on the piston with the markings facing up. Coat the rings with pre-mix oil so they can slide in the groove when trying to install the piston in the cylinder. Always install the piston on the connecting rod with the arrow on the piston crown facing towards the exhaust port.

7. The traditional way to assemble the top end is to install the piston assembly on the connecting rod, compress the rings, and slide the cylinder over the piston. That can be difficult with larger bore cylinders, or if you're working by yourself. Try this method instead: install one circlip in the piston, install the piston into the cylinder with the pin hole exposed, install the piston pin through one side of the piston, posi-

tion the cylinder over the connecting rod and push the piston pin through until it bottoms against the circlip, install the other circlip. It only takes two hands to install the top end using this method and there is less chance that you'll damage the rings by twisting the cylinder upon installation.

8. On cylinders with reed valves and large oval intake ports, take care when installing the piston assembly in the cylinder because the rings are likely to squeeze out of the ring grooves. Use a flat-blade screwdriver to gently push the rings back in the grooves so the piston assembly can pass by the intake port.

9. For steel head gaskets, place the round side of the "bump" facing up. Don't use liquid gasket sealer; use aerosol spray adhesive types instead. For hybrid fiber/steel ring head gaskets, place the wide side of the steel rings facing down.

10. When you initially start the engine after a rebuild, manipulate the choke to keep the engine rpm relatively low. Once the engine is warm enough to take it off choke, drive the vehicle around on flat hard ground. Keep it under two-thirds throttle for the first 30 minutes. Two common myths for proper engine break-in are to set the engine at a fast idle, stationary on a stand, and to add extra pre-mix oil to the fuel. However, when the engine is on a stand it doesn't have any air passing through the radiator and it is in danger of running too hot. When you add extra oil to the fuel you are effectively leaning the carb jetting. This can make the engine run hotter and seize.

Troubleshooting Piston Failures

The process of examining a used piston can tell a mechanic helpful information on the condition of a two-stroke engine. When an engine failure occurs, the piston is likely to take the brunt of the damage. A careful examination of the piston can help a mechanic trace the source of a mechanical or tuning problem. This is a guide for the most common mechanical problems.

Perfect Brown Crown

The crown of this piston shows an ideal carbon pattern. The transfer ports of this two-stroke engine are flowing equally and the color of the carbon pattern is chocolate brown. That indicates that this engine's carb is jetted correctly.

Black Spot Hot

The underside of this piston has a black spot. The black spot is a carbon deposit that resulted from pre-mix oil burning on to the piston because the piston's crown was too hot. The main reasons for this problem are overheating due to too lean carb jetting or coolant system failure.

Ash Trash

This piston crown has an ash color, which shows that the engine has run hot. The ash color is actually piston material that has started to flash (melt) and turned to tiny

flakes. If this engine had been run any longer, it probably would've developed a hot spot and hole near the exhaust side and failed. The main causes of this problem are too lean carb jetting, too hot spark plug range, too far advanced ignition timing, too much compression for the fuel's octane, or a general overheating problem.

Smashed Debris

This piston crown has been damaged because debris entered the combustion chamber and was crushed between the piston and the cylinder head. This engine had a corresponding damage pattern on the head's squish band. The common causes of this problem are broken needle bearings from the small or big end bearings of the connecting rod, broken ring ends, or a dislodged ring centering pin. When a problem like this occurs, it's important to find where

the debris originated. Also, the crankcases must be flushed out to remove any leftover debris that could cause the same damage again. If the debris originated from the big end of the connecting rod, then the crankshaft should be replaced along with the main bearings and seals.

Chipped Crown Drowned

This piston crown chipped at the top ring groove because of a head gasket leak. The coolant is drawn into the combustion chamber on the down-stroke of the piston. When the coolant hits the piston crown it makes the aluminum brittle and it eventually cracks. In extreme cases the head gasket leak can cause erosion at the top edge of the cylinder and the corresponding area of the head. Minor leaks of the gasket or O-ring appear as black spots across the gasket surface. An engine that suffers from coolant being pressurized and forced out of the radiator cap's vent tube, is a strong indication of a head gasket leak. In most cases the top of the cylinder and the face of the cylinder head must be resurfaced when a leak occurs. Most MX bikes have head stays mounting the head to the frame. Over time the head can become warped near the head stay mounting tab, because of the forces transferred through the frame from the top shock mount. It's important to check for warpage of the head every time you rebuild the top end.

Shattered Skirt

The skirts of this piston shattered because the piston-to-cylinder clearance was

too great. When the piston is allowed to rattle in the cylinder bore, it develops stress cracks and eventually shatters.

Snapped Rod

The connecting rod of this engine snapped in half because the clearance between the rod and the thrust washers of the big end was too great. When the big end bearing wears out, the radial deflection of the rod becomes excessive and the rod suffers from torsion vibration. This leads to connecting rod breakage and catastrophic engine damage. The big end clearance should be checked every time you rebuild the top end. To check the side clearance of the connecting rod, insert a feeler gauge between the rod and a thrust washer. Check the maximum wear limits in your engine's factory service manual.

Four-Corner Seizure

This piston has vertical seizure marks at four equally spaced points around the circum-

ference. A four-corner seizure is caused when the piston expands faster than the cylinder and the clearance between the piston and cylinder is reduced. Another common problem of this type is a single point seizure on the center of the exhaust side of the piston. However, this occurs only on cylinders with bridged exhaust ports. The main causes for this problem are too quick warm-up, too lean carb jetting (main jet), or too hot of a spark plug range.

Multi-Point Seizure

This piston has many vertical seizure marks around the circumference. This cylinder was bored to a diameter that was too small for the piston. As soon as the engine started and the piston started its thermal expansion, the piston pressed up against the cylinder walls and seized. The optimum piston-to-cylinder wall clearances for different types of cylinders vary greatly. For example a 50cc composite plated cylinder can use a piston-to-

cylinder wall clearance of .0015 inches, whereas a 1200cc steel-sleeved cylinder snowmobile set-up for grass drags will need between .0055 to .0075 inches. For the best recommendation on the optimum piston-to-cylinder clearance for your engine, look to the specs that come packaged with the piston or consult your factory service manual.

Intake Side Seizure

This piston was seized on the intake side. This is very uncommon and is caused by only one thing, loss of lubrication. There are three possible causes for loss of lubrication: no pre-mix oil, separation of the fuel and pre-mix oil in the fuel tank, and water passing through the air-filter and washing the oil film off the piston skirt.

Composite Flaking

Most two-stroke cylinders used on motorcycles and snowmobiles have composite-plated cylinders. The composite material is made of tiny silicon carbide particles. The electro-plating process enables the silicon carbide particles to bond to the cylinder wall. The particles are very hard and sharp; they don't bond to the ports so the manufacturer or reconditioning specialist must thoroughly clean the cylinder. Sometimes the silicon carbide "flashing" breaks loose from the ports and becomes wedged between the cylinder and the piston. This causes tiny vertical scratches in the piston. This problem isn't necessarily dangerous and doesn't cause catastrophic piston failure, but it should be addressed by thor-

the exhaust side so catastrophic problems will appear there first. There are several reasons for a failure like this. Here are the most common: air leak at the magneto side crankshaft seal, too lean carb jetting, too far advanced ignition timing or faulty igniter box, too hot of a spark plug range, too high of a compression ratio, too low octane fuel.

Amazingly enough this piston shattered and the engine quit without causing any significant damage. Most of the debris was deposited in the exhaust pipe. I flushed the crankcase, replaced the crank seals, bored the cylinder, and fitted a new piston.

oughly flushing the cylinder and ball-honing the bore to redefine the cross-hatching marks. This type of problem can also be caused by a leak in the air intake system. Debris like sand or dirt can cause the same type of tiny vertical scratches in the piston skirt and cylinder wall. However the main difference is the color of the piston crown and spark plug. Dirt will leave a dark stain on the piston and sand will make it look shiny, like glass. That's because melted sand is essentially glass. Normally you will need to replace the piston kit because the scratches will reduce the piston's diameter beyond the wear spec.

Blow-by

This piston didn't fail in operation but it does show the most common problem, blow-by. The rings were worn past the maximum end gap specification, allowing combustion pressure to seep past the rings and down the piston skirt causing a distinct carbon pattern. It's possible that the cylinder wall's crosshatched honing pattern is partly to blame. If the cylinder walls are glazed or worn too far, even new rings won't seal properly to prevent a blow-by problem. Flex-Hones is a product available at most auto parts stores. They can be used to remove oil glazing and restore crosshatch-honing marks that enable the rings to wear to the cylinder and form a good seal. If you purchase a Flex-Hone for your cylinder, the proper grit is 240 and the size should be 10 percent smaller than the bore diameter.

Bridge Point

This piston has a deep wear mark in-line with the exhaust bridge. Two different things can cause a problem like this. The most common problem is that the right-side crankshaft seal is leaking, causing tranny oil to enter the bore. The Ionic charge of the friction present at the exhaust bridge and the oily debris cause an attraction. The oily debris works like an abrasive media to accelerate the wear at the exhaust bridge. An-

Burnt-out Blow-Hole

This piston was overheated so badly that a hole melted through the crown and collapsed the ring grooves on the exhaust side. Normally the piston temperature is higher on

Shattered and Scattered

This piston was allowed to run way past its service life. Too much clearance between the piston and cylinder wall caused stress cracks to form at several points.

other common problem is a lack of proper relief clearance on the exhaust bridge. When a cylinder is replated or overbored, the exhaust bridge must be ground for extra clearance over the bore size. That is due to the fact that the exhaust bridge gets hotter than other areas of the cylinder. The extra relief clearance compensates for expansion. The normal relief clearance is between .001 to .003 inches. Generally speaking the wider the exhaust port in relation to the bore size and the narrower the bridge, the less relief needed. Too much bridge relief will cause the rings to flex the exhaust port and break.

Piston Bounce

Notice the distinct circular line located near the outside of the piston? This was caused by contact between the piston and the cylinder head's squish-band at top dead center (TDC). There are several causes for this problem ranging from worn connecting rod bearings to an improperly modified cylinder head. The optimum clearance between the piston and head at TDC is .040 to .080 inches depending on the displacement of the engine. The larger the displacement the greater the clearance required.

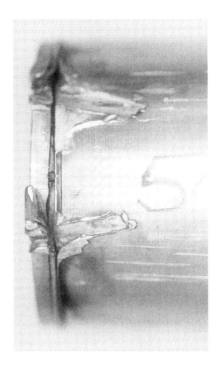

Arrow Forward!

This piston was installed backwards, meaning that the arrow on the piston crown was pointing to the rear of the bike. The ring end gap was aligned with the exhaust port and the rings expanded out of the groove into the exhaust port, thereby causing them to shear-off in the exhaust port. This engine suffered catastrophic damage and required a new cylinder and piston.

Piston manufacturers use a standard of stamping an arrow on the crown that points toward the front of the bike, or the exhaust port. Another indication of the correct piston position is to have the ring centering pins facing the intake side of the cylinder. There is only one motorcycle I've ever known that opposes this rule, the early-model Kawasaki KDX 175. That model has a piston with ring centering pins aligned on both sides of the exhaust port.

Reading Piston Burn Patterns

Reading the burn patterns that naturally form on the crowns of pistons can give a tuner insight into several different aspects of the engine's performance and condition. The color and arrangement of the burn patterns, and the location with regards to the different types of ports, can help determine what changes are needed in order to make the engine run its best.

The piston shown here is from an RM125. The bike was running a bit weak throughout the rpm range. These are some of the observations of the burn patterns and how they relate to the engine's condition and carb jetting.

Zones of the Piston Crown

1. Outer edge: The light gray color indicates lean carb jetting. Mocha brown is the optimum color, but some oils, like Yamalube R, have additives that prevent carbon from forming on the piston crown.
2. Front edge: The two black spots align with the sub exhaust ports and indicate exhaust blowback when the sub exhaust port valves are closed. If the exhaust valves were carbon-seized and stuck closed, the carbon patterns would be much larger.
3. Rear edge: The two small black spots are above the ring alignment pins. The black spots show pressure leakage, possibly from excessive ring end gap. That will enable the combustion gases to escape past the ring gap, leaving a carbon trail in its wake.
4. Rear band: The intake side of the squish-band has some light brown colored patterns. That is the right color for the center pattern when the carb jetting is right. If the color were dark brown that would mean that the engine is running on the rich side or that the engine doesn't run at the right temperature.
5. Center: The center pattern has a shape that can explain how an engine is running. This pattern is shaped like a heart, showing the flow patterns through the transfer ports. Notice the left side is

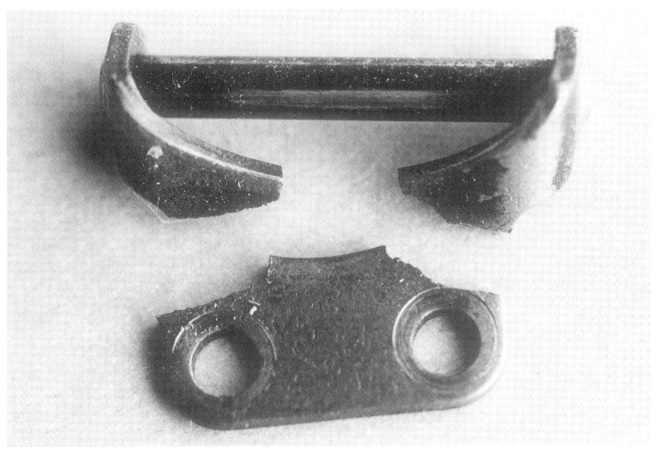

All KX250s use a yoke lever like this to transfer the linear motion of the centrifugal governor into the actuator rod. If your bike ever starts running bad, unbolt the plastic cover on the lower right side of the cylinder and make sure that the actuator rod is moving in accordance with rpm. If not then this yoke lever is probably broken.

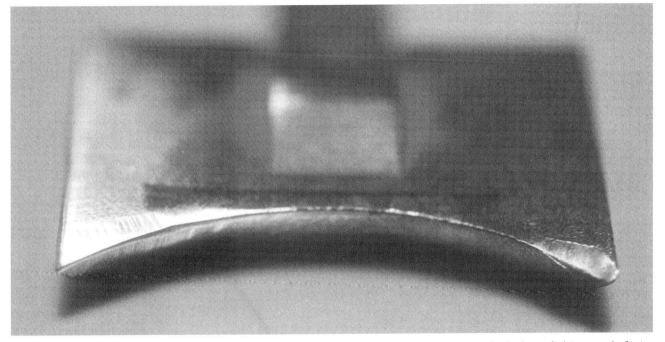

KX250 1993-2000. This is a before and after view of the typical wear damage that occurs to the center valve. The ends develop burrs which increases the friction on the KIPS system. The shiny side was deburred with a grinding and polishing wheel.

1987 Honda CR125 ATAC Test

Question: I have an older CR125 with an ATAC system. That is the one with the big chamber on the front of the exhaust pipe. My question is, how can I test the system to be sure it is working properly?

Answer: To test any of the ATAC systems, start by removing the chamber cover. Then start the engine. The exhaust note should be very loud and exhaust gas should be coming out of the chamber. When you rev the throttle wide open, the valve should close off the chamber and the exhaust should only be coming out the pipe.

1995 KX125 Runs Flat

Question: My 1995 Kawasaki KX125 seems to run flat at the top end. My friend's 1994 KX125 blows mine away in a drag race. Could there be something wrong with my engine's exhaust valves?

Answer: Yes, there is definitely something wrong with the exhaust valves. The 1995 model had a design defect in the governor control that prevents the KIPS valves from opening fully. Replace your governor's ramp cup with the one from the 1994 or 1996 model, both of which carry the same part number.

Top-End Clicking Noise

Question: My 1989 Yamaha WR250 makes a clicking noise from the top end, until about half throttle. It's not a loud scary noise, just annoying because I can't figure out where it's coming from. Any ideas?

Answer: The power valve's stop tab is worn from slamming closed thousands of times. This enables the power valve to rotate further closed at low rpm. The clicking noise is probably from the piston rings striking the power valve. Disassemble the top end and look for shiny spots on corresponding areas of the power valve and the piston. You can use a file to relieve the power valve at the shiny area. This will provide a clearance gap so the power valve does not contact the piston. This same procedure should be performed to YZ and WR cylinders that use steel sleeves, and are overbored for larger pistons.

KX250 1988-92 KX500 1990–2000. This is the bench-top procedure for installing the valves. Install the center first, drop in the drum valves, and link the drive channels on the drum valves with the pins on the center valve. Hold the drum valves up to slide in the rack, push in the seal, and pull the rack out until it stops. Now lower the drum valves onto the rack in the wide-open position.

slightly larger; that indicates that the flow rate of the right-side transfers is greater than the left side. That means that the area and timing of the left-side transfer ports needs to be adjusted to match the right side.

TWO-STROKE EXHAUST VALVES

Three words sum up exhaust valve maintenance: spoogey, gooey, and grungy. If two-stroke exhaust valves didn't have such a dramatic effect on the engine's powerband, then I'm sure mechanics would remove them and beat them to bits with a hammer in frustration, because there is little information given by the manufacturers on how to diagnose and repair the exhaust valve systems on well-used dirt bikes. This section is a guide to the characteristic mechanical problems that occur to the exhaust valve systems of dirt bikes. Plus we'll give you some tips on how to re-time exhaust valve systems.

How Exhaust Valves Work

An exhaust valve system is designed to increase the engine's low-end and midrange power. There are three different designs of exhaust valve systems. The first-generation design uses a variable-volume chamber mounted to the head pipe to change the tuned length of the head pipe. A butterfly valve is used to separate the surge chamber and the head pipe. At low rpm, the valve is open to allow the pressure waves in the pipe to travel into the surge chamber and effectively lengthen the pipe and reduce the pressure wave's magnitude when it returns to the exhaust port. These systems were primitive and not very effective on 125cc dirt bikes. Honda and Suzuki used this type of exhaust valve system in the mid- to late 1980s.

The second-generation design features valves that control the effective stroke and the time-area of the exhaust port. These valves are fitted to the sub-exhaust ports and the main exhaust port. The main exhaust-port valves operate within close proximity to the piston to control the effective stroke of the engine. The effective stroke is defined as the distance from TDC to when the exhaust port opens. At low rpm, the engine needs a long effective stroke, which results in a high compression ratio. At high rpm, the engine needs a shorter effective stroke, longer exhaust duration, greater time-area, and a lower compression ratio. Yamaha used this system starting in 1982 on the YZ250. Honda's HPP system is similar and was used on the 1986–91 CR250 and 1990 to current-model CR125.

The third generation of exhaust valve systems attempts to change the exhaust-port velocity, effective stroke, exhaust-gas temperature, and the pressure of the compression wave. Yamaha and Suzuki started using these systems on their 125s in 1995. Both companies employed a venting system to the outside atmosphere. This is very complex because they are attempting to affect the temperature and pressure of the returning compression wave to synchronize it with the piston speed. The exhaust-gas velocity and the effective stroke are controlled by two oval wedge valves that enter the exhaust port at a 45-degree angle. The wedge valves partially block the exhaust port, thereby boosting the gas velocity. Kawasaki's KIPS system uses wedge valves in the main exhaust port to control the effective stroke, drum valves in the sub-exhaust ports to control the time-area, and a surge chamber to absorb the excess compression-wave pressure at low rpm.

The exhaust valves are opened and closed by a centrifugal governor mechanism. The governor is mounted under the right side-cover and is gear-driven by the crankshaft. As the engine rpm increases, the governor spins, thereby increasing the angular momentum of the four steel balls encased in the governor. The steel balls fit into an angled ramp-and-cup arrangement. A spring is used to provide tension on the steel balls. When the momentum of the steel balls overcomes the spring's tension, the balls force their way up the angled ramp. A spool attached to the ramp enables it to change its linear position with changes in rpm, and the spool is attached to a linkage system that operates the exhaust valves in the cylinder. Factory race teams

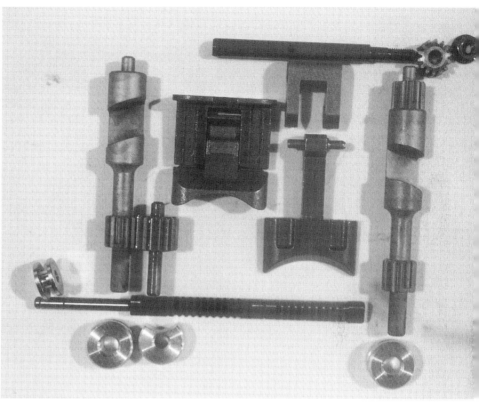

This is a typical KIPS system for the following models: 1992–1997 KX125, 1995-2000 KDX200, 1993-2000 KX250. As you can see there are numerous moving parts. Two racks must be timed with gears to link the main center valves and the drum valves. This is a very good valves system for performance, but it requires a lot of maintenance.

This is the new generation KIPS system used on the 1998 and newer KX80, 100, and 125 models. There are three pieces: a stationary guide, a sliding valve, and a pivoting flapper. This design is mostly self-cleaning and should be checked every time you service the top end. It's normal for a large amount of sludge to accumulate under the valve cover.

The late-model KIPS can be cleaned simply by removing the valve cover and pulling the whole assembly out for service.

have different combinations of springs, ramps, and balls to tune the exhaust valve operation and enhance the powerband.

EXHAUST VALVE TIPS & TUNING

Although exhaust valves use the same essential principles, implementation is different with each manufacturer. Each type has its own flaws and fixes. The list below gives you tips on how to install and service the most common exhaust valves, as well as some tuning tips.

Honda HPP

Honda's HPP system started as a butterfly operated canister mounted between the cylinder and pipe. It served to control the volume and length of the exhaust pipe. It had little effect on the power and most aftermarket pipes eliminated the canister. The butterfly was prone to carbon seizure and required frequent maintenance. The next-generation HPP was used on the 1986-91 CR250. This system featured two sliding valves that operated within close proximity of the piston and effectively varied the exhaust port time-area in accordance with rpm. The square valves moved horizontally through a valve guide. The system was plagued with a mixture of design problems and misinformation on how to service and re-time this complicated exhaust valve arrangement. This section lists some common problems and some tips for timing the system, installing the cylinder, and engaging the HPP mechanism.

Common HPP Problems

Two main problems plague the HPP system: carbon fouling and rack-and-cam-spindle damage. The square shape of the valves contributes to the accumulation of carbon on one corner of the valve guide (stationary part), in the corner of the guide that is directly in the exhaust gas stream, and this causes the valve to become carbon seized. Chamfering the corresponding edge (1mm) of the valve will eliminate this problem. The rack and cam spindles are easily damaged when the cylinder is installed incorrectly, or the HPP mechanism is engaged incorrectly. See the photos for examples of damaged rack and cam spindle parts.

HPP Timing Procedure

Use the following procedure to time the HPP system:
1. Install the HPP valves and levers and tighten the pivot nuts. Place the washer on the stud first, then the lever (marked left and right), and then the flanged center bushing with the flange side facing up.
2. Turn the cylinder upside down. To position the rack correctly, slide it to the left until it stops; then move it right 2mm. Rotate the rack so the square notch faces you. Now the rack is in the correct position so you can install the pinion shafts. Carefully turn the cylinder right

The most common problem with the Suzuki exhaust valve system has to do with the actuating lever spring. On the top right side of the cylinder there is a shaft that the valves are linked to. If you remove the actuating lever the spring may snap loose and cross ends. The spring ends should always be parallel in order for the valves to move.

side up without changing the position of the rack.

3. Close the valves and install the left pinion shaft with the screwdriver slot facing the one o'clock position. Install the right pinion shaft with the screwdriver slot facing the eleven o'clock position (see photo for correct positions). A simple way to determine if the pinions are mis-timed to the rack is to look at the screwdriver slots. The wrong position is with both slots facing twelve o'clock.

Installing the Cylinder and Engaging the HPP Drive

After timing the HPP mechanism, the cylinder is ready to be installed on the crankcases. Here are some tips for installing the cylinder and engaging the HPP drive mechanism:

1. Make sure the reed valve is removed from the cylinder. CR250s have such large intake ports that the rings tend to slip out of the ring grooves during installation of cylinder. This takes the spring pressure off the cam spindle. Now turn the engagement

bolt 1/4 turn clockwise. You should feel it positively lock into a groove and stop. Remember that the HPP engagement bolt is a spring-loaded detent, not a threaded bolt. Slide the cylinder down onto the piston and rings, and use a screwdriver to push the rings back in the grooves until the rings clear the intake port.

2. The HPP mechanism should be engaged while the cylinder is being installed, just to keep the cam spindle in position. The cylinder will stop about 3mm from the crankcases because the cam spindle and the rack are misaligned. Now disengage the HPP mechanism by turning the engage bolt 1/4 turn counterclockwise. Grasp the right-side valve lever and wiggle it; the cylinder should then drop evenly onto the crankcases.

3. Bolt the cylinder down tight. The best way to engage the HPP mechanism is to insert a screwdriver in the right-side pinion shaft and turn it counterclockwise. Now turn the engagement bolt clockwise. You should feel the engagement bolt lock positively in position. If you try to rotate it too far, you will bend the cam spindle and the

system won't work at all, so don't be a hammer-head! The best way to check the HPP system is to remove the left-side valve cover from the cylinder, start the engine and warm it up, then rev the engine. The valves should be fully closed at idle and fully open when the engine is revved.

In 1992 Honda introduced the HPP system currently used on the CR250. This system features a center valve for the main exhaust port and two rotating drum valves to control the flow of the sub exhaust ports. This system also features a return of the old resonator as used on the mid-1980s model. The resonator improves the throttle response and mellows the powerband at low rpm. A thin rod links the valves together and the whole system is mostly self-scraping to prevent carbon build-up.

The inside of the center valve has an elongated passage where the tie rod travels. This elongated passage is prone to carbon build-up over time (1-2 years). The carbon limits the range of movement in the valves. The carbon is easily removed by using a

This is a typical layout of the valves used on the following models: 1989-2000 RM80 1988-2000 RM125, 1989-95 RM250, all RMX. The cylindrical shaped valves are comprised of a stationary guide and a sliding valve. A knob mounted on the top left side of the cylinder provides spring tension. It's common for the left spring to get twisted in half from turning the knob too much or in the opposite direction (counterclockwise).

small-diameter rattail file. The sides of the center valve and the drum valves interface, and that area is prone to carbon build-up too. A wire brush or file is an effective tool in cleaning the exhaust valves.

Here is a simple way to check the operation of this system. On the left side of the cylinder there is a 17mm cap bolt that exposes a straight line mark in the left drum valve. There is a corresponding mark on the cylinder. The "L" mark denotes the low-speed position of the valve and the "H" denotes the high-speed position. To check the HPP, start the engine. At idle the valve should align with the "L" mark. Then rev the engine, the valve should align with the "H" mark. If the angle of the mark on the valve is slightly off, then the valve probably needs to be de-carboned.

This system is very easy to disassemble and can only fit together one obvious way. There are some aftermarket parts to adapt the performance of this system for

different types of dirt biking. Pro-Racing in England makes a spacer for the right-side valve cover. It serves to add volume and length to the resonator part of the system. This is especially suited for enduro riding where a smooth transition to the midrange is important for better traction. ESR (Eddie Sanders Racing) in California makes a replacement HPP system that holds the valves wide-open. The center exhaust valve is thinner, which enables tuners to raise the exhaust port. The ESR system is primarily used for dirt track or kart applications where low-end power is of no consequence.

Whenever the cylinder is installed on the bottom end after top-end rebuilding, the valves need to be put in the closed position. Otherwise the HPP cam spindle that connects the actuator in the cases to the cylinder will get damaged when you tighten down the cylinder. That will also make the valves inoperable. Always check the HPP valve operation after you assemble the top end by

using the inspection cap on the left side of the cylinder.

The CR125 HPP system was redesigned in 1990. Honda chose to use a system similar to the 1986-91 CR250, featuring horizontally sliding valves. This system was plagued with problems over the years. The valves are prone to carbon seizure because the critical square edges face the exhaust stream. If the clips that fit on the ends of the valves vibrate off or if the valve wears too much then the valve can tilt on an angle and strike the piston.

Another common related problem occurs when tuners widen the exhaust port during porting and neglect to grind the valves at the outer corners for piston clearance. There again the piston strikes the valves because they protrude into the bore. In 1998 Honda modified the valves, adding an L-shaped rib that prevented the valves from angling in and contacting the piston. The problem of clearance between the top of the valve and the guide was eliminated so the new-style valves provide more low-end power. These valve and guide sets from the 1998-99 models fit the CR125 models back to 1990.

In 2000 Honda redesigned the CR125 engine and adapted the exhaust valve system used on the RS250 road racer. Honda also used this system on several dual sport and street bikes sold in Asia and Europe. The new system is simple and effective—a wedge-shaped valve pivots at one end, similar to the CR250. The valve is much thicker and can vary the exhaust port's effective stroke, time-area, and duration over a wider rpm range. It's a self-scraping set-up, so maintenance should be greatly reduced over previous models.

Kawasaki KIPS

Kawasaki's KIPS exhaust valve system has gone through a steady refinement of design. Kawasaki uses a different system to suit the needs of the different model bikes. The earliest KIPS design used two drum shaped valves to control the flow of the sub exhaust ports. Opening the ports gave the exhaust port more time-area. The main exhaust port was relatively small with modest timing and duration. A rack and pinion set-up controlled the drum valves, opening them at about 6,000 rpm. Kawasaki uses the rack and pinion design in all their KIPS systems except the 1998 and later KX80-125cc models.

The 1992 KX125 and KDX used the next-generation KIPS that featured a center wedge valve with two side drum valves engaged to a rack-and-gear actuating system. This system was very complicated with all its moving parts. The top and bottom racks had to be synchronized through the left drum valve, which has two drive gears molded in it. The drum valves are made of aluminum. When the drum valve becomes carbon seized, the steel teeth on the rack shear off the aluminum teeth on the drum valve, rendering the drum valve inoporable. Check the condition of the gear teeth every time you do a top-end service, because if one gear fails the whole system runs out of sync. On the late-model 80-125cc KXs, the KIPS is relatively simple, relying on a wedge valve

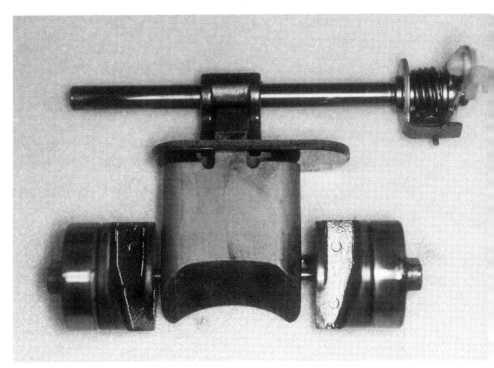

This is a layout of the valves used on the 1996-2000 RM250. It's similar to the Honda and KTM designs.

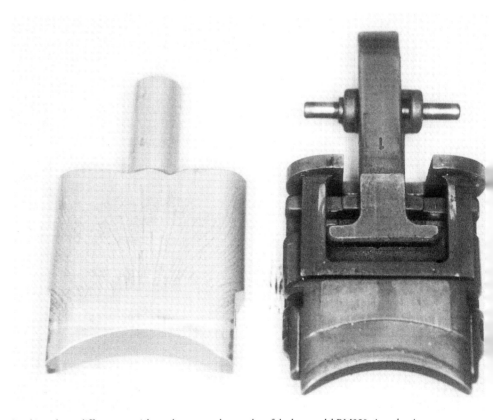

Suzuki used two different materials on the center exhaust valve of the late-model RM250. A steel articulated valve was used in 1997. It worked very well and was durable. The 1996 and later model valves were made of aluminum and hard anodized for wear resistance. These valves are prone to burring at the edges, requiring frequent maintenance.

This is the Powervalve from the 1999 YZ250. It's a two-stage system where the center valve opens first and the sub exhaust valves open later based on the ramp angle of the drive lug, all mounted to a single drive shaft.

and flapper. This system is self-scraping, so it requires little maintenance. In the first year of operation (1998), the KIPS system was plagued with failures such as the pin breaking on the flapper, the valve receding into the cylinder and contacting the piston, and over-extension of the valve causing cock and jam. Pro-Circuit made an aftermarket valve cover with a full stop that prevented over-extension and in 1999 Kawasaki changed the wedge valve and flapper design for more rigidity and that solved all the reliability problems.

The drum valves on the 1988-92 KX250 and 1990-2000 KX500 are also aluminum but have a hard-anodized coating that resists wear. However, the drum valves eventually wear at the drive channels for the center wedge valve, and the sloppy fit between the wedge and drum valves prevents the center valve from fully opening. That is why these bikes get noticeably slower as they get older. There is no preventative cure or aftermarket part. You just need to replace the drum valves when the drive channels wear out.

The 1993 KX250 was the first year for the KIPS system used through present day

models. The system uses a single wedge and flapper valve for the main exhaust port and two drum shaped valves for the sub exhaust ports. The valves are all linked together with two racks and pinions on the right drum valve and a steel gear on the upper rack linking the wedge valve. A left-hand-thread nut retains the gear to the rod that actuates the wedge valve. Check the nut periodically—if the nut loosens, the wedge valves become inoperable. The KX250 KIPS also features two large cavities to allow for dissipation of the compression wave that travels back up the exhaust pipe at low to mid rpm. It's important that the two valve covers on the cylinder are sealed with gaskets and it is normal for large amounts of black sludge to accumulate under those valve covers. It takes years for the sludge to accumulate to the point of adversely affecting performance. The only way to clean out the sludge is to have the cylinder hot-tank cleaned at an automotive rebuilding store.

The 1993–2000 KX250 wedge valve tends to form burrs at the outer edges that face the piston. These burrs prevent the wedge valve from opening fully, and the thin

flap that comprises the exhaust-port roof hangs out into the exhaust-gas stream, producing a shock wave that closes off the exhaust port. File the burrs smooth and check the wedge valve through the full range of movement. The valve pocket in the cylinder gets worn too. Aftermarket cylinder rebuilders like Max Power Cylinders apply a hard coating to that area to reduce wear or build-up material that has worn down from the moving wedge valve.

Another characteristic problem of the KX250 KIPS is broken governor levers. The lever that transmits the movement from the centrifugal governor to the right-side case lever tends to break in half. This piece is located under the right-side cover. If your KX250 suddenly loses top-end power, it's probably due to the actuating lever breakage or the carbon-seizure of the KIPS valves.

1988–92 KX250 and 1990-2000 KX500 KIPS Timing Procedure

The explanation of this procedure, written in the Kawasaki service manual, is confusing. It requires you to time the upper and lower racks at the same instant. My method of timing the exhaust valves is composed of simple steps that enable you to check your work as you go. The 1988–92 KX250 and KX500 use the drive-channel system to actuate the center valve. Here is the best way to time the KIPS on these models.

1. Set the cylinder upside down on a bench.
2. Install the center valve but don't bolt it in!
3. Install the side drum valves and align the drive channels on the drum valves with the center valve, but don't bolt it in!
4. Install the side drums valves and align the drive channels on the drum valves with the engagement pins on the center valve.
5. Lift up the drum valves so the bottoms of the gears are flush with the cylinder base. Take care not to disengage the center valve.
6. Slide in the rack from either side of the cylinder. Position the rack by installing the seal pack and pulling the rack out until it bottoms against the seal pack. This is the full-open position.
7. Drop the drum valves onto the rack so the valves are in the full-open position.

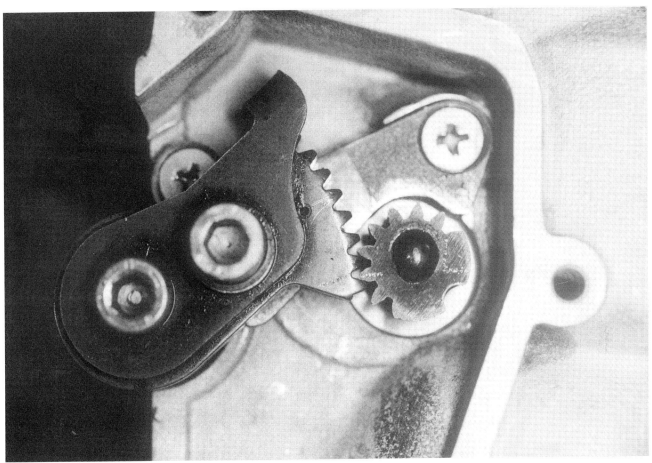

This is a view from the left side of the cylinder of a typical KTM exhaust valve system. The main shaft has a gear plate, which turns the side drum valves. Scribe marks show timing alignment. The plate with the two Allen bolts controls how far the main exhaust valve closes at TDC. That is the stop plate. If you turn it too far, the main valve will contact the piston and damage it.

Don't pay attention to alignment dots or marks on the valve or rack just remember that the valves should be open when the rack is pulled out and closed when the rack is pushed in.

1992–97 KX125 and 1993-2000 X250 KIPS Timing Procedure

The system used on the KX125 and KX250 uses both wedge and drum valves with racks. This is the best exhaust valve system for performance but the most difficult to maintain. Here are some tips for re-timing this KIPS system.

1. Install the wedge valves in the cylinder and the actuating rod and lever. Squirt some pre-mix oil on the parts.
2. Pull the wedge valve into the full-open position, place the gear on the end of the rod, and rotate the gear counterclockwise until the rack butts against the stop plate. Thread the nut on the rod and tighten it counterclockwise because it is a left-hand-thread nut.
3. Place the drum valves into their respective cavities until the top of the gears are level with the cylinder base. Now push the lower rack into place and bolt the seal pack on the rack into the cylinder.
4. Pull the rack out until it stops and push it in 1mm; now it is in the correct position to install the drum valve. Before you push down the drum valves, make sure the wedge valve and drum valves are in the full-open position.
5. Push down the drum valve with the two gears first because it must engage the upper rack and lower rack simultaneously. Take care and be patient. You may have to wiggle the wedge valve yoke to get everything to fall into place. Never hammer the drum valves! Then push down the right drum valve and install the idler gear. Now install the bushings and check the system. The valves will bind and stick if you try to move the valves without the bushings installed, or if the cylinder is facing upside-down.

Test the KIPS in this way: pull the rack outward until it stops, and look through the exhaust port from the pipe side. The valves should be in the full-open position. On cylinders where the base has been turned down more than .010 inches, the drum valve bushings will also need to be turned down to prevent the valves from binding when the cylinder is tightened.

Suzuki ATEV

Suzuki first used exhaust valves in 1985, using a drum valve that uncovered a

Use RTV Ultra Copper silicone sealant on the front exhaust plate of the KTMs.

cavity in the head or cylinder to add volume and length to the exhaust pipe, strictly at low rpm. In 1987 they employed a system that featured two large valves that had multiple functions. This system was used on the 1989-2000 RM80, 1987-2000 RM125, and 1987-95 RM250. The wedge shaped valve was positioned at about a 45-degree angle over the exhaust port. The ATEV system is designed to regulate the effective stroke, exhaust-gas velocity through the exhaust port, and on 1995 and later models it controls the exhaust gas temperature. The ATEV system is self-cleaning in that the valves are scraped of carbon every time they move. Some of the early-model RMs suffered from broken exhaust valves when the stem would detach from the cylindrical wedge. That problem was cured in 1991 when the radius between the stem and valve was increased.

The two common problems that occur with the ATEV are caused by the two following errors in assembling the system:

1. Too much preload on the spring. On the left side of the cylinder is a dial that controls the spring preload for the exhaust valve system. The preload doesn't have that great of an effect on the engine's powerband, but too much preload will prevent the valves from opening, which causes a lack of top-end power.

2. Crisscrossed spring. A centering spring on the right side of the cylinder, located on the rod, actuates the valves. This spring is commonly installed wrong. The spring tabs should be parallel when coupled to the lever and rod. If the spring tabs are crisscrossed, the valve travel will be limited and won't open fully.

In 1996 Suzuki redesigned the RM250 engine, going back to a design reminiscent of the 1987 model RM250. For this model Suzuki modified Honda's HPP design used on the late-model CR250. However a problem plagued this system. Instead of pivoting the center valve, Suzuki chose to slide it in a passageway of the cylinder. The added mechanical friction made the system prone to binding in one position, half-open. This causes the engine to run flat. Another problem was the shape of the valve. The leading edge that faced the piston was too square and sharp. Even when the valve was in the full-open position it caused a shock wave that impeded the outgoing exhaust flow. Grinding the edge smooth reduced the low-end power but helped improve top-end.

In 1997 Suzuki redesigned the center valve, using steel and splitting the valve into two sections, a major and minor valve. They also added a two-stage spring system. With some simple grinding to match the valve to

the exhaust port when fully open, this set-up was a winner! Suzuki chose to redesign the system in 1998-2000 to the 1997 design. The thought was that the steel valve damaged the valve pocket in the cylinder—although simply extending the nickel silicon carbide bore material into the valve pocket would have solved this problem.

Yamaha POWERVALVE

Yamaha was the first motorcycle manufacturer to adapt exhaust valves to two-stroke motorcycle engines. Yamaha's simple design of a cylindrical valve that rotates 1/4 turn to vary the height of the exhaust port requires little maintenance. This system was used on the YZ250 from 1982-98, and on the YZ125 from 1983-93. Occasionally, you have to replace the seals and O-rings to prevent exhaust oil from dripping out of the side of the cylinder.

In 1989, Yamaha added a stop plate to limit the travel of the power valve, primarily so mechanics couldn't install the valve in the wrong position. The stop plate is located on the left side of the cylinder. The valve has a small tab that bumps up against the stop plate to limit the fully open and closed position of the valve. This design enabled Yamaha to position the valve closer to the piston to make it more effective at varying the exhaust-port timing. Unfortunately, the soft-aluminum tab on the valve gets worn, allowing the valve to rotate farther in the fully closed position. Eventually, (after about three years' use) the tab wears enough so the valve strikes the piston, causing damage to the piston. Yamaha's exhaust valve is cheap to replace. I recommend replacing the valve when the tab wears more than .030 inch (.7mm).

In 1994 Yamaha changed the engine design of the YZ125 and included the next generation of exhaust valves. This system used two oval-shaped wedge valves, positioned at a 45-degree angle over the exhaust port. This system was similar to the one employed by Suzuki. Yamaha experimented with resonator cavity volume, and vents for pressure bleed off and temperature control. Overall this is a very reliable system. Occasionally the pins that fit through the ends of the valve to interface with the actuator lever vibrate out causing the valve to strike the piston. Those pins are a press fit but you can add some Loctite Instant Adhesive to the pins for added protection. Yamaha has been concerned with high-rpm valve flutter—they've added springs to the valves to control the flutter, but future innovations could include a positive seal between the valve and the cylinders' valve pocket.

In 1999 Yamaha redesigned the YZ250 engine and exhaust valve system. This model features a powervalve that marks a significant design change, from the company that pioneered the use of exhaust valves on two-stroke engines. Looking more like a Rube Goldberg device, the new powervalve has separate valves for the main (center) and sub exhaust ports (sides). The whole assembly is controlled by one actuating rod, but the side valves open after the main exhaust valve. The side valves are controlled by two wedge-shaped ramps that resemble a shift drum from a transmission. The ramp design offers versatility in tuning. By changing the shape of the ramp, the duration and timing of the sub exhaust ports can be changed to match a rider's ability or the demands of the terrain. So far there are no aftermarket companies making these ramps but you can bet that the factory teams are experimenting with them!

The new exhaust valve system also features an atmospheric vent that not only relieves the pipe pressure wave at low rpm but also introduces cool air into the exhaust system to make the pipe work over a larger rpm range.

KTM 250, 300, 360, 380 1990–97

KTM uses two distinctly different designs of exhaust valve systems. The earlier model uses one large center valve with the actuating rod cast together. Two drum valves control the sub exhaust ports and steel gears are used to interface the main and minor valves. The effective stroke can be adjusted by altering a stop plate on the left side of the cylinder. The governor control in the right-side case has an inspection cap that allows tuners to add thin washers and increase the spring preload in order to affect a change in engagement rpm.

The system is prone to carbon seizure of the steel valves (sub exhaust ports). Also there are rubber O-rings that prevent oil from leaking out the sides of the actuating rod. Those eventually wear out. In order to service this exhaust valve system, you need to remove the cylinder. The main valve and all its hardware can remain bolted together. There is an access cover fastened by four bolts to the front of the cylinder. There is no gasket for the cover, it seals with a non-drying liquid gasket like RTV silicone. The main valve just pulls straight out. The drum valves are held in place by two plates with two tapered panhead Phillips screws. There is a specific procedure for removing these screws. Start by heating the screw heads for two minutes with a propane torch. That will break down the locking agent on the threads. Then use a hand impact driver with a number two Phillips tip. If you strip the heads of the screws (most people do, including me!) then just use a tapered-point punch to spin the screws out. That will destroy the screw, but you should replace the Phillips with a tapered panhead Allen bolt. Take care when handling the stop lever on the left side of the main valve. Before you loosen the two Allen bolts, scribe a line to reference the position of the plate relative to the gear plate. It is possible to adjust the stop plate so far that the valve rotates past the full-closed position and contacts the piston. That would destroy the piston.

The 1998 and newer KTMs have an exhaust valve system that makes use of the resonator concept. That system is so complex that you would need the factory service manual in order to service it.

TWO-STROKE LOWER-END REBUILDING

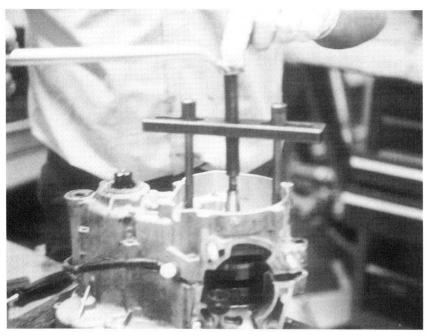

This is a case-splitting tool. The long outer bolts thread in the stator plate mounts. The center bolt presses on the end of the crankshaft and separates the case half from the crank. Motion Pro makes a professional kit for motorcycles and bearing supply or auto parts stores stock similar types of pullers.

R ebuilding the lower end of a two-stroke engine is the procedure that is most often put off until next race/month/season. When you start hearing the engine make a strange knocking sound, it's time to shut it off and tear it down rather than pin the throttle wide open and hope it will just go away! The normal service interval for lower end rebuilding is once a year on engines under 200cc and once every two to three years for 250 and larger engines. While rebuilding the lower end you should replace the ball bearings that support the crankshaft and the transmission shafts, plus the rubber seals. In most cases, the crankshaft will need to have a new connecting rod, pin, bearing, and thrust washers installed. Some manufacturers (Honda) don't sell parts for their crankshafts, only the entire part. However, there are companies that offer higher-quality replacement parts (Hot Rods) to rebuild modern Japanese cranks and vintage Spanish cranks. Although some aspects of lower end rebuilding are very specific to a particular model engine, this section gives you an overview of the general process.

THE RIGHT TOOLS

Engine rebuilding is nearly impossible without the right tools. Some guys try to use the "caveman" method—big hammers and chisels. As a result, they usually do some stupid thing that ruins expensive engine components.

To properly rebuild your lower end, you will need the following tools from the manufacturer: a service manual for torque specs and disassembly/assembly techniques specific to your model engine, a flywheel puller, a clutch-hub holder, a crankcase splitting tool, and a crankshaft installation tool—but I'll show you how techniques for removing the clutch and installing the crank so you can save money on those tools.

You will also need an air- or electric-powered impact wrench to remove the nuts that retain the flywheel, clutch, countershaft sprocket, and primary gear; a parts washer with solvent to clean the engine parts; a hydraulic press to remove and install the bearings because a hammer will only damage them; a propane torch to heat and expand the aluminum crankcases to remove or install the bearings because they have an interference fit (meaning that the bearing is a slightly larger diameter than the hole that it fits into); a digital caliper to measure certain engine parts and compare them to the minimum wear specs listed in the service manual; a variety of tools such as wrenches and sockets; and soft tools such as brake cleaner, thread locking agent, penetrating oil, seal grease, and gasket sealer.

A simple way to hold the engine while you work on it is to make an open square box from wood blocks. A universal box for any engine can be made from 2x4-inch blocks with the dimensions of the box being 5x10 inches. CC Specialty makes a ball-vise for $100 that is convenient if you plan to rebuild engines frequently. To permanently remove the temptation to use steel hammers when rebuilding engines, buy a plastic mallet. Snap-On makes a lead-filled plastic mallet that works excellent. The last thing you will need to rebuild an engine is several parts storage bins. I prefer to separate the engine's components into separate bins—top-end parts, electrical parts, clutch parts, shifter parts, transmission, and crankcase bolts. This enables me to keep the parts organized for quick assembly. I also puncture small holes in the bottom of the bin so I can pour parts cleaning solvent into the bins to clean the parts. Then there isn't any chance of the parts becoming lost in the bottom of the parts-washing tank.

Top-End Disassembly and Inspection

Refer to the sections on top-end rebuilding and exhaust valve servicing for more information on this topic.

Bike Blows White Smoke

Question: My old YZ250 smokes so much that I'm embarrassed to ride it. The front of the pipe drools oil out the manifold, and the engine fouls plugs fast. What could be causing this problem, and how can I fix it?

Answer: Your bike may be drawing trans oil into the crankcases and burning it in the combustion chamber. You should monitor the trans oil level to confirm this suspicion. The crankshaft main bearings are probably worn out and the crank is wobbling at high rpm, allowing oil from the trans to slip past the right-side crank seal. Lower ends don't last forever! It's about time that you rebuilt the lower end with new main bearings and seals and perhaps even rebuild the crank with a new rod kit. Otherwise, you can just live with the problem and keep adding trans oil. Eventually, the crank will be stressed so hard that it will seize the lower end. The average labor charge for a lower end rebuild (assuming you take the engine out of the frame) is $100 plus parts, and crank rebuilding is about $45. Average parts tickets range from $75 to $275.

Crankshaft Balance

Question: I have a 1991 Kawasaki KX500, and I have been told that it would benefit from crankshaft balancing. How is this done and who offers this service? Also, since the engine is apart, is there anything else I should examine?

Answer: There are a few different terms used to describe tuning techniques performed to crankshafts:

"Truing" is a procedure where you rotate the left and right crank halves about the big end pin to align the halves together. Truing is the most common procedure performed to crankshafts. When a new connecting rod kit is installed, the crank must be trued. If you are only replacing the crankcase main bearings the crank alignment must be checked and trued if necessary. Worn main bearings can cause a crank to go out of true.

"Balancing" is a procedure where you change the balance factor of the crank. The balance factor is the relationship between the reciprocating mass of the piston and part of the rod assembly and the rotating mass of the crank weights. The motorcycle manufacturers set the balance factor of their crankshafts based on the riding habits of the average buyer for a given model. The balance factor of the KX500 is set for about 5,000 rpm. The KX500 is one of the most widely adapted dirt bikes. People ride KX500s in tight woods for trail riding, desert racing, hill-climbing, motocross, and even road racing. A good engine tuner may want to have the balance factor changed to make the engine vibrate less in the rpm band you use most. There are three companies well known for crankshaft balancing: Falicon in Florida, Redline in Wisconsin, and Rick Petersen Motorsports in California.

If your KX500 is vibrating excessively or wearing out main bearings quickly, your bike might be suffering from a problem common to KX500s that are over-revved often. The main bearings that support the crank are pressed into cast-iron races that are pressed into the crankcases. These races can become elongated, allowing the bearings to wobble and wear out prematurely. If your bike has this problem, you would have to replace the crankcases or have them resleeved. Rapid Precision Machine in Massachusetts offers the crankcase resleeving service for $50 per sleeve.

Bad Vibrations

Question: My 250 vibrates so bad that I can't keep my left boot on the footpeg when I free rev the engine. Do you think there might be a problem inside the engine?

Answer: Don't start that bike! The crankshaft main bearings could be worn, allowing the crankshaft to wobble in the crankcases, thereby causing the vibration. Also, check the flywheel. Look for cracks in the outer shell, around the rivets. Bring your engine to a skilled dirt bike mechanic and have him check it out for you.

Electrical System Disassembly and Inspection

Use an impact wrench to remove the flywheel nut. Don't be tempted to jam a screwdriver in through one of the holes in the flywheel to prevent it from spinning. That will damage the coils under the flywheel. K&N makes a threaded flywheel puller that has left-hand threads to fasten to the flywheel and a right-hand-threaded bolt to push on the crankshaft. Put a dab of grease on the flywheel end to prevent the bolt from galling and damaging the machined center on the crankshaft end (if the center is damaged, it is much more difficult for a technician to true the crank). It's OK to tap on the end of the tightly threaded puller with a plastic mallet.

Here is a tip for removing stuck flywheels. Use a propane torch to heat the center hub of the flywheel. Take care not to shoot the flame through the holes in the flywheel. Then spray penetrating oil between the crankshaft end and the flywheel. This should loosen the flywheel enough for the puller to pop it off.

When the flywheel comes off, inspect the center-hub rivets and look for tiny cracks in the hub around the rivets. Replace the flywheel if there are any cracks. Big-bore bikes may have problems with shearing flywheel Woodruff keys, especially on the KX500 and YZ490. The problem is that the flywheel is not matched to the crank at the taper, but that can be corrected, using the following procedure. Remove the Woodruff key and apply grinding paste to the crank's taper. Hands press the flywheel onto the crank and turn it back and forth for 5 minutes. This will hone down the high spots on the surfaces of each part so the flywheel won't ever loosen up and shear the Woodruff key. After matching, clean the parts thoroughly with contact cleaner.

Once the flywheel nut is removed, this is how a flywheel extractor is used. The standard tool has two sets of threads, coarse and fine. The fine threads of the tool are left-hand threads so you have to turn it counterclockwise to thread it onto the flywheel. Once it threads on until it stops, hold the flywheel side of the tool with a large crescent wrench. Thread in (clockwise) the center bolt with a socket and ratchet. Always use grease on the extractor tool's crank-bolt, and apply heat and penetrating oil to a stuck flywheel before you resort to using a hammer!

Clutch Disassembly and Inspection

There are a number of things to check on the clutch, and you will need a factory service manual for specifications on the wear limit of the clutch parts. Some of the things you want to inspect include the clutch springs for free length, the clutch plates for thickness, clutch plates for any broken plates, the outer pressure plate for a sizable ridge worn in that would indicate that the plate is too thin, the inner hub and outer basket for chatter marks, the clutch basket's aluminum housing and the primary gear for excessive free-play between the two, and the center bushing (measure its diameter). A worn bushing will cause a variety of problems, including broken clutch plates. See the section on clutch rebuilding for more details.

Shifter, Kickstarter, and Primary Gear Disassembly and Inspection

You will have to remove the shift shaft, power-valve governor cartridge, and the primary gear that is bolted to the end of the crankshaft. The best way to remove the primary-gear bolt is with an impact wrench. There is no factory holding tool for this gear; it's just an accepted practice to use an impact wrench. If you are only going to change the main bearings, you don't need to remove the kickstart cartridge or the shift drum and spring-loaded shifting mechanism.

If the flywheel has chronic problems with staying tight or shearing keys, then you need to lapp it with valve grinding compound. Wipe a dab of the gritty compound on the flywheel taper. Then twist it several times on the taper of the crank so as to mate the surfaces and make them flatter.

Some tuners go for every advantage. These crank and tranny parts have been coated with a low friction material called tungsten disulfide, brand name WS2, from Micro Surface in Morris, Illinois. The drive train accounts for about 15 percent power loss due to friction.

This steel slug is being heated with a propane torch so it can transfer heat to the inner race of the main bearing, causing it to expand. The process takes about five minutes.

Splitting the Crankcases

Remove all the case bolts, and install the case-splitting tool onto the left-side crankcase. The puller's two bolts thread into the stator-plate mounts. The center bolt of the puller threads up against the crankshaft end. Apply some grease to the end of the crankshaft so the puller's tapered bolt doesn't gall the end of the crankshaft. Slowly tighten the puller bolt and tap around the outside of the cases with a plastic mallet. This will help break the bond of the case alignment pins. If the cases start to split apart with an uneven gap from front to rear, then tap on a part of the right-side crankcase with a plastic mallet. You may also have to tap on the countershaft, but be careful because you could break the bearing support ring that is cast into the case.

To remove the transmission shafts, you need to first remove the shift forks. Pull the rods that hold the forks, and then pull out the forks. Place the forks onto the rods, and set them in a parts bin in the order that they fit in the engine. The rod with the outside of the right countershaft bearing is very vulnerable on Hondas. Pay attention to the placement of shims on the ends of the transmission shafts; sometimes they will stick to the bearings and fall out later when you are washing the cases.

Transmission Disassembly and Inspection

There are three shift forks in the transmission, and they are marked "L" for left

A propane torch and a can of brake cleaner are useful tools when rebuilding lower ends. Big rubber bands are good for holding all the gears and bushings on the shafts so they don't get misplaced.

and "R" for right. They each have a different radius, so you can't install them in the wrong position. Visually check the sides of the shift forks for blue marks. That would indicate that the forks are bent and need to be replaced (RM250s and KX500s are notorious for bending shift forks). Now remove the transmission shafts, paying close attention to shims that may be stuck to the case bearings. Visually inspect the gear engagement dogs for wear. The female and male

dogs will have shiny spots on the corners if they are worn. Also, the bike will have the tendency to jump out of gear during acceleration. The best way to keep the gears and shims on the transmission shafts is with rubber bands.

Crankshaft Removal and Inspection

Sometimes, the crank will be difficult to remove from the right-side main bearing (on all engines except Suzukis). Never strike the

137

end of the crank with a metal hammer; try a plastic mallet first. If that doesn't work, then thread the primary-gear nut on to protect the threads and use a hydraulic press to remove the crank. Measure the rod clearance to determine if it needs to be rebuilt. Check the crankshaft run-out and true it if necessary before installation. See the section on crankshaft repair if your inspection reveals a problem.

This is the Kawasaki wedge tool. It wraps around the rod and supports the crank from being tilted if you have to tap it into place with a mallet.

Yamahas and Kawasakis do not use center crankcase gaskets. You must use a thick non-drying sealer like Yamabond or Liquid Gasket 1104. Smear it on evenly with a business card or a clean finger.

Bearing Removal and Installation

The best way to remove or install bearings is by heating the aluminum crankcases with a propane torch, and then using a hydraulic press to gently push them out. Never pound the bearings out with a hammer and punch. The outer race of the bearing is the only part of the bearing where a press slug should be placed. Large sockets or discs work well as press slugs. Placing the new bearings in the freezer for two hours and heating the cases with the torch will enable you to install the bearings without a press. Fit the bearings into position with as little stress as possible exerted on the crank ends. Some manufacturers make special tools that wedge in between the flyweights so you can press the crank into place (Kawasaki). Other manufacturers use a threaded tool that draws the crank into the bearing.

Crankshaft Installation

Here is a simple way to install the crank. Place the crank in a freezer for two hours so it contracts in size. Get a cylindrical piece of aluminum with the same diameter as the inner bearing race. Heat and expand the bearing's inner race by heating the aluminum slug with a propane torch for 5 minutes while it rests on the inner race of the right-side main bearing. Drop the cold crank into the hot right main bearing. Now repeat the procedure for the left main bearing, and prepare to assemble the cases.

Assembling the Crankcases

With the crank and transmission fitted into the right crankcase, you're ready to assemble the cases. Kawasaki and Yamaha use non-drying sealer as a center gasket between the crankcases. Apply the sealer to one side of the case. Spread it evenly with a business card and let it set up for about 10 minutes. Next, place the left case over the crank and transmission cases, press the cases toward each other to within 5mm of sealing, install the bolts that fasten the cases together, and slowly tighten them while maintaining an equal gap between the cases. You may need to tap the case lightly because you are trying to align eight different cylindrical pieces all together (crank, transmission shafts, shift-fork rods, shift drum, and case alignment

pins). Once the case bolts are snugly tightened, try to turn the crankshaft and the transmission shafts. The transmission should turn easily, and the crankshaft should turn with some resistance. Using the plastic mallet, tap lightly on the transmission shafts while spinning them. Do the same with the crankshaft, tapping on both ends. The crankshaft may make a sharp cracking sound. That is good because it means that the crankshaft has centered between the main bearings. Now torque the bolts on the cases.

Bench Testing

When you get the lower end together and the cases are sealed tight, install the shifting mechanism and turn the clutch shaft while clicking through the gears. The transmission is your main consideration when bench testing.

Final Assembly

Assemble the rest of the engine components, mount the engine in the frame, hook up all electrical wires, control cables, and linkages. Torque all the mounting bolts, and then you're ready to break in your rebuilt engine.

Breaking In a New Bottom End

The new lower end will need some patient break-in time. The best way is to let the engine idle for three separate 10-minute sessions with a 20-minute rest period between sessions. You don't need any extra pre-mix oil because the engine load is minimal when the engine is idling.

CRANKSHAFT REPAIR

Crankshaft-related problems can cause the most expensive engine damage. Consider that at 10,000 rpm, the piston moves up and down in the cylinder 166 times per second. The rod bearing and the crankcase main bearings support the reciprocating mass of the piston and rod. If you don't keep your air filter clean, the dirt will wear out the bearings causing the crank and piston to whip around unsupported and destroy the inside of the engine. All of this can happen in a matter of seconds in a 125cc engine. There are several ways for you to check the condition of the engine bearings, and you should do so, fre-

Engines with case reed induction will have gaskets with tabs to stabilize the gasket during crankcase assembling. The tabs have to be shaved even with the gasket surfaces using a razor blade or gasket scraper.

Once the cases are assembled and the bolts are tight, tap on each side of the crankshaft until the gap between each side of the cases and crank is equal. You may hear a sharp pop. That is a stress relief sound from the large ball bearing mains adjusting to the side load.

Measure the connecting rod's side clearance by inserting a feeler gauge between the flyweights and the side of the rod. Compare the feeler gauge measurement with factory dimension specs.

Grasp the rod and try to pull it up and down. Don't be too concerned with the radial movement; the rod is supported on needle bearings. You shouldn't feel any up and down play in the rod.

quently, to prevent catastrophic engine damage. Here are some tips for monitoring the condition of the crankshaft.

Checking for Crankshaft and Bearing Damage

Use these techniques for checking the condition of lower end parts such as the connecting-rod bearing, main bearings, and flywheel rotor.

Flywheel Movement

Grasp the flywheel with your hand and try to move it up and down and in and out. If you feel any movement, the main bearings are worn out. Remove the flywheel and the stator plate. Check the left crank seal for fuel leakage. This seal is blown, and dirt was drawn into the engine past the seal. Usually a bike will bog at low speed or heat-seize the piston on the exhaust skirt when the left crank seal leaks.

Connecting-Rod Movement

Grasp the connecting rod and try to pull it straight up and push it down. It is normal to feel some radial play because the rod bearing is a needle bearing. You should-

n't feel any up and down play. If you do, rebuild the crank. The side clearance between the rod and the thrust washers is a good indicator of rod-bearing wear. Use a feeler gauge to measure the side clearance. The factory service manual lists the maximum side-clearance specification for your model of bike.

Shattered Flywheel

Flywheels can occasionally come apart. The reason for this is worn main bearings. The crank is supported by the primary drive gear on the right side of the engine.

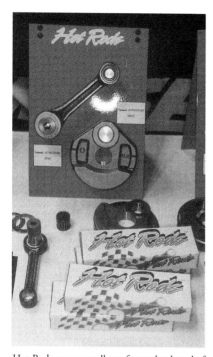

Hot Rods are an excellent aftermarket brand of connecting rods. They make crank parts for motorcycles, ATVs, and PWC.

Press the new pin into one crank half. Put a dab of white grease on the pin first.

When the main bearings wear, the crank deflects more on the left side where the electrical components are mounted. When the flywheel is allowed to gyrate, the flywheel rivets will eventually shear.

Crankshaft Rebuilding Techniques

Before you decide to have your crankshaft rebuilt, do a survey on the exact cost of buying a new crank assembly as opposed to the parts and labor for rebuilding. Check the crankshaft ends for hammer marks or peening. When the machined centers of the crankshaft ends are distorted or marred, the crank cannot be set in a truing jig and is nearly impossible to align. If the ends of your crank are marred, you should buy a new crank. You must also evaluate the technician who will perform the rebuilding service. If he doesn't have the proper training or special tools, then he can't do the job! Use this section as a guide to evaluating the quality of a crankshaft rebuilding company. If you have a Suzuki or Yamaha, you will find that it is much cheaper to rebuild the crank than to buy a new one. In contrast, Kawasaki and Honda crankshaft assemblies are relatively inexpensive.

The Right Tools

To rebuild a crankshaft, you need special tools. The two most important and expensive tools are a 30-ton hydraulic press (about $500) and a truing jig (about $750). It is possible to use a lathe as a truing jig but only when the crank is set between two live centers. You cannot clamp one side of the crank in the chuck and one end in the center and expect to get an accurate deflection measurement; the deflection of the crank is redirected, and the crank reads true when it is far out of true. Other tools needed are a small square, a scribe, a dial indicator and stand, a brass hammer, a steel wedge such as a chisel, and a variety of rectangular steel blocks and pins so you can secure the crank in the press during assembly. Mud Creek Engineering in Michigan (517) 676-9534 makes a great tool ($800) that allows you to assemble the crankshaft in perfect alignment; no additional truing is needed. The tool uses bushings to align the crank journals as the crank is pressed together.

Honda CR Crankshafts

Honda cranks have thin, bell-shaped sheet-metal covers pressed onto flyweights. About 1/3 of the crank periphery (around the crank pin) is hollow, so you cannot use the impact method to align a Honda crank. You must use the RCE tool to align the crank. Honda doesn't offer OEM replacement connecting rods, but Hot Rods have an aftermarket rod kit available for late-model Japanese dirt bikes, including Honda CRs.

Step-by-Step Crank Rebuilding

The following step-by-step procedure tells how a technician would rebuild a crank using conventional jigs and a truing stand:

1. Before disassembling the crank, the technician places a square against the side of the flyweights and scribes two parallel lines, 180 degrees apart, across the face of the flyweight. These alignment marks will help the technician align the crank upon assembly. Now the crankpin can be pressed out of the flyweights and all of the old parts should be discarded. Never reuse the old connecting rod, bearing, pin, or thrust washers.

2. The technician then applies a thin layer of assembly grease to the bearing surfaces of the crank pin, bearing, thrust washers, and rod. After the grease has been applied, the crank pin can be pressed into one of the flyweights. The washers, bearing, and rod are then placed onto the crank pin.

3. The technician heats the other flyweight's pinhole with a propane torch for about 3 minutes. This will expand the diameter of the pinhole and reduce the need for excessive pressure to assemble the crank. He then uses the square to align the scribe lines on each flyweight so the crank is assembled very close to true.

4. As the crank is pressed together, the technician uses a feeler gauge to monitor the clearance between the connecting rod and the thrust washer. The proper clearance is listed in the service manual. The manual also lists an overall crank width spec that can be measured with a caliper.

Once the rod is pressed into one crank half install the rest of the rod assembly including the bearing and washers. Place a machinist's square alongside the crank halves to align the free half before pressing in on the rod.

This is the RCE tool. The crankshaft can be pressed together true with this excellent tool that features a sturdy jig frame and bushings to align the crank halves.

Truing the Crank

1. During the truing process, the technician supports the crank between live centers.

2. Knife-edged bearings must be used if the machined centers of the crank ends are damaged. Dial indicators are used to measure the run-out of each crank end and the side run-out of the flyweights.

3. If the crank has side run-out, then the flyweights aren't parallel and must be adjusted before the crank ends can be trued. This is accomplished by hitting the wide side of the flyweights with a large brass hammer, and then wedging the flyweights apart at the narrow side with a large tapered chisel and hammer. It sounds very caveman-like, but this is the way the pros do it. Of course, the crank must be removed from the jig before the run-out can be adjusted; otherwise the dial indicators and jig centers will be damaged. The crank ends have run-out because the flyweights aren't parallel and must be rotated about the crank pin. This is accomplished by striking the flyweight at the exact point of the greatest run-out, with a brass hammer, while holding the opposite flyweight in hand. It doesn't take must force to rotate the flyweight into true.

4. Now you may understand why we must be careful how the crank is installed into the crankcases during engine assembly. It is very easy to throw the crank out of true if you beat the hell out of it and the cases during assembly!

BASIC TWO-STROKE TUNING

Changing the powerband of your dirt bike engine is simple when you know the basics. A myriad of aftermarket accessories is available for you to tune your bike to better suit your needs. The most common mistake is to choose the wrong combination of engine components, making the engine run worse than a stock engine. Use this section as a guide to inform yourself on how changes in engine components can alter the powerband of your bike's engine. Use the guide at the end of the chapter to map out your strategy for changing engine components to create the perfect powerband.

TWO-STROKE PRINCIPLES

Although a two-stroke engine has fewer moving parts than a four-stroke engine, a two-stroke is a complex engine with different phases taking place in the crankcase and in the cylinder bore at the same time. This is necessary because a two-stroke engine completes a power cycle in only 360 degrees of crankshaft rotation, compared to a four-stroke engine, which requires 720 degrees of crankshaft rotation to complete one power cycle. Two-stroke engines aren't as efficient as four-stroke engines, meaning that they don't retain as much air as they draw in through the intake. Some of the air is lost out the exhaust pipe. If a two-stroke engine could retain the same percentage of air, it would be twice as powerful as a four-stroke engine because it produces twice as many power strokes in the same number of crankshaft revolutions.

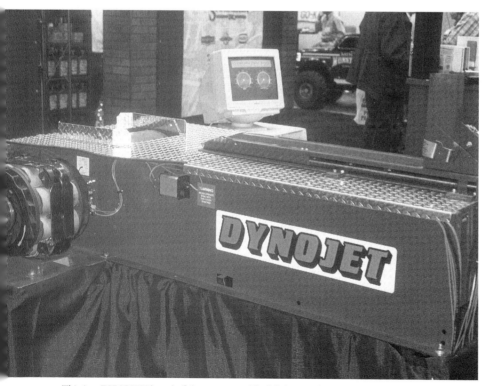

This is a DYNOJET brand of dynamometer. The bike's rear wheel spins a 900-pound steel drum. An Eddy-current generator measures torque, rpm, and as many other sensors as you want to interface with the PC software.

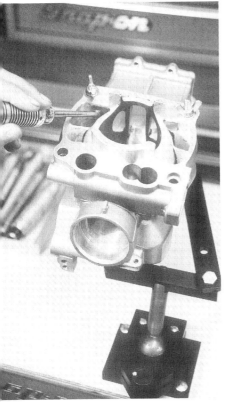

This is a cylinder mounted in a ball-vise. The cylinder is being ported with CC Specialty porting tools. They have the biggest, most complete supply of porting tools.

The following explains the basic operation of the two-stroke engine:

1. Starting with the piston at top dead center (TDC 0 degrees) ignition has occurred and the gases in the combustion chamber are expanding and pushing down the piston. This pressurizes the crankcase causing the reed valve to close. At about 90 degrees after TDC the exhaust port opens, ending the power stroke. A pressure wave of hot expanding gases flows down the exhaust pipe. The blow-down phase has started and will end when the transfer ports open. The pressure in the cylinder must blow-down to below the pressure in the crankcase in order for the unburned mixture gases to flow out the transfer ports during the scavenging phase.

2. Now the transfer ports are uncovered at about 120 degrees after TDC. The scavenging phase has begun, meaning that the unburned mixture gases are flowing

Powerband Questions

Question: I have a couple of questions about powerbands for you to answer. What exactly are they and where on the bike are they located? How do powerbands work?

Answer: The powerband of a motorcycle is a term that describes the usable power produced over an rpm band. The rpm band is about 3,000 rpm wide on a mini or 125cc bikes and as much as 5,000 rpm on a 250cc engine. In magazine test articles, powerbands are usually described in one of the following terms: wide, narrow, pipey, torquey, or over rev.

The powerband is often confused with the power valve. The power valve is a device that is fastened to the exhaust port in the cylinder. The power valve adjusts the exhaust-gas velocity and effective power stroke of the engine so it produces a wider powerband. A centrifugal governor that is gear-driven from the crankshaft primary gear operates the power valve. The power valve starts in the low or closed position. As the rider twists the throttle and the engine rpm is raised, the power valve adjusts the exhaust-port size in accordance with engine rpm. The precise control of the power valve gives the widest powerband, and that is good.

Some manufacturers' power-valve designs are better than others, but the best-performing power-valve systems require the most maintenance. Periodic cleaning of the power valve will ensure that the engine will have the widest possible powerband.

Flywheel Weights on a 125cc Bike

Question: I have a 1994 CR125 that I use to race motocross. I have a question. What advantages would I get from putting on a heavier flywheel? I understand it helps with wheel spin (the main reason I'm considering one), but will it affect my throttle response in areas where it's important like, say, in whoops? Also, will it affect my top-end power? I want to have less wheel spin to drive out of corners faster, but I don't want to lose throttle response over lips of jumps and in whoops. Is the flywheel weight my dream come true?

Another question, are there any advantages to weld-on models or bolt-ons?

Answer: A flywheel weight can only be effective if the engine has enough torque to control it. If you are having problems with too much wheel spin, then install a flywheel weight. The advantage to a thread-on flywheel weight is that if it doesn't work, you can just remove it. Weld-on flywheel weights are permanent.

"Blueprinting" is a slang term used to describe the process of removing all the burred edges, matching the gaskets, and matching the crankcase and cylinder transfer ports. By matching one case half to each side of the cylinder, a tuner can easily mark and grind the mismatched areas of the cylinder and cases.

Another blueprinting tip is to turndown the base of the cylinder on an expanding mandrel, to set the base perpendicular to the bore. Normally it takes only about .004 inches to square the cylinder. If you take more material it will serve to raise the compression ratio and turbulence in the head, and lengthen the effective stroke. That helps low- to midrange power, or serves to tame down a pipey powerband.

Flow bench testing two-stroke cylinders enables tuners to test and balance the flow rates of the transfer ports. The cylinder flow adapters are made of plastic and sealed with grease.

out of the transfers and merging together to form a loop. The gases travel up the back side of the cylinder and loop around in the cylinder head to scavenge out the burnt mixture gases from the previous power stroke. It is critical that the burnt gases are scavenged from the combustion chamber, to make room for as much of the unburned gases as possible. That is the key to making more power in a two-stroke engine. The more unburned gases you can squeeze into the combustion chamber, the more the engine will produce. Now the loop of unburned mixture gases has traveled into the exhaust pipe's header section.

3. Now the crankshaft has rotated past bottom dead center (BDC 180 degrees) and the piston is on the upstroke. The compression wave reflected from the exhaust pipe is packing the unburned gases back in through the exhaust port as the piston closes off the port at the start of the compression phase. In the crankcase the pressure is below atmospheric, producing a vacuum, and a fresh charge of unburned mixture gases is flowing through the reed valve into the crankcase.

4. The unburned mixture gases are compressed, and just before the piston

reaches TDC the ignition system discharges a spark causing the gases to ignite and start the process all over again.

HOW TO CHOOSE A POWERBAND

By making changes in engine components, nearly every Japanese dirt bike has the potential for two types of power. The engine can be tuned for midrange and high-rpm power or for low-end and midrange power. The midrange and high-rpm bike will have little or no low-end, hit explosively in the midrange, and have an abundance of top-end power that can be overrevved. This kind of power can put you out front in the straights, but it is harder to control and will tire out the rider more quickly. Expert outdoor riders tend to use engines tuned for high-rpm power.

An engine can also be tuned for low-end and midrange. Such an engine will have plenty of power down low, a beefy midrange, and a flat top-end. Supercross and enduro riders favor this kind of power. It is easy to use, and gives the rider confidence. Most riders can see faster times or just have more fun with more low-end and midrange.

With tuning, you can change your motorcycle's powerband to somewhere between one of these extremes. Only a few riders use the extremes. Professionals on outdoor

tracks—especially 125cc European Grand Prix bikes—use engines that are almost all high-rpm power. These machines are extremely fast and require highly talented professionals to make the most of them. Enduro riders in extremely slippery, technical conditions use bikes tuned for lots of low-end. Trials riders use bikes that are tuned for nothing but low-end.

Generally speaking the higher the powerband peak (both in horsepower and rpm) the narrower the powerband. Conversely the lower the power peak the wider the powerband. Sometimes you can get the best of both worlds. Exhaust valve systems have made the biggest difference in widening the powerband. Innovations in exhaust pipe design and ignition systems have also contributed to making two-stroke engines as tractable as four-stroke engines.

Riders should choose a powerband according to their skill level, terrain obstacles, and maintenance practices. Here are some tips on how to select the right powerband for you.

Skill Level

Generally speaking, beginning riders need low- to midrange powerbands while expert riders can benefit from top-end powerbands. There are exceptions, though.

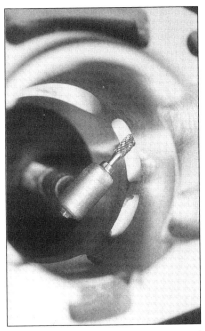

A right angle porting tool is needed to make real porting changes. Making careful modifications in the port height and angle entry is the hardest part of porting.

An inside caliper is used to measure the chord width of a bridged exhaust port. The maximum width of a bridged port is 95 percent and an oval port is 70 percent.

Supercross bikes have low- to midrange powerbands because the steep, far-spaced jumps are positioned so close to the turns. Keep in mind that low-end to midrange powerbands are typically easier to use. In conditions where traction is minimal and the terrain is particularly technical, low-end power will allow

TUNING FOR SPECIFIC POWERBANDS

This chart is designed to give you some general guidelines on different powerbands and the changes required to the individual engine components. For specific recommendations on your model bike, refer to the chapters on tuning tips.

Component: Cylinder Head
Low to Midrange: 9.5:1 compression ratio, squish band 60% of bore area
Midrange and High-Rpm: 8:1 compression ratio, 40% squish

Component: Cylinder Ports
Low to Midrange: Exhaust port 90 ATDC, transfer ports 118 ATDC
Midrange and High-Rpm: Exhaust port 84 ATDC, transfer ports 116 ATDC

Component: Reeds
Low to Midrange: Dual-stage or .4mm fiberglass petals
Compromise: Thick carbon fiber petals
Midrange and High-Rpm: Large area 30-degree valve

Component: Carburetor
Low to Midrange: Smaller diameter or sleeved down carb (26mm for 80cc, 34mm for 125cc, 36mm for 250cc)
Midrange and High-Rpm: Larger carb (28mm for 80cc, 38mm for 125cc, 39.5mm 250cc)

Component: Pipe
Low to Midrange: Fatty or Torque
Midrange and High-Rpm: Desert or Rpm

Component: Silencer or Spark arrestor
Low to Midrange: Short, small diameter
Midrange and High-Rpm: Long, large diameter

Component: Ignition Timing
Advance timing
Low to Midrange: Stock timing
Midrange and High-Rpm: Retard timing

Component: Flywheel
Low to Midrange: Add weight
Compromise: Stock flywheel
Midrange and High-Rpm: PVL internal flywheel

Component: Fuel
Low to Midrange: Super unleaded 93 octane
Midrange and High-Rpm: Racing fuel 105 octane

you to keep the bike under control and ultimately go faster. Also, torquey bikes are more fun to ride casually. Expert and top-level riders need high-end power to be competitive, but the extra juice can easily slow down lesser riders even in good conditions, and is a handicap in slippery, difficult conditions.

Terrain Obstacles

This term describes a wide variety of things ranging from the soil content to the elevation changes and the frequency of jumps and turns on a race track. Low- to midrange powerbands work well on soil like mud and sand. Tight tracks with lots of off-camber or difficult corners will favor low-end to midrange power. Smoother, broader powerbands work well for enduro or trail riding over a wide variety of terrain and soil conditions. Midrange to top-end

powerbands work best on terrain with loamy soil, long fast uphills, and fast sweeping turns.

Maintenance Practices

Generally speaking, powerbands designed for low- to midrange require less engine maintenance than powerbands designed for high rpm. High-rpm powerbands usually require frequent use of the clutch in order to get the engine up into the rev range where the powerband is most effective. An engine that sustains high rpm requires more frequent replacement of parts such as piston and rings, reeds, crankshaft bearings, and clutch plates. Also the carb jetting becomes more critical. If the main jet is one size too lean, the piston can seize. High-rpm powerbands have high compression ratios so fuel selection is critical. Most

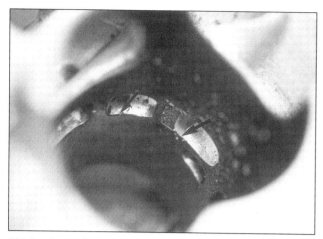

This is a view inside the cylinder, focusing on the port windows at the cylinder bore. The gray areas of the transfer ports are epoxy filler materials. The arrows show the change in side angle entry. Epoxy is added to ports to affect multiple changes. The volume of the epoxy raises the primary compression ratio (crankcase vs. cylinder volume), and the shape of the epoxy reduces the port-time-area, and short-circuiting.

This photo shows the ducting side of the transfer ports. Here a pottery art tool is used to fill epoxy in key areas of the ports. This work serves to boost the crankcase compression to give the powerband more low end.

tuners recommend racing fuel because the specific gravity of fuels such as these doesn't vary with the season like super unleaded pump fuel.

TUNING GUIDE TO PERFORMANCE MODIFICATIONS

When deciding what to do to your engine, you first need to decide what you want. What kind of riding do you do? What level of rider are you? How much money do you have to spend? Also, remember that you need to bring the bike to peak stock condition before you add aftermarket equipment.

This section lists each performance mod and describes how to modify each system for the performance you want.

Cylinder Porting

The cylinder ports are designed to produce a certain power characteristic over a fairly narrow rpm band. Porting or tuning is a metal-machining process performed to the cylinder ports (exhaust and transfers) that alters the timing, area size, and angles of the ports to adjust the powerband to better suit the rider's demands. For example, a veteran trail rider riding an RM250 in the Rocky Mountain region of the United States

will need to adjust the powerband for more low-end power because of the steep hill climbs and the lower air density of higher altitudes. The only way to determine what changes will be needed to the engine is by measuring and calculating the stock engine's specifications.

The most critical measurement is the port's time-area. A port's time-area is a calculation of a port opening's area and timing in relation to the displacement of the engine and the rpm. Experienced tuners know what exhaust and transfer port time-area values work best for different purposes (motocross vs. enduro, for example).

These are rubber molds of cylinder head combustion chambers for Honda CR125s. The mold on the left is from a 1987 model. It had a wide squishband and good low-end hit. The center mold is from a 1989 model. Good top-end overrev with a sacrifice down low. The mold on the right is a total hemispherical shape from a 1983 model. This is an ideal shape but too prone to gasket leaks.

This is how solder is used to measure the squish clearance (clearance between the piston and squishband of the head). By bending the solder into an "L" shape and inserting it into the spark plug hole, you can kick-over the engine and measure the thickness of the crushed solder.

This head has a centered spark plug hole and can easily be threaded to a mandrel and turned in a lathe. This photo shows the squishband being machined.

In general, if a tuner wants to adjust the engine's powerband for more low to midrange, he would do the following two things:

1. Turn down the cylinder base on a lathe to increase the effective stroke (distance from TDC to exhaust-port opening). This also retards the exhaust-port timing, shortens the exhaust-port duration, and increases the compression ratio.

2. Narrow the transfer ports and re-angle them with epoxy to reduce the port's time-area for an rpm peak of 7,000. The rear transfer ports need to be re-angled so they oppose each other rather than pointing forward to the exhaust port. This changes the flow pattern of the transfer ports to improve scavenging efficiency at 2,000 to 5,000 rpm.

For both of these types of cylinder porting changes to be effective, other engine components would need to be changed as well.

Cylinder Head Modification

Cylinder-head shape also affects the powerband. Generally speaking, a cylinder head with a small-diameter, deep combustion chamber and a wide squish band combined with a high compression ratio is suited for low-end and midrange power. A cylinder head with a wide, shallow chamber and a narrow squish band and a lower compression ratio is suited for high-rpm power.

Cylinder heads with wide squish bands and high compression ratios will generate high turbulence in the combustion chamber. This turbulence is termed maximum squish velocity (MSV) and is rated in meters per second (m/s). A cylinder head designed for Supercross should have an MSV rating of 35m/s, whereas a head designed for motocross should have an MSV rating of 25m/s. The only way to accurately determine the MSV rating of a head is by measuring some basic engine dimensions and inputting the numbers into a TSR computer program called SQUISH.

In the model-tuning-tips sections of this book, the SQUISH program was used to calculate the modified head dimensions.

Aftermarket companies like Cool Head also offer cylinder heads, which have different cartridges to give different cylinder head shapes. The various head cartridges have different combustion bowl shapes, compression ratios, and MSV ratings. The head cartridges are incrementally different, corresponding with powerbands ranging from extreme low-end to high rpm.

Crankshaft Modification

There are two popular mods that hop-up companies are doing to crankshafts: stroking and turbo-vaning.

Stroking increases the stroke of the crankshaft, which increases the displacement of the cylinder and boosts the midrange torque power but decreases the rpm peak. Two techniques are commonly used to stroke two-stroke crankshafts: welding closed the old big-end hole and re-drilling a new big-end hole or boring the pin hole larger and welding an eccentric flange to each crank half.

Turbo-vaning a crankshaft is an old, discredited technique that allegedly improves the volumetric efficiency of the engine by fastening scoops to the crank. Every decade some hop-up shop revives this old idea and gives it a trendy name. These crank modifications cause oil to be directed away from the connecting rod, and often the vanes will detach from the crank at high rpm, causing catastrophic engine damage. My advice: Don't waste the $750!

Carburetor Modification

In general, a small-diameter carburetor will provide high air-mass velocity and good flow characteristics for a low- to mid-rpm powerband. A large-diameter carburetor works better for high-rpm powerbands. For 125cc engines, a 34mm carburetor works well for Supercross and enduro and a 36 or 38mm carburetor works best for fast motocross tracks. For 250cc engines, a 36mm carburetor works best for low- to mid-rpm powerbands, and a 39.5mm carburetor works best for high-rpm powerbands.

Recently there has been a trend in the use of airfoils and rifle boring for carbs. These innovations are designed to improve airflow at

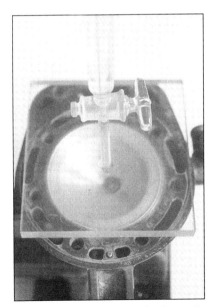

The volume of the combustion chamber can be measured with a graduated cylinder or burret, and a flat plate of Plexiglas.

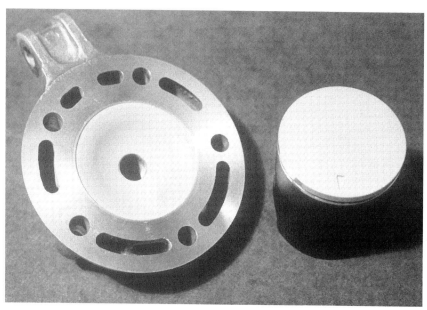

There is a lot of talk about thermal barrier coatings. TBCs are supposed to trap more heat in combustion and insulate the water jacket to reduce bleed off of heat. However it actually takes a very thick coating on the piston crown and combustion chamber to get even a small gain in performance. The dark coating on the piston skirt in the photo is a polymer with molybdenum. It sprays on like paint and is baked to improve adhesion.

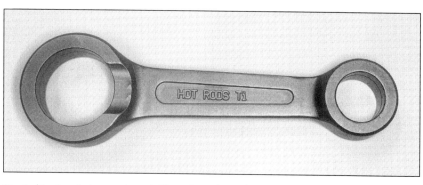

Hot Rod is a brand of connecting rod. It's an aftermarket replacement kit for crankshaft rebuilding. A recent trend in connecting rods is material. This prototype titanium connecting rod is about 20 percent lighter than a steel rod.

low throttle openings. Some companies like Performance Engineering in Florida offer a service to overbore the carb and they include inserts to reduce the diameter of the carb. For example, a 38mm carb for a 250cc bike will be bored to 39.5mms and two inserts will be supplied. The carb can then be restricted to a diameter of 36 or 38mm. Not every carb can be overbored. The maximum diameter of the carb cannot exceed the width of the slide. Otherwise air will by-pass the venturi and the engine will run too lean. There are two ways to overbore a carb, by stripping it down and turning it on a lathe (Keihin PWK and Mikuni round slide), or by milling it on a vertical mill using a rotary-table. The rotary-table method is necessary for carbs where the needle jet cannot be removed (Keihin PJ and Mikuni TMX). Whenever a carb is overbored the jetting must be richened to compensate for the loss of intake velocity.

Aftermarket Reed Valves

Like large-bore carburetors, bigger reed valves with large flow area work best for high-rpm powerbands. In general, reed valves with six or more petals are used for high-rpm engines. Reed valves with four petals are used for dirt bikes that need strong low-end and midrange power. Three other factors must be considered when choosing a reed valve: the angle of the reed valve, the type of reed material, and the petal thickness. The two common reed valve angles are 30 and 45 degrees. The 30-degree valve is designed for low-end to midrange power and the 45-degree valve is designed for high-rpm power. Two types of reed-petal materials are commonly used, carbon fiber and fiberglass. Carbon fiber reeds are lightweight but relatively stiff (spring tension) and are designed to resist fluttering at high rpm. Fiberglass reeds have relatively low spring tension so they instantly respond to pressure changes in the crankcase; however, the low spring tension makes them flutter at high rpm, thereby limiting the amount of power. Fiberglass reed petals are good for low-end to midrange powerbands, and carbon fiber reeds are better for high-rpm engines. Regarding longevity, the fiberglass reeds tend to split whereas the carbon fiber reeds tend to chip.

Some aftermarket reeds, such as the Boyesen dual-stage reeds, have a large, thick base reed with a smaller, thinner reed mounted on top. This setup widens the rpm range where the reed valve flows best. The thin reeds respond to low rpm and low-frequency pressure pulses. The thick reeds respond to higher-pressure pulses and resist fluttering at high rpm. The Boyesen RAD valve is different than a traditional reed valve. Bikes with single rear shocks have offset carbs. The RAD valve is designed to evenly redistribute the gas flow from the offset carb to the crankcases. A RAD valve will give an overall improvement to the powerband. Polini of Italy makes a reed valve called the Supervalve. It features several mini sets of reeds positioned vertically, instead of horizontally (as on conventional reed valves). These valves are excellent for enduro riding because they improve throttle response. In addition, tests on an inertia chassis dyno show the Supervalve to be superior when power-shifting. However, these valves don't generate greater peak power than conventional reed valves.

Aftermarket Exhaust Pipes

The exhaust pipes of high-performance two-stroke engines are designed to harness the energy of the pressure waves from combustion. The diameter and length of the five main sections of the pipe—head pipe, diffuser cone, dwell, baffle cone, and stinger—are critical to producing the desired powerband. In general, aftermarket exhaust pipes shift the powerband up the rpm scale. Most pipes are designed for original cylinders, not tuned cylinders.

There are two reasons for buying an aftermarket pipe: to replace a damaged pipe or to gain performance. The stock exhaust pipes of most late-model Japanese dirt bikes offer excellent performance. In fact, many aftermarket pipes are just copies of OEM pipes. The reason nobody buys OEM pipes is because they are way too expensive. There are several different manufacturers of pipes in the world. Generally speaking, the pipes manufactured in Europe (SPES, DEP Sport, MESSICO, HGS) offer greater high-rpm performance at a much higher price ($350) than the American pipes (FMF, PC, Dyno-Port, Bill's, R&D). The European pipes are designed to work in conjunction with ported cylinders whereas the American pipes are designed to work with stock cylinders.

Pipes are available in two types of material, steel and aluminum. The steel pipes are made in bare and plated finishes. Plated pipes require no maintenance whereas bare metal pipes require constant maintenance to prevent corrosion. FMF's new Burly pipe is made of thicker steel and resists rock dents. There is no performance difference between the two finishes. The energy of the finite amplitude waves reflecting through the pipe is not affected by surface finish. However, sharp edges and abrupt transitions between sections of the pipe affect the fuel/air particles carried by the waves.

It is possible to determine how the shape of the pipe will affect the performance of your bike. The pipe manufacturers label their pipes with terms that describe the pipe's effect on the powerband. Terms like "Fatty, Supercross, and Torque" are associated with enhancements in the low to midrange of the powerband. Terms like "Desert, motocross, or RPM" are associated with enhancements in the upper midrange and top end of the powerband. Generally speaking, pipes with designations such as this work well with cylinders and heads

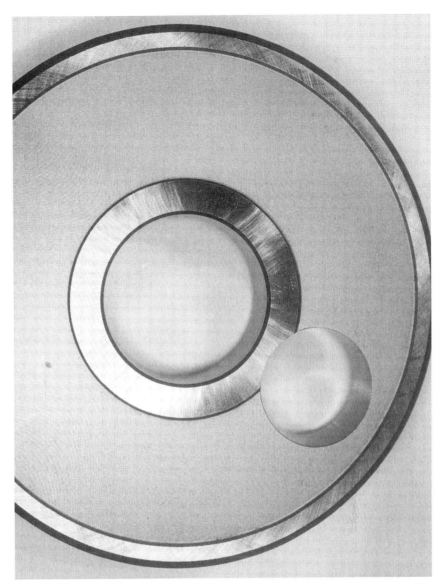

The stroke of an engine is based on the center to center distance of the crankshaft journal and the connecting rod hole. The greater the distance the greater the stroke. For every 1mm that the center distance changes, the stroke increases 2mm. The rod length has nothing to do with the stroke length. Long rod kits don't boost the displacement of the engine.

tuned for the same type of powerband. It is unusual for an "RPM" pipe to work well with a "torque" cylinder.

Aftermarket Silencers

Silencers come in all sorts of shapes and sizes. The idea is to use the silencer to maximize the pressure and velocity in the pipe. That profile will be different for powerbands and riders' demands. Too much pressure in the pipe at high rpm will radically increase the temperature of the piston crown and could cause the piston to seize in the cylinder.

Designing the silencer is the final step when developing a pipe package. Silencers are designed on the dyno and verified on the race track. Generally speaking if you buy an aftermarket pipe, buy the silencer to go along with it. Some popular silencers have optional end caps that have spark arrestors built in to them.

Flywheel Weights

A heavier flywheel will smooth out power delivery. The flywheel is weighted to improve the engine's tractability at low to mid-rpm.

This crankshaft has welds fusing the crank halves and the connecting rod pin to prevent the crank from slipping out of true.

Flywheel weights are best for powerful bikes with decent low-end and an explosive hit. The weight will smooth out the hit and reduce wheelspin, which will improve your drive out of corners. One popular myth associated with flywheel weights is that they increase low-end power. If an engine doesn't have enough low-end torque in the first place it will be worse with the extra flywheel weight.

Two different types of flywheel weights are available: weld-on and thread-on. A-Loop performs the weld-on flywheel weight service. Steahly is a company that makes thread-on flywheel weights. This product threads on to the fine left-hand threads that are on the center hub of most Japanese magneto rotors. Thread-on flywheel weights can only be used if the threads on the flywheel are in perfect condition. The advantage to weld-on weights is they can't possibly come off.

Modern bikes use external rotor flywheels. They have a larger diameter than internal

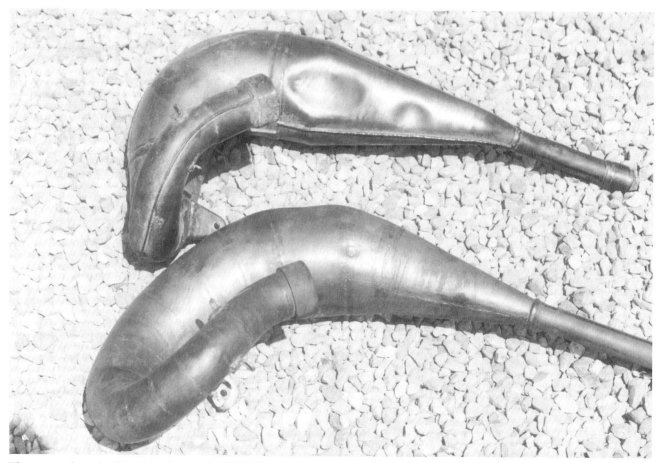

These are two distinctly different pipes for a Honda CR125. The one on top is an HRC high rev pipe and the other one is a DOMA sand pipe. The obvious differences are in the overall length and the size of the head pipes.

rotor flywheels so they have greater flywheel inertia. PVL makes an internal rotor flywheel that gives quicker throttle response.

Ignition Timing

The ignition timing has a minimal effect on the powerband. Retarding the timing has the effect of reducing the hit of the power-band in the midrange and extending the top-end overrev. *Overrev* is a slang term that de-scribes the useable length of the powerband at high rpm.

The scientific reason for the shift of the powerband to extremely high rpm is that the temperature in the pipe increases with the re-tarded timing. That is because the burn cycle takes about 55 degrees of crankshaft rota-tion. When the timing is retarded the burn cy-cle starts later and continues into the pipe. Raising the exhaust gas temperature raises the velocity of the waves to be more synchro-nous with the piston speed and port timing of the cylinder.

Advancing the timing has the effect of increasing the midrange hit of the powerband, but makes the power flatten-out at high rpm. The reason is that the relatively long spark lead time enables for a greater pressure rise in the cylinder before the piston reaches TDC. This produces more torque in the midrange but the high pressure contributes to pumping losses at extremely high rpm.

Engine Management Systems

Motorcycle engines have always been at the forefront of engine design. The next leap will come in the form of engine management systems that control the ignition system, power jet, exhaust valves, and resonator tem-perature and pressure. Right now we're see-ing new products like programmable or switchable ignition boxes. In the near future we'll see a continual stream of products that will culminate in a direct-injected two-stroke engine with a management system that coor-dinates the ignition, intake, exhaust, and ul-timately the powerband with just a tweak of your thumb.

The Optimum GP Control package for the Suzuki RM250 is a kit that includes a handlebar switch, KX250 carb with pumper and throttle position sensor, and a computer that fits under the seat on a hinged plate.

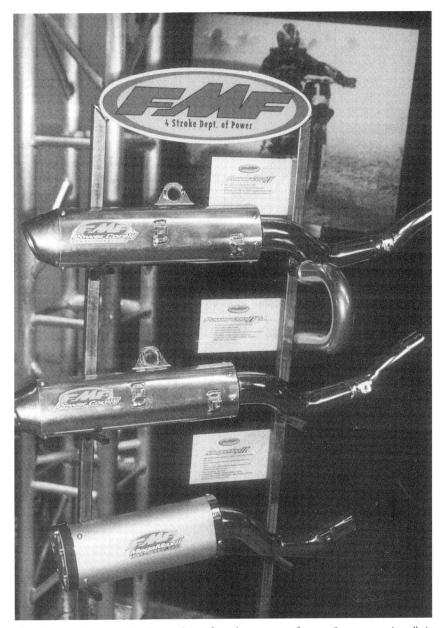

If you buy an aftermarket pipe buy a silencer from the same manufacturer. Some companies sell si-lencers in different lengths and have optional spark arrestor caps that can be quickly fastened to the end of the silencer.

This unit coordinates the ignition system with the carb's fuel pump. The handlebar switch offers 42 different positions and the jetting and ignition can be adjusted on the fly. There is also a separate "Holeshot" switch that pro-vides smooth power delivery and better trac-tion. You can also program it with a PDA and change things like the engine's ability to per-form on less expensive fuel. The Kawasaki Keihin electronic carb with the throttle posi-tion sensor is ideally suited for computer con-

trol and especially coordination with other things like exhaust valve systems.

There are less expensive aftermarket parts like igniter boxes. FMF sells the Wolf brand igniter box that features adjust-on-the-fly timing. Products such as these offer a choice of an advanced curve for better midrange and one with a retarded curve for better overrev. Normally these products sell for about the same price as the OEM igniter box.

FOUR-STROKE ENGINES

This is the intake valve. There are excessive carbon deposits that cause a flow problem at low valve lifts. The deposits are due to a worn valve stem seal, which enabled oil to burn on the valve. This valve can be cleaned with a wire brush bench grinder.

Four-stroke engines are very reliable, but when they finally break down, there are so many engine components that problems can be hard to diagnose. A four-stroke engine has more moving parts than a two-stroke engine, especially in the top end of the engine. Components such as the valves, guides, piston, and rings wear at different rates based on service intervals and riding use. For example, if you run the engine with a dirty air filter, the piston and rings will wear faster than the valves. Conversely, if the valve-to-tappet clearance is too tight and the valves hang slightly open from the valve seats, the valves are subject to being overheated by the high combustion temperature and pressure. So how are you supposed to diagnose top-end engine components without totally disassembling the engine?

There is a simple diagnostic test that can be performed to any four-stroke engine that enables you to determine the condition of the top-end components. That test is the leak-down test.

LEAK-DOWN TESTERS

A leak-down tester is a device that provides a regulated pressurized air source to the cylinder through a hose threaded into the spark plug hole. A leak-down tester has two pressure gauges, one for controlling the test pressure and one for monitoring the percent of airflow that leaks past the worn engine components. These types of testers are available from Snap-On tool dealers or auto parts stores. You will also need an air tank with 100 psi or an air compressor. Leak-down testers come with a variety of adapters that thread into any size of spark plug hole. Leak-down testers sell for $50–$150.

How to Test

First, attach your compressed-air source to the tester and set the regulator control so the gauge needle reads 100 percent. Thread the adapter hose into the spark plug hole. Turn the crankshaft so the piston is at TDC on the compression stroke. Attach the adapter hose to the leak-down tester. The compressed air will fill the combustion chamber. If there is a pressure leak, then the leak-down tester's gauge will show the percentage of loss.

The normal amount of pressure leakage is 1–8 percent. If the percent of leakage exceeds 10 percent, then you need to find and repair the leak. The most apparent places to track down a leak are at the crankcase breather, the carb, and the exhaust pipe. The following are some tips on diagnosing leaks for the top-end engine components.

Piston Rings

If the piston and rings are worn, pressure will seep past the rings and into the crankcases. When the pressure is too great it pushes crankcase oil out at two places, the rubber crank seal and the breather hose that connects to the air box. An oil leak at the crankshaft seal (behind the ignition rotor) is a telltale sign of worn rings. Excessive oil in the air box is another sign. Check the air box and filter for oil residue. With the leak-down tester installed and pressure in the cylinder, remove the breather vent hose from the air box. Cap your thumb over the end of the hose and feel for leaking air pressure.

Valve-to-Seat Leaks

Most pressure leaks are the result of carbon build-up on the valves. This occurs when oil leaks past the valve-stem seals, burns, and accumulates on the valve seat. This wedges the valve open slightly, causing the leak. When this happens to the intake valves, the engine may make a coughing sound at idle. The coughing noise indicates that a small amount of combustion gases are flowing backwards in the intake port and into the carburetor. The back flow of gases caus-

To check the valve to guide clearance, extend the valve out of the seat about 10mm and try to wiggle it in any direction. Excessive movement means that the guides need to be replaced.

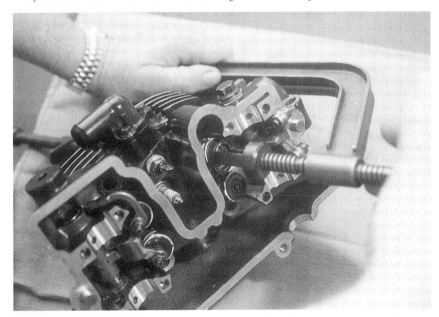

On all four-stroke dirt bikes, you need a special tool to remove the valve springs. Automotive tools are too big and won't fit. Kiowa makes kits with a G-clamp and several different sized tips to fit the wide range of dirt bikes.

es a surge in the carb and momentarily stops the fuel from flowing. Remove the air box and the exhaust pipes, and then connect the leak-down tester to the engine and pressurize the cylinder. Then, cup your hand over the end of the carburetor or exhaust port and feel for leaking air. You will probably be able to hear the sound of the leaking air quite easily.

Fixing the Leaks
Piston, Rings, and Cylinder Bore

The average service interval for a dirt bike's piston and rings is about 3,000 miles. After 3,000 miles, you probably will need to overbore the cylinder for an oversize piston because cylinder bores become worn in a taper, or slightly out-of-round pattern. Some tuners

This is a YZ426. The valve clearance is measured by inserting a feeler gauge between the shim cup and the camshaft.

There are two ways to install the piston assembly in the cylinder. The first is to pin the piston to the rod and lower the cylinder onto the rod. A hose clamp or a universal ring clamp can be used to compress the rings to slide the assembly into the cylinder.

prefer to overbore cylinders to boost the engine's displacement or compression ratio. If the rings are leaking on a relatively new bike (less than 1,000 miles) it's probably due to improper break-in procedure. If an engine isn't broken in properly, oil will burn into the cross-hatch grooves in the cylinder walls. This forms a glazing that prevents the rings from sealing properly. The best fix for this problem is to replace the rings and hone the cylinder bore with a Flex-Hone. Flex-Hones are made by Brush Research in Los Angeles, California. Flex-Hones are made of hundreds of silicone-carbide balls mounted to plastic stems and fastened to a center shaft. They don't remove metal like a mandrel hone, but Flex-Hones remove the burned-oil glaze and polish down the surface of the bore so the rings can seal properly.

Valves and Seats

Fixing this problem can be as easy as replacing the stem seals and cleaning the valves with a wire brush. However, if the valve has been wedged open by the carbon for many engine running hours, then the valve and seat surfaces are probably burnt and pitted. In this case, the valve-seat angles will need to be refaced and the valves replaced. Whenever the valves are removed, I recommend lapping the valve to the valve seat with fine lapping compound. Auto parts stores sell kits with fine lapping compound and a suction-type valve-lapping tool. The tool looks like a round rubber tentacle. You just put a dab of lapping compound on the valve seat and squish the lapping tool onto the valve face. Then turn the tool back and forth for about 2 minutes until the lapping compound polishes the valve-to-seat interface.

Get Help Fast!

If you don't have the specialized knowledge or the tools to perform a leak-down test on your bike, then bring it to a motorcycle shop. A leak-down test takes about an hour and shops charge between $30 and $60. A leak-down test is much less expensive to do during a tune-up because the technician will already have the valve cover removed to set the tappet clearance. Performing a leak-down test once a year will keep you informed on the condition of your bike's engine.

COMMON PROBLEMS

A word of caution to all of you slackers who refuse to work on your bike until it breaks down. Here are some examples of what can happen when simple mechanical problems manifest into catastrophic engine damage.

Tight Valves

If the tappet clearance is inadequate, the valves may hang open when the engine is running at peak temperatures. The exhaust valves may get so hot that they break apart, causing catastrophic engine damage. Leaky intake valves may cause a back-fire that ignites unburned mixture gases in the air boot and air box, thereby starting a fire!

Worn Spark Plug

Over time, the spark plug gap will increase due to erosion of the electrode and ground arm. The greater the spark plug's gap the greater the voltage required to arc across the gap. This raises the temperature of the electrode and ground arm, eventually causing the metal to fracture. If the spark plug's tiny ground arm breaks off, it could wedge itself between the valve and valve seat, causing the valve to break apart. Spark plugs last as long as 60,000 miles on

Advanced Cam Timing

Question: I'm having a problem with my KLX250. I rebuilt the top end, and the bike was slower. I performed a leak-down test, and the pressure was leaking past the exhaust valves. Is it possible that I could have bent both of the exhaust valves but not the intake valves? If not, what could be the problem?

Answer: It's likely that the cam timing is advanced one tooth. That would make the engine sluggish. Another reason why I think it's a timing problem is this: When you perform a leak-down test you set the crankshaft to TDC on the compression stroke. If the cams were mis-timed, then the exhaust valves would be cracked open causing the pressure leak.

Motor-Oil Question

Question: I bought a brand-new bike and broke it in with a synthetic motor oil. Now, the bike has less than 1,000 miles, and it leaks oil at the crankshaft seal and it runs like it's jetted rich. I thought I was being careful with my new engine's break in, but obviously I did something wrong. Any clues?

Answer: Synthetic oil is not for breaking in engines. The extreme "slipperiness" of synthetic oil prevents the rings from seating and allows the combustion gases to pressurize the crankcase. The pressure escapes through the crankcase vents and drags some oil with it. The crankcase vent is attached to the air box, so the excess oil coats the air filter and effectively makes the engine run richer. To this problem, hone the cylinder with a Flex-Hone and replace the rings. Clean the air filter of the excess oil and break in the engine with petroleum-based motor oil.

Four-Stroke Choke System

Question: I just bought a Yamaha XT225. When I first start the bike with the choke engaged, the engine idle is very high, and if I put the bike in gear it bogs and stalls easily. After a few minutes, it works fine. Does my bike have a problem, and should I worry about it?

Answer: Your XT225 is a street-legal bike with a four-stroke engine. These bikes are often jetted leaner than two-stroke dirt bikes because street-legal bikes have to meet EPA pollution standards. When you first start your bike, you must engage the choke to provide the engine with a rich fuel-air mixture. That is why the engine idle is so high. The engine must be allowed to warm up to operating temperature before you can try to ride it. If the engine is too cold, it will bog or stall, and the piston could expand too fast and temporarily seize to the cylinder bore. Spend the extra time to warm up your bike properly. Once the engine comes up to operating temperature, you must disengage the choke or the engine will cough and sputter from the excess fuel.

Black Smoke Exhaust

Question: I have a 1987 XR250R that has suddenly started to run rich in the midrange. The bike was running fine one day and the next weekend it started running badly. If I hammer the throttle it screams until it levels off, then it spits, sputters, and blows black smoke out the pipe. It idles smoothly, though. I wonder if the diaphragm is bad. I checked for holes in the diaphragm but didn't find any. Your help would be appreciated.

Answer: If the diaphragm was perforated, the engine would bog badly on acceleration and probably wouldn't even run off the choke. The black smoke that comes out the pipe is partially burned fuel. Your bike is running very rich for one or more reasons. Check these parts of the fuel system:

1. Check the fuel tank and carb vent hoses. If the hoses are clogged, that will cause a fluctuating-fuel-supply problem.

2. Remove the float bowl and check to see if the main jet is threaded into the needle jet.

If the jet unthreaded due to vibration, there would be no way to meter the fuel through the carb at full throttle, which would cause a rich running condition.

3. Check the air filter. If the filter is clogged with dirt, that would also cause a rich condition.

4. Check the choke mechanism. If it is a butterfly type, the actuating mechanism could be faulty. That might allow the choke to be engaged, causing the rich running condition.

These are the four most common problems with fuel delivery systems that cause rich running conditions. If you don't think you have the tools or special knowledge to carry out these mechanical tasks, then look to a dirt bike mechanic in your area or to a Honda dealer.

DR250 Jetting Problems

Question: I'm having all sorts of problems jetting my DR250. I ride my bike at an altitude of about 2,000 feet here in Oregon. Shouldn't I have to lean the jetting for high altitude? I put an aftermarket muffler on it, and the instructions said to increase the main jet three sizes and shim the needle. Where do I get shims for the needle? Now the bike pops when I let off the gas, and it's driving me nuts! I tried putting a larger pilot jet in the carb to stop the popping, but my dealer gave me a jet that doesn't look the same as the one I took out. My stock jet has tiny holes in the side of the jet. Are the holes good or bad? What effect would lighter vacuum springs have? Should I drill big holes in the side of the air box and remove the snorkel to let in more air?

Answer: Let's tackle the popping problem first. You were correct to increase the size of the pilot jet, but I suggest turning the airscrew clockwise to further richen the low-speed mixture. Another cause of popping could be that the exhaust valve lash is too tight. Set the cold valve lash to .004 inch. The holes in the pilot jet are aeration holes to help the fuel atomize as it goes up the pilot circuit. Pilot jets with holes are better.

The shims for the needle are listed on the Suzuki parts microfiche for the four-stroke street bikes. Shims are available in packages of four. You'll have to do trial-and-error testing to determine the correct

(continued on page 156)

number of shims, but four shims would be the maximum. You shouldn't have to compensate for altitude under 2,000 feet. A lighter vacuum spring will effectively make the 1/4- to 1/2-throttle jetting richer. Opening up the air box or removing the snorkel will only make the engine run leaner, plus you will change the tuned length of the intake tract. If you want to do any mods to the intake system, call the guys at Cycle Gear. They make a special air box and jetting kit for the DRs.

Four-Stroke Oil Question

Question: I have a question about oils. If I put Bel Ray gear lube in my Husky 610, will it make the clutch work smoother when the engine gets hot?

Answer: Bel Ray gear oil is designed for the transmissions of two-stroke engines. They have a sealed crankcase and use pre-mix oil in the fuel to lubricate the crankshaft. Four-stroke engines have a common oil supply for the transmission and crankcase. Therefore, you must use oil designed to lubricate the top-end parts and the crankshaft. Don't put any type of gear oil in the crankcase of your four-stroke engine. Gear oil will cause the piston rings and cylinder walls to glaze with a burned-on layer of oil. The engine will lose compression and foul plugs, plus it will be very hard to start. Just keep using 10-40 motor oil.

Four-Stroke Backfiring

Question: Recently I bought my first four-stroke dirt bike, a KTM400LC. I have about 1,600 miles on the bike, and now it has a problem. When I shut off the throttle the engine backfires. What could be causing this problem, and how can I fix it?

Answer: Don't confuse backfiring with popping. A small amount of popping is normal on a four-stroke engine. Normal means two pops when decelerating with a warm engine. Backfiring means a flame or smoke puff shoots out of the end of the pipe and the engine kills. Popping can be traced to one or both of two possible problems.

1. The pilot jet is too lean. The pilot jet is the only jet in the carb that feeds fuel to the engine when you shut the throttle. The popping indicates a lean condition.

2. The exhaust valve lash is too tight, causing the valve to be slightly open when the engine gets hot. This allows combustion gases to escape past the valve and out the exhaust pipe. This is most likely the problem with your bike. KTM recommends that you have a factory-trained technician set the valve lash (clearance) after the initial break-in of 500 miles. As the engine breaks in, the valve settles deeper into the valve seat of the cylinder head, and the valve lash is decreased. If you don't have the valve lash set correctly, the exhaust valves will eventually become overheated and permanently damaged. If the intake valve lash is too little, the engine will make a coughing sound from the carb at idle speed.

Lead Additive for Four-Strokes?

Question: My local auto parts store stopped selling lead additive for fuel. Is it safe to ride my XR200 with unleaded fuel?

Answer: All four-stroke Japanese motorcycle engines produced after 1975 do not require lead in the fuel. The manufacturers use Stellite-coated valves. The lead will only damage the Stellite coating and make the valve seat erode. The lead causes a chemical reaction with the Stellite under heat and pressure. If you think your valves might be damaged, you can visually inspect the seat contact point on the valve for tiny dots. That would indicate that the valve is damaged and needs to be replaced.

---

some automobiles, but only a fraction of that in a motorcycle. Modern motorcycle engines have high compression, high-turbulence combustion chambers that produce spark plug temperatures between 1,800 and 2,300 degrees Fahrenheit. Most manufacturers recommend changing the plugs every 1,000 miles.

Worn Piston

A worn piston has excessive clearance to the cylinder wall. This causes an increase in crankcase pressure, which forces some oil out the breather vent. When too much oil is lost, the remaining oil's temperature will rise, causing a breakdown in lubrication. Eventually, the piston will shatter from the vibration. The shattered fragments of the piston fall into the crankcase and can damage the crankshaft and gearbox.

FOUR-STROKE TOP-END REBUILDING

A four-stroke engine is more difficult to rebuild than a two-stroke engine because there are more moving parts in the engine's top end. Here is a guide to rebuilding the top ends of single-cylinder four-stroke engines.

Before you disassemble the engine, you need to do a pressure leak-down test to determine what top-end parts are worn. See the previous section for detailed instructions.

Before you attempt to disassemble the engine, you should remove the fuel tank and pressure-wash the engine and upper frame. This will help prevent dirt from falling into the disassembled engine. The following section details the procedures for rebuilding the top end of a single-cylinder four-stroke engine.

Tools and Materials

You should have the following tools and materials before you begin: new top-end gasket kit, service manual, torque wrench, oil drain pan, spray penetrating oil, spray cleaner, plastic mallet, assorted wrenches and sockets, parts bins, clean towels, measuring caliper, Flex-Hone, and drill.

Tear Down

Start the engine disassembly by removing the inspection caps from the left-side engine cover. One is located in the middle of the cover, which allows access to the crankshaft bolt. This bolt retains the flywheel and will be used to rotate the crankshaft to get the piston in the proper positions while rebuilding the top end and timing the camshaft. The crankshaft should only be turned in the normal direction of rotation;

otherwise, the cam-chain tensioner could be damaged. The other inspection cap is mounted in the front of the engine cover, and it allows you to see the TDC stamping mark on the side of the flywheel. This is an important reference mark when timing the camshaft during top-end assembly. Then, remove the spark plug, exhaust pipe, carburetor, cam cover, and oil lines.

Camshaft Removal and Reference Marks

After removing the cam cover, rotate the crankshaft so the TDC mark on the flywheel aligns in the center of the inspection window. The camshaft should not be depressing the valves; if it is, rotate the crankshaft another revolution, and the piston will be at TDC on the compression stroke. All Japanese four-stroke single-cylinder engines are designed for camshaft installation at this crankshaft position. Look at the reference marks on the right side of the camshaft drive sprocket. Compare these marks with the ones in the service manual or make a drawing for your own reference. Normally, there is a straight line on the sprocket that aligns with the gasket surface of the cam cover. Pay close attention to these marks because you will have to align the camshaft upon assembly and to synchronize the crankshaft to the camshaft. Failure to do this properly will cause engine damage! To remove the camshaft, you may have to remove the sprocket from the camshaft, depending on your model engine. If you do remove the sprocket take care not to drop the sprocket alignment pin into the crankcases.

Head Removal

Now, you can remove the cam-chain tensioner, head, and cylinder. The head and cylinder are fitted with alignment pins, so it may be difficult to remove these parts. Never use a screwdriver or chisel to split the head and cylinder apart because that will damage the gasket surfaces. Instead, use a dead-shot plastic mallet to split the engine components apart. The cam-chain guides are just plastic bars that either fasten or are wedged into place. Tie a piece of wire around the cam chain to prevent it from falling into the crankcases.

If you don't have a ring compressor you can use this simple method. Turn the cylinder upside-down. Use your thumbs to squeeze the rings into the grooves and into the bore. Make sure that the ring ends stay within 60 degrees of rotation. If the compression rings directly overlap that will cause blow-by into the crankcases.

Cleaning and Inspection

Clean the engine parts in mineral-spirits solvent to remove the oil. Carbon build-up can be removed with spray oven cleaner. After cleaning, rinse the parts with detergent and water. If you don't have the proper tool to compress the valve springs, bring the head to your local franchised dealer and pay them to remove the valve springs. Warning: Automotive-type valve-spring compressors may not fit the tiny valve retainers of motorcycle engines and may damage the cylinder head. Take care to keep the sets of valve springs and retainers together, matched to the sides they were removed from. To check the valve-to-guide clearance, extend the valve from the seat 10mms, grasp the valve head, and try to move it side to side. If you feel excessive movement and the backside of the valve is covered with carbon deposits, then the valve guide and seal are worn and must be replaced.

Next, clean the valve with a wire brush and check the valve seat for pitting or a sharp edge. The pitting indicates that the Stellite coating on the valve is destroyed, and a sharp edge indicates that the engine was over revved and the valve springs floated, causing the valve to hammer up against the seat (common on KTM 400LCs). Stellite valves cannot be refaced on a valve grinding machine because that would remove the Stellite coating. The

The YZ and KLX models use this type of shim cup. The small disc is the shim and it fits in the valve collet; the cup covers it to keep it in place. These shims are available from franchised dealers.

This is a Blue-Point brand leak tester. Metered compressed air goes into one side of the tester and cylinder pressure leakage feeds back to a gauge. Leakage of 20 percentage or more represents a serious engine problem.

only option is to replace the valve. All Japanese four-stroke engines use Stellite-coated valves, but European bikes do not.

Measuring the Piston and Cylinder

An easy way to measure the piston and bore diameters is with a digital caliper. Calipers cost about $125 and are very accurate. Measure the piston at its widest point, near the bottom of the skirt, and compare the measurement to the minimum-diameter spec listed in the service manual.

A mechanical stethoscope can help you isolate worn engine parts by listening through the metal at key points near bearings, rocker arms, and the cam chain.

This is what happens when you try to ride your four-stroke dirt bike forever without maintenance! The valves broke apart, smashed through the piston crown, and wedged between the rod and the piston.

Measure the bore at the bottom of the cylinder because bores tend to wear fastest at that point. Some mechanics prefer to measure the cylinder bore with a dial-bore gauge. This is a precision measurement device that enables you to check the out-of-round and taper of the cylinder. Most motorcycle machine shops will do this service for free in an effort to get your business for overboring. If you have the tool, it only takes 10 seconds to check the size. The piston rings can be measured by inserting them into the cylin-der bore evenly, then measuring the end-gap with a feeler gauge. If you go through the trouble to disassemble your engine, you may as well replace the rings.

Cylinder Honing

If the cylinder does not require boring, you should hone it before reassembling the engine. The best tool for de-glazing a cylinder bore is a ball-hone. The flexible aluminum-oxide balls remove burnt oil and refinish the crosshatch marks that are so important for proper ring sealing. Ball-hones are available from Brush Research Co. under the product name Flex-Hone. These hones work great for both two- and four-stroke engines. Cylinder honing is performed by chucking the hone in a drill, coating the cylinder with penetrating oil, and spinning the hone in the cylinder while rapidly moving it up and down in the cylinder for 30 seconds. Clean the cylinder in detergent and water, dry it, and spray it with penetrating oil.

Ready for Assembly

There are several different methods for installing the piston and rings into the cylinder. The Japanese motorcycle manufacturers make a special tool for squeezing the rings, but it is expensive and cumbersome. My method is as follows: Install the piston onto the connecting rod and lock in the circlips. Align the end gaps of the rings so they don't overlap each other and cause a loss of compression or oil. Buy a hose clamp that is slightly larger than the piston diameter from an auto parts store. Clamp it snugly around the piston rings. Make sure that some part of the piston is exposed above the hose clamp. This will act as a pilot to guide the piston into the bottom of the cylinder evenly so the rings don't break upon installation. Grasp the cylinder with one hand and center it above the piston. Use your other hand to support the underside of the piston. Push the cylinder down onto the piston until the hose clamp slides down past the rings. Now, remove the hose clamp. Bolt down the cylinder head and install the cam-chain guides.

Timing the Camshaft and Crankshaft

The cam chain may have some slacking links below the sprocket on the crankshaft, so grasp the chain and pull it taut while turning the crankshaft until the TDC mark on the flywheel is centered in the inspection window of the left-side engine cover. Install the cam, paying attention to the alignment marks. The cam shouldn't be depressing the valves. Install the sprocket but don't lock the tabs on the bolts yet. Install the cam-chain tensioner and release it so it tensions the chain. Now, rotate the crankshaft two revolutions and check the alignment marks. You may find that the marks are slightly off, indicating that the cam sprocket must be moved one tooth on the cam chain. This is a common problem because the cam-chain tension was loose when the cam sprocket was installed because the tensioner wasn't installed yet (it is impossible to get the cam sprocket onto the cam with the tensioner installed). To re-align the cam chain to the sprocket in the proper position, you must remove the cam-chain tensioner and repeat the process. After the camshaft and crankshaft are aligned properly, apply a locking agent to the threads of the bolts that fasten the sprocket to the camshaft, then lock the tabs over the bolts.

Checking the Valve Clearance

There are two types of valve trains on modern four-stroke dirt bikes. The most basic is a rocker arm with a threaded adjuster bolt and nut, the more advanced high performance system uses a shim cup arrangement. A small steel shim with a precise thickness is positioned between the valve and the cup. The cup rides against the cam.

The valve clearance is measured when the engine is cold and the cam lobe is facing away from the actuator (rocker arm or shim cup). Normally the clearance should be .004-inch for exhaust valves and .002-inch for intake valves. The exhaust valves require more clearance to compensate for heat expansion since they run at a higher operating temperature than the intake valves. A generic procedure to measure the valve clearance is to rotate the crankshaft to the TDC position on the compression stroke so both valves are closed, then measure the clearance with a feeler gauge. Models like the YZ400 that use shim cups require a special feeler gauge set that is very narrow.

Generally speaking you can expect the rocker arm valve trains to increase in valve clearance over time, and the shim cup valve trains to decrease in valve clearance over time. The reason for this is simple: The rocker arm systems wear and the shim cup systems stay constant in dimension. The valve is slowly wearing and moving deeper

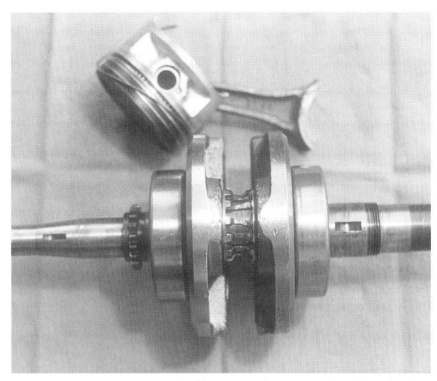

This engine lost lubrication and the crankshaft bearings melted, causing the rod to wobble and bend.

into its seat. That causes the valve clearance to decrease. When an engine is constantly overrevved the valve bounces off the seat and clearance is decreased quickly. Engines with worn valve seats tend to pop on idle because gases are escaping past the valve seat.

Adjusting the rocker arm systems is easily accomplished using a feeler gauge and a set of wrenches. Adjusting the shim cup systems is much more difficult and requires removal of the camshaft to gain access to the shim, which is placed under the cup. Manufacturers offer a narrow range of different thickness shims. The original shims are on the thick side of the range to allow for adjustment. When the clearance requires an extremely thin shim, it's an indication that the valve is worn from bouncing. In that case the valve would need to be replaced and the seat refinished.

One caution when attempting to adjust the valve clearance of the shim-cup style systems: Your local dealer probably won't have the shims in stock and will need to

special order the parts. I suggest that you first measure the clearance and then remove the cams to access the shims. The shims are marked with a size number; write that number down corresponding to the valve for future reference. That way when you periodically check the clearance, if it's tight or loose you'll have an indication of what shim to order in advance.

Break-In Procedure

If you ball-honed the cylinder, no special ring break-in procedure is necessary. Just go easy on the throttle for the first ride. If the cylinder was overbored you will need to break in the engine in three separate sessions of 20 minutes each, with a 20-minute rest period between each session. In the first session, never exceed 1/2 throttle and third gear. In the second and third sessions, never exceed 3/4 throttle and fourth gear. Rev the engine up and down while shifting gears. Ride the bike on flat, hard ground (mud and sand exert too much of a load on the engine and can make it overheat easily).

WHEELS, TIRES, & BRAKES

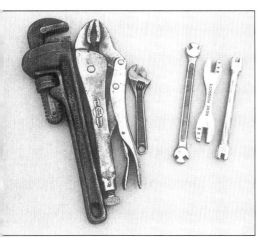

Right and wrong tools. The right tools (on the right) are case hardened and have wide wrench flats.

Wheels, tires, and brakes make our bikes roll, stick, and stop. How effectively these things happen depends on how true you keep the wheels, the types of tires you choose, and how often you service the brakes. This chapter gives you helpful tips that will save you money on catastrophic failures and reduce the time spent working on your bike so you can spend more time riding it!

HOW TO FIX WHEELS

Your bike's wheels are your safety net. When you land from a big jump and the suspension bottoms, the wheels are the only things that keep you and your bike from smashing into the ground. Yet hardly anyone checks the spoke tension between rides. That is the only way you can prevent catastrophic damage to the wheels. This section is a comprehensive wheel maintenance guide that covers the spectrum from routine spoke tensioning to total lacing and truing. The information presented is applicable to the older-style, angle-head spokes and modern straight-pull spokes.

Right and Wrong Tools

Tools such as vise grips and adjustable wrenches are the wrong tools to use on spokes because they will deform the flats on the spoke. Spoke wrenches are the right tools to use; they are designed to tightly fit the spoke flats, so you can tighten the spoke without the chance of stripping the flats. A new tool hit the market in 1999, a spoke torque wrench. It's a good tool for guys who have difficulty judging spoke tension. However if the spoke threads start to corrode, you'll have to apply much more torque at the nipple in order to get the same spoke tension.

Basic Tensioning Tips

Take care when tensioning spokes. If you over-tighten the spokes, the rim could crack at the weld line. A little loose is better than too tight.

Apply penetrating oil to the threads of the spoke before attempting to tighten the spokes. Power-washing a bike can cause the threads to corrode. The penetrating oil breaks down the corrosion on the threads.

Tighten every third spoke 1/4 turn, starting with the spoke nearest the air valve. After three revolutions you will have tensioned the spokes equally. The spoke threads on from the inner-tube side of the tire, so when you look at the spokes from the rim center, you need to turn the spoke nipple counterclockwise to tighten it.

Lacing and Truing Wheels

The following wheel-lacing procedure is for wheels with inner and outer spokes. Wheels with inner and outer spokes are more difficult to service than straight-pull spokes. The inner/outer-spoked wheels require you to remove four spokes just to install one new one. Inner/outer-spoked

Over-tightening the spokes can cause the rim to crack.

The inner spokes must be installed first because they have limited movement.

Most modern wheels use straight pull spokes where the head angle is very slight. Older bikes use two different spokes, inner and outer. The outer spokes have a sharper head angle.

wheels have two different styles of angled heads, one for the inner spokes and one for the outer spokes. Straight-pull spokes do not have angled heads, so they are easy to remove and replace individually. However, the truing process is the same for either type of wheel.

1. Wrap a piece of masking tape around the crossed spokes before you remove the

spoke nipples. This will make it easier to re-lace the spokes into the proper rim holes. The spoke with the 110-degree bend is an inner spoke. The spoke with the tighter, 90-degree bend is an outer spoke. Wheels with modern straight-pull spokes have only one type of spoke.

2. Place the spokes in the hub and swing them into position. Spokes next to each other

cross four other spokes. This is called a "cross-four" pattern and is the standard spoke pattern for dirt bike wheels.

3. Place the rim over the top of the hub and spokes. Start by installing one inner spoke into position and lace all the inner spokes around the rim. Take care that you lace the spoke through the spoke hole on the correct side of the rim. Do the initial spoke tightening with a screwdriver. Thread all the nipples onto the spokes an equal number of threads. Repeat the process for the outer spokes.

4. Mount the wheel in a truing stand, and then fix a dial indicator stand onto the truing stand and against one side of the rim. Tighten the spokes 1/4 turn, alternating every third spoke, until all the spokes are tight. Use the dial indicator to check for run-out; adjust the spoke tension so the rim has no more than .020 to .050 inch run-out.

What to Do About Dented Rims?

There is no way for you to remove the dents from your rims; you will have to replace them. Excel rims are much stronger than OEM rims. Your spoke wrench may be the reason that you are stripping the flats on the spoke nipples. I use a Rowe spoke wrench that has wide flats that are case-hardened. Tallon Engineering in England and Buchanan Wheel in California offer stainless steel spoke nipples for all popular brands. Buchanan also makes custom spokes to fit

Initially use a screwdriver to thread the spokes to a common thread length. Then tighten the spokes with a proper wrench, tightening every third spoke 1/4 turn until all the spokes are the same tension.

This is a wheel truing stand and a dial indicator. This is the most accurate way of truing the hop and the side to side run-out.

Before you try to remove a bearing, first remove the seal and use a propane torch to heat up the hub around the bearing to make it easier to break loose from the hub.

applications like fitting smaller rims for dirt track racing. Buchanan's telephone number in California is (626) 969-4655.

WHEEL BEARING REPAIR

Top GP mechanics replace the wheel bearings after every race. In racing, you need every small advantage. Less demanding riders might only need to replace their bike's wheel bearings once a race season. This section's tips show you how to check and change your wheel bearings the easy way.

Basic Cleaning and Inspection

1. The seals in the hubs can be removed, cleaned, and greased many times before replacement is needed. You should also clean out the area between the seal and the sealed bearing. Now you can check the condition of the bearing.
2. Place your finger on the inside race and try to spin it. If the bearing is worn out, it will be hard to turn. Check for excessive movement in the race. A wheel bearing should never have any movement!
3. Wheel bearings have interference fit into the hubs. That means that the bearing is larger than the hole it fits into in the hub. The hub must be heated with a propane torch in the area around the bearing so that the hub will expand enough to allow the race to be removed.
4. After the hub has been heated with a propane torch for about 3 minutes, use the following procedure to remove the bearings. From the backside, position a long drift-rod onto the inner race of the bearing and strike it with a hammer; rotate the position of the drift-rod around the circumference of the race so you push the bearing out of the hub evenly.
5. The wheel-bearing assembly consists of two seals on each end, two wheel bearings, and one axle spacer. After removing one bearing, pull out the axle spacer. Then remove the second bearing. Notice how dirty and corroded the bearings and spacer become when the seals fail.

6. Clean the inside of the hub, and then heat it with a propane torch for about 3 minutes, just prior to installing the bearing.

7. One side of the bearing is sealed (the side that faces out). Before installing the bearings, pack the open side with white-lithe or moly greases.

8. Use a hammer and a bearing driver to install one bearing. Universal bearing/seal driver kits are available from auto parts or industrial-supply stores. Drive the bearing until it's completely bottomed into the hub. Now install the seal with a dab of grease to prevent water from penetrating the bearing. Install the axle spacer, and then install the second bearing until it is fully seated. Install the second bearing's seal with a dab of grease, and you're done!

Damage Control

Imagine that your wheels have the most catastrophic bearing failure and the bearing cups in the hub get damaged. That would mean that the bearing cup is worn oblong and won't retain the bearing tightly in the hub. Normally, you would have to buy a new hub, but a company in New England offers a service to repair worn bearing cups. Rapid Precision Machining bores and sleeves a bearing cup for only $50.

TIRES

The tires of a dirt bike are particularly important because of the terrain that we ride on. You can have a bike with the most expensive suspension revalving and a powerful engine, but if the knobs are all rounded off you'll still end up on your butt. In the European motocross GPs, riders and mechanics regard tires as a suspension component. They are constantly fiddling with different tire patterns, compounds, and hybrid mousse inserts just to get a slight competitive edge. I try not to let tires dominate too much of my mechanic duties, and I refuse to be intimidated by a chunk of rubber. This section gives you information that will make tire selection and tire changing a lot less stressful.

Put the wheel on a flat surface, tilt the punch on an angle, and tap it with a hammer. Keep turning and impacting all around the bearing until it comes out.

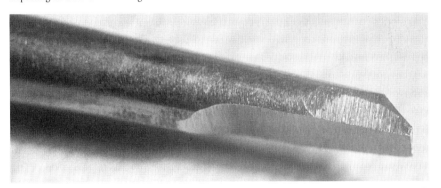

This wheel-bearing remover is hand-ground from a tapered punch. The relief on the tip enables the punch to offset the floating bushing and contact the inner race of the wheel bearing.

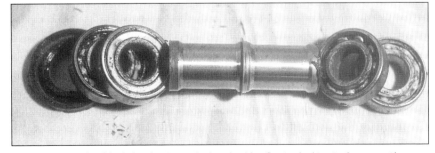

This is what's inside of the hub; a bearing on both ends with a floating bushing in the center. Always replace the seals whenever you change the seals.

Rapid Precision Machine offers a service to rebuild hubs with sweat-fitted bronze bearing races.

These are the tools you'll need to change a tire. Tire irons should be smooth and rounded at the edges. The longer curved irons have the best leverage but they won't fit in a tool bag. A valve stem remover, liquid soap or talcum powder, a pressure gauge, and a compressed air source. If you're on the trail or at the races, you can use air cartridges. Cartridges are available from motorcycle or bicycle shops.

TIRE CHART

Hard	Intermediate	Soft
Clay, Churt, Dry Dirt	Loamy Soil, Some Rocks	Sand, Mud, Rocks
K490/K695	K755/K737	K752/K752 Dunlop
M23/M22	M57/M58	M25/M26 Bridgestone
MT460	MT32	MT320 Pirelli
14–12 psi	12–10 psi	10-8 psi

The first set of numbers is for the front tire and the second set is for the rear tire. The same follows for the recommended tire pressure.

Tools for Home and Trail

You will need the following tools to change a tire: a 12mm wrench for the rim lock and the Schraeder valve, a valve-stem tool, an air pressure gauge, a set of short and long tire irons, a compressed air source, and a bottle of spray detergent. If you want to put together a collection of tools that fit into your trail-riding tool kit, get two short tire irons, a valve-stem tool, pressure gauge, a bar of soap, and Moose Racing's compressed air cartridges.

Changing Tires

Changing tires without tearing the bead or pinching the inner tube is just a matter of technique. You can struggle with the task, or you can use your head and stay patient. Here are some tips that I've learned over the years.

You will need the following tools: a 12mm wrench, valve stem tool, air pressure gauge, long and short tire irons, and spray detergent (warm, soapy water in a spray bottle works just fine).

First, loosen the rim lock and remove the valve-stem nut. Then break the bead using the following technique: place the wheel on a flat surface, and put one foot on the rim while using the other foot to press down on the sidewall of the tire. Remember to protect the disc rotor with a piece of cardboard, so the ground doesn't scratch it.

The proper technique for removing one side of the tire goes like this: Insert the curved end of the tire iron between the tire and rim and pulled back at a 45-degree angle to the rim while inserting another iron about 3 inches away. Then pull back the first iron to the rim while setting the second iron at a 45-degree angle. Remove the first iron and insert it again, 3 inches away from the second iron, and the process is repeated. At some point you will be able to use your hands to remove the tire. The fewer times you insert the tire irons, the less the chance of pinching the tube. I prefer to use the shorter tire irons for the front tire because the sidewall of the tire is thinner and requires less force to lift it off the rim.

After you have lifted one side of the tire over the rim, reach inside the tire and remove the tube and rim lock. Then, you can

I use a plastic bowl to cover the sprocket so it doesn't get damaged while changing the tire.

Once you break the bead away from the rim, insert one iron in the tire at a time, folding the tire over the rim alternating every few inches until the tire is two-thirds the way off.

Next grab the tire with one hand while holding the spokes with your other hand. Slip the tire off the rest of the way and remove the rim lock and inner tube.

Original wheels come with rubber rim-bands. Some mechanics like to replace the rim band with duct tape to prevent water from seeping into the tire.

use the long tire irons to remove the tire. This is the proper technique: Grasp the rim with one hand and cross your other hand over and insert the flat side of the iron between the tire and rim. Once you bend the iron over as far as it will go, you can usually grasp the tire with your hand and push it downward to remove the tire all at once.

Before you try to install the tire, elevate the wheel by putting it on top of a rigid plastic or steel bucket. To install the tire, first put the rim lock into the rim and the rim band over the lock to hold it in position. Spray detergent on the inner side of the tube to prevent it from being pinched by the rim and irons. Spray some detergent on the inside of the tire's bead. This will help it slide on to the rim. Use the short irons to carefully install the tire over the rim. Then rest both irons on each side of the rim lock and push it up into the tire past the bead.

Remember to thread the lock nut on a few threads to the rim lock before popping the rim lock past the bead. Otherwise the rim lock could fall into the tire, making it difficult to install in the hole of the rim. Start

These are three different rear tire tread patterns. On the left is a paddle tire designed for sand. The tire in the center has widely spaced knobs which works best in mud. The tire on the right is a Pirelli bi-directional type. The bi-directional can be installed so the tread pattern's direction of rotation suites either intermediate or hard packed terrain.

When installing the tire, start by putting the tire on the rim then insert the lock and the inner tube. It helps to lube the tire with soap to prevent the tire iron from pinching the tube.

at the rim lock and work over to the air valve, then around the rest of the tire. Try to roll the tire's bead on with your hand before using the tire irons. Every time you use the tire irons you run the risk of puncturing the inner tube. When I first started working in motorcycle shops in the early 1970s, motorcycle tire machines had not yet been invented. The service manager wouldn't let the mechanics use tire irons to install tires. We had to roll the entire bead of a street tire or knobby with our hands. It's possible, but only with the right technique.

Tread Patterns, Compounds, and Pressure

There are many different tread patterns and compounds for off-road tires. In general, hard compounds are better for soft terrain such as mud and sand, and soft compounds are better for hard terrain such as clay. Regarding tire patterns, the best patterns for hard-packed surfaces are ones with tightly spaced low-profile knobs. That way the soft compound short knobs can conform to the terrain surface without breaking loose. In the 1995 Supercross season, Jeremy McGrath had great success using Dunlop's dual sport tire (K940) on the tracks with hard-packed clay surfaces. The best tire patterns for soft terrain are ones with tall knobs that are widely spaced. That way the hard compound knobs can penetrate the terrain surface and resist becoming clogged-up, due to the open area between the knobs. The latest trend in tires is a reversible type to cover intermediate and soft terrain. Pirelli was the first to offer this type of tire.

A tire's air pressure can be adjusted to take advantage of the tire's tread pattern and compound. In general lower pressure is used for soft terrain because that allows the tire to conform to the ground for maximum traction. On a muddy surface there aren't as many sharp-edged bumps and it's difficult to get big air over jumps, so it isn't necessary to use high air pressure to prevent the tube from being punctured. However, on hard-packed or rocky surfaces, it's necessary to run higher pressure for three reasons: to resist punctures from hard landings, to keep the tire from spinning on the rim lock, and to make the soft-compound tire conform to proper profile.

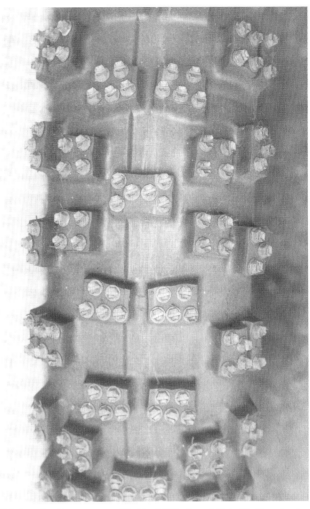

These are the two basic types of front tire tread patterns. Soft terrain tires (left) have widely spaced, tall, pointy knobs. Tire tread designed for hard packed terrain is closely spaced, low profile, with more surface area of knobs.

This is an ice tire custom modified by Jeff Fredette. Jeff double lines the tire and installs 800 sheet metal screws into the knobs. This tire produces more traction on ice than a sharp knobby does in dirt.

Here are some guidelines for selecting the proper models of the most popular brands of tires—Pirelli, Dunlop, and Bridgestone—along with some recommendations on air pressure.

Puncture Protection

There are some precautions that you can take to insure against punctures. Heavy-duty inner tubes should be used on every bike, except minis and 125s, that are raced competitively in motocross. The reason is that the tubes are heavy and pose a bit of drag on these small engines. In some forms of racing such as desert events held in rocky terrain, the risk of puncture is great, even with heavy-duty tubes. For this situation you may want to

use either a mousse tube or a combination mousse and inflatable tube such as the Dunlop Crescent mousse. Many off-road racers riding large-displacement bikes choose to install mousse in the tires. The mousse is a dense, closed-cell-foam tube that does not deflate when punctured. Mousse also gives the tire some extra protection from rock impacts. The mousse enables the tire to absorb the impacts of rocks instead of bottoming and deflecting in a random manner. Mousse tubes do have some disadvantages, however. They are prone to shrinkage, and they have a high cost per usage ($175 each for about 1,000 miles). The Dunlop Crescent mousse product sells for about $120 and is available for both front and rear tires.

Snow and Ice Tires

Riding in snow and ice can be as much (if not more) fun than riding typical terrain. It also can be a way for riders in northern climates to stay sane during the winter. With good tires, the effect is not all that different from riding on loose sand.

Winter conditions can vary drastically. Off-road bikes can't handle extremely deep snow, but studded tires allow the bike to navigate 12 inches of snow and less with ease (not to mention throwing huge amounts of roost). Also, ice riding and racing is generally good as long as the ice is safe, and is basically flat-tracking (although you can find heaved ice to jump under the right conditions).

167

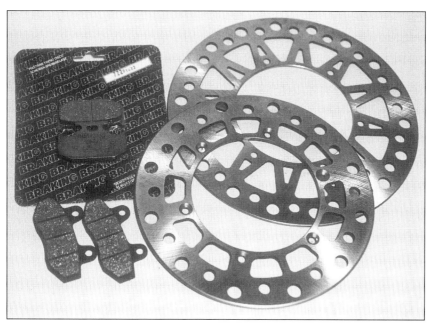

This is a Braking brand disc kit. Braking discs are made of stainless steel so they don't corrode and resist bending. Braking also makes oversized discs for better stopping power.

In this photo the brake pins are being removed with an Allen socket.

Ice Studs

There are several different ways to get good traction in frozen conditions. The most common is to screw ice studs into your tires. The aftermarket studs are better than regular sheet metal screws for several reasons. For one, they are actually unfinished sheet metal screws. The finishing process smoothes the surface of the screws, which reduces the traction they give. Also, the aftermarket screws are coated, making them more durable than regular sheet metal screws. Use the pattern shown in the photos to install these screws.

Keep in mind that screws will eventually round off and will pull out of the tire on occasion. Replace the screws regularly as you ride.

Trelleborg Ice Tires

Former national enduro champ Kevin Hines recommends Trelleborg tires for winter trail riding. He says Trellys have the best compound and stud arrangement. The studs are carbide-tipped points molded into the knobs. Trellys are very durable and cost about the same as a tire and liner with 800 screws (under $200 each).

Ice Racing Tires

Jeff Fredette is an avid ice racer, besides being the "King of KDXs." Fredette was one of the first racers to use a 21-inch front wheel for ice racing. I remember when he showed up for a race at a popular circuit outside the Chicago area, back in 1980. That circuit attracted the local hard-core dirt-track racers. People thought Fredette was lazy because he just studded-up the stock tires of his Suzuki PE175. He left the lights on the bike and everything. People weren't laughing much when he kicked their asses by holding the inside line!

Fredette's reasoning was that the wide-spaced knobs of the 21-inch tire are ideal for penetrating the top layer of snow and ice debris that covers the corners of an ice-racing track. Since then, he has become a well-known ice tire expert.

Fredette sets up his own tires for oval-track ice racing. He lines his tires with old street tires. He first strips the sidewalls and bead off these street tires with a carpet knife. He lines the rear with an 18-inch street tire and uses a 21-inch Harley-Davidson tire to line the tire up front. The lining keeps the points of the screws from rupturing the tube.

He places only the tread of the street tire into the Kenda Ice Master trials tire. The tread pattern and compound of the Kenda tire are excellent for holding the 800 5/8-inch Kold Kutter brand screws that provide the traction on ice and fasten the Kenda and street tire liner together.

You might think, "Hey what's the big deal? You just get a screw gun and jam a bunch of sheet-metal screws into a set of tires." You might be able to get away with that for riding around the cow pasture, but to be competitive in ice racing, you'll need to do more. The alignment of the screw heads is critical because it is the edges and corners of the screws that help the tire gain traction on the ice. The edges of the screw are used for a paddle effect and the corners are positioned to bite when the tire is leaned over in a turn. Each of the 800-odd screws must be threaded into the tire perpendicular to the knob with a screw gun (see photograph).

BRAKE SYSTEMS

The elements and the laws of physics punish the brakes of a dirt bike. The disc brake pads push against a disc that is sometimes covered with water, mud, and sand. Consequently, dirt bike brake systems wear much faster and need much more maintenance than the brake systems on cars or street bikes.

In racing, the front brake is primarily used to slow the motorcycle. The rear brake is used to change a bike's attitude over jumps by creating a torque reaction. The rear brakes can also be applied lightly to keep the rear end of the bike tracking straight through whoops sections. Dragging the brakes quickly wears out the pads, so you should check them often. The friction from dragging the brakes also creates a lot of heat, and that heat transfers through the caliper piston and into the brake fluid. This heat rapidly breaks down the fluid, so it, too, must be checked often.

Weak Front Brakes

Question: The front brake on my KX250 is weak. I change the fluid often and have tried different types of pads. Nothing helps much. I power-wash the brakes after I ride, just to keep out the dirt. What do I need to do to fix this bike's brakes?

Answer: Power-washing the brakes with soap is a bad thing. The soap film attacks the adhesive in the pad and bonds to the ridges in the disc. Soap can also glaze the disc. You can deglaze the disc with medium-grit sandpaper, or there are companies that can re-surface the disc. The best cure is to install a Braking stainless-steel disc and a set of composite or metallic pads.

Brakes Get Hot and Lock-Up

Question: The disc brakes on my bike start to get hot and lock-up. The pads get wedged against the disc and I can't even turn the wheel until the brakes cool down. I have to bleed out some brake fluid when it gets real bad. What do you think is wrong with my bike's brakes?

Answer: This is a common problem. The two brake pins that the pads slide on become grooved and prevent the pads from moving away from the disc when the brake lever is released. Try replacing the pads and pins and changing the brake fluid to a DOT 4. The best fix for preventing the problem of grooved brake pins is stainless steel pins made by WER (Works Enduro Rider). They make these pins with hex heads too, so they are easy to remove when changing brake pads.

Kevlar Brake Pads Wear Too Fast

Question: I put a set of expensive Kevlar brake pads on my bike and they are shot after only a few rides. The material is still on the pad, but I have to pull in the lever really hard just to get them to lock up. What gives?

Answer: I'm guessing that you are a real power-washing freak. That is a sure way to damage Kevlar pads. The strong detergents that the commercial power-washing systems use can damage the Kevlar material used on the pads. The detergent bonds to the pads and causes them to form a low-friction glaze. That is why the pad material has not worn down but the pad won't grip the disc. Don't try to file or sand the pad; just get a new set, and wash your bike with water only!

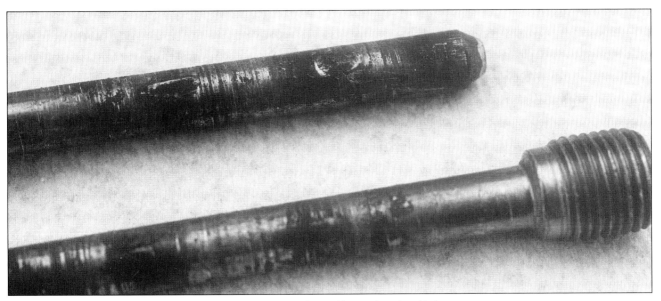

This is a close-up view of the brake pins. Look for wear spots and divots that could cause the pads to bind.

Once the brake pins are removed the pads can be removed.

This is a severely worn brake pad. All that is left is the backing plate.

In addition to normal maintenance, you can also tune your brakes in a number of ways. Manufacturers make different pad material to improve longevity in various riding conditions. Metallic pads work best in sandy conditions, and composite pads offer superior braking power. There are different types of discs, too. This section will give you all the basics of brake-system repair, maintenance, and tuning, along with some tips on trouble shooting braking problems.

Basic Cleaning and Pad Replacement

The following are some basic tips on checking and changing brake pads. If you are having a specific problem with your brakes, see the troubleshooting guide listed at the end of this chapter Always review the factory service manual for your model bike before attempting any service procedures.

1. Before you attempt to change the brake pads, first power-wash the brakes clean with water (no soap). The high-strength detergents used in power-washers can damage the caliper seals, disc surface, and even attack the bond used on the pad, so avoid spraying the brakes when you wash your bike. Next, clean the dirt from the inside of the Allen-head caliper screws with a pick or brake cleaner. This will ensure that the Allen wrench gets a rigid grip and doesn't strip the screw when you go to remove it.

2. Remove the brake pins and check the pin's surface for divots, dents, and corrosion. These surface blemishes can cause the pads to drag when the brakes get hot. Replace the pins at least once per year, and never apply grease to the pins!

3. After you have removed the brake pins, you can remove the caliper and pull out the pads. Check the pads for glazing or wear. If the pads are worn out, replace them.

4. Re-install the pads, calipers, and pins, and tighten all the screws. Always depress the brake lever several times after you have installed the wheels. This will enable the brake pistons to pump up to the pads.

Fluid Replacement

The brake fluid should be changed at least two times a year. Race mechanics change the fluid on their bikes every two races. There are two methods for replacing the brake fluid and bleeding the brakes: pump-and-purge or with a hand-operated vacuum pump.

The Pump-and-Purge Method

If you don't have a brake bleeder tool, this is the best method to change brake fluid.

1. Remove the master-cylinder cap, and top the cylinder with brake fluid.

2. Put a six-point box-end wrench on the bleeder valve located on the caliper. Slip

a 10-inch-long piece of clear plastic tubing over the end of the bleeder valve.

3. Slowly pump the brake lever and hold it fully engaged; then loosen the bleeder valve a quarter of a turn for one second before tightening the valve.

4. While frequently checking fluid level in the master cylinder and topping it off as necessary, repeat Step 3 until the fluid coming out of the tube is clean and clear and without bubbles.

5. Remove the hose, snug down the bleeder valve, top off the master cylinder, and replace the master-cylinder cap.

The Hand-Pump Method

A brake bleeder tool will speed up your brake fluid change. Use the following method to change your oil with the tool.

1. Connect a collection tank between the pump and a hose attached to the bleeder valve.

2. Remove the master-cylinder cap. Be prepared to constantly replenish the master cylinder with brake fluid during the bleeding process.

3. Loosen the bleeder valve a half turn and use the vacuum pump to slowly pump the fluid through the brake system. Don't forget to replenish the master cylinder!

4. When the fluid coming out of the bleeder valve looks clean, clear, and free of bubbles, stop pumping and snug down the bleeder valve.

5. Detach the pump from the bleeder valve, replenish the master cylinder, and replace the master-cylinder cap.

Troubleshooting

Problem: The brakes drag when they get hot.

The old-style system is a drum brake. These systems have to be serviced after every ride in wet conditions. Normally you have to clean the brake pad dust out of the drum and lightly sand the glaze off of the shoes. Don't use compressed air to clean out the dust; the particles are carcinogenic.

Solution: The brake fluid could be saturated with water. It's best to change the brake fluid twice a year.

Problem: After only 15 minutes of riding, the rear brake pedal has no free movement and the brakes are very sensitive.

Solution: The brake pins could be bent or have divots that cause the pads to drag against the disc. The heat is transferred through the caliper piston and into the brake fluid. The water in the fluid boils and expands, and that causes a lack of free movement at the brake pedal. Check the brake pins and change the fluid.

Problem: The brake lever or pedal pulsates when the brakes are applied.

Solution: The disc is bent and is pushing the piston back into the caliper. This force is transferred into the pedal/lever, making a pulsation for every revolution of the wheel. Replace the disc because it cannot be repaired.

Problem: The front brake pads wear on an angle.

Solution: The front caliper carrier bracket is bent; replace it.

Problem: The brakes make a squealing noise.

Solution: The discs and pads have a thin film of glazing on their surfaces. The glazing could have occurred from leaking fork seals, power-wash detergent, or chain lube accidentally sprayed on the disc. Medium-grit sandpaper can be used to remove the glazing off the surface of the discs and pads. Afterward, clean the discs with brake cleaner—never with a detergent!

Chapter 11

TUNING TIPS FOR HONDA DIRT BIKES

2000 HONDA CR125

Flaws: weak powerband
Fixes: exhaust valve modification

After being criticized for having an antiquated engine with a high maintenance exhaust valve system, Honda made a bold change in the top end of the CR125. The cylinder is nearly identical to the RS250 roadracer design. There is a new exhaust valve that has only three main parts. The valve varies the effective stroke, port time-area, and duration. It's a great design except for the shape, which is easily fixed. Overall Honda made a good decision to update this model. The new top end has a lot of potential.

Best Value Mods

Engine: porting and exhaust valve mods
Suspension: springs for your geared weight

Carb Jetting

The stock jetting is too rich at about 1/3 throttle. You can use the optional leaner needle (#70) and a 340 main jet as the baseline settings.

Cylinder Mods

The cylinder is nearly identical to the RS250 roadracer design. The exhaust port and valve can be modified in a number of different configurations. For more top-end power raise the exhaust port to 27.5mm from the top of the cylinder. Also drop the outer edges of the exhaust port 5mm.

Exhaust Valves

As noted above, the new valves are a great design except for the shape, which is easily tuned. Honda did tuners a favor by making the valve halves so large and restrictive. The valves can be ground to different profiles. In stock form the valves don't allow for enough blow-down timing from 4,500 to 8,000 rpm prior to when the valves flip wide open. A simple way to advance the exhaust valves is to make a bushing for the stop-pin to limit how far the valves close. A bushing with a 7mm diameter, placed over the top of the original stop pin, is ideal for most riders.

Crankcase Mods

The 2000 CR cylinder has the same transfer ports as the RS roadracer. However the interface with the crankcases is grossly mismatched. The cylinder hangs over into the cases. If you're looking for more top-end power the cylinder ports should be ground larger to fit the cases. If you're looking for strictly low-end power, then apply epoxy to the cases to blend into the cylinder ports.

Overbore Kits

It's possible to overbore and electroplate the cylinder to a 56mm bore. That boosts the displacement to 133cc and takes the engine to the AMA limit for modified amateur racing. The cylinder requires porting to take advantage of the bigger piston. The exhaust port needs to be raised to 27.5mm, widened to 53mm, and the edges dropped 5mm to conform to the profile of the front transfer ports. No head mods are needed for the 2mm oversize piston and the raised exhaust port.

1998-99 HONDA CR125

Flaws: weak top-end power
Fixes: Cometic base gasket and head mod

The 1998 CR125 was the greatest evolutionary design leap. With an aluminum frame, five-speed gearbox, and a new exhaust valve system Honda came under criticism from the motorcycle press. The frame followed the same concept as the CR250, and has proven itself reliable and rigid. The five-speed gearbox enabled Honda engineers to widen the gears, making the tranny more reliable. Earlier models tend to break first gear, which is part of the main shaft. This failure occurs most often when aftermarket clutch plates were installed with stiffer springs. The new HPP exhaust valve system cured a two-fold problem related to performance and reliability. The new HPP eliminates blow-by over the valves and prevents a worn valve from contacting the piston.

Best Value Mods

Engine: Cometic gasket, bigger carb, CR250 air-boot

Suspension: Pro-Action revalving

New HPP

The new exhaust valve system solves a number of maintenance and performance problems with the HPP system. The new valves feature an L-shaped guide rail that prevents the valve from contacting the piston after it wears. The new design also seals properly in the closed position for more compression and better low-end power. Some of the magazines claim that the bike doesn't have enough top-end power. That is due to the lower exhaust port height of the new HPP valves. The effective stroke is longer and the compression ratio is lower so the engine can run on pump gas.

Cylinder

The cylinder porting and casting quality is excellent. All you need to do is experiment with the cylinder height. That involves swapping base gaskets of different thickness. Cometic makes base gaskets in the sizes of .010, .020 (stock), and .039 inches. If the thinnest gasket is installed, the engine's powerband will be shifted down the rpm scale, good for tight stadium racing. There is no head modification needed. However if you install the thickest gasket, you'll need to modify the head. If you really want to get the cylinder ported here are some guidelines. Widening the exhaust port will only cause the valves to snag the ring. The transfer ports can be raised to 41.25mm for the front set and 42mm for the rear set. This gives more top-end power. Grinding the valve guides on an angle so the port height measures 28.5mm from the top of the cylinder can effectively raise the exhaust port.

Motocross World of England specializes in big wheel CR minis. They make all sorts of custom parts like pipes, plastic, graphics, and clutch covers.

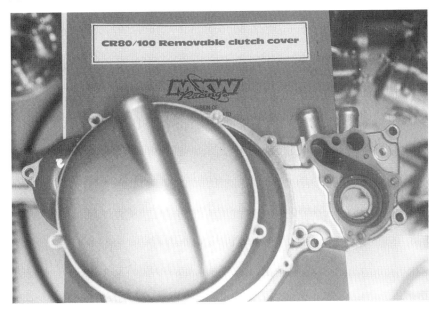

This is the MXW removable clutch cover for CR80s.

Head

The head's gasket surface can be turned-down as much as .024 inches (.6mm) in order to raise the compression ratio to compensate for the Cometic .039 base gasket.

Exhaust Plugs or Valves?

The HPP valve system maximizes the powerband by adjusting the time-area of the exhaust port to the engine's rpm. If an engine is to be tuned for maximum top-end power and the application can sacrifice some low-end power, then exhaust valve plugs are the best choice. On dirt track motorcycles and shifter-karts, I install plugs because the engine is used in a narrow high-rev range. The manufacturer of the aluminum exhaust plugs is Boyesen Performance. The plugs are installed in place of the HPP valves. The exhaust port height can be raised to 28mm measured from the top of the cylinder. That

SRS is a company in Italy that makes trick parts for CR125s, including carbon fiber guards, cylinders, heads, and side covers.

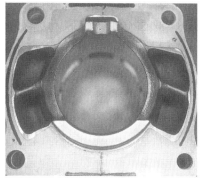

This is a view of the mismatch between the cylinder and base gasket for a 2000 CR125. The gasket matches the crankcases, so you can see how the cylinder grossly overlaps the cases. In porting, these ports are ground to fit the cases.

will really make the engine rev. By removing the exhaust valves you can also remove the powervalve governor that drives off the crankshaft. That serves to reduce drag and friction on the crank and yield an extra horsepower.

Carb and Air-Boot

The 1998 CR can gain more top-end by installing the intake set-up from a CR250. Parts like a Keihin PJ38 carb with the air-boot from a 1998 CR250 will boost maximum airflow through the engine. A carb from a 1990-96 CR250 will fit the best. The baseline jet settings for that carb are 58 Slow jet, 1468 Needle P-2, 170 Main jet. The Honda part

2000 Honda CR125 Exhaust Port and Valve Mods

Raise exhaust port to 27.5mm

Lower the outer edges 8mm

Re-profile the exhaust valve 2mm

This is a drawing of the 2000 CR125 cylinder porting and valve mod. The valve mod helps the midrange acceleration.

number for the needle is 16012-KS6-004. The 1999 CR125 already uses the larger air-boot but still needs the larger carb.

1992-97 HONDA CR125

Flaws: carb jetting off, clutch fades, rims dent easily

Fixes: richen jetting, install steel clutch plates, lace-up Excel rims

The CR is regarded as the best 125 of the early to mid-1990s. These models had their share of problems, but overall this was the most reliable 125cc motocross bike. Simple problems such as carb jetting can be adjusted with just a needle and main jet change. The clutch performs better with steel plates and frequent oil changes. The stock rims are very soft and dent easily when riding in rocky conditions. It's best to replace them with Excel rims once they are dented.

The CR engine can be modified to be a better enduro bike, or have the raging top-end power for GP motocross. Whatever type of dirt riding you do, the CR125 can be modified to suit your riding demands.

Best Value Mods

Engine: 1468 Needle for carb, RAD Valve, 53-tooth rear sprocket

Suspension: stiffer fork springs

Supercross or Enduro Powerband

If you want to increase the low-end and midrange power of your CR125, these following modifications are the hot ticket. These are great for Supercross, where you need quick bursts of power, or enduro riding, where mellower power is better for navigating snotty trails. Also, these modifications are well suited to lower level riders. The bike will be easier to ride, with the sacrifice of some top-end power.

HPP Valves

The exhaust valve guides of the 1993 to 1997 models are manufactured with such a high opening, that when the valves are closed the exhaust gases can bypass over the top of the valves. For more low-range to midrange power, install the exhaust valve assemblies from the 1999 CR125. These parts are very expensive at about $150 but it really helps the low-end power. Honda part numbers: Left 14700-KZ4-000, Right 14600-KZ4-000.

Head Mod

The 1990 and 1991 models had domed pistons and hemi-shaped combustion chambers. The 1992 model was the first year of the flat top piston design. Never mix heads and pistons on the earlier and later CRs or engine damage can occur. The 1990 and 1991 cylinder head can be improved by turning down the face of the head 0.028 inch or 0.7mm. Then the squish angle must be cut at a 10-degree angle, with a deck height of 0.020 inch or 0.5mm. On the 1992 and later models, the spark plug doesn't thread in flush to the combustion chamber. The top of the spark plug lug should be turned down on a lathe 1mm. The compression ratio and squish band width are good, so no other mods are needed.

Reed Valve

The Boyesen RAD Valve makes a tremendous difference in the low- and midrange of the powerband and is a must for enduro riding.

Exhaust Pipe

The best pipe for these engine mods is a Dyno-Port low-end pipe.

High-Rev Powerband

The stock engine peaks at about 10,500 rpm. To be competitive in the national championships or GPs, the engine must have a powerband that starts at 9,500 and peaks at 12,500 rpm. Modifying the CR for that extra elusive 2,000 rpm is very expensive and requires total engine disassembly and special machining. This is a parts list of the engine components, and an explanation of how they are tuned to work together: 1992 CR125 cylinder No. 12110-KZ4-860, 1991 Head No. 12200-KZ4-730 38mm PJ Keihin carb, aftermarket pipe and silencer, and carbon fiber reeds.

The 1992 CR125 cylinder has more aggressive exhaust and transfer port timing than the 1993 and 1994 models. You can use the 1993–96 HPP valves, but you need to switch to the domed piston and head. The

On most CR250s made after 1989, the spark plug hole is too long, preventing the spark plug from threading completely into the combustion chamber. The arrow marks the point where metal can be turned down from the top of the plug hole. Use a thread-chaser to clean the threads after machining.

domed set-up enables more efficient cylinder scavenging at high rpm. The carbon fiber reeds are less prone to fluttering and the larger carb is needed to boost the rpm peak of the engine.

Crankcase Mods

The cases must be machined for a larger intake port with better flow up to the transfer ports.

Reeds

Carbon fiber reeds should be used because stock reeds start to flutter at about 10,700 rpm. Carbon fiber reeds produce excellent top-end power without fluttering.

Head and Piston

The domed piston has a slight advantage at extremely high rpm. Use a Wiseco Pro-Lite and the 1991 head.

CR125 Carb Jetting

Here are some specs on a starting point for carb jetting. The specific gravity is different from North America and Europe so European jetting specs will need to be slightly richer. American carb jetting for 36mm PJ Keihin using 93-octane pump gas with a pre-mix ratio of 40 to 1: Air-screw 1.5 turns, slow-jet #58, needle #1468, main jet #168. European specs for unleaded premium petrol, 40 to 1 pre-mix: Air-screw 1. 5 turns, slow-jet #62, needle #1468, main jet #178.

Baseline carb specs for a 38mm PJ Keihin are one step richer on the slow and main jets using the 1468 needle.

CR Clutch Tips

Never install stiffer clutch springs in a CR125. The clutch is designed to slip when the gears engage on up shifting. This helps reduce the impact on the transmission. Stiffer clutch springs could accelerate wear on the transmission because of the increased load. Steel clutch plates wear slower and don't contaminate the gear oil. However they do increase the drive train inertia, just like a flywheel weight. The effect of the heavier steel clutch plates will help you hook and stay in control in slippery hard-packed tracks but the bike will feel a bit slower to respond in deep sand or where you have good traction. The additional weight of steel clutch plates can make the bike a bit easier to ride, as well. When the stock clutch basket wears out replace it with a Hinson racing clutch. The Hinson clutch basket is made of better material and hard anodized with Teflon.

Pro Circuit makes extra wide footpegs for big guys.

The 1997 and 1998 CR250s have a lower primary compression ratio than the 2000 model. To boost the throttle response I add a putty-type epoxy to the bridges of the transfer ports. The epoxy also changes the flow pattern of the gasses entering the cylinder bore.

Big Bore Kits

Wiseco makes two oversize piston kits in the sizes of 56mm (133cc) and 58mm (144cc). Any oversize piston kit will require modifications to the cylinder ports, head, and exhaust valves. Cometic makes special oversize head gaskets to fit bigger bores. Forward Motion Racing specializes in big bore kits using Wiseco pistons.

1985-89 HONDA CR125

Flaws: left-side crankshaft seal leaks, clutch plates wear out
Fixes: replace seal often, install Barnett steel plates

Honda really perfected the 125 in the late 1980s. Here are some general things to pay close attention to or modify for better performance.

Best Value Mods

Engine: 53-tooth sprocket, 1468 carb needle

Suspension: shock revalving, stiffer fork springs

Gearing

A good baseline for gearing on all models should be 13/53 for motocross and 12/52 for Supercross and enduro. Ideally, adjust by single teeth on the rear for slightly different tracks and conditions.

Carburetor

A 36mm works best. Use these jetting specs: 58 slow-jet, 6 slide, 1468 needle, and 168 main jet (vary slightly according to elevation and extreme air temperature differences).

Crankshaft

The left-side crankshaft seals wear out quickly because the left-side cover is flimsy. Replace the seals often; otherwise, the piston could overheat and seize on the exhaust skirt. The 1987 model's crankshaft was updated to a stronger design. The new connecting rod uses a 15mm pin, so you must change the piston with the crankshaft. Both parts are standard on the 1988 model.

Cylinder Interchange

The 1989 cylinder is Nikasil plated and it will fit the 1987 and 1988 models (which are not plated).

Clutch

Replacing the aluminum clutch plates with steel plates makes the clutch last longer and doesn't hurt performance. Never install stiffer springs in the clutch of a CR125 because it will cause first gear drive to fail. That gear wears quickly on these bikes normally, and it is part of the clutch shaft so it is expensive to replace.

Reeds

Honda doesn't make replacement reeds for their bikes, so use Boyesen reeds.

ATAC System

The exhaust valve on the 1987–97 models can be damaged on installation. The right-side valve end has a flat machined on it, and if you tighten the actuator lever too tight, it can round the flat edge. This causes the valve to hang open and raise the exhaust-gas temperature at high rpm, eventually causing the piston to seize.

Shock

The rear shock can be modified for better handling on the 1985–88 models. These types of shocks use the straight shims. The rebound-valve stack has two transition shims, one in the middle and one closest to the piston. Put both transition shims between the number 26 and 27 shim from the piston. After this, the shock will handle square edged bumps much better.

1997-2000 HONDA CR250

Flaws: piston and ring design, secondary coil
Fixes: Wiseco piston, replace coil when misfire starts

The 1997 model was the first generation of advanced ignition systems. The traction control concept of monitoring rpm changes versus time is good, but Honda missed the mark on the 1997 model. It needs a steeper advance curve in order to give the powerband a hard-hitting mid-range, like previous models were famous for. The 1998 model had a slight change in the cylinder head and the ignition. The 1999 model had a different cylinder with porting that was a bit too mellow for most riders. A few mechanical problems that have surfaced with time are failure of the ignition coil and the piston ring. When the top coil fails the engine starts misfiring, then loses spark completely. The piston ring tends to spin around the ring groove after the centering pin works loose from the piston. The best solution to these problems is to keep a spare top coil in your toolbox and replace the stock piston often or switch to a more durable Wiseco piston. The 1997 model was the first year for the aluminum frame. By 2000 Honda changed the frame at the front down tube and lengthened the swingarm. Some of the problems on early models involved clearances at the motor mounts and head stays. That could easily be fixed with shim washers to take up the gap. Lengthening the swingarm helped the handling on the 2000 models. Handling on earlier models can be improved with revalving. For information on the engine, look at the next section on the 1992-96 models.

Best Value Mods

Engine: Wiseco Extreme Lite piston, Cometic thin base gasket

Suspension: Revalving

Secondary Coil

The 1997 CR250 had a problem with a bad batch of secondary coils. That is the coil mounted on the left side of the frame that connects to the spark plug. A clear symptom of a faulty coil is a high rpm misfire and hard starting. Eventually the coil fails completely and the engine loses spark. In 1998 Honda cured the problem with a better quality coil.

Carbs

In 1997 and 1998 Honda used an electronic carb that monitored rpm with a black box. This system was sensitive to a couple of problems. The wire connector was located on the outside of the frame and was prone to water seepage. The black box was sensitive to electrical noise and it's very important to use a resistor spark plug to reduce the interfer-

The new CR aluminum frames need protection from rocks. Get a fabricator/welder to TIG weld a 1/8-inch plate between bottom frame rails.

ence. The symptoms of a faulty solenoid are a lean bogging in the mid-range during hard acceleration. If this happens, it's best to just disconnect the wire connector and install a richer jet needle, like a 1368.

1992-96 HONDA CR250

Flaws: chain and sprockets wear, cylinders break, rear suspension kicks

Fixes: loosen chain tension, use 1999 cylinder, revalve shock

There is hardly any difference between the 1992–96 engines, so the mods listed will apply to the previous models. The focus of our engine mods will be to make the CR easier to ride for motocross riders and especially great for enduro riders.

Best Value Mods

Engine: carb jetting, flywheel weight

Suspension: Revalving

Crankcase Mods

The 1992 CR250 has a problem of poor oil flow between the trans and clutch cavity. On any dirt bike, when the clutch is spinning it forces the oil into the transmission. There has to be passageways that link the trans and clutch cavities so the oil can circulate and cool the clutch. Starting in 1993 Honda bored two more oil flow passages in the right-

side crankcase, linking the two cavities. If your 1992 CR250 is burning up clutch plates frequently, drill two 8-mm holes in the right case half to provide a passage for the oil.

Carburetor

The jetting needs to be richened to a #1368 needle and a #185 main jet.

Cylinder Head Modification

Index the spark plug depth by turning down on a lathe. The spark plug lug must be turned down .040 inch. If the cylinder base hasn't been yet turned, then .5mm can be turned off the cylinder head gasket surface. This will reduce the minimum clearance space from between the piston and head, increase the compression ratio, and give a stronger pulling powerband for more torque.

Cylinder Tuning

The original Honda castings are excellent and the port timing is consistent. However a big increase in low-end torque can be gained with the proper use of epoxy and a right-angle hand-grinding tool. This work is better left to professional tuners. The cylinders are interchangeable between the 1992–2000 models. The 1995, '96, and '99 cylinders are the best because of the smaller exhaust and intake ports. These cylinders have the best timing combination and the most sealing surface

HONDA FAQs

Retro Honda Cartridge Forks

Question: I have a question about an older bike. I have a 1985 CR250 and I'm looking for better performance from the forks. Is there a cartridge-fork kit for these older bikes?

Answer: The Race Tech Emulator Valve is well known as a fork kit for modern mini-cycles, and it fits into the older non-cartridge forks. The kit is easy to install because it just slides in from the top of the fork and is held in place by the fork spring. When you install the Emulator Valve, clean the fork's internal parts. Check and replace the fork bushings and seals and add new fork oil. New fork springs will reduce front-end diving and headshake at the end of fast straightaways. All fork-spring manufacturers have recommendations for the correct spring rate for your model bike and your riding weight. Guides such as these are published and printed in catalogs.

1995 CR Fork Recall

Question: I heard that Honda issued a recall on the 1995 CR's forks, in March of that year. What is the problem with the forks? Did Kawasaki and Yamaha issue similar recalls on their Kayaba forks? I just bought a used 1995 CR250 and I want to find out if the forks were ever fixed.

Answer: The problem with the 1995 Honda Kayaba forks is a possibility that a limited number of fork tubes weren't heat-treated properly. The defective fork tubes can crack near the bottom of the tube where the axle clamp is fastened. If you have a 1995 dirt bike with Kayaba forks, check with your local franchised dealer. Your bike's serial number is registered with the manufacturer. Dealers have access to a computer record of what factory directed recalls or updates need to be performed with your bike.

A similar problem of loose or broken front axle clamps can occur with riding use. Check your older bike by removing the front wheel. Grasp the fork tube with one hand and the axle clamp with the other hand. Try to flex the two apart. Check for looseness or clicking noises. Look for hairline cracks in the aluminum clamp. Also check the axle, when it is clamped to the fork. If it's a loose fit, the axle and fork tube will need to be replaced because there is no way to repair this type of damage.

1989 Shock Rebound Adjuster Seized

Question: I have a 1989 CR250, and the rear shock's rebound adjuster is seized. I can't turn it with a screwdriver. What's wrong?

Answer: The problem you describe is common for Showa shocks on 1986–89 CR250s and CR500s. The rebound adjuster consists of a fine-threaded screw and a ramp-shaped nut. Condensation causes the fine threads to become corroded, and the corrosion keeps the adjuster screw from turning. It is possible to remove the rebound adjuster cartridge and clean the threads of the screw so the adjuster works. This task requires that you discharge the nitrogen gas pressure from the shock's bladder. If you do not have the special tools or knowledge required to service suspension components, then don't try to repair the adjuster. Instead, trust the job to a professional suspension technician

1996 Keihin Carburetors

Question: I heard that some of the 1996 bikes have a Keihin carb that has an extra jet. How does this carb differ from current production carbs?

Answer: The 1996 Suzuki RMs and Honda CRs sport the new Keihin carbs. This carb uses an old idea of an auxiliary main jet to deliver more fuel during sustained full throttle running. Many companies sell aftermarket accessory kits that offer the same benefits. These products work excellent for desert riding. Terry Varner of FMF makes a system that allows you to adjust the fuel flow as you ride. It is a very popular kit with desert racers.

area for the rings. The 1999 cylinder has extremely small exhaust ports and has smooth power delivery. I think that it works great on the 1997 and '98 models to tame them down. However many people complain that the 1999 model is flat on top end. For the 1999 model I recommend raising only the sub exhaust ports to 39mm measured from the top of the cylinder. The smaller intake port doesn't hinder performance and is stronger to reduce piston skirt wear. The cylinders with the smaller intake port are easier to install because the rings are less likely to pop out of the grooves when sliding the cylinder down on the piston. More crankcase compression is gained by applying the epoxy on alternate sides of the separating bridge. This also changes the flow-pattern up through the transfer ports and into the cylinder bore. Flow-shaping is also performed on the rear transfer port window exit angles. This cylinder will peak at 7,500 rpm and work great with the stock pipe, stock or spark arrestor silencer, and intake system. To attain the optimum compression ratio and exhaust port's time-area on the 1992-94 model cylinders, the cylinder base must be turned down (.5mm) on a lathe. Now the transfer ports must be raised to a dimension of 58mm measured from the top of the cylinder.

Flywheel Weight

The final component for tuning is the flywheel weight. Tuners normally overlook this component. Dave Watson teaches riding schools in England. Dave thinks that flywheel weights make the power delivery easier for most riders to handle. Especially junior and vet motocross riders, or trail riders.

Swingarm

The 1992 CR250 had a problem with cracks forming in the swingarm. The swingarm can be gusseted for added strength. The biggest cause of a cracked swingarm is too little chain slack. Take care when adjusting the chain, it's better to be a bit loose than tight.

1990-91 HONDA CR250

Flaws: leaky air boot, carbon seized HPP valves, fork debris

Fixes: seal boot, chamfer HPP valves, Eibach springs and Pro-Action preload cones

These bikes were very reliable but had some handling problems that are easily fixed. The engines produced good torque but the exhaust valve system is difficult to service. Here are some fix-it and tuning tips for these models of CR250s.

Best Value Mods

Engine: carb jetting, flywheel weight

Suspension: aftermarket springs, Pro-Action cones

HPP Valve Mods

The HPP valves are prone to carbon seizing; see the recommendations listed in the chapter on exhaust valve servicing.

Carb Jetting

Here are some jetting specs when using a 40 to 1 pre-mix ratio with 93 octane-unleaded fuels and an NGK BP7ES spark plug: 55 slow jet, 1369 needle in the third position, and a 175 main jet.

Air box sealing

The air-boot-to-air-box flange must be sealed on the older CRs. The best sealer to use is weather-strip adhesive because it isn't fuel soluble. Never use silicone sealer because the fuel will deteriorate the sealer and allow water and dirt to enter the air box.

Cylinder Tuning

There are some simple mods that can be performed to the cylinder with just a file. The casting flaws around the boost ports should be removed for smoother flow through the intake and the HPP valve guides should be matched to the exhaust port. This is a critical area of the cylinder because even a small mismatch can cause a shock wave that effectively blocks the exhaust port. Other more difficult mods include raising the transfer ports to 58mm from the top of the cylinder, turning down the cylinder base 0.5mm, and narrowing the rear transfer ports as listed in the paragraph for the late-model CRs.

Head Mods

The top of the spark plug lug must be turned down on a lathe 3mm to allow the spark plug to thread down flush into the

The aluminum frames need attention at the engine mounts. If you notice an excessive gap when the bolts are loosened, a shim should be installed to tighten the gap. Washers can be used for shims and Kawasaki lists thin shims in their parts book for the KX250.

combustion chamber. This mod improves throttle response and reduces spark plug cold fouling.

Flywheel Weight

The CRs benefit from a flywheel weight. Sixteen ounces is the standard size that companies such as A-Loop or Steahly use for their products, although they will have several options available. In general, heavier weights are better for enduro and off-road while lighter weights are geared toward motocross or Supercross. For novice and intermediate riders, the heavier weights can work very well. Power delivery is just a bit more manageable and low-end is greatly improved. The result is the bike is easier to control yet delivers the same amount of horsepower.

There are two different types of flywheel weights, weld-on and thread-on. A-Loop performs the weld-on flywheel weight service. Steahly makes thread-on flywheel weights. This product threads onto the fine left-hand threads that are on the center hub of most Japanese magneto rotors. Normally the threads are used for the flywheel remover tool. Thread-on flywheel weights can only be used if the threads on the flywheel are in perfect condition. The advantage to weld-on weights is they can't possibly come off.

Big Displacement Kits

If your cylinder's plating is worn and needs to be repaired, consider a Wiseco big oversize piston kit. Wiseco offers pistons in the size 265cc for AMA legal competition in the 250 classes. This kit requires modifications to the exhaust valves.

Ignition Timing

Advancing the ignition timing gives the CR more midrange hit in the powerband. Normally Honda stator plates aren't adjustable. To make the plate adjustable you need to file the plate 1mm at the lower bolt hole. This will enable you to rotate the stator plate clockwise to advance the ignition timing.

Crankshaft Seal

The left-side crankshaft seal is prone to failure. Honda redesigned the seal in 1992. The main reason that the seal fails is due to dirt and water entering the ignition cover Boyesen Engineering makes an aluminum cover that seals properly. If your CR bogs at low rpm, the seal is probably blown and needs to be replaced.

Fuel Tank Insert Nuts

The fuel tank insert nuts are square shaped and pressed into reliefs in the plastic

This is the Service Honda CR500AF. It's a hybrid based on the CR250 chassis and CR500 engine.

The big CRs went through an amazing design evolution in the late 1980s. The suspension on them went from drilled passageways and squirting fork oil to upside down cartridge forks and a rear shock with technology rivaling an Ohlins. The CRs changed more in 5 years than they did in the previous 12 years since their inception. There are many innovative products built by European and American companies to bring the mid-1980s CRs into the 1990s. The CR250s can be improved greatly. The 1986 and 1987 models shared the same exhaust valve system, and this was a very controllable motorcycle. However, the HPP system requires frequent service. Here is a survey of the products and mods for these timeless motorcycles.

Best Value Mods

Engine: 1369 carb needle, chamfer HPP valves, T-vents in carburetor

Suspension: fork springs, check linkage bolts

CR250 Exhaust Valves

The earlier models (1984–85) have a butterfly valve linked to a can at the exhaust manifold to increase the volume of the header pipe at low rpm and boost the low-end power. The butterfly valves are prone to carbon build-up, which locks the valve in the open position and reduces the top-end power of the engine.

Suspension

Honda had problems determining the proper fork-spring preload on the early cartridge forks. They used too much on production bikes, sometimes as much as 30mms! The proper amount is 5–15mms. The best fork spring rates to use are 0.40–0.41 kilograms for the CR250 and 0.44 kilograms for the CR500. The Race Tech Emulator Valve is about the only aftermarket accessory that you can use to improve the handling of the older CRs. It's the closest thing to a cartridge fork.

Linkage

Other trouble points include the suspension linkage and the floating rear drum brakes of the 1985 and 1986 models. The 1988 CR250 had chronic problems with bent rear-shock-linkage bolts, until Honda re-

---

fuel tank. When the scoop bolts are over tightened, the insert nuts tend to spin in the tank when the bolt is removed. That makes it impossible to remove the radiator scoop. The solution is to remove the insert nut and epoxy bond it back in place. Removing the nut will be difficult. I use an air impact wrench to spin the bolt fast, while using a large flat screwdriver to pry off the scoop, just behind the insert nut. Take care not to puncture the fuel tank. Once you remove the scoop and insert nut, you can grasp the square insert nut with a wrench or channel -lock pliers and remove the bolt. Apply a dab of Duro Master-Mend epoxy to the insert nut and the relief in the fuel tank. Press the insert nut in place for about 15 minutes.

Forks

These cartridge forks have the early-model valve design with the small-diameter piston. They are prone to clogging with metal debris. These forks have to be disassembled and cleaned often. The main sources for the metal debris are the springs and the spring preload cones. The springs have a coating that flakes off. The preload cones are made of steel with sharp-machined edges. That cone fits into the spring and aggravates the flaking problem. The solution is to use Eibach brand fork springs. They are powder-coated with a flexible material that doesn't flake off. Pro-Action makes an aluminum preload cone

that doesn't wear or vibrate like the stock steel cone. Performing these two mods will save you money in fork oil changes and improve the bike's handling.

Some suspension companies offer the service of hard anodizing for the fork parts. On bikes produced after 1989, most of the fork parts are hard anodized from the manufacturer. Hard anodizing prevents the aluminum parts from wearing prematurely. This service is used for repair of the slider tubes on the 1990 and later CR250 models.

Many companies make aftermarket base valve kits for cartridge forks. These products offer improvements in performance because of changes to the piston design and the valve shim stacks. If you are going through the expense of installing a base valve kit, make sure that the fork springs are matched to your riding weight, skill level, and the base valve kit. Companies such as Race Tech provide a tuning manual with their Gold Valve products. The tuning manual provides guidelines on spring rates and valving changes for a variety of different rider profiles.

1985-89 HONDA CR250 & CR500

Flaws: soft fork springs, magneto covers leak, air boot leaks

Fixes: stiffer fork springs, Boyesen magneto cover, seal air boot

designed the parts and added flanges to the heads of the bolts. The part numbers for the new bolts are H/C 2976678 and H/C 2976686. The CR linkage requires careful attention and frequent lubing. A seized linkage can put an enormous strain on the frame, causing everything from cracks in the frame to leaks at the head gasket.

Rear Wheel

In 1989 Honda redesigned the rear hub to be lighter. It was too weak and shattered. Honda had a recall campaign in Europe but not in America. The 1990 hubs looked similar to the 1987 hubs, with a conical taper compared to the straight-diameter hub of the 1989 model. Tallon makes an excellent replacement hub that is far stronger than the stock hub.

Ergonomic Changes

Some simple bolt-on parts for the rest of the chassis include wider footpegs, stiffer seat foam, a skid plate to protect the frame, and a cable to prevent the rear brake lever from tearing off in berms.

Engine

The only real change to the CR500 in the late 1980s was the addition of water-cooling. The air-cooled models suffered from detonation, and the cylinder head had to be modified to lower the compression ratio and narrow the width of the squish band.

Spark Plug

The best spark plug heat range is an NGK BP7ES.

Carb Problems

The carb's fuel-inlet needle and seat wear out quickly because of the vibration, causing the engine to flood when the bike is dropped. Change them every season.

Silencer

The later-model CR500s suffered from chronic breakage of the silencer core. The silencer needs to be packed often; otherwise' there is nothing to protect the core tube from vibration.

Reed Valve

In 1986, Honda put a plastic insert in

This is Scott Summer's last air-cooled XR. Scott and his dad make all sorts of trick parts for these bikes. Summer's Racing Concepts can be reached at 800-221-9752.

the reed valve to boost the velocity by stuffing the dead-air space. Aftermarket "reed stuffers" are available from FMF. Boyesen reeds are a good investment because the reed stop plates block the cylinder's rear boost port. Boyesen reeds are more responsive than original Honda reeds and they don't require the stop plates.

Carburetor

Jetting for the 1986–91 models burning 93-octane pump gas and a pre-mix ratio of 40:1 should be 55 slow jet, 1369 needle, and 172 main jet. Take care setting the float level and replace the inlet needle and seat every year. Changing to a modern T-vent system for the carb is also beneficial. In this way, if you ride through mud your bike won't vapor lock because the mud splattered up under the bike blocks the carb's float bowl vents.

Ignition System

The ignition systems require frequent maintenance in the form of cleaning the inside of the flywheel. The dirt and water that get drawn in from the plastic side cover cause the coils to break down, the flywheel to get corroded, and the left-side crankshaft seal to wear. Boyesen Engineering makes aluminum side covers that seal better than the stock plastic ones, plus they function as a heat sink to transfer damaging engine heat away from

the ignition. Ignition coils and spark plug caps tend to break down on the CRs.

Air Box

The air-boot flanges on the CRs tend to leak after you pressure-wash the bike with strong detergents. Reseal the air boot with weather-strip adhesive, available from auto parts stores.

1990-2000 HONDA CR500

Flaws: abrupt powerband, headshaking
Fixes: lower compression ratio, stiffer fork springs

The CR500 hasn't changed much in the past 5 years and there is a lot you can do to this bike. The engine hits abruptly and riders complain that it is hard to ride on slippery surfaces. Here are some mods that will help the engine pull smoothly from low-end and rev out further.

Best Value Mods

Engine: DEP Sport pipe and silencer
Suspension: fork springs

Carburetor

A 39.5mm Keihin PWK carb will add 3 horsepower to the top end and make the engine pull cleanly off the low end. Sudco sells an aftermarket PWK or you can use a carb from a KX500 1992 and later.

Cylinder Head

Reshaping the transition between the combustion chamber and the squish band can be accomplished by turning the head on a lathe. Set the tool angle to 25 degrees and cut into the squish band starting 15mm from the edge of the chamber. Install a projected nose spark plug such as a NGK BP6ES.

Cylinder

The hook angles of the rear transfer ports should be filled with epoxy so the transfers are aimed at each other instead of towards the exhaust port. The narrower the port, the smoother the low-end power. The minimum chordal width of each rear transfer port is 10mm. Raise the exhaust port 1.5mm and widen the two ports 4mm on each outer edge. The steel sleeve should be matched to the aluminum casting because

SRC makes a brace for conventional forks.

it is very rough from the original manufacturing process. Polish the port edges with fine grit sanding paper. That will improve piston and ring life.

The bore of the cylinder should be monitored for out-of-round wear and taper wear. I have had the best luck running oversize Wiseco pistons, set to 0.004-inch piston to bore clearance.

Exhaust System

Pro-Circuit, FMF, and DEP Sport make excellent pipe and silencer combinations for the CR500.

Fork Springs

Riders who weigh over 170 pounds may want to switch to a stiffer spring rate (23–25 pounds). If bottoming and headshake occur frequently, that is a sign that you need stiffer fork springs and higher fork oil level. The highest fork oil level is 120mms, for the minimum air space and highest pressure.

1990-2000 HONDA CR80

Flaws: fork damping
Fixes: Emulator Valve

This bike hardly changed from 1987 to 1995. The engine was excellent, a design far ahead of its time, but the chassis and the suspension were archaic. The swingarm on the early models was stamped sheet metal and clipped together. Later, Honda changed to a conventional welded design. The forks are simple oil-orifice, damper rod type. This suspension set-up is the single biggest hindrance to an aspiring mini racer. The biggest problem with the CR is the spring rates of the forks and shock. Pro-Action makes a selection of different springs, calibrated accurately. Ask a suspension tuner for his recommendations on both front and rear spring choices, based on the rider's weight, height, and ability. Heavier or especially tall riders will need stiffer springs, for obvious reasons.

Forks

Riders who use the front brakes hard will need stiffer fork springs to prevent the front end from diving abruptly in braking bumps. These forks are damper rod, not cartridge, forks. There are two ways to change the damping rate: either change the viscosity of the oil (SAE 10 wt.) or vary the diameter of the hole in the damping rod. Changing the oil height will only change the bottoming characteristics of the fork but not the damping. In 1994 a new product became available for CR forks. It's called the Emulator Valve, and Race Tech makes it. This valve improves the damping of the compression and rebound circuits, emulating the effect of cartridge forks. The valve costs just over $100 and is easy to install. The Emulator Valve fits between the fork spring and the damper rod of each fork leg. For a more detailed view of exactly how the Emulator Valve is installed, visit the "Moto Professor's" Web site at www.motocross.com/motoprof.

Shock

The low-speed compression damping is too soft. Try adjusting the clicker to between 4-6 clicks out.

Big Wheel Suspension

Most riders will benefit from stiffer springs on both ends. Companies like Race Spec and Pro-Action specialize in hard-to-get springs for minis. The rear shock needs more compression damping because the longer swingarm causes the shock's shaft speed to be slower. Also the rebound damping is too stiff. Try adjusting the clickers to remedy these problems.

Cylinder

The port timing of the stock cylinder is OK for most riders. For expert riders, I suggest widening the right rear transfer port to 17mm, the same width as the corresponding left rear transfer. The exhaust port can be raised to a maximum height of 24mm, measured from the top of the cylinder. These mods will help top-end power. One common problem to watch for on all CR80s is chronic head gasket leaks. The problem is not the head or gasket, it's the top of the cylinder. The surface has imperfections all around the stud holes and the water ports. The way to fix this problem is to start by removing the studs, then lapp the top surface of the cylinder on a flat surface using medium grit sandpaper as an abrasive medium.

1987-95 HONDA CR80 BIG-WHEEL & 100CC CONVERSIONS FOR ALL YEARS

The big-wheel CR80 became available in 1996. Before then, if you wanted to build a super mini, you had to buy special chassis parts only available in England.

Dave Watson of Race Spec in England makes a big-wheel kit for all CR80s prior to 1996. The kit consists of rims, spokes, Bridgestone tires, swingarm, and fork caps. The fork caps extend the fork tubes to accommodate the 19-inch front wheel. If you use this kit, consider using stiffer springs. The longer swingarm places greater leverage on the shock spring.

Wiseco makes a Pro-Lite piston kit to convert the 82cc cylinder to 99cc. This kit is designed for use with overboring and electroplating. Cometic makes a steel head gasket to fit the larger 51mm bore size. This 100cc conversion also requires a modification to the cylinder head. Some companies are offering larger pistons for the CR, but that can present many other problems related to crankshaft balance and the demands on the cooling system. The Wiseco 99cc piston makes the engine more reliable than stock!

HONDA XR TUNING

with Scott Summers and Fred Bramblett

Honda XRs are used for everything from play riding to hare scrambles to desert racing. They are perhaps the most bulletproof and widely used dirt bikes on the planet. Although enduro and trail riders have been using XRs for decades, Scott Summers, one of the best off-road riders in the sport, has put a number one plate on the flanks of an XR600 for several times in the 1990s and has demonstrated that XRs are capable of much more than just plunking down trails or crawling through the woods. He and his mechanic Fred Bramblett are not your typical rider-mechanic duo. They are motorcycle innovators. They've devised some interesting innovations for the XR line of Hondas. They've tested just about everything possible for XRs. Whether they are racing the Baja 1000, the ISDE, or cow-trailing through the deep woods of Kentucky, they know the set-up that works

best. Here are some of their tips on products to improve the longevity and performance of the XR line of motorcycles.

ROUTINE MAINTENANCE

These are some of the maintenance tasks that you will need to perform after every hare scrambles race or long trail-riding weekend.

Engine
Air Filter

Clean the air filter and the air box after every ride. Check the filter for excess oil build-up near the point where the crankcase vent enters the air box. If the rings are worn, crankcase oil will flow up the vent and into the air box and coat the filter. This can cause a rich fuel jetting condition.

Oil and Filter

Change the crankcase oil after every two rides and the filter on every other oil change. Check the wire mesh screens that are mounted in the bottom of the frame and in the crankcase. If you ride a mud race and have to fan the clutch often, the fiber clutch plates can start to disintegrate and pollute the crankcase oil. These particles will become trapped in the wire mesh filters. You should clean these filters at least twice each year.

Lube the Cables

Lube and adjust the clutch and throttle cables. Remember that the clutch cable free-play will be reduced as the clutch plates wear.

Valve Adjustment

The XRs don't need frequent valve adjustment, but keep in mind that the valve lash will be reduced as the valve and seat wear. Check and adjust the valve lash every 200 miles or after every fifth riding weekend.

Chassis
Chain and Sprockets

Clean the chain and sprockets after every ride, then lube the chain and check the free-play. Inspect the sprockets for chipped teeth, caused by rocks. Check the alignment of the rear chain guide. Sometimes rocks or ruts can bend the guide, causing the guide to push the chain out of alignment with the rear sprocket. This problem can cause the chain to derail.

Keep It Greased

The XRs have grease zerks mounted in the swingarm and linkage pivots. You should grease the zerks after every other ride for two reasons: to force water and dirt from the bearing cavity and to lube the bearing. Fred Bramblett fits grease zerks to the neck of the XR frame, to provide grease to the steering head bearings. The zerks are mounted to the frame and the races are notched to allow the grease to enter the bearing. The service interval for greasing the steering head bearings is every four rides. That may seem frequent, but consider that the XR holds the crankcase oil in the frame. When the oil gets hot the frame temperature rises and the grease in the steering head bearings can melt disperse from the bearing.

Spokes

Because the XR is a fairly heavy dirt bike, the spokes require frequent attention. Check the spokes after every ride and don't be tempted to over-tighten the spokes. That can cause the rims to crack.

Brake Fluid

Change the brake fluid after every four rides. Use Dot 4 fluid.

Damage Control

The XR models are well-developed bikes that are extremely reliable. The one fault that even great bikes can't escape is their ability to survive a crash. Crashing is one thing that all dirt bikers do from time to time. The rider-mechanic team of Summers and Bramblett have bumped their heads together to come up with a line of products that help make the XR more resistant to crash damage. They've come up with some interesting innovations to improve the XRs. Their products are available through Summers Racing Concepts (800) 221-9752.

Foot Levers

The shift and brake levers are reinforced to prevent them from bending, but are also designed so they break off clean to minimize

This is the SRC chain guard.

damage to more expensive components. For example, the shift lever is designed to break clean at the shift shaft during really hard impacts. In that way the shift shaft doesn't bend or damage the crankcases. A stainless steel cable wraps around the end of the levers and connects to the frame, to prevent tree branches from becoming wedged between the side covers and the levers. The cables also serve to

prevent the levers from snaring when riding through deep ruts.

Wire Protectors

The Summers team noticed a common problem with XRs. It is common for the wires and rubber plug that exit from the right-side engine cover to get snared by branches and yanked out of the side cover. This allows the crankcase oil to leak out of the side cover and eventually cause catastrophic engine damage. The guys developed an aluminum guard to protect the wires from tree branches. The guard just bolts on to a few of the side cover's mounting screws, and silicone seal is applied to further insulate the wires.

Chain Guard

The original chain guard should be modified to allow the chain to derail downward, if the chain is forced off the sprockets or breaks. It is possible for the chain to bunch-up and break the crankcases with the original guard design.

Fork Brace

A special fork brace was developed for the conventional cartridge forks used on the XR650L, XR600, and the new XR400. The brace reduces the front wheel deflection when riding over ruts or over large rocks.

XR Performance Options

If you are considering bolt-on performance parts or high-performance services for your XR, you need to consider your riding demands and the type of terrain that you ride on. There are myriad products available for the XR, products designed to suit a wide variety of different applications. Here is a survey of the different engine components, and how certain products are designed for either high-speed off-road or slow-speed woods riding.

Cooling Systems

There are two ways to improve the cooling systems of air-cooled engines: welding additional fins to the head and cylinder or in-stalling an oil cooler. The oil cooler is the most efficient set-up for reducing the engine temperature. The weld-on fin set-up is commonly used on desert racers that run at high speeds where there is more free air available to take advantage of the additional fins. XR's Only and Ballard Cycles sell the weld-on fin kits. Lockhart makes an aftermarket oil cooler, or you can adapt the OEM oil cooler from the XR250 to the XR600.

High-Compression Piston

Wiseco makes an optional high-compression piston for the XR600. Higher-compression pistons are generally more beneficial for slow-speed woods riding or high altitude riding.

Carburetor

The stock carb works great for woods riding and many riders prefer a larger, 41mm carb for desert racing. The White Bros. 41mm carb kit gives an increase of about 4 horsepower and 6 mph. However, this larger carb sacrifices slow-speed throttle response that is important for woods riding over muddy or rocky terrain.

Head Pipe

There are three types of head pipes: straight, tapered, and oversized. All OEM head pipes are straight. The XR head pipes are two different lengths. This effectively widens the powerband at low rpm with a sacrifice in peak power. The Summers team uses the tapered head pipe marketed by Yoshimura. A tapered head pipe improves scavenging efficiency and reduces pumping losses because the pipe draws out the exhaust gases rather than relying on the piston to pump out the cylinder. Typically, tapered head pipes can cause odd jetting problems, but Fred Bramblett says that he hasn't experienced any jetting problems with the Yoshimura pipe. Tapered head pipes work best with OEM cams or ones with slightly retarded exhaust timing. Oversize head pipes are generally used in conjunction with big bore kits, or for high rpm applications such as desert racing or DTX.

Tailpipe

There are two types of tailpipes: straight through silencers and spark arrestors. Some riding areas and racing organizations require the use of spark arrestors on off-road motorcycles. Check with the rules before you purchase an expensive aftermarket tailpipe. Straight through silencers provide the right flow characteristic and resultant backpressure to produce maximum power over a wide rpm band. Spark arrestors have a series of baffles that prevent particles of combustible gases from exiting the tailpipe. The Summers team uses the Yoshimura tailpipe for closed course racing.

Camshaft

The Summers team uses the stock XR cam for hare scrambles and enduro racing, and the HRC cam for desert racing. The HRC cam has a higher lift and longer duration. Most aftermarket cams offer 2-4 degrees of duration over OEM cams. Increasing the duration generally improves peak power but changing the overlap of the intake and exhaust has a more dramatic effect on the powerband. Decreasing the overlap improves low-end torque with a sacrifice of peak power, while increasing the overlap improves peak power with a sacrifice of low-end power.

Chapter 12

TUNING TIPS FOR KAWASAKI DIRT BIKES

1998-2000 KAWASAKI KX125

Flaws: too high compression, exhaust valve sticks open
Fixes: head mods, Pro-Circuit valve cover, stiffer springs

The 1998 model represented the latest generation of the KX125. Although it had some minor problems it was a significant change over the previous generation. The 1998 model started with problems like being sluggish and sprung soft, but by the time the 2000 model was released the magazines were praising it as the best bike of the class.

Best Value Mods

Engine: head mods, Pro-Circuit pipe, silencer, and valve cover
Suspension: stiffer springs, Pro-Action Incremental Valving

New KIPS System

The 1998 model was the first year of the new exhaust valve system. Initially Kaw had a recall on the valves because they would seat deeper into the valve cavity and eventually contact the piston. Another common problem is breakage of the pin the flapper valve pivots on. The most chronic problem is the valve sticking wide open. Pro-Circuit makes a replacement valve cover that includes a stopper to prevent the valves from opening too far and jamming. The 1999 model featured a huge improvement in the exhaust valve. It is thicker, so the low-end power is improved and built more heavy duty. Unfortunately the new valve won't fit in the older 1998 cylinder but the entire 1999 cylinder and valve will fit on the 1998 crankcases.

Head Mods

The compression ratio on the 1998-99 models is good for a typical MX or enduro engine but makes the powerband run flat at high rpm. Modifying the head for greater chamber volume will improve the top-end power but reduce the low-end power. Normally, I just narrow the squish band by 2mm on a lathe by setting the tool angle to 22 degrees and cutting into the bowl. Afterwards the head can be polished with some medium grit sandpaper to remove the tool marks.

Cylinder Porting

With the 1998 cylinders, tuners tried all sorts of things, such as lowering the transfers by turning-down the cylinder base, widening the exhaust port, narrowing the exhaust bridge, and even grinding the exhaust valve cavity deeper near the bore so the flapper valve would open the port completely. In 2000, Kaw seems to have got the porting right. They dropped the transfer ports and raised the exhaust. If you're looking for more low-end power you can have the cylinder turned-down .75mm and the head's squish band machined for a 1mm recess. For more top-end power, just experiment with layering base gaskets.

Suspension
Forks

In 2000 Kaw changed the forks in a subtle way. In an effort to make the forks more like twin chamber designs, they added a rubber gas bladder to separate the air space from the oil to prevent mixing or aeration of the oil. In the summer of 1999, Ricky Carmichael's factory bike was seen with hose connections to the fork caps. The fork caps were plumbed with hoses that attached to a central gas accumulator. That way the forks would be more balanced. It was a new use for a tried-and-true idea.

1997 KAWASAKI KX125

Flaws: sluggish acceleration, soft front end
Fixes: igniter box, stiffer fork springs

Just when the 1996 model was starting to perform as well as the 1994 model, Kaw took a step back with the 1997 bike. Overall it's a reliable bike and performs well as a trail bike. But for MX it doesn't accelerate as quickly as some of the other bikes and the suspension is too soft because Kaw chose to use progressive-rate fork and shock springs. Early and later models used straight-rate springs. The acceleration shortcoming is due to a combination of things like the cylinder, ignition, and crankshaft.

Best Value Mods

Engine: 1996 ignition box, porting for low end
Suspension: straight-rate fork springs

Ignition

The black box on the 1997 model is programmed for a conservative advance curve. That hurts the midrange hit that is so critical on technical tracks. The 1996 model black box works much better (No. 21119-1453). When switching to the '96 black box, for best results advance the ignition timing to the far mark stamped on the stator plate.

Cylinder and Head Mods

The '97 cylinder is nearly identical to the 1995-96 models. These models suffer the same problem: The transfer ports open too soon. In order to lower or retard the transfer ports' opening timing, the cylinder base must be turned down on a lathe by .6 mm. The exhaust ports must be raised to 28 mm, measured from the top of the cylinder. The cylinder head's squish band must be relieved by .5 mm. The angle of the cut on the squish band is 7 degrees.

Lighter Crankshaft

Although Team Green in America recommends installing the 1996 model crankshaft

when the 1997 crank wears out, I don't think the difference in weight is worth the expense. The lighter 1996 crank makes the engine rev quicker (No. 13031-1407), but lacks the ability to control wheel-spin in slippery track conditions like the '97 crank. You choose which crankshaft might benefit your riding situations.

Forks

The forks work pretty well for most riders. Use Team Green's recommendations on determining which spring rate is best for you.

Shock

There are two ways to make a bike turn tighter: use different pull rods in the linkage, or extend the shock travel. Both methods enable the rear end to ride higher, and transfer more weight to the front end. Pro-Circuit and DeVol Racing offer aftermarket pull rods. The simplest way to lengthen the shock travel is to install two 18X.3mm shims between the top-out plate and the shock shaft.

Check Link Bolt

Check the torque of the linkage bolts—that is the only chronic problem with the KX—otherwise the bike is extremely reliable and inexpensive to maintain. Check the entire bike's bolts between races, and use non-permanent locking agent on the threads of the bolts and screws.

1993-96 KAWASAKI KX125

Flaws: stiff rear suspension
Fixes: revalve softer

The KX125 peaked in 1994. The 1996 model used the same linkage ratio and power-valve governor. The 1996 model was the first to use the new Keihin carb with airfoils. The 1993 model had the best top-end power but the later models had much wider powerbands. The good thing about Kawasakis is that you can mix and match OEM engine components to change your bike's powerband. For example, when converting a 1993 model for enduro riding, use the 1995 cylinder, head, piston, and wedge valves. The following are some tips on changing the KX125s engine for different types of powerbands.

This is a view of the KX60 boost ports and how they fit with the crankcase.

Best Value Mods

Engine: cylinder porting
Suspension: Pro-Circuit link rods, shock revalving

Supercross/Enduro Powerband

The stock 1994 and newer intake parts and pipe are ideal for Supercross, enduro riding, or novice motocross. These tuning components have a peak of about 9,600 rpm. The 1993 and older intakes were designed for a 13,000-rpm peak. However, the 1993 cylinder and head can be greatly improved. Using TSR design software, I examined the 1993 cylinder and found that the rear transfer ports are too big. Also, the exhaust-port timing is very radical. The solution is to turn down .7mm from the base of the cylinder. This will retard the port timing and boost the compression ratio. Then remove the same amount of metal from the cylinder head's squish band to maintain the proper piston-to-head clearance of 1mm.

Next, use epoxy to re-shape and narrow the two rear transfer ports. The width of each rear transfer port should be 14mms, and they should be aimed directly at each other. This will improve the gas flow between 3,000 and 8,000 rpm and make the engine pull strong in the midrange. You won't have to fan the clutch with this little tractor!

Cylinder Interchange

The cylinders of the 1993 and 1994 models interchange. The 1993 cylinder is best for high rpm because of the size of the transfer and exhaust ports. Also, the exhaust duct on those cylinders is round instead of the smaller oval diameter of the 1994 cylinders. The 1994 cylinder is best for low-range to midrange, plus there is greater sealing surface for the piston and rings, so they last longer. The cylinder heads do not interchange because of flat versus domed pistons and water spigot positions of the different model years of KX125s. The 1995 KX125 cylinder will not interchange with earlier models because the center wedge exhaust valves are thicker.

Hi-Rpm MX Powerband 1994–96 KX125

The biggest improvement you can make in the top-end power of the 1994–96 KX is to switch to some engine parts from the 1993 KX. Parts such as the intake system will enable the 1994–96 models to rev to 12,500 rpm. The 1995 model needs different power valve governor parts because that year's design was faulty and prevented the KIPS valves from opening fully. Here are some tips on modifying the KX125s for more top end.

Carburetor

Use a 38mm Keihin PWK. The carb's air-boot spigot will need to be turned down and cut shorter to fit into the 1994–96 air boot. The 1994 model uses a small-body (35mm) Keihin PWK carb, and it can be bored to a maximum of 37mm.

Intake System

The reed valve from the 1993 KX is designed for better flow at high rpm, much bet-

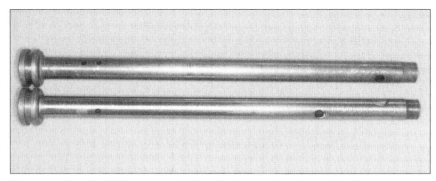
These are the Terry-Kit KX60 damper rods. They offer improved damping and 1-inch longer travel.

ter than the four-petal reed valve introduced in 1994. Install the 1993 reed valve and intake manifold (Kawasaki part numbers 12021-1085 and 16065-1246) in later-model KXs. The crankcases will need to be modified to accept the larger reed valve.

Crankcase Mods

In order to install the bigger reed valve from the 1993 model, the engine must be disassembled to modify the crankcases. It is necessary to remove about 0.080 inch or 2mm from the top and bottom of the reed valve cavity in the crankcases.

Air Box

The side panel ducts must be cut away with a hacksaw to enlarge the air ducts to the air box. You can also remove the clear-plastic splash shield from the front, top edge of the air box; this will also improve airflow.

Cylinder Head Mods

The squish band in the cylinder head is too wide to be revved to 12,800 rpm! Narrow the squish band's width to 5mms, using a lathe.

Ignition

The igniter box from the 1996 model should be installed on earlier models because the timing curve is better suited to a high-revved engine.

Power-Valve Governor

The governor is a spring-loaded centrifugal device controling the KIPS exhaust valve position in relation to engine rpm. When the engine gets to 8,000 rpm, the power-valve governor's steel balls develop enough centrifugal force to overcome the ten-

sion of the spring. The 1995 model had a two-stage ramp cup, designed to widen the powerband. Unfortunately the second angle of the ramp cup was too steep, so the governor never fully shifted. This prevented the exhaust valves from opening fully. The 1994 and 1996 models use ramp cup No. 49111-1051. It's best to switch to that part on the 1995 KX125.

Link Stay Bars

Pro-Circuit makes link stay bars for the 1993–96 bikes. This changes the rear ride height and transfers the weight differently, so the bike turns tighter. Caution: Because of the wide production tolerances on Japanese dirt bikes, you need to check the clearance between the aftermarket stay bars and the swingarm through the total rear wheel travel. You have to do this with the shock removed, and file the stay bars or swingarm if either part contacts the other.

Rear Shock

The original shock compression valving is too stiff. It must be revalved softer. Not only does this mod improve the bike's handling, but it also reduces shock fade. Shock fade is less likely because revalving the shock for softer/faster compression damping lowers the velocity of the shock fluid. Enzo Racing in America sells a thick foam bottoming cone and an extended reservoir cap for Kayaba shocks. The foam cone helps prevent the shock from bottoming hard and causing damage to the shock's internal parts. The reservoir cap allows for more oil volume, which will extend the amount of time before the shock fades.

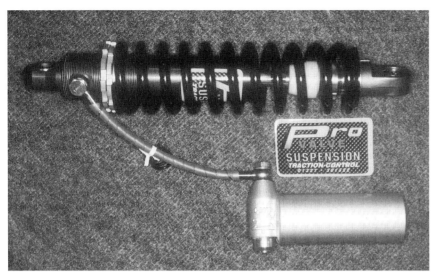

Pro Racing in England makes a Kayaba shock for the KX60. The shock features a remote reservoir and adjustable compression and rebound damping.

1992 KAWASAKI KX125

Flaws: chronic connecting-rod failure, carb bogging, shattered pistons
Fixes: install a Hot Rod kit, change carb jetting, fix crankshaft problem

This model featured a redesigned engine and chassis. As with most first-year bikes, it was plagued with mechanical problems. The following is a guide to fixing the common problems of the 1992 KX125.

Best Value Mods

Engine: 1990 igniter, porting
Suspension: fork springs, better fork bushings

Carb Jetting

Team Green recommends a 162 main jet and a NORH needle #16009-1707.

Crankshaft

The original connecting rods are sensitive to breakage if the engine is over revved. The original rods didn't have enough torsional stiffness. Kawasaki later produced a better-quality connecting rod and bearing, but the Hot Rod kit is a better design.

Cylinder and Head

The 1992 model cylinder and head won't interchange with any other models.

The best tuning mods are to turn-down 0.5mm from the cylinder base, and narrow the width of the rear transfer ports with epoxy, to a total width of 16mms. This gives more low-end power and reduces the need to overrev the engine.

Gearing

Gear up to a 51-tooth sprocket.

Forks

The fork spring rate should be at least 0.38 kilograms. The bushing in the forks that support the piston rod in the top of the damping rod wears out fast and causes a loss of rebound damping. The forks top out fast and hard, often making a clunking noise. The bushings can be replaced with accessory parts. See the cartridge-fork section for information on how to change the bushings.

1990-91 KAWASAKI KX125

Flaws: water and air leaks, frame breakage, rough acceleration
Fixes: lap crankcases and epoxy casting imperfections, gusset frame, jet carb

If you could combine the best parts of each of these models you'd have a great bike. The following are some tips on how to prevent mechanical failures and improve performance with Kawasaki parts.

Best Value Mods

Engine: Boyesen RAD valve, carb jetting
Suspension: frame gusseting

Carb Jetting

Stock pilot jet, 1.5 turns out on the airscrew, CA6 slide No. 16025-1164, an N84C needle No. 16025-1164, stock or one size larger main jet.

Ignition

The igniter box from the 1990 KX125 has a timing curve designed for high rpm, while the 1991 model is designed for an enduro-type of powerband. If your 1991 KX coughs and sputters when you accelerate out of a turn or pops at high rpm, then the 1990 igniter will work best for you. The Mitsubishi stator-plate coils suffer from moisture build-up and breakdown. Look to a service company to repair the coils. The best method for insulating the wires to protect them from moisture damage is a process called "wet wrapping." The copper wire is fed through a bath of resin and then wrapped on to the coil. Shoup Enterprises in Colorado specializes in repairing coils.

Ignition Timing

Here is a simple way to fine-tune your ignition timing without buying expensive measuring gauges. Remove the magneto cover from the left side of the engine. Looking directly at the stator plate from the left side of the bike, imagine that the stator plate is a clock. If you turn the stator plate clockwise you will advance the ignition timing. This makes the engine hit hard in the midrange but fall flat on top end. If you turn the stator plate counterclockwise you will retard the ignition timing. This makes the bike smoother in the midrange and rev higher before falling flat. Kawasaki has provided reference marks on the crankcases and the stator plate so you can gauge how far to rotate the stator plate without damaging the engine. Normally, enduro and Supercross riders prefer to advance the ignition timing, while motocross, grass track, and kart racers prefer to retard the ignition timing.

Interchanging Top-End Parts

The major difference between the KX125 models from year to year is the piston and head design. Never mismatch pistons and cylinder heads from 1990 and 1991 models. The concave design of the 1990 model offers better performance but suffers from head gasket leaks. The 1991 model used an alignment pin between the cylinder and head. All the 1991 KX parts will fit the 1990 model and offer greatly improved reliability.

Reed Valve

Boyesen's RAD valve makes a big difference on these models because the stock reed valve has too much flow area and a high-rpm peak. The RAD valve gives more torque before coming on the pipe, so the bike gets better traction out of corners. It will also save you money in clutch plates!

Clutch Tips

For best longevity, use steel clutch plates and springs from the KDX 200. EBC and Barnett make accessory clutch kits with excellent materials and stiffer springs. Barnett plates have wider tabs on the fiber plates, so they resist grooving the clutch basket.

Cylinder Mods

The weakness of the 1990 and 1991 cylinders is the timing of the exhaust and transfer ports. There isn't enough time for the exhaust gases to depressurize the cylinder before unburnt mixture gases flow from the transfer ports. The machining procedure that cures this problem is to turn down 0.5mm from the cylinder base, raise the exhaust port to 26mm from the top of the cylinder, and install a No. 046 head gasket from Kawasaki.

PAX Racing makes these triple clamps that feature a wide range of handlebar positions.

Crankcase Mods

The 1990 and 1991 models suffered from casting flaws in the front corners of the crankcase ports. The casting holes can be plugged by applying epoxy to the area affected. Also, take care when tightening the oil drain plug. The casting on the crankcase for the drain bolt hole is very thin. It's easy to crack the plug hole from over tightening the bolt.

Clutch and Shifting Problems 1990–96 (all models)

The following are some ways to improve the clutch performance and ease of shifting:

1. Drill two small-diameter holes into the female splines of the clutch hub, and then chamfer the holes with a triangular file. This will improve the oil flow to the metal clutch plates and reduce the galling to the clutch hub. This mod also gives you a better feel when fanning the clutch through the turns.
2. The stamped-steel plates attached to the shift shaft should be thoroughly chamfered and polished. This reduces the friction on the plates, so they can slide together easier, making for quicker shifts.
3. File and polish the edges of the shift star that is bolted to the end of the shift drum. The shift star relies on a spring-loaded roller to keep the transmission in gear.

1985-89 KAWASAKI KX125

Flaws: lack of low-end power, clutch problems

Fixes: Boyesen reeds, lap crankcases, Barnett plates and springs

The late-1980s KX125s were great bikes, real workhorses. Sure they had some problems but what bike doesn't? Here are some tips for improving the longevity of these bikes.

Best Value Mods

Engine: Boyesen reeds, carb jetting
Suspension: Race-Tech Emulator Valve, Excel rims

Air Leaks

Like all Kawasakis they had characteristic air leaks at the crankcases because Kaws don't use center gaskets; instead, they use a non-drying sealer. Lapping the crankcases makes a big difference in low-end power and engine longevity.

Cylinder Mods

The 1986 model was the slowest 125 of that year. Best mods included turning down 1mm from the cylinder base and machining the head 1mm at the squish band.

Silencer

The silencer core from the 1985 model should also be used on the 1986 model (order Kawasaki part No. 49099-1113).

Soft Rims

The 1986 and 1987 models had problems with the front rims cracking at the weld. Replace the stock piece with a Tallon or Excel rim.

1988-89 KAWASAKI KX125

The 1988 and 1989 models had a new engine design that featured the concave piston design and multiple transfer ports, along with a new triple-exhaust valve system. This was a fantastic engine design with an infinate amount of potential! The 1988 and 1989 models can be improved in the following ways:

Carburetor

The carb's needle-jet primary hood (the half-cylinder-shaped piece sticking up into the venturi) should be filed down 1.5mms. This will make the engine run leaner in the midrange.

Head Gasket Leaks

The cylinder head on the 1988 model had chronic head-gasket leaks that would eventually cause the piston to crack off at the top ring groove. The solution is to fit the head and cylinder with alignment pins, which came standard on the 1989 model. Another way to fix the head-gasket problem is to drill out the head stay bolt hole larger and install a Nylok nut and two large-diameter washers. The Nylok nut allows you to tighten the head stay bolt to a lower torque value without the bolt falling out. This enables the bolt to flex from the top shock mount forces but not affect the cylinder head.

1997-2000 KAWASAKI KX250

Flaws: power hits hard, shifting sticky, soft forks

Fixes: porting, updated detent spring, stiffer fork springs

The KX has a hard hitting midrange with weak overrev. That combined with the new close ratio gearbox makes a rider short-shift too much. By duplicating the exhaust porting of the '97 CR250, the KX can be made to rev more like the Honda. That is exactly what Kaw changed on the 2000 model.

Best Value Mods

Engine: porting
Suspension: fork springs

Cylinder Porting

There are two distinctively different porting jobs that I perform on the KX250. The most popular porting gives a powerband that starts pulling early and has a smoother transition into the midrange. The other porting gives more top-end overrev.

Smoother Broader Powerband

These porting mods include extensive use of epoxy in the rear transfer ports to redirect the flow and raise the crankcase compression ratio. None of the port heights are changed, just balanced from side to side.

More Overrev Powerband

These porting mods involve some critical machine work that requires a right angle porting tool. The sub-exhaust ports must be widened and raised 2mm. The main exhaust port must be ported to an oval shape. The transfer ports need to be ported to heights of 58mm for the front ports and 58.5mm for the rear ports.

Piston and Head Mod

The stock piston and head offer a high compression ratio, so there are no mods needed. However, if you want a quicker revving engine, consider the new lightweight flattop piston from Wiseco. The new piston kit is designed to combine a flattop crown with super-lightened skirts (Wiseco No. 704PS). Wiseco originally designed this piston for Team Kawasaki. This new piston is designed

for high-maintenance racing use. It's much lighter than the standard domed piston. The flattop design has greater mechanical efficiency than the standard dome design. The flattop crown makes it necessary to perform a modification to adjust the cylinder head's combustion chamber and squish band to suit. The gasket surface of the head must be turned-down on a lathe by 2.5mm. Then the squish band must be re-cut at a 4-degree angle. The depth of the squish band, measured from the gasket surface is .25mm. Switching to a projected insulator spark plug (NGK BP7EV) will improve throttle response between 1/4 and 1/2 throttle.

Shifting Woes

For the 1997 model, if you're having problems shifting from first to second, or if the tranny pops out of gear often, then replace the shift detent spring with Kaw part No. 92145-1063. For any other year KX, the problem could be as simple as clutch debris collecting in the cases near the shift drum or shift linkage. You can simply remove the right-side engine cover and spray some brake cleaner at the shift drum to flush out the debris. Changing the tranny oil more often will help too.

Suspension

Forks

The fork springs are too soft for most riders who weigh more than 160 pounds. Change to a set of .41 Kilogram springs.

Shock

Set the race sag to 95mm. The valving is pretty good and lengthening the shock's travel will improve the front end. The simplest way to lengthen the shock travel is to install two 18 X.3mm shims between the top-out plate and the shock shaft.

1993-96 KAWASAKI KX250

Flaws: frame breakage, poor low-end power, and weak front brake

Fixes: gusset frame, cylinder porting, and braking front disc

The 1993 KX was the first year of the new engine. The main difference was the KIPS valve system. A more efficient wedge

On the early-model KX80 and all models of KX60, there are three plastic plugs located around the main bearing in the crankcases. Sometimes they can leak. Apply a dab of epoxy over the outside of the plug to better seal it.

valve design was adapted because the old system was prone to mechanical failure and excess noise. The new KIPS system would have problems of its own, but it is still the best exhaust valve design for two-stroke engines. The new chassis was narrower and the top shock mount was made integral to the frame. In 1994, Kawasaki changed the steering head angle of the KX250. They changed the rake angle so the bike would turn better at slow speeds. The rear shock valving is generally stiff while the spring is soft for riders over 175 pounds. Here are some of the mods that I recommend for the KX.

Best Value Mods

Engine: cylinder porting, Boyesen RAD valve

Suspension: Braking oversize front disc kit, aftermarket brake hose

Cylinder

I recommend raising the sub-exhaust ports to 40mm from the top of the cylinder and transfer port heights to 58mm. The rear transfers will need to be narrowed with epoxy (4mms) and re-angled so they are aimed towards each other. If you are really after the maximum power, consider having the cylinder plated to a tighter piston-to-cylinder wall clearance of .0025 inch. The stock clearance runs .004–.006 inch. The cylinders for the different years of KXs won't interchange. The 1993 and 1994 are similar and the 1995 and newer models are similar. The intake

1994 KX250 Frame Cracks

Question: I have a 1994 KX250. I'm a heavy rider and I jump my bike high and bottom hard. My bike's frame has developed several small hairline cracks in areas such as the footpegs, top shock mount, and the link stay mounts. I've never had the suspension serviced. Would shock revalving help remedy this problem? Does anyone offer a frame repair service for Kawasakis?

Answer: Considering that you are a big guy and rode the wheels off that bike for two seasons, I'd say your KX held up pretty good. When the suspension bottoms, that puts a greater stress on the frame, so factory race teams employ professional fabricators to improve the strength of production frames—and you can too. Many plates are welded to key areas of the frame to form gussets. The areas of the KX frame to gusset include footpeg mounts, upper shock mounting bracket, and the bottom cradle of the frame. TUF Racing can gusset your KX frame.

Regarding the revalving question, yes, your shock could be tuned to prevent the hard-bottoming problem. Be prepared to buy a different shock spring (about $100) to match your riding weight. Since your shock has never been serviced, it will need a new seal pack and perhaps a piston seal (about $75). A professional suspension tuner will require your input to determine the best valving changes to complement your riding style.

KX Chain Slapping

Question: I have a 1992 KX125 and when the chain gets too loose it slaps up against the inside edge of the sub-frame. I'm afraid it's going to wear through and weaken the expensive sub-frame. What can I do to protect the sub-frame from chain wear?

Answer: Go to your local hardware store and buy a short piece (6 inches long by 1/2 inch wide and 1/8th inch thick) of aluminum corner stock. Rivet the aluminum piece to the inside edge of the sub-frame. That way the chain will rub against the aluminum stock rather than your sub-frame. However if the sub-frame is already damaged, don't rely on the aluminum stock to act as a patch. Instead replace the sub-frame with an OEM part or a Pro-Circuit accessory sub-frame.

KX Sloppy Pipe Fit

Question: My KX250 has a lot of oil drooling out from the point where the pipe fits into the cylinder, and when I rev the bike you can see exhaust smoke seeping from the manifold. I've tried sealing it with RTV orange silicone but it keeps blowing out. I've replaced the O-rings on the exhaust pipe twice. Could the cylinder be worn out and if so, is there an inexpensive way for me to fix this?

Answer: It is common for the steel exhaust pipe manifold to wear the aluminum spigot on the cylinder, causing the pipe to seal poorly and drool out unburned exhaust gases. And yes there is an inexpensive way to fix the problem. Innovation Sports makes a special non-hardening putty sealer that you can wrap around the manifold to improve the seal. The putty withstands the high exhaust gas temperatures and is reusable. This product can be ordered from your local dirt bike dealer through Parts Unlimited or White Bros. distributors.

KX500 Gear Popper

Question: My 1992 KX500 pops out of gear after I shift into third and nail the throttle. I know it's not the way I'm shifting it, because it only happens in third gear.

Answer: Hey pal, transmissions don't last forever, especially on a bike with man-sized power! This is actually a common problem with KX500s. The shift fork that controls the third gear cluster gets worn or slightly bent before the other two shift forks. The reason is you shift up and down past third gear more often than the other gears. Replacing the shift fork requires that the crankcases be split. If the engine has never been rebuilt, then you should at least replace the crankshaft main bearings and the four bearings that support the two gear shafts in the crankcases. Replace the entire set of three shift forks because the others are probably worn out too. The average labor cost from a dealer would between $90-150. Parts would be about $250.

KX Loose Clutch Parts

Question: I just took apart the clutch on my 1982 KX80, and all the bolts were loose. The center nut that holds the clutch to the main shaft was ready to fall off. I just rebuilt the clutch two weeks ago; how could everything come loose so soon?

Answer: The manufacturer recommends applying a thread-locking agent (such as Loctite blue) to all the nuts and bolts in the clutch. There is a lot of vibration and sudden movements in a clutch, so a worn out clutch will just rattle apart. Sometimes, the center bearing and clutch hubs get deep wear marks in their moving surfaces, and that can also cause a clutch to fail. It's best to have a technician examine your clutch basket, hub, spring length, and the clutch plates' thickness. Change the oil every month of riding, and use good hypoid gear oil such as Bel Ray or Spectro.

KDX Electrical Problem

Question: My 1989 KDX200 cuts out at high rpm on flat ground or at lower rpm when I try to take a hill. The spark plugs tend to foul quickly too. What could it be?

Answer: The problem might be that the spark plug is too cold of a heat range or the spark plug gap is too large. The higher you rev the engine, the greater the voltage needed to arc across the spark plug's electrode and ground arm. Also, whenever the load on the engine is too great (hill climbing) the cylinder pressure increases, thereby raising the required voltage for spark. Electrical components fail with time, but here is a simple way to eliminate the spark plug as the cause of your bike's problem. Use this spark plug and gap: NGK B8ES gapped at .020 inches. Use a feeler gauge to set the gap accurately. If your bike still has problems, you should have a Kawasaki service technician perform an electrical test on the bike. Sometimes it's as simple as a bad kill switch, or it may just need a thorough cleaning and reseal the wire connectors. If the problem is a defective electrical component, such as a black box or stator coils, then performing an electrical test with the Kawasaki Factory igniter box simulator and a multimeter is the only way to test your bike's electrical system. Proper testing will save you money on trial-and-error replacement of expensive electrical components.

Popping on Bumpy Ground

Question: I have a 1989 KX125, and it has the weirdest problem. When I ride on flat ground it runs great, but when I ride over whoops or a series of square-edged bumps the engine cuts out. My local dealer checked the ignition system with an ohms meter and said it was OK. He cleaned the wire connectors and set the ignition timing to factory specs, but my bike still has the same problem. Could it be carb jetting?

Answer: Your dealer was right to check the ignition components with an ohms meter. That is the standard test used to determine if electrical components are good or bad. Loose or corroded wire connectors, spark plug caps, and kill switches can also be weak links. Sounds as if the obvious things have been eliminated, so it's probably the black box. This box contains all the circuitry to vary the ignition-timing curve over the entire rpm range. A liquid epoxy is poured into the black box to insulate the chips and diodes of the circuitry from water or vibration damage. Sometimes, air bubbles develop in the black box before the epoxy hardens. Without solid support and protection from the epoxy insulating material, the chips and diodes vibrate loose, opening the circuit and causing the ignition to lose spark. This can happen when you land from a big jump or ride over a series of bumps at speed. There is no way to repair a black box; the only option is to replace it with a new one.

Kick Starter Slips

Question: I have a 1990 KDX200. The kick starter seems to work intermittently. It will kick a few times with compression, then go flat-kick straight through. Is the spring going bad here? What part in the kick-start mechanism needs replacing?

Answer: When you engage the kick-start lever, a spring pushes on a ratcheting gear. Perhaps the spring is broken, or worse, the splines on the kick-start shaft could be stripped. The only way to determine the exact problem is to remove the right-side engine cover and check the kick-start shaft assembly. The assembly has a spring that hooks into a hole in the right crankcase. Unhook the spring and pull the assembly out of the case. Visually check the thin coil spring and the shaft splines for wear. Those parts will just slide off the backside of the shaft. The ratcheting gear and the shaft have tiny dot marks that align together. Make sure they are aligned when you assemble the kick-start shaft.

KDX Hop-Ups

Question: I am trying to improve the power on my 1995 KDX200. I have installed a FMF pipe and silencer, a Boyesen RAD valve, and a Wiseco Prolite piston. I would like to gain some bottom and midrange power, and more revs. The bike runs like it has a rev limiter. Could you give me some advice on porting specs? My thoughts were to open up the boost ports. Is it possible to open them too much? I'm also considering modifying the head. How high can I increase the compression ratio and still run the bike on pump gas? How much can I raise the KIPS auxiliary exhaust ports?

Answer: You have the right combination of aftermarket products to give the engine a wider powerband. Regarding the flat top-end problem, check the spark arrestor to make sure the packing hasn't blown out of it. Check the exhaust valves too; make sure they aren't carbon-seized. That problem will prevent the valves from opening and choke off the exhaust flow. As far as cylinder porting is concerned, you can match and polish the entire sharp edges in the ports, but don't enlarge the boost ports. That will cause a loss of low-end power. Don't attempt to turn down the cylinder base on a lathe. That model's exhaust valve system is gear driven and removing material from the cylinder base will change the gear lash. The KDX cylinder head design will run on super unleaded premium but the KDX engine is sensitive to overheating when you increase the compression too much. Raising the sub-exhaust ports .020 inches or .5mm will give a slight increase in top-end power without losing any low-end power.

Justifying the 240 Kit on the KDX

Question: After suffering "sticker shock" at the new bike prices I decided to keep my old 1985 KDX200, which I have ridden very little and is in excellent shape.

I am interested in improving its performance and remembered an old *Dirt Bike* article about boring such a bike out to 240cc. My question concerns whether you would recommend performing this type of work? I want the job done correctly with quality parts.

I received a brochure from a company that advertised a complete price of $590 to install the 240cc kit. This includes a sleeve, Wiseco piston, head gasket, and labor. Is that a good price and are there any other costs to consider? I don't want to put too much money into this old bike.

Answer: The 240cc kit makes the engine in your 1985 KDX vibrate badly at high rpm because of the greater reciprocating mass (piston assembly). The carburetion becomes erratic at idle, but it makes awesome low- to midrange power. If that's what you're looking for, then go for it!

As far as the method of installation, steel sleeves are inefficient liners for cylinders. I prefer the method of overboring and electro-plating the cylinder instead of sleeving. That way there are no heat transfer problems and you don't have to spend extra money porting the cylinder because there is no steel sleeve to match.

Max Power Cylinders is a motorcycle cylinder reconditioning company that electroplates cylinders with nickel and silicon-carbide (about $175). You can buy the Wiseco piston kit and the head gasket from LA Sleeve (about $100), but don't buy the sleeve—you won't need it with plating. You'll have to do some other mods along with overboring the cylinder. The cylinder head will need to be machined for the larger bore size and the chamber volume will need to be adjusted for the corrected compression ratio. The crankcase will need to be modified to accommodate the larger piston, so figure on that labor and parts too. A 36mm carb makes the engine perform better with the larger displacement, so consider that too.

Increasing the displacement of an engine requires attention to other engine components besides the top end. Consider those factors in the total cost when trying to justify the money on such a project.

tract is shorter on the 1995 cylinder. The exhaust duct is a smaller diameter, and won't fit with the earlier-model pipes.

The 1995 cylinder is great for enduro and Supercross but the small exhaust duct limits its top-end potential. All of these cylinders have casting slag in the Boyesen ports (located between the intake and transfer ports). You can use a rasp file to remove the slag and enlarge the port to the standard casting lines. Enlarging the port too much doesn't benefit performance.

The best option for an oversized piston is the Wiseco 74mm kit which increases engine displacement to 310cc. The kit fits 1993–2000 KX250s and requires modifications to the exhaust valves and cylinder head. Cometic makes a special head gasket for this kit.

Cylinder Head

There is no need to turn down the cylinder head of the 1994 model for more compression. Now you can just use the optional, thinner head gasket available from Kawasaki (Part No. 11004-1240).

KIPS Valves

Previous model KX250s had a two-piece KIPS actuating rod. The fit between the two pieces was loose and that caused a variance in the KIPS valve range of movement. In 1994, Kawasaki redesigned the rod as one piece. Kawasaki recalled early production models in the United States and installed an upgraded rod. This part fits 1992 and 1993 KX250s. Because the KX250 uses a relatively stiff power valve governor spring, the link-plate tends to crack. If your older KX has sluggish performance, check the link-plate. It is located under the right-side engine.

Another common problem with the KIPS wedge valve was burred corners. The exposed corners of the wedge valve get heated from the exhaust gases while striking the flapper plate. This causes the ends of the wedge valve to develop burrs. The burrs limit the travel of the wedge valve. The wedge valve is prevented from closing to the stop, so the powerband feels weak on the low end. At high rpm, the wedge valve is prevented from opening fully. That makes the engine run flat at high rpm because the flapper is hanging out in the exhaust gas stream. The wedge valve should be checked when servicing the top end. Grasp the KIPS rack and move it through its travel, opening and closing the exhaust valves.

Frame Breakage

The 1994 model had characteristic frame breakage on the gusset plate for the rear shock mount. That is due to the too stiff high-speed compression valving in the shock. The frame instead of the shock absorbs too much energy. The valving on the 1995 model was softened to fix this problem. To improve the frame, I suggest adding gusset plates to key areas such as the footpeg brackets and the top shock mount.

Chain Roller Problem

The 1994 KX250 has a design flaw in the placement of the upper chain roller. The roller is mounted too close to the air boot. The roller doesn't even free wheel and when the chain contacts the roller it spins it, causing it to wear away the air boot. Eventually the air boot develops a hole and debris is drawn into the engine, causing a seizure. The solution is to turn down the chain roller's outer diameter on a lathe so it can free wheel.

Big Brakes

Braking offers a special front brake kit for the KXs. This kit was developed for Mike Kiedrowski and Mike LaRocco when they were teammates for Kawasaki. Many other factory race teams use oversize front and rear Braking discs kits. The KX disc is 20mm larger, making it 260mm in diameter. The kit includes a caliper mounting bracket, the disc, and a set of pads. Braking discs are laser cut from stainless steel and textured for a consistent finish.

If you want to improve the front braking power of your old KX and don't want to spend much money, try a WP replacement brake line. These hard plastic lines don't expand like the stock brake line so the brakes feel less spongy and more like a Honda's brakes. Another simple mod to the brakes is stainless steel hex bolt pins for the brake pads. Moose Racing and WER offer these aftermarket brake pins. These items resist forming divots as the brake pads are engaged and released. Stock Kawasaki brake pins tend to form divots that prevent the brake pads from sliding away from the disc. Typical symptoms of this problem are stuck brakes.

Gearing

Switch to a 50-tooth rear sprocket and this bike will pull stronger through the loamy bends and steep uphills. This works on KX250s 1990–95.

Rear Suspension

The rear shock spring is too soft for riders who weigh more than 170 pounds. A 5.2-

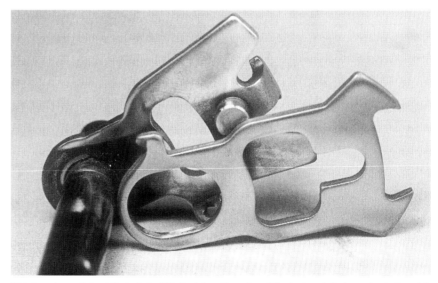

This is a photo of the shift shaft for KX dirt bikes. One plate slides back and forth on the shaft, and is spring-loaded. These parts are stamped from steel so one edge is rounded and the other is sharp. This shift shaft has been deburred and polished; that makes the shifting action more positive with less effort.

kilogram spring is the best choice. The compression valving should be changed for softer high-speed compression when you switch to the stiffer spring.

1991-92 KAWASAKI KX250

Flaws: cylinder wears fast, front end steers slow
Fixes: replate the cylinder, Terry triple clamps

These bikes had much-improved frames but different cylinders. The 1991 cylinder needs Boyesen boost ports added to the intake port, for more midrange power. Both cylinders have large intake ports that caused the piston skirts to wear and crack prematurely. Later models had bridged intake ports that solved the piston wear problem. KXs are noted as bikes that handle well at higher speeds. However this makes the bike steer wide in tight slow turns.

Best Value Mods
Engine: Boyesen RAD Valve, KIPS valve mods
Suspension: revalve shock, Terry triple clamps

Steering
The KX fork rake angle is greater than that of a Honda CR. This makes the bike stable at speed but is difficult to turn tightly. Terry Products developed a triple clamp set for the KX, which has a rake angle 2 degrees less than stock. This product works on 1991–93 KX250s. They even make a kit for 1994–95 models, but Kawasaki reduced the rake angle on these frames in production. The Terry Triple Clamp kit requires you to press out the original stem, and press the stem into the Terry bottom clamp. This task requires straight jig fixtures and a 20-ton press. Better to trust this job to a professional who has the tools and knowledge. The Terry clamps sell for $250 and the labor is about $50.

Cylinder
I recommend getting the cylinder nickel silicon-carbide plated (Max Power, US Chrome, or Aptec). There are some options for oversize piston kits. La Sleeve makes a 295cc piston kit and Klemm makes a 310-cc kit that includes a sleeve. The 295cc piston

can be used in a plated cylinder but the 310cc requires the use of a special sleeve that can only be installed by Klemm.

1990 KAWASAKI KX250

Flaws: abrupt powerband, frame breakage
Fixes: lower compression ratio, use shims on engine and shock mounts

This bike was a hard-hitting screamer with an abrupt powerband. The best way to tame it down and get some traction is to clean up the jetting, and install a flywheel weight. This was the first model with the upside down forks and the perimeter frame. These frames were notorious for cracking near the top shock mounts and the steering head bearing cup.

Best Value Mods
Engine: carb jetting, flywheel weight
Suspension: gusset frame

Carb Jetting
Install these jets in the carb: 6.0 slide, and a N87C jet needle. The Boyesen RAD Valve is designed to improve the low-end and midrange power. The compression ratio of the stock engine is too high. Installing the optional thick head gasket available from Kawasaki, or a Cometic fiber gasket can lower it.

KIPS Valves
Adding two shims next to the spring can increase the power valve governor spring tension (Kawasaki part No. 92026-1238). This will stall the KIPS valves from opening until a higher rpm. Adding a flywheel weight will reduce wheel spin and soften the hit in the midrange.

Flywheel Weight
Adding weight to the flywheel will reduce the wheel spin and soften the abrupt hit in the powerband. If you use a KX250 for DTX or micro sprint racing, don't use a flywheel weight. Flywheel weights put a greater strain on the main bearings on engines that are over revved.

Ignition Timing
Try retarding the ignition timing. This will reduce the hit in the powerband and make the engine run cooler. Kawasaki makes it easy to

change the timing. They scribed marks in the stator plate and a reference mark on the crankcase. Loosen the stator plate mounting bolts and rotate the stator plate counterclockwise to the far mark (about 1mm).

Frame Breakage
That is a big problem on this bike because the top shock mounts were put under a compression load when the top shock bolt was tightened.

The shock mounting plate can be spaced away from the frame with washers to reduce the compression load on the shock bolt. The frames usually broke at the shock mounting plates, bottom motor mounts, and the top steering race in the neck. Gussets could be added to the frame to strengthen it and a weld-on skid plate actually worked the best to hold the frames together. Refer to the chapter on frames for more information on strengthening frames with gussets.

1985-89 KAWASAKI KX250 & KX500

Flaws: frame breakage, KIPS valve wear, shock-absorber wear
Fixes: gusset frame, replace KIPS valves, replace shock bushings

Best Value Mods
Engine: thick head gasket, carb T-vents
Suspension: Braking oversize disc brakes, gusset frame

Frame Breakage
Tabs and mounting brackets tend to break away from the frame tubes because these parts were MIG welded on the assembly line. Always have the parts TIG welded and gusseted. Reinforcing the footpeg brackets, engine mounts, top shock mount, and neck are very important. Welding a sheet of .6mm stainless steel to the bottom of the frame will act as both a gusset and a skid plate to strengthen and protect the frame.

Shock Problems
Because of strong demand, companies are making seal and bushing kits for the rear shocks. If the shock body has worn out, the best option is to buy a reconditioned Ohlins

Another component of the shifting mechanism is the star. It fits on the end of the shift drum and the detent roller puts pressure against the star so the tranny stays in gear once you've shifted. The edges of the star can be polished on a Scotch-Brite wheel mounted in a bench grinder.

shock. These shocks are totally rebuildable and have better damping than stock shocks.

Front Forks

Non-cartridge forks can be made to work similarly to modern forks with a Race-Tech Emulator Valve.

Brakes

The bolts that support the brake pads tend to develop divot marks with prolonged use. Replace them with WER or Moose Off-Road stainless steel hex-head bolts. A simple way to eliminate the spongy feel of the brakes is to use a White Power hard-plastic brake hose. If the discs are glazed they will make a squealing noise when the brakes are applied. The discs can be re-surfaced on a surface-grinding machine. Look to a machine shop for this service. Change the brake fluid every three months for best results. Use Motul 300C brake fluid.

Carburetor

If your KX bogs when riding over whoops or when landing from big jumps, fit double vents to the carb as on the 1995 models. There are aftermarket kits or you can get two 1/8-inch-diameter brass T-fittings and hoses from a pet shop. They sell them for aquariums. Route one set of hoses down and one set up under the fuel tank or into the air box. You can improve the low-end power of the

1990 KX250 by installing an N87C needle and a No. 6 slide.

KIPS Valves

The two drum valves of the KIPS system tend to wear at the drive channels for the center valve. The center valve is steel and the drum valves are just hard-anodized aluminum, so the drum valves wear quicker. When the drum valves wear too much, the center valve remains in the closed position all the time, and that can reduce top-end power.

Check and clean your exhaust valves frequently (see section on exhaust valves for specific instructions) and replace the drum valves periodically.

Crankcase Main Bearings

If your bike has a lot of vibration, the crankshaft's main bearings may be worn, or worse yet, the crankcase races may be oblong shaped. If you disassemble the engine, and the main bearings just fall out of the cases, then the races are worn. The bearing races are made of cast iron, and they tend to wear into an oblong shape. It is possible for a machine shop to fit steel races to the crankcases, and this is usually less expensive than buying new crankcases. This problem is common on KX500s.

Gearbox Problems

KX500s that are raced for two or more seasons tend to develop transmission problems. It is characteristic for them to jump out of third gear. Rounded engagement dogs on the third gear drive and bent shift forks usually cause the problem.

Piston Cracking

The KX500s have problems with pistons cracking at the intake skirt because the stock cylinders wear quickly. This problem is eliminated when the cylinder is plated with Nikasil.

KX250 Compression Ratio

The KX250s have a very high compression ratio. This can lead to a variety of problems, among them, head gasket leaks. Using two head gaskets is a simple way to reduce the compression ratio and the possibility of head gasket leaks.

Reed Petal Breakage

The big bore KXs tend to chip the stock carbon fiber reed petals at the outer corners. This problem can make the engine hard to start, bog at low rpm, and pop at high rpm. The solution is to replace the stock reeds with Boyesen Dual-Stage or Aktive reed petals. They are more durable and increase low-end power.

Clutch Lurching

Kawasaki clutches need stiffer clutch springs. Look to aftermarket companies such as Barnett or EBC for springs. One way to reduce lurching of the clutch is to radius the edge of the clutch actuator rod with a file. This will make it engage smoother. Switching to automatic-transmission fluid will help the clutch work better because these types of oil are designed to work with fiber-to-steel clutch plates.

1990-95 KAWASAKI KX500

Flaws: third gear engagement dogs wear, powerband flattens out

Fixes: replace third gear, install thicker head gasket

How do you improve the perfect open bike? It's tough! The only way to improve this bike is too focus on suspension tuning and regular maintenance. Make sure the fork and shock springs are matched to your weight. Use guidelines for setting race sag and determining the proper spring rates as listed in the chapter titled "Baseline Settings." If you want to make your KX500 turn tighter for tracks with many off-camber turns or for enduro riding, then a Terry Kit triple clamp kit will do the job. This triple clamp kit will reduce the steering head angle 2 degrees. Ty Davis, the famous off-road racer, developed the triple clamp kit.

Best Value Mods

Engine: thicker head gasket
Suspension: proper springs

Transmission

The KX500s have a characteristic problem of developing worn engagement dogs on third gear. The occurs because riders often load the engine the hardest while riding in third gear.

Engine Mods

If you want to get a smoother low-end pulling powerband with more overrev, install two optional, thick head gaskets (Part No. 11004-1186) and an aftermarket exhaust pipe.

1998-2000 KAWASAKI KX100

Flaws: sluggish powerband
Fixes: porting, bigger carb

This latest generation of KX100 featured a new exhaust valve system. That feature wasn't well received because it didn't give significant performance gains. Plus the system was plagued with design problems that included frequent breakage of the flapper part of the valve.

Best Value Mods

Engine: porting, 28mm Flatslide PWK Keihin carb, FMF pipe
Suspension: springs

Cylinder Porting and Head Mods

Since the 100 cylinder is just a bored-out 82cc cylinder, the ports are too small for such a large piston. Key areas like the transfer ports and exhaust outlet and bridge must be machined to let the gases flow through the cylinder. When I port a KX mini cylinder, I use an old exhaust pipe flange fitted to the exhaust outlet. This helps me cut the appropriate material out of the cylinder. The exhaust bridge can be narrowed to 2mm wide and the outer top corners of the port can be blended for better flow and less chance of ring scuffing. The exhaust port height can be raised to 25mm and the transfers to 35mm. The rear transfer ports can also be widened 1.5mm towards the front transfers. The head doesn't need any modifications unless you are building the engine for strictly low-end power.

Alternative Big Bores

The KX is a prime platform for a big bore because the crankshaft can be stroked easily and Wiseco makes piston kits 2mm larger than stock. The maximum displacement possible from a KX100 is 121cc. RPM in Covina, California, offers bore-and-stroke engine

This is the detent, consisting of a spring-loaded lever and a roller that engage the star. In 1997 Kawasaki used a softer spring to make shifting easier; instead it popped out of gear easily.

mods for the KX. However, anytime the engine is modified for more displacement, the stress on the engine parts becomes significantly greater and the longevity compromised.

Aftermarket Carb

The best choice of an aftermarket carb is the Keihin PWK 28mm.

1994-97 KAWASAKI KX100

Flaws: mismatched ports, soft forks, under-carbureted
Fixes: port cylinder, stiffer springs and base-valve kit, 28mm carb

The KX100 cylinder can be improved greatly. Kawasaki used the stock 80cc cylinder casting and bored and plated it for a larger piston. The problem is, they use a pipe designed for an 80cc engine, and the ports aren't corrected to suit the flow of a larger piston. One simple mod can be performed to the cylinder for better throttle response. Drill two 6mm holes on each side of the intake port into the transfer ports. These are called Boyesen ports, named after the

prolific inventor. The KX80 already has them. Also, use a file to widen each exhaust port to a total of 27mm wide (measured with a thin plastic ruler conformed to the bore). Set the height of the exhaust to 25mm from the top of the cylinder. A simple bolt-on item that gives smoother power with more top-end is a 28mm carb. Both Mikuni and Keihin have carb kits available.

Best Value Mods

Engine: 28mm carb
Suspension: base valve kit

Ported Piston

A boost port can be added to the intake side of the piston; use a KX80 piston as a model for duplication.

Hot Suspension Mods

The big-wheel KX100, introduced to America in 1994, has upside-down cartridge forks. The compression damping of these forks can be greatly improved by installing the compression base valve from the 1992 Yamaha YZ125. Pro Racing makes a tuned aftermarket base valve for the KX big-wheel forks.

1998-2000 KAWASAKI KX80

Flaws: sluggish power
Fixes: porting

The new exhaust valve system was designed to make the KX mini competitive with the RM but it takes too much energy to drive the powervalve governor mechanism so it slows the engine down. Porting for more top-end power helps overcome the drag from the governor. Overall this bike has better suspension than previous models. There are more springs available for the forks and shocks, plus the forks have modern valving that can be tuned.

Best Value Mods
Engine: porting
Suspension: springs

Cylinder Mods
Porting this cylinder is a bit tricky and should be left to professionals. Like the 100 cylinder, I use an old exhaust pipe flange to carefully match the junction of the exhaust port and the pipe. Then I raise the exhaust port to 24.5mm and widen each exhaust port 1mm, and narrow the bridge 1mm. The intake and exhaust bridges are very critical because the edges need to be deburred to minimize the wear on the piston and rings. The transfer ports should be matched for a height of 35.5mm.

Ignition Changes
Just rotating the stator plate to Kaw's prescribed marks will have a slight effect on the power. Advancing the timing will benefit most riders. FMF and Mimic make switchable CDI boxes that enable a big change in the powerband.

1990-97 KAWASAKI KX80

Flaws: air leaks, connecting rod bearings, lacks low-end power
Fixes: seal casting plugs and lap crankcases, pre-mix ratio to 20:1, cylinder and head machining

The KX performs consistently, handles well, and is reliable. However, many riders complain that the KX80 can't run with an RM80 from corner to corner. That is because the RM has power valves that give the RM80 more low-end torque. The following are some tips on making the KX more competitive with the RM's engine.

Best Value Mods
Engine: 28mm carb
Suspension: Eibach fork springs

Cylinder and Head Mods
The KX80 can be given more low-end and midrange-bursting power by turning down the cylinder base on a lathe. This retards the port timing. The stock port timing is too radical for the loamy technical tracks of the Midwest and eastern United States. Turn 0.028 inch or 0.7mm from the base. The cylinder head must also be turned so the deck height from the gasket surface to the start of the squish band is 1mm. The squish angle should be 10 degrees and 5mm wide.

Carburetor
For more top-end power, install a 28mm Keihin PWK carburetor, available from Carb Parts Warehouse.

Crankcases
The crankcase halves are sealed on Kawasakis with a non-drying sealer rather than a paper gasket. As the bike gets older, forces acting on the frame strain the engine mounts and the crankcases, and the crankcases sometimes begin to leak. I recommend lapping the crankcase halves whenever the main bearings are replaced. Kawasaki dealers sell a non-drying gasket sealer called Three Bond #4. It's the same substance as Yamabond, sold at Yamaha dealers. Apply a thin, even coating of the sealer on both sides of the case halves. A business card is a good tool for spreading the sealer evenly across the gasket surface. Let it air dry at 70 degrees Fahrenheit for 10 minutes before assembling the engine.

Another problem affecting the crankcases of KX80s is that the casting plugs vibrate loose. The plugs are positioned around the outside of the main-bearing race. Spread a thin, even layer of epoxy over the plugs to seal them from leaking. Use Duro Master Mend epoxy.

Connecting Rod Bearings
The connecting rod bearing is prone to failure from lack of lubrication. Run a pre-mix ratio of 20:1 and jet the carb accordingly (richer).

Suspension
The 1990s line of KX80s was steadily improved. The forks use a Travel Control Valve, which is similar to Race Tech's Emulator Valve so there is no need for any expensive mods. Just spring the bike for the rider and change the suspension fluids every 10 races or 20 running hours.

Forks
The forks need stiffer damping for aggressive riders. Switch to 15-weight fork oil and tighten the pre-load spring on the travel control valve, one turn clockwise. Riders who weigh more than 120 pounds should change to a stiffer spring rate.

Shock
The shock suffers from too soft, low-speed compression and rebound. Try setting the race sag to 75mm, the compression adjuster to 5 clicks out, and the rebound adjuster to 6 clicks out.

1985-90 KAWASAKI KX80 & KX100

Flaws: crankcase air leaks, cylinder wears quickly
Fixes: epoxy and lap cases, electroplate cylinder

Kawasaki struggled for years developing its KX80 into the excellent bike that it became in 1990. Problems with design and materials plagued this model. Common problems included broken frames, crankcase air leaks, and scored cylinders. The frame can be gusseted with mild steel plates at the bottom motor mounts and the steering head. The crankcases can be lapped on a surface lapping plate. It's best to lap the cylinder base surface and the crankcase-mating surface. Use Yamabond as a sealer between the crankcases. The cylinders of the older KX80 had a problem of the rings rotating past the ring centering pins and snagging on the rear transfer port edge. The ring centering pins were positioned incorrectly on the piston, too close to the port edge. Wiseco pistons have the pins

If an old KX125 develops a chronic head gasket leak or breaks the rear studs from the cases, I recommend elongating the head stay brackets like the one on the right. Then you need to install large diameter washers on each side of the bolt and use a NYLOK nut. The nut allows you to tighten the bolt snug without any chance of it falling off. Enabling the head stay to flex a bit will reduce the twisting forces on the head.

centered on the bridge between the ports. The standard Kawasaki electrofusion plating wears out quickly. It's best to re-plate the cylinder with Nikasil or ceramasil. If you're looking for more performance from the engine, Boyesen reeds make a big improvement over the stock fiberglass reeds. Also, there is a big mismatch between the exhaust port and the exhaust pipe. I use an old pipe flange as a guide for the grinding tool. This mod works on all KX80s and KX100s through present-day models.

Best Value Mods

Engine: Boyesen reeds, cylinder plating
Suspension: suspension service

2000 KAWASAKI KX65

Flaws: poor powerband
Fixes: porting and head mods

Kawasaki revamped the KX65 in 2000, changing the chassis and the engine from the old KX60. Basically the new chassis was a scaled-down version of the KX80. This model has much better handling and braking. Unfortunately the engine isn't on par with the chassis. The new cylinder and head offer greater potential when ported.

Best Value Mods

Engine: Turn down cylinder base, raise exhaust port, and re-cut the recess in the head 1mm.

Cylinder and Head Mods

The basic problem with the KX65 is that the exhaust port is too small and low, and the transfers are too high. That means that the blow-down timing is too short, causing burnt and unburnt gases to mix in the cylinder. This causes the engine to bog in the midrange and misfire on top end. A simple way to fix this problem is to turn down the cylinder base 1mm, raise the exhaust port to 22mm from the top of the cylinder, and recess the squish band in the cylinder head 1mm at a 10-degree angle. You can also turn down the top of the spark plug hole 1mm to enable the plug to thread flush to the combustion chamber.

1990-99 KAWASAKI KX60

Flaws: cylinder ports vary, crankcase plugs leak, forks too soft
Fixes: adjust cylinder ports, epoxy plugs, install Terry fork kit

The only significant changes to this engine have been igniter boxes with different ignition curves. In the past I've recommended mods such as raising and widening the exhaust ports and grinding by-pass ports in the intake sleeve of the cylinder. Those mods still work well, and we have some updates that include raising the crankcase compression ratio. In the United States the latest rage is to overbore the cylinder 2mm, and plate the cylinder to fit the Wiseco Pro-Lite piston 648P8. That's possible because the AMA rules allow cylinders to be overbored 2mm. In England it's now possible to boost the displacement of the 1999 and older KX60s to 65cc. This requires cylinder boring and plating of the cylinder to fit the 2000 KX65 piston.

In England, it's possible to fit a centrifugal clutch to a KX60, to help a rider make the transition from auto to shifting on a larger bike. The kit is available from Moto X Rivara.

Best Value Mods

Engine: cylinder porting, Boyesen reeds

Suspension: Terry fork kit and stiffer springs

Reeds

There are some simple things you can do to boost the midrange power. One is to install a set of Boyesen dual-stage reeds to help the low- to mid-throttle response.

Cylinder Porting

The KX60 cylinder can be modified to suit a wide variety of riders. The following are some set-ups for beginner and expert riders. If you have a good set of files, you can match the exhaust ports to .845 inch or 21.5mm, measured from the top of the cylinder. Each exhaust port should be 21mm wide, measured on the circumference of the bore. To change the heights of the transfer ports, you'll need a right-angle die grinder. Set the transfer port heights to 1.265 inches or 32mm, measured from the top of the cylinder. To make crankcase boost ports, use a round file to grind channels in the intake side of the cylinder sleeve. These ports (5mm wide and 3mm deep) will enable gases to flow directly through the transfer ports for more midrange power. This procedure can be done for all model years of KX60s.

The set-up for low-end porting is more difficult than for top-end porting. The cylinder base must be turned down .010 inch or .25mm to retard and reduce the exhaust timing and duration. Also, the transfer ports must be modified for lower time-area. This is accomplished by applying epoxy to the rear transfer ports and narrowing them 3mm, measured on the circumference of the bore.

Pipes

For more top-end overrev, use a tuned pipe such as those from FMF, Pro-Racing, or R&D Racing.

Piston Port

Drill a 6mm hole in the intake side of the piston, centered between the ring alignment pins and just below the bottom ring groove. This will help the top-end power.

Carburetor

The stock carb is too small for expert riders who need top-end power. The KX80 carb (26mm on 1990–96 models) fits into

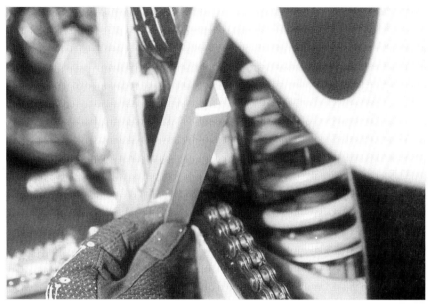

This aluminum channel strip can be riveted to the left backside of the sub-frame to protect it from chain-slap.

the intake and air boots of the KX60. This carb needs only minor jetting changes to adapt to the KX60.

Crankcases

The crankcases have three casting plugs positioned around the main bearings. Occasionally, these plugs leak, so it's best to smear some epoxy over the plugs from the outside of the crankcases.

Forks

If you are a relatively large rider or are aggressive with the front brake, you should switch to the optional stiff fork springs (Kawasaki part No. 44026-1175) to reduce front-end diving. Terry Kit in America makes an aftermarket fork kit that increases the forks' travel by 20mm and offers better damping characteristics. The kit includes damper rods with different sized holes for the rebound and compression damping. It's possible to improve the damping using the stock fork parts. This mod involves welding three holes closed in the damper rod, and relocating the compression holes. Braze both compression holes closed (holes located near the bottom of the damper rod). Then drill one 5mm hole positioned 46mm from the bottom of the damper rod, and one 5mm hole opposite of the first hole and 66mm from the bottom of the rod.

This mod gives the forks more low-speed compression. To improve the rebound damping, braze one of the rebound holes (the ones closest to the top of the damper rod). Use 10-weight fork oil after performing these mods.

Shock

The stock shock design doesn't allow for maintenance or valving. Companies like WP, Ohlins, Works Performance, and Pro-Racing make aftermarket shocks that can be serviced and revalved. Switch to one of those brands if you are interested in enhancing the rear suspension.

Swingarm

Novation Racing makes an aluminum swingarm that eliminates the linkage system and saves 4 pounds. Check out the Web site at www.novationracing.com

1983-96 KAWASAKI KDX200

with Jeff Fredette

Jeff Fredette is a veteran enduro rider who has raced the ISDE 16 times. He's finished all 16 times and scored 10 Gold medals, 5 Silver medals and 1 Bronze medal. Jeff's company, Fredette Racing Products, specializes in Kawasaki KDX 200 models. Jeff

offers a wide range of parts, accessories, and high performance services. Jeff answers tech questions over the phone, and these are the answers to the most popular topics. He's also got a 2-hour video on KDX repair and tuning and he answers questions on an on-line forum, www.dirtrider.net.

Front Suspension
1983–85

Use the stock fork springs for riders up to 180 pounds. Over that weight use 0.32-kilogram springs with 5-weight oil and a fork oil level of 5.5 inches measured with the springs out and the forks bottomed.

1986–88

The best fork oil weight to run is 7.5 (mix 5 and 10 Wt. 50/50). Run an oil level of between 4.75 to 5.5 inches. The forks are characteristically harsh on small rocks and for the best performance they need to be revalved. The use of progressive rate fork springs is recommended on all models for heavier riders (over 170 pounds). The stock fork springs sag over time. The maximum distance that the forks should sag under the bike's own weight is 3/4 inch.

1989–93

These forks are a little soft. Switching to stiffer springs makes a big improvement. For riders who weigh up to 170 pounds, we recommend .33-kilogram springs from the 1988 KDX. For heavier riders we recommend progressive springs 18-26 pounds. Try setting the compression adjusters 6-11 clicks out. If that still isn't to your liking, I offer revalving for the forks.

1995–96

The stock forks are sprung and valved for a 130-pound rider. For riders between 140 and 190 pounds, switch to 21-pound springs; riders over 200 pounds should use 23-pound springs. Set the oil level to 100mm and the compression adjuster to between 10 and 18 clicks out. The Race Tech Gold Valve kit works well with my shim placement specs.

Rear Suspension
1983–85 KDX

I use the stock spring and set the damper to position #2 for fast riding such as whoops and position #3 for slower riding over rocks. I set the sag to 1/2 inch unladen (the bike's own weight only) for riders under 175 pounds, and 1/4 inch for riders over 175 pounds.

1986–88

I used the stock shock valving with good results. The settings that worked best were 1/2 inch unladen sag for most riders and no sag for riders over 200 pounds. Compression damping settings were best at 3 clicks out for fast whooped out courses and 12 clicks out for tight woods and slow riding over rocks. Run the rebound adjuster at 2.5 turns out. Have the shock oil changed frequently (every 1,000 miles) to prevent shock shaft wear.

1989–93

The stock spring and shock valving is good if dialed-in properly. Start with a fresh oil change. Set the sag to 3.75 inches (with rider and fuel tank full). Set the compression clicker to 6 for fast terrain and 10 for slow terrain. Set the rebound clicker to 8 for fast terrain and 12 for slow terrain.

1994–96

The stock spring and shock valving work well for riders who weigh 170–200 pounds. If you were lighter or heavier than that, you would benefit from a different spring. Lighter riders should use a 4.8-kilogram spring and heavier riders should use a 5.2-kilogram spring. When you ride on fast terrain, set the compression adjuster to 8 clicks out, set it to 16 clicks for slow terrain. Set the rebound adjuster in the same way, more damping at higher speeds.

Engine Performance
1983–85

The stock pipe works best with an Answer products SA silencer. The cylinder ports should be cleaned and matched and the carburetor jetting should be as follows: 1983:150 main jet; 1984-85: 35 pilot jet and a 280 main jet.

1986–88 KDX

The biggest improvement in performance is had by changing the silencer. The Answer SA Pro works well with an FMF pipe. Cylinder porting (clean casting and match port heights) will tame the hard-hitting powerband and give more low and top end. Carburetor

jetting is as follows: 1986–87 models: 30 pilot jet, p-2 needle clip position, 330 main jet; 1988 model: 48 pilot jet, p-3 needle clip position, 155 main jet. When performing a top-end rebuild, the factory service manual doesn't explain the KIPS valve timing procedure. The dot marks on the drum valves align with the ring mark on the actuator rod (rack). To check your work, when the actuator rod is pulled out to the stop the valves should be open and when pushed in the valves should be closed.

1989–94

These modifications work best to improve the powerband over the entire rev range: FMF pipe and a straight-through silencer, Boyesen RAD Valve, cylinder porting. Carburetor jetting: 48 pilot jet, 1173 needle in the middle clip position, 158 main jet, and turn the air-screw to 1.5 turns out.

1995–96

The 1995 model was the first year for the new KX style exhaust valve system. The new design utilizes a wedge valve for the main exhaust port. This design enables better control of the effective stroke and compression ratio over a wider rpm band. The best mod is an FMF pipe. A silencer would be the next best choice. If you can run a straight-through silencer, use the FMF. If you need to run a spark arrestor, use an FMF or an Acerbis 035. The next mod you consider should be cylinder porting. The cylinder needs the casting marks smoothened and polished for more power throughout the band, especially on top end. A Boyesen RAD valve gives a modest gain in performance. If you are having problems with clutch slippage, switch to stiffer clutch springs (Kawasaki OEM No. 92144-1484). Run the trans oil level on the high side of the sight window. That will also help reduce the noise from the clutch side of the engine.

General Tips
1983–85

The clutch basket nut and crank gear nut are likely to come loose. It is best to apply a thread locking agent such as Red Loctite to the threads and check them for tightness periodically. Keep the ignition clean and dry. Condensation can cause coil breakdown.

This 1991 KX250 and all KDX250 cylinders are missing the boost ports that link the intake and transfer ports. In this photo a 3/8-inch drill is used to make the ports.

Shoup Enterprises in Colorado can re-wind the Mitsubishi stator plates for a fraction of the cost of a new replacement. Make sure you Loctite the kickstand bolt! The rock screen on the headlight makes a great headlight lens cover. Just bend the tabs to remount over the lens.

1986-88

The rear brakes need more return spring action. This can be done with a conduit connector attached to the brake cam bolt with the "C" of the conduit connector facing the rear. Take an old inner tube and make some rubber bands from it. Run them toward the swingarm and tap a bolt in the swingarm to anchor the rubber bands. Kawasaki brake shoes last the longest. Disc brake conversion kits can be had for about $400 from Fredette Racing.

1989–94

Loctite the left footpeg, kick stand, and kick starter nuts, and the odometer reset knob screw. These are costly parts to replace if you lose them! To cut the handlebars down, use a pipe cutter. That will enable you to remove the end plugs easier. Flush and replace the brake fluid monthly with Dot 4 brake fluid to prevent brake fade.

Chapter 13

TUNING TIPS FOR SUZUKI DIRT BIKES

1997-2000 SUZUKI RM125

Flaws: 1997-99 piston and cylinder breakage
Fixes: weld-narrow exhaust port and replate

In 1997 Suzuki made their latest generation of the RM125. With conventional twin chamber forks and revised frame geometry these bikes have excellent turning and handling characteristics. The bottom end of the engine is essentially the same. The cylinder is similar to the design from the early 1990s. By 2000, Suzuki had managed to perfect the cylinder for a wide powerband and great longevity. More recent models have the new generation of electronic carbs where fuel is pumped into the venturi during the midrange.

Best Value Mods

Engine: cylinder plating, Wiseco piston
Suspension: revalve shock for more rebound, stiffer fork springs

Cylinder Mods

The new 125s have a redesigned cylinder that is a hybrid retro design with a new-style exhaust valve and a 1992 cylinder port design. The extra set of sub-exhaust ports was eliminated because of chronic problems with the plating flaking off between the exhaust ports. The 1997 and '98 models had their own flaws. In an effort to get enough exhaust area to compensate for the sub-exhaust ports, the main exhaust ports were widened to 95 percent of the bore's total width. If the piston and ring were not changed often enough, the ring would eventually break and tear up the bore.

The maximum chordal width of the exhaust ports for reliable running is 51.5mm, measured from the widest outer edges of the exhaust ports. That is the same spec as the 2000 cylinders. In the United States, many tuning shops are widening ports too far. Caution: Don't exceed the maximum chordal width spec or the rings could be prone to accelerated wear. If you have a '97 RM125 cylinder that was modified by a tuner for a wider exhaust port, it's possible to repair the cylinder by welding corners of the exhaust port, thereby narrowing the port. Max Power and Aptec offer this service along with their replating service.

If you want to get more midrange and top end from the 1997-99 cylinders, it's as simple as raising the exhaust ports. The highest that you can raise the exhaust ports is 28mm, measured from the top of the cylinder.

Head Mods

When you raise the exhaust port you have to turn down the sealing surface of the head. In this way you can compensate the compression ratio in accordance with the change in effective stroke. When you raise the exhaust port to 28mm, turn down the head .6mm.

Clutch

Never use aftermarket clutch plates and springs in this bike. I tested two popular kits and the springs were either too stiff or the plate thickness was incorrect. When the stock basket wears out, replace it with a Hinson Racing clutch.

Forks

Just set the oil level to 210mm and install stiffer fork springs if your weight is a factor (over 160 pounds in riding gear).

Shock

The stock shock has too much low-speed rebound (LSR). To compensate, you should set the race sag to 95mm and the rebound adjuster to 6 clicks out. If you have to switch to a stiffer spring because of your weight, then you'll definitely have to get the shock revalved for more rebound damping. Another thing to consider is frequent oil changes, like every 20 riding hours. The bushings are very soft on these shocks and wear quickly.

1990-96 SUZUKI RM125

Flaws: nylon reeds crack, air box leaks
Fixes: carbon fiber reeds, seal the air box

The RM125 went through some big changes in the early 1990s. The 1989–92 models are similar in that they have the same generation engine and chassis. The 1993 model featured the redesigned frame, inspired by the testing done by Donnie Schmit and Stefan Everts when they won world championships in the early 1990s. The 1993 model handled better through whoops sections, and when the Twin Chamber forks were introduced in 1994, it made the Suzuki the best handling 125. The 1993 cylinder featured the new sub-exhaust ports. The port timing on these new-style cylinders has too much transfer port time-area, so the powerband is flat in the low end and hits hard when the exhaust valves open at 8,000 rpm. Here are some tips on improving the RMs.

Best Value Mods

Engine: carbon fiber reeds, cylinder mods
Suspension: shock revalving

Suspension

The suspension on the RMs is very good. The rear shock, however, needs more rebound damping. This can be improved with revalving or with an aftermarket piston and valve kit such as one from Pro-Action.

Ignition

The new digital ignition system on the 1994–96 models will fit on the 1991–93 models. It must be used as a set (stator and igniter box). The old-style ignition suffers from high-rpm misfiring over 12,000 rpm, which builds heat and eventually overheats the igniter box.

Intake System

The old-style nylon reeds were prone to cracking. They needed to be checked. The new carbon fiber reeds help the top-end over-rev. Aftermarket carbon fiber reeds are good replacements for the 1990–93 reed valves. The air box doesn't seal very well at the junction of the boot and the box. Reseal this junction with weather-strip adhesive.

Cylinder and Head Mods

The engine has a similar powerband to the other 125s. It can be modified for more low end with a hard midrange burst from 3,000 to 9,800 rpm or for a strong-pulling upper midrange with more peak horsepower from 8,800 to 12,500 rpm. The first powerband is ideally suited for Supercross, intermediate motocross, or enduro racing. The second powerband is for top experts only! Here are some guidelines for building each engine.

Low/Mid Powerband

The cylinder base must be turned down .032 inch or .8mm on a lathe, to reduce the exhaust port duration. Then the transfer ports must be raised to 42mm from the top of the cylinder. The rear transfer ports should be redirected to oppose each other rather than hooking towards the exhaust port.

Hooked ports waste fuel by short circuiting it out the exhaust port before the engine comes on the pipe. Because the cylinder base was turned down, the cylinder head's squish band must be remachined so the piston doesn't contact the head. The distance from the gasket surface to the squish band should be 1.2mm and the squish-band angle (10 degrees) should be matched. Boyesen reeds or a RAD-Valve will match the intake system to the new powerband. Final mod, set the power valve spring tension to one turn clockwise from zero.

Top-End Powerband

The main exhaust port must be raised to 28mm from the top of the cylinder. The two sub-exhaust ports must be widened 1mm each. Turn down the cylinder head .5mm at the gasket surface. Install a 38mm PJ Keihin carb and start with these jets: 60 slow jet, 5 slide, 1469 needle-middle position, and a 175 main jet. The Messico GP pipe makes 2 horsepower more than the next best pipe. Messico pipes are made in Italy. All of these mods will help the RM produce an honest 36 horsepower at the rear wheel. That is about 6 horsepower more than original with these mods.

ATEV

The 1995 RM125 has a new generation exhaust valve system that features bypass ports that vent gas pressure waves out the exhaust valve chamber. I recommend installing an automotive PCV check valve to prevent water from being drawn up the vent hose. The vent hose is mounted to the upper left side of the cylinder. Insert the PCV valve halfway up the vent hose. This will prevent any debris from being drawn into the cylinder. These new exhaust valves will interchange with older models but they don't offer any advantage.

Clutch Problems with 1993–96 RM125

Heavy clutch action with a low trans oil level will make the clutch cover wear out at the bushing where the actuating lever seats. This allows the actuating lever to wobble, causing poor clutch action. The symptoms of a worn cover are dragging, slipping, and difficulties adjusting the lever play. It's impossible to fit a needle bearing to the cover because there isn't enough cover material to fit the bearing. You just have to replace the cover when it wears out.

A Note on the 1996 RM125

The 1996 model used the bypass ports in the exhaust valves just like the 1995 model. The main difference is in the shape of the exhaust valves. In an effort to improve the low-end power of the RM125 cylinder, the new-style exhaust valves are oval in shape and have a flat edge that makes them seal closer to the piston. This lengthens the effective stroke and gives the engine better low to midrange power with a slight sacrifice of top-end power. The cylinder and head mods listed for the 1995 and earlier models work well on the 1996 model too. However, it isn't possible to interchange the 1996 and later cylinders with the 1995 and earlier models.

1985-89 SUZUKI RM125

Flaws: chronic piston seizures, ATEV breaks, linkage seizes
Fixes: thick sleeve and Wiseco piston, use 1990 valves in 1989 RM125s, grease bearings

These bikes were plagued with all sorts of problems ranging from chronic piston seizures to broken exhaust valves and corroded swingarm and linkage bearings.

Best Value Mods

Engine: Wiseco piston and cylinder sleeve
Suspension: grease linkage frequently

RM fuel valves are notorious for leaking, and on some early-model 250s, had poor overall flow. This valve is made by Pingel in Wisconsin.

Top End

The cylinders can't be bored past .5mm or .020 inch; otherwise, the cylinder sleeve becomes too thin and it can't transfer out the heat properly. You must have the cylinder sleeved if you need to bore beyond .5mm. The aftermarket sleeves are much thicker than the one in the stock cylinder. Aftermarket sleeves can be overbored as much as 2mm when using Wiseco pistons. RM125s

suffer from exhaust valve problems. The old-style drum valves become carbon-seized, so they must be cleaned often. The 1989 and 1990 models crack at the stems, causing them to fall into the cylinder bore and crash into the piston.

Crankshaft Seal

The left-side crankcase seals are prone to failure so they should be replaced every 10 engine running hours.

Swingarm

The swingarm bearings and linkage are prone to corrosion, so grease them often.

1996-2000 SUZUKI RM250

Flaws: weak suspension linkage, exhaust valve system problems

Fixes: monitor linkage for cracks and lubrication, polish exhaust valves

In 1996 the RM250 was *Motocross Action*'s Bike of the Year. It was the most improved bike of its class, but every new generation model has its share of problems. The 1996 RMs were delayed because the top shock mounts were welded on to the frames in the wrong position. Soon after the bikes were released, the shock linkage was recalled. Suzuki replaced the original linkage with a new and improved unit. The new unit still requires frequent maintenance and it should be inspected for cracks near the pivot holes. The 1996 engine is a close copy of the Honda CR250 engine, with a 66.4x72 bore and stroke and a cylinder reed valve. Some riders complain that this model doesn't have enough top-end power, but woods riders favor the excellent low-end to midrange power. Here are some tips for improving the 1996 RM250.

Best Value Mods

Engine: cylinder porting
Suspension: shock revalving

Exhaust Valve System

Although Suzuki copied Honda's cylinder design, they couldn't infringe on the patents of Honda's HPP system. The one thing Suzuki couldn't copy was Honda's excellent exhaust valve system. The 1996, 1998-2000 center exhaust valve is made of aluminum that causes a shock wave in the exhaust port, when the valve is in the high rpm position. This design is also prone to carbon build-up and erratic operation. The center valve doesn't fully recede into the roof of the port, leaving the flat edge of the valve exposed to the exhaust stream. It is possible to radius the bottom edge of the valve to improve the top-end power, but with a sacrifice of low-end power.

Another common problem is carbon build-up on the actuating rod that links the side drum valves to the center valve. The rod is exposed to the exhaust stream on each side of the center valve. This exhaust valve system requires frequent cleaning. You can polish the sharp edges of the valves, in order to reduce the friction, but take care not to remove the brown colored hard-anodized coating that protects the valves. Over time the center valve will become so worn at opposing corners that it will be prone to jamming in one position. Suzuki designed a stiff return spring for this new valve system. The spring, located behind the indexing knob on the right side of the cylinder, should be set to one turn clockwise from zero tension.

The articulated steel exhaust valve of the '97 RM is a better design than the single stage aluminum valve. I'm sorry that Suzuki only used it for one model year. The steel valve has two stages, like the RMX design. This is intended to give the engine a smoother powerband, but there are some simple mods to perform before this system works as well as the system on the CR.

The biggest improvement in top-end power can be had by grinding smooth the minor center valve so it conforms to the exhaust port roof. The stock design allows the valve to protrude out into the air stream and impede the outflow of the exhaust. It's easy to polish down the sharp edge with a round file. Start by removing the cylinder, turn it upside down on a bench top, and open the exhaust valves to the max. File down the portion of minor exhaust valve that extends into the port. Take care not to let the file touch the plated cylinder bore. That could cause the plating to chip and damage the bore. After you've finished, disassemble the exhaust valve system and clean out all the metal particles. The exhaust valve spring tension is critical. Set the minor valve spring tension (upper knob) to _ turn clockwise. Set the major valve spring tension to _ turn clockwise. If the spring tension is too tight, the valve's opening timing will be retarded, causing a detonation noise while accelerating through the mid-range. Sometimes excess spring tension can prevent the valves from opening, depending on the amount of carbon build-up on the valves.

Cylinder

The cylinder porting is very good, a close copy of the CR. However if you want more top-end power, raise the sub-exhaust ports to 39mm measured from the top of the cylinder. The 1998 model has a very small main exhaust port. It can be widened and raised to the same height as the sub-exhaust ports. On the 1999-2000 models Suzuki copied the KX250 cylinder design. Unfortunately the bridges that support the intake port tend to cause piston seizures. I figured out how to fix that problem by gusseting the bridges to increase rigidity and prevent them from flexing into the piston. However the cylinder needs to be replated in order to repair the weak intake bridges. The modified height of the transfer ports should be 58mm measured from the top of the cylinder.

Head Mods

In 1998 Suzuki switched from a dome shaped piston to a flattop design that works real well. Wiseco makes a flattop piston for the 1996-2000 RM250 (Wiseco part No. 705PS). When this piston is used on domed heads, it requires that the head be modified in the following manner: Turn down 2.5mm from the sealing surface. Set the tool angle to 4 degrees, set the squish recess depth to 1mm, and cut the squish angle until the tool blends into the chamber bowl.

Carb

Riders at high altitude or warm climates complain of rough running when accelerating out of turns. The reason is the carb's slide cutaway is too rich. The cutaway can be modified by filing and polishing for a finished depth of 7mm. Take care when performing this mod because a rough edge can cause the throttle to stick open.

Clutch

Most pros switch to a Hinson Racing clutch basket and pressure plate, combined with KX250 plates and springs (Kawasaki Fiber plates part No.13088-1105; Metal plates No. 13089-1066; Springs #No. 92144-1351). This set-up resists lurching, and slippage is better than the original clutch parts.

Suspension
Forks

Set the oil height to 210mm and adjust the clickers for conditions.

Shock

Set the sag to 95mm, and set the rebound adjuster to six clicks out.

1993-95 SUZUKI RM250

Flaws: rich carb jetting, front end dives, clutch plates break

Fixes: lean jetting, revalve rear shock and shorten, install Barnett or 1996 KX250 clutch plates and FMF aftermarket pressure plate

Suzuki changed the crankcases and added more flywheel weight in an effort to reduce the hard hitting midrange. The cylinder hasn't changed since 1992. This cylinder has such large transfer ports that it can't pull the extra flywheel weight and this makes the bike seem as if it has no low-end power. In 1995 Suzuki redesigned the exhaust valve system to use bypass ports in an effort to gain low-end power. In 1996 Suzuki changed the entire engine design to one that was very close to the current model Honda CR250. The bore and stroke was changed to 66.472mm. The cylinder was changed to the old reed valve in the cylinder design used in 1988. A new exhaust valve system was employed, but it is prone to carbon seizing. Also this exhaust valve design hinders the top-end power potential of this model. Here are some things you can do to tune the RM.

Best Value Mods

Engine: aftermarket silencer, cylinder porting

Suspension: revalve and shorten shock, stiffer fork springs

Intake System

Because of the angle of the stock reed valve, the reed petals tend to flutter badly at about 7,000 rpm. Replacing the petals with ones made of carbon fiber will help. The carb jetting is a bit too rich. I've had the best luck with a Honda CR needle No. R1368N with the clip in the middle position, and a 185 main jet. This needle is leaner than stock and the main jet is richer. Combine this with an NGK BP7EV spark plug and your RM will run smoother and crisper through the rev range. The stock air box is prone to water seepage. The air box should be sealed at the seams with duct tape.

Silencer

The original Suzuki silencer is poorly designed. Changing to an aftermarket silencer will dramatically improve the power over the full rev range.

Cylinder Porting

If you want a strong pulling powerband with more low end and a smoother midrange with loads more top-end over rev, then the cylinder has to be ported. The exhaust port must be raised to 37mm from the top of the cylinder and widened 2mm on the outer edge of each exhaust port The transfer ports are too large and that makes the stock RM flat at low rpm (under 4,000 rpm). Narrow the set of rear transfers 6mm (each port) at the back corner angles, and direct the ports to flow straight across at each other. This procedure must be done with epoxy since it is nearly impossible to fill the ports with molten aluminum during TIG welding.

Exhaust Valve Precautions

The two most common mistakes made with Suzuki's ATEV exhaust valve system are turning the spring preload knob too far clockwise (which puts too much tension on the valves and then they won't open at all—maximum preload is 1.5 turns clockwise from zero preload), and installing the right-side shaft spring in a crisscross position (that spring is designed so the spring tabs are parallel to each other).

1995 Exhaust Valve System

This system features bypass holes drilled in the exhaust valves. The exhaust gases are allowed to enter the chamber cover and provide resonance. However there is a serious design flaw. This chamber is vented to the atmosphere, allowing hot exhaust gases to escape out the black rubber vent hose fastened to the left side of the cylinder. The pressure waves present in the exhaust gases travel to the end of the tube and reflect back into the cylinder, drawing cold air and debris into the cylinder. It's best to block the vent tube with a bolt, tapped into the cylinder casting. There is a tube on the right side of the cylinder to vent excess transmission oil gases and water condensation. I recommend installing an automotive PCV valve. Make sure the PCV valve has hose ends of 1/4th inch. Connect the PCV valve in the middle of the left side vent hose. The PCV valve is a one way valve. Position the PCV valve so the flow is outward. This will prevent debris from being drawn up the hose and into the engine.

Trans Oil Filling

Suzukis tend to lose trans oil from the countershaft seal or it leaks into the crankcases through the right-side crankshaft seal and is combusted in the engine. You can tell when the seal is blown because the exhaust pipe will billow out white smoke, spark plugs will be fouled, and oil will drip from the pipe. Install 1,000cc of oil in the transmission and change it every 10 engine running hours.

Rear Frame Support

The support bar that bridges the rear frame tubes is vulnerable to being dented by the seat base when a rider lands hard from a jump. The frame support bar should be reinforced by welding a piece of steel flat stock on top of the existing support.

Rear Suspension

The rear shock has too much travel and that causes the weight bias to transfer forward. The common solution employed by suspension tuners is to shorten the shock travel. The shock travel can be shortened by inserting shims (8mm in total thickness) between the shock seal assembly and the bottoming plate. Of course the shock must be disassembled to do this mod and you should entrust this work to a skilled suspension tuner.

Gearing

The rear sprocket should be changed to a 50-tooth. Check the sprocket bolts frequently because they are prone to vibrating loose.

1990-92 SUZUKI RM250

Flaws: clutch problems, rich jetting, loose primary gear bolt

Fixes: replace needle bearing, leaner slide, replace bolt

These were fairly reliable bikes in their time. They have good suspension components that can be greatly improved with revalving. The forks need stiffer springs and the compression valving must be softened. The rear shock needs more rebound damping and that has always been a characteristic problem with Suzukis. The engines had some chronic problems such as clutch failures, leaky seals, and piston failures. Suzuki has redesigned these OEM parts for better reliability.

Best Value Mods

Engine: install a 4.5 slide in the carb, Boyesen RAD Valve

Suspension: soften fork compression, install 0.41-kilogram fork springs

Carb Jetting

The carb jetting is too rich. I recommend using a #40 pilot jet, 4.5 slide, position three on the needle, and a 320 main jet. Install a NGK BP7ES spark plug or the equivalent heat range in another brand of plug.

Silencer Mods

Shorten the silencer 50mm to improve the power throughout the rev range. This is easy to do on RMs because it is a straight silencer. Mark 50mm from the end of the silencer body (not the end cap). With the silencer assembled, use a hacksaw to cut the silencer. Then grind off the rivets from the end cap. Pack the silencer with new packing material (Silent Sport packing) and put the end cap on the body. Mark the holes for the rivets and drill three new rivet holes in the silencer body. Then install new rivets.

Chronic Clutch Problems

If your RM is having chronic problems of breaking clutch plates the problem might be that the center bushing and needle bearing is worn. This causes the clutch basket to wobble, putting a strain on the steel plates. Barnett clutch kits have wider tabs on the fiber plates and reduce the gouging that occurs in the fingers of the clutch basket.

Cylinder and Head Mods

The main difference between the early- and late-model RM250 cylinders is the size of the exhaust port outlet. It is larger on the early models. Suzuki wanted to boost the midrange torque of the later models so they reduced the size of the port, thereby boosting the exhaust gas velocity. That mod is nearly impossible to do on the early-model cylinders. However turning down the cylinder base 1mm will improve power throughout the rev range. The exhaust and transfer ports have the same dimensions as the later-model cylinders, so modify the ports as listed in the 1992–95 RM recommendations.

Loose Primary Bolts

The bolt that retains the primary gear on the crankshaft tends to come loose. If the bolt ever comes loose, replace it with one from a 1995 model and apply a thread locking agent to the bolt and torque it to factory specs.

Reed Valve

A Boyesen RAD valve improves the low- to midrange power of the RM250 and is one bolt-on item that is really worth the money.

1985-89 SUZUKI RM250

Flaws: cylinder plating chips, ATEV spring fails, bushings wear

Fixes: electroplate cylinder, replace spring, service bushings

During the late 1980s the RM250 was transformed from a wide, top-heavy trail bike to a sleek racer that carves a tight line. Here are some tips for improving the longevity and performance of the RM250.

The 1987 and 1988 models were very similar and represented a major design change over the 1985 and 1986 models. *Dirt Rider* magazine rated the 1987 RM250 as the best bike of the class. These bikes had conventional cartridge forks and a modern tapered-shim shock-valve design. If you are currently riding a 1987–88 RM250, your bike may have some of these symptoms: front forks rebound too fast, exhaust smoke is ex-

cessive, powerband is flat, and spark plugs foul easily.

The 1989 and 1990 models are narrow bikes with low centers of gravity. They featured the original inverted cartridge forks, a case-reed-valve engine, and the new TMX Mikuni carb. These models had a hard-hitting powerband, and the suspension worked well for aggressive riders. Characteristic problems include clutch plate breakage, the transmission pops out of second and third gear, spark plug fouling at low speeds, and rear shock kicking.

Best Value Mods

Engine: cylinder plating
Suspension: Braking oversize disc

Cylinder Plating

The boron-composite cylinder plating material tends to flake on the 1987–89 models. Examine the intake side of the cylinders for wear. The cylinders can be repaired with nickel silicon-carbide plating from companies such as Max Power, Aptec, or US Chrome.

Exhaust Valve System

The exhaust valves tend to accumulate thick oil deposits that eventually lock the valves in the closed position. When this happens, the engine will run flat at high rpm. Remove the cylinder and clean the valves with oven cleaner, detergent, and water. Manually operate the exhaust valve control lever and make sure the valves move with the lever. There is a spring on the lever, so it can move even if the valves are seized. If the exhaust valve spring tensioner (located on the upper left corner of the cylinder) is turned too far clockwise, then the valves will be sprung in the closed position. If your RM has been overbored and has an aftermarket steel sleeve installed in the cylinder, then the exhaust valves must be filed for adequate clearance.

Loose Primary Bolts

The bolt that holds the gear on the right side of the crankshaft tends to vibrate loose. When it backs off the threads, it prevents the exhaust valve governor control from operating the exhaust valves. The best fix is to remove the bolt and clean the bolt and crankshaft threads. Then apply a thread-locking

agent such as red Loctite, and torque the bolt to factory specs.

Excessive Spark Plug Fouling

If your RM pumps out exhaust smoke like a mosquito abatement truck and fouls spark plugs, then the right-side crankshaft seal is probably blown. This is a common problem that is cheap and easy to fix. The seal costs about $10. The right-side engine cover and clutch must be removed so you can access the primary gear. The seal is under the primary gear. If you do not have a clutch-holding tool or access to pneumatic impact wrenches, then bring your bike to a mechanic. This is a simple mechanical procedure, but it is dependent on the use of the right tools.

Clutch Plate Breakage

If your RM is breaking clutch plates periodically, then the bushing and needle bearing for the clutch basket may be worn, allowing for excessive axial movement of the clutch. This bushing and bearing should be replaced every two riding seasons. Another cause of clutch-plate breakage is a clutch basket with deep groove marks caused by the fiber plates. When the clutch is disengaged, the plates just stick in the grooves, causing the clutch action to be "grabby." Sometimes, you can fix the problem by filing down the edges of the grooves in the clutch basket. In most cases you should replace the worn clutch basket as a set with a new bushing and bearing.

Missed Shifts

The 1989–92 RM250s sometimes developed shifting problems from down-shifting too often with too great of an engine load. The problem is caused by worn or bent shift forks. The shift forks should be replaced every time the lower end of the engine is rebuilt or every two riding seasons.

Suspension Rebounds Too Quickly

The forks and the shock can slowly develop too fast of rebound damping for the same reason: the bushings are worn out. If the forks make a clanking sound on the upstroke or cause your forearms to pump up severely, then the bushings on the piston rod are so worn that the oil bypasses the piston, thereby reducing the damping effect. The

RM Clutch Plate Breakage

Question: My 1990 Suzuki RM250 suffers from chronic clutch-plate breakage. What could the problem be?

Answer: The fiber plates on RM250s break when there is too much radial movement between the clutch basket and shaft. There are two main causes of this excess movement: worn bushing and bearing (located between the clutch basket and main shaft), and a loose primary gear. You can check these parts by trying to wiggle the clutch basket while bolted to the shaft. Excess movement indicates that the bushing or bearing is worn. To check the primary gear, remove the clutch basket and try to twist the gear back and forth. The gear is rubber-mounted so it will move slightly, but if it moves a lot, the rubber bushings are probably worn. The only way to fix this problem is to replace the clutch basket.

RMX Gears in an RM

Question: I trail ride a 1992 RM250. I realize this bike was designed for motocross but I ride on some fast trails and I need a wider 5th gear. I tried fiddling with the gearing but it affected the bike too much for tight woods riding. I called my local Suzuki dealer and asked if 5th gear from the RMX would fit in the RM transmission, he said he didn't think so. Any suggestions?

Answer: I checked the Suzuki part numbers for the trans shafts and gears. Your Suzuki dealer is right, the shafts are different. You could swap the entire trans, but that would be expensive. A-Loop sells drop-in 5th gear sets for about $100. They make these gears for the CR and the RM.

RMX Rebound Adjusters Won't Stop

Question: I rebuilt the forks of my RMX250 for the first time and now one of the rebound adjusters won't thread down to the zero position, it just keeps turning. What did I do wrong and how can I fix it? I hope I didn't mess up the forks.

Answer: Don't ride your bike until you fix this problem! It is likely that the piston rod was not threaded completely into the fork cap before the jam nut was tightened. The rebound adjuster screw has nothing to stop against. If the jam nut loosens, the piston rod will unthread from the cap and the loose parts will flop around inside the fork tube causing major internal damage to the fork. Fix this problem a soon as possible! If you don't trust your mechanical abilities, trust the work to a qualified suspension technician.

piston-rod seal band and bushing are only available with the repair service from companies such as Pro-Action, White Bros., Race Tech, and Scott's.

Bigger Brakes

Oversize brake discs can give a boost in braking power. The front end especially benefits from this mod. A company called Braking makes oversize disc and caliper bracket kits for the front end of the 1989–95 RMs.

Mikuni Carburetor Update

The 1985–88 RM250s had the Mikuni TM carb. Later models had TMX carbs. These carbs do not have an idle adjustment. If you are trail riding and would like the convenience of a bike that idles, then you need a Mikuni TMS carb, available from White Bros. If your RM bogs when landing from big jumps, then add a Boyesen Super Bowl and T-vent kit.

1989-99 SUZUKI RMX250

Flaws: weak power, chain guides bend, brakes weak

Fixes: gusset chain guide brackets, Braking disc

The RMX hasn't changed much over the years. The chassis and suspension have evolved slower than the RM. The main difference between the engine of the RM and RMX is the top end and transmission. The RMX has a superior exhaust valve design but the RM has a better cylinder and head design. The RMX has lower gear ratios for first and second and a higher ratio for fifth gear.

Best Value Mods

Engine: head mod, Cometic gaskets, FMF Fat Boy pipe

Suspension: steering damper

Top End

The RMX cylinder needs a wider exhaust port and smaller transfer ports. The compression ratio is very low. There is a simple solution, advance the port timing with a thicker base gasket (1mm, .039-inch) and a thinner head gasket (.25mm, .010-inches). Cometic sells these gaskets individually. If you want to have the cylinder and head machined, widen the exhaust ports (2mm, .080-inches) on each outer edge. The rear transfers can be epoxied in the back corners. The head can be turned down (.75mm, .030-inches). These mods are for a stock base gasket and a 1989 RM250 head gasket or the Cometic equivalent. The exhaust valve system on the RMX uses a dual-stage valve design. It's great for smooth power delivery but requires frequent maintenance in the form of cleaning. There are two long coil springs that exert tension on the secondary valves. Those springs get clogged with carbon. Pay special attention to cleaning those springs when servicing the exhaust valve system.

Carb

A 39.5mm Keihin PWK is the best performing carb for the RMX. It has an idle circuit that makes it more controllable at low throttle openings and the throttle response is smoother.

Pipe

FMF Fat Boy or Burley pipe and silencer.

Kick Starter

The kick starter knuckle joint tends to wear prematurely, allowing the kick starter lever to flop around. Unfortunately there is no aftermarket replacement part. You have to keep the knuckle joint clean and oiled with chain lube.

Brakes

A Braking oversize disc is recommended for the front. Braking discs are laser cut from stainless steel and offer better longevity and stopping power than OEM discs. Moose Racing hex-head brake pins are more durable than the OEM pins, plus they're easier to remove.

Chain Guide Mods

The chain guide is mounted to the swingarm with straight tabs. There is no support to prevent the tabs from bending inward and guiding the chain off center. Pete recommends butt-welding triangular tabs on the chain guide tabs and the swingarm. Aluminum covers for the guide aren't really effective until the mounting tabs are improved.

1990-2000 SUZUKI RM80

Flaws: magneto cover leaks, pistons wear fast
Fixes: Boyesen magneto cover, Wiseco Pro-Lite piston

This bike is a great design that suffers from one big problem: poor quality materials used in the engine components. The forks are a little soft too. Here are some tips on improving the longevity of the RM80.

Best Value Mods

Engine: Boyesen magneto cover
Suspension: Emulator Valve, fork spring preload

Engine

The cylinder bore and the crankshaft bearings wear out quicker than on other Japanese dirt bikes. The cylinder uses a steel sleeve that can be rebored to accept oversize piston and rings. Wiseco Pro-Lite forged pistons are much better quality than original cast Suzuki pistons. The cylinder can only be overbored twice, any larger and the liner can't transfer out the heat and the engine will lose power. The cylinder has rough transitions between the liner and the ports. Removing the burrs from the ports and turning down the head .010-inches will help broaden the powerband. Don't waste a lot of money on porting because the cylinder won't last forever!

The connecting rod and main crankshaft bearings need to be changed at least once a racing season. The water pump impeller is made of plastic and tends to melt when the engine gets really hot. Boyesen Engineering makes an aluminum impeller that pumps more volume of water and won't melt from the hot coolant.

Magneto Leaks

Replace the magneto cover with one made of aluminum. This will help seal water out from the generating coils, a common cause of ignition failure. Boyesen Engineering sells aluminum magneto covers for RM80s.

Forks

The forks need stiffer springs but no manufacturer makes springs for the RM80. However most tuners add 10mm-long aluminum spacers between the fork caps and the springs. Race Tech's Emulator Valve significantly improves the fork damping. Change the fork oil to 10 weight for Emulator valves, and 15 weight for the stock forks.

Shock

The best mod for increasing the service life and the performance of the shock, is to plate the inside bore of the shock body with Apticote 2000 nickel silicon-carbide. Pro-Action offers this service.

Chapter 14

TUNING TIPS FOR YAMAHA DIRT BIKES

1997-2000 YAMAHA YZ125

Flaws: requires frequent top-end service, forks bottom

Fixes: replace the piston kit every 15 hours of running, stiffer fork springs and hydraulic anti-bottoming device

This bike is widely considered to have the best engine in its class, but it sacrifices some reliability. A couple of key areas to watch are the top end, connecting rod, and frame. The 1999 cylinder had the best performance but was most prone to failure. The 2000 model cylinder is the best overall design and includes a new exhaust valve design. The frames are prone to cracking when the bikes are jumped too hard and key bolts are left loose like the engine mounts and swingarm pivot. Refer to the frame chapter for tips on inspecting and strengthening frames.

Best Value Mods

Engine: Wiseco Pro-Lite piston kit, weld cylinder exhaust bridge

Suspension: Magnum anti-bottoming fork accessory, weld frame cracks

Cylinder

The cylinder's exhaust port is very wide. The exhaust port's bridge has a weak spot, about 10mm down from the top of the port. The problem is that the exhaust valve pockets are machined too deep and intersect the bridge, causing its thickness to be reduced at a critical point. The bridge is prone to cracking at this point if the piston seizes. It's best to replace the piston rings every 5 hours of engine time. If the exhaust bridge cracks it can be repaired by a company that specializes in electroplating. The bridge needs to be welded and made wider (3mm). This mod will require you to fit the exhaust valves. You'll have to chamfer the corner of the valves that butt the exhaust port's bridge. If you don't grind the valves properly, they won't close all the way.

Crankshaft

Another significant design error lies in the crankshaft. A two-stroke crankshaft has less mass on top near the pinhole to compensate the balance factor of the reciprocating mass of the connecting rod and piston assembly. Manufacturers use different designs to fill-in the void around the pinhole.

Honda fits sheet metal covers around the crank. Kaw and Suzuki use lightweight aluminum slugs. Yamaha uses plastic slugs. The problem seems to be that the plastic slugs are fitted so closely around the pinhole that they shroud the big end bearing from getting enough lubrication. The crank gets hot around the big end and the plastic starts to swell-up, thus compounding the problem. Eventually the plastic melts and flows into the big end bearing, causing the bearing to fail. This is my solution to the problem. Disassemble the crank to replace the rod assembly. The melted plastic must be removed with a die-grinder and a large fluted tool-bit. Bevel the plastic slug at a 45-degree angle all around the pinhole to allow more area for the pre-mix to lubricate the big end bearing. Removing plastic from the slug does lower the crankcase compression ratio and that causes a slight loss of low-end power, but reliability is worth the sacrifice in performance.

Carb

The carb jetting on the 1999 model has too rich of a slide. Switch to a 7.0 slide if your bike has a bog when fluctuating the throttle over whoops and through turns.

Forks

These are the best performing forks for a 125. However some riders complain about the metallic clunking noise when the forks are bottomed out. Yamaha switched to an elastomer foam bumper for the anti-bottoming device. Hydraulic products work much better. Devol Racing has a product called the

This is the old-style gear for the YZ80 1993-95. Although they aren't prone to problems, the tips of the gear teeth can wear. The Yamaha replacement part is case-hardened much better.

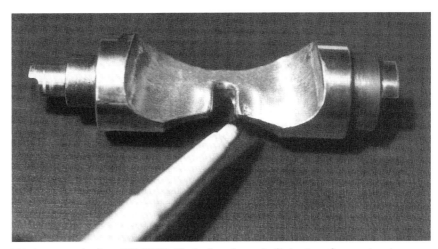

This is a powervalve for a 1993 YZ125. The leading edge can be filed so it conforms to the exhaust port and maximizes the flow out the exhaust port.

Magnum. It is an anti-bottoming device that fits inside the cartridge. It requires specialized knowledge of cartridge forks to install the device so it's best to rely on a suspension technician who has the proper tools. Take care to use the correct spring rate for your geared weight and riding style. If the front fork race sag is less than 30mm, switch to a softer spring rate. If the race sag is more than 55mm, switch to a stiffer spring rate.

Shock

The stock shock valving is very good and it's not likely that you'll need to have it revalved.

Frame

The frame is especially prone to cracking at the footpeg mounts. The best preventive maintenance is to reinforce the footpegs with gusset plates welded under the footpegs and along the frame tubes. Another trouble spot is the lower engine mounts. They are only spot-welded on one side of the plate. Find a skilled fabricator in your local area to reinforce the footpeg and engine mounts.

1994-96 YAMAHA YZ125

Flaws: frame tabs crack, chronic coolant leaks

Fixes: gusset frame, install head alignment pins

This bike is a good design. The exhaust valve system is similar to the RM in that it reduces the volume of the exhaust port and boosts the port velocity at low rpm. This system was refined each model year, to improve performance and reduce the need for maintenance. The 1994 model had some teething problems. Yamaha redesigned the connecting rod and bearing to reduce premature failure. The problem of second gear seizures was remedied in the 1995 model. The frame on the 1995 model was gusseted in several places because the 1994 model developed cracks at the radiator mounts, top shock mount, and footpegs. That problem can be easily corrected with frame gusseting. The YZ cylinder and head need alignment pins because the forces from the head stay can cause chronic coolant leaks. This problem manifests into erosion at the top edge of the cylinder, damaging the Nikasil plating.

The powerband is similar to that of the other 125s, good midrange, but falls flat at 10,600 rpm, making 29 horsepower at the rear wheel. Don't believe the exaggerated horsepower claims of some Japanese manufacturers. They all make this same peak power at nearly the same rpm. The YZ has great low- to midrange power, making it an ideal trail bike. If you want to make your YZ competitive in motocross, you have to do mods to the cylinder and head, plus add a pipe and silencer.

Best Value Mods

Engine: FMF pipe and silencer
Suspension: Eibach fork springs

Shifter Mods

Over the years Yamahas have been criticized as being hard to shift. Polishing the shifting mechanism and drilling oil holes in the clutch hub will help, but the best product on the market is Race Tech's external shifter mechanism. It's fairly expensive but many riders swear by it. This product enhances the leverage ratio of the shift lever.

Forks

The Kayaba forks have great damping but the spring rate is set for a fairly light rider (160 pounds). If you have any problems with head shaking or front end diving when braking for turns, consider stiffer fork springs.

High-RPM Powerband

The set-up for producing top-end power from the YZ is similar to the other 125s, but much less expensive than the Honda.

Cylinder and Head

The cylinder and head designs of the 1994−96 models are similar, but these specs on the exhaust port and head are applicable to those models. The cylinder transfer ports have the right profile but the exhaust port needs to be raised and widened for a 12,500-rpm peak. The exhaust port must be raised to 28mm from the top of the cylinder and enlarged 1mm on each side. The head should be machined for a higher compression ratio. If your YZ125 suffers from chronic coolant loss, you should machine the squish

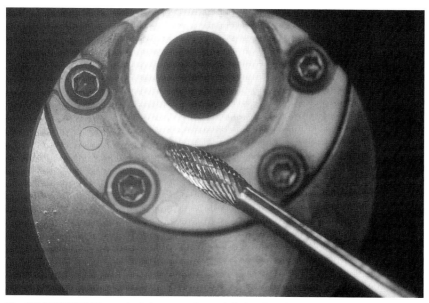

The 1996-2000 YZ125s use plastic inserts on the crankshaft. When the big end bearing fails the plastic melts around the rod faces. In that case the plastic slag must be ground off.

band's recess in the head to .75-1.0mm. This will help keep the engine from developing coolant leaks because it reduces the pressure on the O-ring in the cylinder. Also you should elongate the head stay bolt hole to allow for a bit of movement in that area of the motor mount. Older bikes especially need more clearance at the head stay because the frames tend to get deformed from too many hard landings.

Piston Interchange

The 1998 model piston has a boost port in the intake side that improves top-end over-rev and helps the piston run cooler. The 1998 and newer pistons use a smaller pin and a bearing with thicker needle bearings. The pin is lighter and the bearing will take a higher load than the old-style bearing. These parts can only be used as a set. The Wiseco order numbers are a 726P8 piston kit and a B1038 needle bearing.

Exhaust System

The stock silencer is too restrictive for a high revving engine. In 1994, World Champ Bob Moore and Motocross Des Nations Champion Paul Malin used FMF pipe and silencers.

Intake System

The intake system is the next component to be modified. You'll need to upgrade to a 38mm carb (Mikuni Jetting: 20 pilot, 4 slide, 63 needle, 360 main jet).

Install carbon fiber reeds (.5mm thick) or a RAD valve, because the stock reeds start to flutter badly and restrict the intake flow at 11,200 rpm.

Crankcase Porting

This final mod is optional but it makes a significant difference. The crankcases are slightly mismatched to the cylinder, and the transition between the intake port and the crankcase ports can be improved with filing and polishing.

1992-93 YAMAHA YZ125

Flaws: flat power, ring pins vibrate out
Fixes: match power valves, Wiseco Pro-Lite

The 1992 and 1993 model cylinders were similar to the 1990 model.

Best Value Mods

Engine: power valve matching, carb jetting
Suspension: basic servicing

Power Valve Mods

Matching the power valve to the exhaust port can have big gains in performance, when the valve is fully open. The power valve governor control is located under the right-side

engine cover. Installing a ramp-cup and spring from earlier-model YZs can help the midrange power. Yamaha part numbers for these parts are 90501-30742-00 ramp-cup, 3XJ-11912-00 spring.

Piston

A Wiseco piston should be installed because the piston ring alignment pins tend to fall out of the OEM pistons after sustained over-revving of the engine.

Head Mod

The squish band of the cylinder head needs to be narrowed to 6mm, measured from one side of the chamber. This work can be performed on a metal lathe. If you raise the exhaust port, you'll have to reduce the volume of the cylinder head to a total of 9cc.

Cylinder Mods

Recommended cylinder mods include turning down the cylinder base .5mm, and raising the exhaust port to 26mm from the top of the cylinder. Apply epoxy to the hook angles of the rear transfer ports. These mods reduce the time-area of the transfer ports and increase the exhaust port. This will help the bike accelerate harder in the midrange with more top-end over rev.

Carb Jetting

Recommended baseline jetting for the 36mm Mikuni carb: 20 pilot jet, 4.5 slide, 56 needle, and a 310 main jet.

Reed Valve

The Boyesen RAD valve works well for overall power gains and Carbontech carbon fiber reeds work well for high rpm powerbands.

1990-91 YAMAHA YZ125

Flaws: weak low-end power (1991 model)
Fixes: change gearing, reeds, and 1990 Power Valve parts

The 1990 top-end parts are regarded as the best-tuned components Yamaha ever designed for the YZ125, and the 1991 model was notorious as the worst. Where the 1990 engine was great for motocross, the 1991 had a narrow, hard-to-use powerband. The weak low end made 1991 YZ125s slow out of turns. Changing to a lower final drive ratio and installing Boyesen reeds helps a lot. On the 1991 model, it's best to switch to the ramp cup and spring from the 1990 power valve governor. The 1991 model used a two-angle ramp cup that actually works well on the 1992–93 models.

Best Value Mods

Engine: 1991-model Boyesen Reeds, 1990 Power Valve parts, 11-tooth countershaft sprocket

Suspension: basic servicing

Cylinder Interchange

If you have a 1991 model and need to replace the cylinder, consider switching to the 1990 model parts. You'll need to change the cylinder and power valve as a set.

Gearing

Some other simple ways to get more low- to midrange power from either of these models is to use a front sprocket that is one tooth smaller.

Reeds

Boyesen Dual Stage reeds will dramatically improve the YZ's low-end power.

1985-89 YAMAHA YZ125

Flaws: weak clutch, engine bogs
Fixes: Barnett clutch, carb jets

The 125s from the late 1980s suffered from drive train problems. The clutches didn't get enough oil flow, the clutch springs were too soft, and second gear was prone to breakage. In addition, the Mikuni carb had bogging problems when landing from jumps. The following is an overview of how to fix these bikes.

Best Value Mods

Engine: T-vents for carburetor
Suspension: regular service

Clutch

The clutch is easy to fix. Stiffer clutch springs and better-quality plates such as the ones found in Barnett clutch kits will fix the slipping problem. Polishing the clutch-actuating rod helps, too. Yamaha recommends drilling two oil holes (1/16 inch diameter) in each of the female splines of the inner clutch hub. This helps the oil flow, keeping the clutch plates cooler.

Second gear drive and driven gears are prone to breakage. The best precaution is to use the clutch when downshifting and change the transmission oil often. The gear ratios are very wide between first and second gear and these engines don't have much low-end power. If you are having problems bogging the engine out of turns, switch to a 12-tooth countershaft sprocket.

Carburetor

The carb on the 1986–88 models was prone to bogging and starvation problems. Make sure the float level is set parallel to the float bowl base and use these jets as a starting point: 45 pilot, 4 slide, Q-0 needle jet, 290 main jet, and a 3.5 inlet needle and seat. Install the modern T-vent set-up.

Reed Valves

The FMF RAM valve works well on YZ125s. Use the short rev plates for more low-end power.

1999-2000 YAMAHA YZ250

Flaws: wheel spin, flat top end
Fixes: flywheel weight, raise exhaust port to 39 mm

These models were the first with the new engine. The bore and stroke were changed to the same as all other 250s. The old engine was a square bore and stroke and the new engine is over-square, meaning that the stroke is longer. The new exhaust valve system is similar to the CR and RM design, with the exception that the sub-exhaust ports open at a higher rpm than the center valve. This bike is an excellent effort and there is very little to do to it except for adjustments like personal preferences.

Best Value Mods

Engine: flywheel weight
Suspension: springs for your weight

Cylinder and Head Mods

The sub-exhaust ports can be raised to 38mm from the top of the cylinder for more top end and the head can be turned down 5mm at the gasket surface. This set up requires race

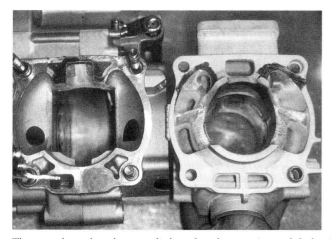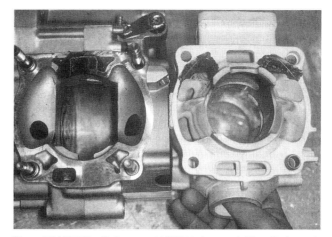

These two photos show the extra cylinder and crankcase porting needed when installing a 1994 YZ250 cylinder on a 1996 YZ250 lower end. The cylinder needs the boost ports enlarged and the crankcase needs a center port added.

The mid-1980s to 1990s model YZs used an aluminum sleeve nut on the steering head. These may be difficult to remove because of corrosion. Apply a dab of Anti-Seize or moly grease to the sleeve nut before installing it on the steering stem.

gas to run properly. The engine tends to be explosive in the midrange. A flywheel weight will make the power more tractable.

Big Bore 275cc

It's possible to overbore and electroplate a YZ cylinder for a displacement of 273cc. The piston is from a Honda 4-wheeler and is made by Wiseco (Part No. 526P8) and is 69.5mm in diameter. This mod requires that the exhaust valves and head be clearanced for the larger piston. These mods make the engine ideally suited for Vet MX or GNCC racing.

1997-98 YAMAHA YZ250

Flaws: soft top end, wheel spin

Fixes: port cylinder, raise compression, flywheel weight

Yamaha redesigned this engine, particularly the cylinder and head. The new cylinder has transfer ports similar to a Honda, the most copied design on the market. The new reed valve is excellent and you won't have to worry about it protruding into the rear boost port like previous models.

However, Yamaha chose very conservative transfer port timing. Here are the mods for the cylinder and head.

Best Value Mods

Engine: Cometic thick base gasket .039, flywheel weight

Suspension: set sag and clickers, stiffer fork springs for riders over 180 pounds.

Cylinder

Raise the transfer ports 1mm or use the optional thick base plate marketed by Yamaha. The use of the plate requires you to turn down the head 1mm. The sub-exhaust ports have been raised to the spec that we published in previous tuning tips, but the powervalve's sub-exhaust channels have been altered to retard the port's opening timing. You can use a round file to adjust the sub-exhaust channels on the powervalve, for more top-end power. Modify the channels to open sooner by filing the leading edge of the powervalve 4mm at a 45-degree angle. Don't be tempted to raise the main exhaust port like Yamaha recommends in their published Wrench Reports. That mod will only make the plating peel from the port, causing cylinder failure.

Head Mods

If you are using just the stock Yamaha base gasket, the most you can turn down the head is .5mm. No adjustments to the squish band depth or angle are needed. If you want to install the Wiseco flattop piston, (No. 706PS), turn down the head 2mm, set the squish band depth to 1mm, and set the squish band angle to 4 degrees.

Forks

The fork valving is pretty good in stock form. Heavier riders will need to change up to a stiffer spring rate like a .41 Kilogram. The fork oil level works best at 90mm. Set the compression clicker from 4 to 8 clicks out.

Shock

Set the race sag to 95mm for best results. The rebound adjuster is very sensitive to changes. The rebound adjuster works best in the range of 4 to 8 clicks out. Set the compression adjuster to 12 clicks and experiment from there.

1997-98 YZ250 '94 Cylinder and Long Rod Kit

There's been a lot of hoopla in the magazines about things like "Long-Rod" kits and the 1994 YZ250 cylinder. In 1997 Yamaha riders Kevin Wyndam and Ezra Lusk used long-rod kits and 1994 cylinders on their factory bikes. The magazines never explained what the individual parts do, and how they affect performance. The 1994 YZ250 cylinder didn't utilize a resonator like the newer models. The resonator improves the low end of the powerband, before the power valve opens (6,000-8,000 rpm). The 1994 YZ had a powerband with a hard midrange hit. It also had a lack of low-end power. Great for pro riders but bad for trail riders. The '94 YZ cylinder had larger transfer ports, and an additional boost port linking the crankcase to the intake side of the cylinder. When combined with the 1989 YZ250 connecting rod, and crankcase mods to feed the boost port, the 1994 cylinder conversion can make the 1997-98 YZ250s into powerful midrange performers.

Building a factory replica YZ like this isn't cheap. The average price is about $1,600. It requires total engine disassembly and a new exhaust system. Here is a short explanation of the key components to this expensive conversion and how to get the most from the investment in parts.

Rod Ratios

Connecting rods are all about time and leverage. On a two-stroke engine, changing the connecting rod length affects a number of other components. The term *rod ratio* is the connecting rod length (center to center) vs. the length of the stroke. Generally speaking, the higher the rod ratio (longer connecting rod) the better suited the engine will be for more high rpm power. Here is a brief explanation of how it works.

When the piston reaches bottom dead center of the stroke (BDC), the longer connecting rod will cause the piston to accelerate faster on the upstroke. The rapid changes in crankcase volume cause the reeds to open to their maximum flow-area. When the piston rises to top dead center (TDC), the longer rod will dwell the piston at TDC for a longer period of time than a shorter rod. By dwelling the piston at TDC, a greater pressure rise could occur inside the combustion chamber, before the piston starts on its down stroke.

What Changes What?

Using a longer connecting rod makes it necessary to install a spacer plate under the cylinder, with a thickness equal to the difference between the stock and longer connecting rods. The common misconception is that a longer rod gives the engine more displacement. It doesn't increase the displacement because the stroke length can only be changed at the crankshaft flyweights. That is called "stroking" a crankshaft, because the distance from the center of the crank to the big end pin is relocated farther away from the center. The biggest change in the engine comes from the increase in crankcase volume and the resultant decrease in the primary compression ratio. This may cause a loss of throttle response and low-end power. Some tuners use epoxy to line the walls of the transfer ports in an effort to decrease the crankcase volume and raise the primary compression ratio.

Cylinder Interchange

Although the cylinders are the same height, the powervalve, ports, and exhaust spigot are all different. In order to install a 1994 YZ250 cylinder on a later model, you have to swap the exhaust pipe flange or buy a pipe from Pro-Circuit. Check on availability of the pipe first. The transfer ports at the crankcase side are much different, requiring both the '94 cylinder and the later-model cases to be matched as a set. The powervalve and head from a '94 cylinder must also be installed. Regarding reed valves, the Boyesen or the V-Force is a better choice over stock valves.

1992-96 YAMAHA YZ250

Flaws: shock linkage, reeds, detonation, lean jetting (Mikuni carbs)

Fixes: DeVol linkage, Boyesen reeds, #59 Needle and 400 main jet for Mikuni only

This engine and chassis have great potential for improvement. The stock engine has a hard midrange hit but falls flat at high rpm. The stock chassis has a shock linkage system with a high rising rate ratio. This makes the rear end handle harshly when accelerating out

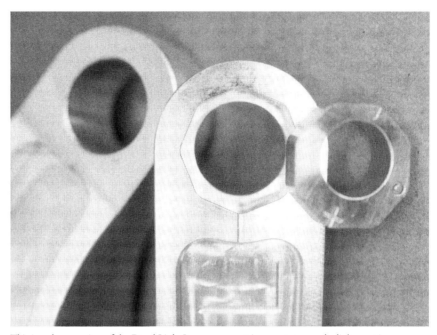

This is a close-up view of the Devol Link. It uses an eccentric mount to vary the linkage ratio.

of turns. The carb jetting on the models with Mikuni carbs (1994 and earlier) were jetted too lean. The Keihin carb was introduced in 1995 and the standard jetting is very close to optimum. The 1995 model featured an updated exhaust valve system. The new system used a surge chamber for low rpm. This helped soften the midrange hit but the power valve is still susceptible to wearing, as were the earlier models. The 1996 model featured a new chassis with a shock linkage system similar to the DeVol design. The top end was changed too. Yamaha changed the cylinder head design to one with greater piston-to-head clearance. This mod reduces the need for race gas. Here are some tips on improving the handling and powerband of the YZs.

Best Value Mods

Engine: Boyesen reeds, head mod
Suspension: DeVol linkage

Shock Linkage

DeVol Engineering has developed a rear suspension linkage kit. This kit improves the rear suspension by eliminating the mid-speed damping spiking causes when going in and out of turns. DeVol changed the linkage ratio curve to be more linear. This reduces the shock shaft speed into a range where the stock shock can be adjusted to handle the braking

and acceleration bumps that lurk in the bends of a race course!

Intake and Carb

The best products for better engine performance are the Boyesen Superbowl and RAD Valve. The original reed valve peaks and starts to flutter at only about 7,000 rpm. The RAD Valve has a wider flow-range so it extends the top end. The new float bowl design prevents the fuel from foaming and starving the engine.

Cylinder and Head Mods

The port timing of the original cylinder makes the powerband come on abruptly and fall flat early. Careful use of epoxy and a grinding tool could transform the cylinder into a wide, stronger pulling engine, with more top-end potential than any of the other bikes. An easy way to extract more top-end from the YZ250 is to grind round the lower side of the oval exhaust port outlet. This will reduce the exhaust gas velocity and improve flow at high rpm. Regarding the porting, the best mod for gaining top end is to raise the sub-exhaust ports to 38mm, measured from the top of the cylinder. The squish velocity rating of the stock head is very high, too high for premium-unleaded fuel. The stock engine detonates in the midrange due to the high compression ratio and squish velocity. The solution is to narrow

On the 1987-1994 model YZ250s, the center reed stops partially blocked the rear boost port in the cylinder. This is a mod for the stock reeds. Boyesen Dual-Stage reeds worked much better and that kit eliminated the reed stops altogether.

This is an aftermarket crankcase breather filter fitted to the YZ400.

the cylinder head's squish band 9mm, measured from one side of the chamber.

Ignition timing

Set the ignition timing to .8mm BTDC. This will eliminate any chance of pinging but unfortunately reduces the midrange hit in the powerband.

Cylinder and Head Mods 1996

The 1996 model cylinder and head have less transfer time area than the previous models. You can adjust the ports to the same specs as the earlier models; by raising the transfer ports 1mm. The cylinder head can be turned-down .020 inch or .5mm on the face.

Power Valve Mod for WR250

Many riders complain that the powerband on the WR is difficult to ride on slippery off-cambers because the power "hits" too hard. Part of the reason is that the power valve snaps open in a narrow rpm band. The power valve timing can be easily changed using a file. To mellow the WR's powerband, you need to file open the sub-exhaust ports, on the power valve. This will enable those ports to open sooner and slowly bleed-off some of the combustion pressure before the big exhaust port opens. This is the same principle that the 1995 YZ YPVS is based on.

Carb Jetting

The carb jetting for the Mikuni was too lean. The needle and main jet can be richened to a #59 needle and a 400 main jet. This makes the engine rev higher with more power. The Keihin carb used on the 1995 and later models is jetted very close and only needs changes to suit local conditions.

Reeds

The next time you remove the cylinder from your YZ or WR, turn it upside down and look up the rear crankcase boost port. You'll notice that the reed stop plates block the upper and lower ports. Install a set of Boyesen reeds because they don't require the use of the reed stop plates and that will enable the boost ports to flow as they were intended to.

Clutch Mods

You can make the clutch easier to pull by rounding the edge on the actuating lever. Oil circulation holes can be drilled in each female spline on the clutch hub. I recommend using Cratex rubberized abrasives and an electric drill, to polish the splines on the clutch hub. This will make the clutch plates react quicker without generating excess friction. The 1994 Yamaha *Wrench Report* recommends replacing the thrust washer that fits between the crankcase

and the clutch basket with part No. 2K7-16154-00-00. This thrust washer is 1mm thinner and will improve the leverage at the handlebar.

Power Valve Governor

In 1994, Yamaha switched to a five-ball ramp from a four-ball ramp in the power valve governor mechanism. This mechanism is located under the right-side engine cover. Yamaha recommends switching to the old four-ball ramp because the extra 5th ball makes the power valve open too soon. This effect is beneficial to enduro riders but motocross riders will notice that the engine is sluggish when shifting from third to fourth gear on uphills. The balls are the same dimension for 1990–94, so all you need to change is the ramp and discard one of the ball bearings. The Yamaha part No. is 5X5-11911-01-00 (Retainer).

YZR Long-Rod Kit

Yamaha markets a kit that includes a longer connecting rod, a spacer plate for the cylinder, and longer power valve linkage. The long rod yields benefits for engines designed for high rpm. With a longer connecting rod, the piston will accelerate quicker from BDC, causing the reeds to open further. The rod spends more time at TDC, which enables the flame front to spread across the chamber before the piston moves on the down stroke. The spacer plate raises the cylinder to lower the primary compression ratio (increase in the volume of the crankcase) and positions the cylinder for the proper port timing. This kit is intended for expert level motocross and DTX racing. This mod works well with other components such as aggressive porting, 39.5mm carb, and a high-revving pipe.

1991-92 YAMAHA YZ250

Flaws: forks rebound fast, rear end kicks, engine pings and detonates

Fixes: replace fork bushings, install DeVol linkage, richen jetting and modify cylinder head

These models don't handle as well as the next generation of YZs but they had good engines with strong low-end power. These bikes are an excellent second-hand bike and can be bought for bargain prices.

The WR250 used engine designs that were a generation behind the YZs (until 1994). Many of the mods and accessory parts recommended for the YZ250 will work well on the WR250.

Best Value Mods

Engine: Boyesen RAD valve
Suspension: stiffer fork springs

Exhaust System

The stock exhaust system doesn't work very well. Pro Circuit makes an excellent pipe and silencer for this bike that improves the power all throughout the rev range.

Intake System

Replace the stock reeds with Boyesen dual-stage reeds and discard the stock reed stops. The reed stops block the rear boost ports.

Forks

Change to a set of .41-kilogram Eibach forks springs. If the forks rebound too fast and make a clanking noise, then the piston rod bushings are worn out. That is a common problem. The oil bypasses the rebound piston and flows past the bushing, thereby eliminating most of the damping effect. The bushings must be replaced as a set and they are available from aftermarket companies such as Pro-Action, Race Tech, and Pro-Circuit.

Rear Suspension

DeVol makes a linkage kit for this bike that will make the older YZs handle almost as well as the 1996 YZ. The rear shock should be revalved in conjunction with the DeVol linkage kit. Check the chrome finish on the shock shaft because they are prone to peeling. Check the bottom of the shock linkage because the links hang so low on a YZ, and they are prone to cracking when the bike is bottomed out.

Cylinder Head Mod

The squish band of the cylinder head is too wide and causes the engine to ping in the midrange. Using a lathe, narrow the squish band to a width of 9mms, measured from one side of the chamber. This mod also helps top-end power and makes it possible for the engine to burn super unleaded premium fuel.

Power Valve Problems

The power valve has a stop-tab on the left side that controls the full open and closed positions of the power valve. The power valve is made of aluminum and the stop plate is made of steel. The aluminum tab wears, allowing the power valve to rotate open and closed too far. When the valve closes too far it contacts the piston and could cause the piston rings to break. Inspect the tab of the power valve; if it has worn more than 1mm replace it.

Sleeve Nut

The aluminum sleeve nut that retains the top tapered bearing on to the steering stem tends to seize to either the stem or the top clamp. Remove the sleeve nut and apply anti-seize or moly paste to the inside and outside of the nut. If the nut is seized on your bike, the best way to remove it is to apply heat with a propane torch and spray penetrating oil on the nut. Caution: Never spray the penetrating oil at the torch because it is a flammable liquid.

1985-90 YAMAHA YZ250

Flaws: rod breakage, shift centering gets loose
Fixes: monitor rod clearance, epoxy pin

Yamaha has always had a great 250. Every year the development team focuses their attention on making the bike perform better and last longer. Overall, the YZs are durable bikes. The following is a list of some areas to pay careful attention to.

Best Value Mods

Engine: Boyesen boost ports, Boyesen reeds
Suspension: Emulator Valve, chain buffer

Crankshaft Connecting Rods

Before 1990, the YZ250 had a 130mm-long connecting rod that was prone to breaking 10mm below the small end. This happens when the connecting rod's side clearance is allowed to wear past the manufacturer's service limit. In 1990, Yamaha shortened the rod to 125mm and that fixed the problem. Unfortunately, you can't interchange the rods. Just monitor the rod's side clearance and replace it when it becomes worn.

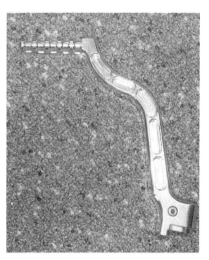

Pro-Tech makes billet kick-start levers for the YZ400/426.

Boyesen Ports

On the 1985–90 models, there is only one port linking the intake to the transfer ports. On these models, drill an additional hole (1/2 inch diameter) on the opposite side of the existing hole and install Boyesen reeds. The midrange power will be greatly improved.

Shift Centering Pin

On the right side of the crankcase, behind the shift lever, there is a steel pin that is used as a pivot for the shift-shaft spring. The fit of the pin in the cases is loose, and they can fall out, causing the shift lever to flop around. The best fix for this problem is to smear a dab of epoxy on the pin to hold it into the case. Be sure to clean the surfaces first or the epoxy won't adhere.

Noisy Chain Buffers

The chain buffer blocks on the 1988 YZs were made of a hard, durable material. Unfortunately, the chain makes a horrible slapping noise when it hits the buffer block. Switch to the block from the 1989 model. It is made from a softer material.

Clutches

The 1988 YZ had an inferior clutch pressure plate design. Switch to the 1989 part. It has stronger ribs on the backside. The later part makes it easier to adjust the clutch to prevent dragging and slipping. Stiffer clutch springs will also help.

This is a view of the fuel injection components for the Optimum GP Control kit for the YZ400/426.

Forks

The best mod for the damper rod forks (before 1989) is a Race Tech Emulator Valve.

Rear Shock

In the mid-1980s YZ250s used a component called a B.A.S.S. system. That device was activated by the foot brake through a cable. The cable operated the compression valve of the rear shock. It was designed to adjust the shock damping when riding through whooped-out straights while dragging the rear brake. The B.A.S.S. system required constant adjusting, cleaning, and servicing, and the cable adjuster was prone to corrosion failure. Most suspension technicians disable the B.A.S.S. system when servicing these shocks. Another characteristic problem with the YZ shocks is shock-shaft corrosion. This problem is aggravated by lack of oil-changing service. The shaft starts to turn blue and the chrome peels off the shaft, eventually causing seal failure. Change your shock oil often.

Transmission Problems

Put your YZ up on a stand. With the engine off and the trans in neutral, try to rotate the rear wheel. If it is very difficult and there is a lot of drag, it could be a sign that the bearing that supports the left side of the clutch shaft could be working its way out of the crankcases and rubbing up against second-gear drive. Eventually, the bronze bushing inside the gear will seize to the shaft. Whenever you have the engine apart for new bearings, replace the left-side clutch-shaft bearing and use a sharp drift-rod to stake it to the cases. This will prevent it from sliding out toward the gear.

Electrical Problems

The biggest cause of hard starting is a poor ground at the secondary coil (top coil under fuel tank). Remove the coil and file the frame tabs where the coil mounts. Another common problem is high resistance in the generating coils (coils behind flywheel). The coils can be repaired for half the price of a new stator plate assembly.

1993-2000 YAMAHA YZ80

Flaws: poor low-end power, non-adjustable forks
Fixes: cylinder and head mods, adjustable base valve

Although the YZ80 is a good bike for expert mini riders due to an abundance of high-rpm power and good suspension, it has too little low-end and midrange for most riders. The problem is a combination of radical port timing and high gearing. Like most of the minis, the YZ doesn't have the quick response to keep up with the RMs out of turns.

Best Value Mods

Engine: cylinder and head mods
Suspension: base valve kit

Cylinder Mods

Here is a way to get more midrange from the YZ80. Turn down the base of the cylinder .028 inch or .7mm and remove the same amount from the squish band of the cylinder head. This retards the port timing and reduces the port duration, plus increases the compression ratio.

Intake

Install a set of Boyesen dual-stage reeds.

Gearing

The stock gearing is too high and should be changed to 12/52, for quicker acceleration. Expert riders prefer changing to a larger carb (28mm flatslide Keihin) for more overrev.

Gearbox

Earlier models had problems with wear on the gear teeth of second gear. Yamaha has since improved the gear and pulled all the old parts from stock. If you ever have to split the cases for engine rebuilding, check the gear teeth for wear. The wear pattern looks like corrosion. Replace the worn gear and the corresponding gear.

Clutch

Yamaha recommends switching to stiffer clutch springs. The part is No. 90501-216A6.

Forks

The forks can be improved greatly by installing an adjustable base valve kit. This makes the forks plusher. There are two options for base valves: 1992 YZ125 OEM base valve or a tuned valve from Pro-Racing or Race Tech. The stock fork and shock springs are too soft for most riders. The way to check the spring rate is to set the race sag to 75mm in the rear and check the unladen sag (bike's own weight without rider). If the unladen sag is under 10mm, then you need to install a stiffer shock spring. The front fork sag should be between 20 and 30mm. If the forks sag more than 30mm then you need to install stiffer springs.

1993-2000 YAMAHA YZ100 CONVERSION

If you want to convert a YZ80 into a big wheel 100, it is possible with a combination of aftermarket engine and OEM parts.

Engine Mods

There are several different kits on the market with displacement sizes suited to different racing associations. The most deluxe kit is the one from R&D Racing. It's 112cc and includes total engine mods and comes with a pipe and carb. Expect to spend about $1,800.

There are less expensive 100cc kits, made by Wiseco and L.A. Sleeve. Those kits require the cylinder to be bored, ported, and electroplated. Stock gaskets can be used but the head must be enlarged to accept the 52mm piston. The crankcases must also be

This is a close-up view of the handlebar switch for the Optimum GP Control system for the YZ400.

modified because the piston skirt contacts the exhaust side of the cases. It's possible to just mask off the crankshaft and grind the minor areas of the cases away for piston clearance. Other additions to the 100cc conversion include a flat-slide Keihin 28mm carb and an R&D pipe and silencer.

Chassis and Suspension

Yamaha's accessory divisions YZR offers an extended swingarm and wheel kits that include rims and spokes. In order for the YZ to be legal for racing in the super-mini class, it needs a longer wheelbase and bigger wheels. Normally when you switch to a longer swing arm you'll need to switch to stiffer springs front and rear.

1998-99 YZ400

Flaws: too-lean jetting
Fixes: carb jetting

Best Value Mod

Engine: Hot Start Button, jetting
Suspension: springs

The best-selling MX bike has had thousands of magazine pages written about every aspect of maintenance and performance. With the huge range of accessories available, you can get carried away buying things for this bike. So rather than focus on particular accessories, let's look at the basics affecting reliability.

Carb Jetting

The stock jetting on the 1998 was a bit lean, especially for loamy terrain and cold climates. Good baseline settings are a 50 pilot jet, a 185 main jet, and adjust the air and fuel screw to tune it in. The accelerator pump needs periodic cleaning; dirt and water seep past the rubber boot and slow down the action of the pump. For more information about this high maintenance carb, look to the chapter on carbs.

Hot Start Button

The Hot Start Button from Terry Products is a handlebar control for the carb's air by-pass system. The Hot Start Button makes it easier to restart the bike in a hurry, and can be used to lean the jetting. The Button has a wide range of incremental movement. If you're riding at a steadily increasing altitude, you could adjust the carb jetting for the less dense air by cracking the Button open.

Flywheel Weight

In rocky or slippery terrain, the YZ may be prone to stalling or too quick wheel spin. You can buy flywheel weight that bolts on to the perimeter of the stock flywheel.

Clutch Breakage

Riders with tendencies to fan the clutch frequently should change the aluminum clutch plates for steel ones. If the plates shatter, the debris tends to flow to the oil sump screen causing it to clog and reduce lubrication.

Crankcase Breather

The crankcase vent hose exits from the top of the engine. That hose needs a filter at the end to reduce the dust that collects in the hose. K&N make a stainless steel filter, marketed mainly for sport riders. Look to a road bike shop for the crankcase vent filters.

Big Bore Kit

The 1998 and 1999 YZ400 cylinders can be overbored 2mm to 94mm for a total displacement of 420cc. The 2000 YZ426 cylinder casting is much thicker than the earlier models. Wiseco makes a 97mm piston kit for the YZ426 that boosts the displacement to 450cc. It is possible to install the 2000 cylinder on the previous models of YZ400,

but in order to use the Wiseco 97mm piston, you have to install a rod kit from a YZ426 because the small end pin is larger. The Wiseco 97mm kit is part No. 4698P8. Cometic makes a corresponding gasket kit.

Pistons

Wiseco makes the oversize piston kits in the stock and high compression models. The sizes range from 94 to 97. The compression ratios are 12.5:1 (part No. 4649) and 13.5:1 (part No. 4650).

Higher compression pistons are a good product for high-altitude correction, and give more low- to midrange torque. The 13.5:1 pistons perform best using VP C-18 fuel. That fuel is blended for pro-stock drag racing and improves the throttle response.

Aftermarket Engine Management Kits

Optimum Power Technologies offers an engine management solution for YZ400/26. This system includes a generator, DC power system, complete ignition system, throttle body, and fuel pump. The unit features total control of the ignition and fuel system via a handlebar switch.

A laptop or PDA can be used to diagnose the system and make programming changes. You can even download ignition and fuel maps from Optimum's Web site.

That way you can customize the fuel and ignition systems to suit a variety of aftermarket components or displacement sizes.

Gearing

Most riders increase the size of the rear sprocket to as many as 54 teeth, depending on the local riding conditions.

Suspension

Overall, the shock spring and valving are stiff and the forks are soft. This bike needs balanced springs front to back. A simple rule of thumb is: Riders with geared weight under 165 pounds need softer fork springs and riders with geared weight over 175 pounds need stiffer fork springs and revalving.

For heavier riders the bike may seem to ride pitched forward. If the front race sag is 2 inches or greater, then the springs are either sacked out or too soft for your weight.

United States

AC Racing
12145 Slauson Ave. • Santa Fe Springs, CA 90670
310-945-2591
Races stands, skid plates, specialty parts for KTM 50 SXR, and more.

Acerbis USA
9402 Wheatlands Ct, #A • Santee, CA 92701
Plastic handguards, SIDI boot distributors, more.

Action Sports
7170 Hwy 10-114 • Menasha, WI 54952
920-996-9480 • www.actionsports-usa.com
Jim Leach runs a full service dirt bike shop and used bike mecca.

Advanced Sleeve Corp.
9348 Mercantile Dr. • Mentor, OH 44060
440-354-3440
Manufacturer of OEM and aftermarket cylinder sleeves for two- and four-stroke engines.

Aktive Reeds
1862-B Tollgate Rd. • Palm, PA 18070
215-541-0430 • www.aktive.com
Manufacturer of aftermarket reed petals.

A-Loop Racing
3911 Norwood Dr. • Littleton, CO 80125
303-791-3104 • www.a-loop.com
Manufacturer and distributor of weld-on flywheel weights, lighting kits, off-road accessories, XR fuel tanks, and freestyle mx accessories.

American Motorcycle Institute
800-881-2264 • www.amiwrench.com
A training school for motorcycle mechanics.

Andrews Motorsports
251 Goodman Rd. • Concord, NC 28027
704-782-6134
Curt Andrews is an engine and suspension tuning specialist. His brother, Mike, runs a series of off-road riding schools.

Applied Racing Products
1115 Industrial Ave. • Escondido, CA 92029
760-743-8190 • www.appliedracing.com
Manufacturer of specialty hard parts such as clamps for Answer Prolite handle bars, aluminum and titanium bolts, and trick parts for 50cc MX bikes.

Aircone, Inc.
240 Elliott Rd. • Henderson, NV 89015
702-566-1077
Manufacturer of exhaust system parts. Will roll expansion chamber cones based on TSR layout specs.

Atomic 22
6821 Fleur Dr. • Des Moines, IA 50315
515-285-4332 • www.atomic-22.com
Manufacturers of specialty parts for motorcycles.

Baja Designs
7558 Trade St. • San Diego, CA 92121
800-422-5292 • www.bajadesigns.com
Dual sport conversion kits.

Barr's Kaw/KTM
1701 S. Stoughton Rd. • Madison, WI. 53716
608-222-6800
A Kaw/KTM dealer in south central Wisconsin.

BBR Motorsports
www.bbrmotorsports.com
Manufacturer of aftermarket aluminum frame kits for four-stroke dirt bikes.

Barnett
2238 Palma Dr. • Ventura, CA 93003-5733
805-642-9435 • www.barnettclutches.com
Manufacturer/distributor of aftermarket clutch parts.

Berg Racing
714-754-1918
CNC aluminum parts and carbon fiber guards for dirt bikes.

Big Gun
909-948-7029 • www.biggunexhaust.com
Tuned exhaust systems for 4-stroke dirt bikes.

Bill's Pipes
Norco, CA • 909-371-1329
Exhaust system manufacturer.

Boyesen Engineering
8 Rhoades Rd. • Lenhartsville, PA 19534
800-441-1177 • www.boyesen.com
A manufacturer of reed valves, reed petals, magneto covers, float bowls, and Twin-Air filters.

Boyesen Racing
7699 Hilltop • New Tripoli, PA 18066
610-298-3383
The performance division of Boyesen, Wes Gilbert builds custom racing engines for bike and karts.

Brush Research
213-261-2193
The manufacturer and distributor for Flex-Hones. A product used for cylinder bore deglazing.

Buchanan Spoke & Rim
805 W. 8th St. • Azusa, CA 91702
626-969-4655
Manufacturer of spokes and rims.

Bumpsticks
2450 Johnson Rd. • Huntington, MD 20639
410-535-0625
Repair and modification of engine and suspension components for dirt bikes.

CC Specialty
6035 CC Lane • Lawrenceburg, TN 38464
800-762-6995
Distributes tools for modifying four-stroke cylinder heads and two-stroke cylinders.

Carb Parts Warehouse
7777 Wall St. • Valley View, OH 44125
440-524-1599 • www.carbparts.com
Mail-order distributor of Mikuni and Kehin carburetors and parts. Specializes in pre-jetted oversized carbs for dirt bikes.

Carbontech
61 Capay Circle • San Francisco, CA 94080
800-776-4089 • www.carbontech.com
Manufacturer of carbon fiber reed petals and exhaust silencers.

CEET
1220 Liberty Way • Vista, CA 92803
619-599-0115
Manufacturer of seat covers, seat foam, and more.

Cernic Cycle
500 Cooper Ave. • Johnstown, PA 15906
814-539-4114 or 800-CERNIC5
Mail-order retailer of Honda and Suzuki OEM parts. Also sells engines, salvage parts, and riding gear.

Chaparral
555 S. H St. • San Bernadino, CA 92410
909-884-3183
Mail-order company offering discounts on name brand accessories and aftermarket products.

Clark Manufacturing
29032 S. Salo Rd. • Mulino, OR 97042
503-829-2156
Aftermarket manufacturer of fuel tanks for dirt bikes.

Cometic Gasket
8090 Auburn Rd. • Concord, OH 44077
440-345-0777 • www.cometic.com
Manufacturer of aftermarket engine gasket kits. Also offers small runs of custom gaskets.

Crank Works
5345 Kyrene Rd. Ste. 32 • Tempe, AZ 85283
www.crankworks.com
Crankshaft rebuilding and stroking.

CRE Imports
54 Spectacle Pond Terr.
E. Wareham, MA 02538
508-295-0812 • www.elineaccessories.com
Distributor of Italian-made accessories for Honda enduro bikes. Lighting kits, exhaust systems, and big-bore kits for Hondas.

Cycle Gear
303 43rd St. • Richmond, CA 94805
510-412-4327
Mail-order company; aftermarket products.

Cycle Suspension Service
12 Davidson Rd. • Colchester, CT 06415
860-537-4306
Manufacturer of aftermarket suspension accessories.

DeVol Racing
741-D Stevenson • Enumclaw, WA 98022
360-825-2106
Manufacturer of frame guards, glide plates, radiator guards.

DG Specialty
1230 La Loma Cir. • Anaheim, CA 92806
Manufacturer of aftermarket performance parts. Offers hop-up parts for vintage MX bikes.

DGY Racing
216 Ogden Ave. • Downers Grove, IL 60515
630-971-2602
A multi-franchise dealer offering custom order dirt bikes by mail.

DRN
Dirt Rider.Net • www.dirtrider.net
The largest most organized web site for information about dirt bikes.

Dirt Cycles Salvage
3A Landing Lane • Hopedale, MA 01747
508-478-5700
Salvage parts for dirt bikes, available by mail.

DSP
714-985-0342 • www.dspracing.com
Carbon fiber and titanium parts.

Dyno Port
1896 Townline Rd. • Union Springs, NY 13160
315-258-5618
Manufacturer of aftermarket exhaust systems. Also offers engine performance services.

E&K Cycle Sales
205 E. Jefferson • Sweet Springs, MO 65351
816-335-4481
Salvage and new parts for Hodaka motorcycles.

Emig Racing
203 Walnut • Grain Valley, MO 64029
816-847-1100
Gary Emig performs high quality mods on dirt bikes, and CNC machines triple clamps and other aftermarket billet parts.

Enduro Experts
459-J Pole Bridge Rd. • Cardiff, NJ 08232
Experts in the preparation of enduro bikes.

Enzo Racing
17658 San Candelo • Fountain Springs, CA 92708
714-964-8010
Mail-order service and parts for Kayaba suspension.

E-Rider
9396 Wilson Mills Rd. • Chardon, OH 44024
440-286-6273 • www.erider.ws
Specialty manufacturer of KTM hard parts.

FMF
18033 Santa Fe Ave.
Rancho Dominguez, CA 90221-5514
310-631-4363 • www.fmfracing.com
Exhaust systems, reed valves, and suspension components. Mail-order service for two-stroke cylinder porting, Pro-Action suspension franchise.

Factory Connection
10 Crossroads Ind. Pk. • Rochester, NH 03867
603-335-7023 • 800-221-7560
Suspension repair and tuning services for all brands of components.

Factory Direct
1355 Pullman Dr. • El Paso, TX 79936
915-858-3365
www.factorydirectperf.com
Distributor for MSD Ignition products.

Factory Pipe
150 Parducci Rd. • Ukiah, CA 95482
707-463-1322
Manufacturer of aftermarket exhaust systems.

Falicon
1115 Old Coahman Rd • Clearwater, FL 34625
813-797-2468
Repair and stroking of crankshafts.

Forward Motion Racing
www.ericgorr.com
Author Eric Gorr's company, specializing in technical videos, computer design and machining services for motorsports racing engines, cylinder rebuilding and tuning.

Fox Racing
15850 Concord Circle • Morgan Hill, CA 95037
408-776-8800
Off-road riding gear and apparel, videos, more.

Fredette Racing Products
31745 Dixie Highway • Beecher, IL 60401
708-946-0999
Repair and tuning of Kawasaki KDX and KLX.

GPS Racing
20 Main St. • Wannamingo, MN 55983
507-824-3999
Race Tech suspension center.

Graydon Proline
15935 Minnesota • Paramount, CA 90723
(310) 531-7142
Aluminum sub-frames, more.

Great Escape
4507 Ray St. • Crystal Lake, IL
815-459-8111
Tom Zont provides full service and tuning plus OEM KX and RM parts and accessories.

H&H Cycle Center
Rd1 Bx568 • Osceloa Mills, PA 16666
814-339-6424
Repair and machine shop, parts and accessories, for new and vintage motorcycles.

H&H Worldwide • Douglasville, GA 30134
8820 Bright Star • Douglasville, GA 30134
770-920-1371 • www.ktmworld.com
Franchised dealer for European motorcycles. KTM specialists.

Harbor Freight Tools
3491 Mission Oaks Blvd.
Camarillo, CA 93011-6010
Mail-order company specializing in low-cost measuring and machine tools.

Hinson Racing
1630 W. 11th St. Unit E • Upland, CA 91786
909-946-2942 • www.hinsonracing.com
Manufacturer of billet clutch parts.

Ico Racing
504-882-3107
Manufacturer of off-road computers.

IMS
6240 Box Spring Blvd. • Riverside, CA 92507
909-653-7720 • www.Imsproducts.com
Off-road accessories.

JMS
114 N. Arch St. • New Carlisle, IN 46552
219-654-8589
A complete dirt bike tuning and rebuilding shop. Dyno testing facilities.

JN Innovations
2415 Radley Ct. #3 • Hayward, CA 94545
510-783-5332
Suspension service.

JT Motorsports
5708 Urbana Pike • Frederick, MD 21701
301-846-4318
Kawasaki, KTM, and Suzuki dealer located in the Baltimore area.

Japan Motors
741 Yarmouth Rd. • Hyannis, MA 02601
508-778-7211
Specialists in big bore kits for two-stroke dirt bikes.

Klotz
P.O. Box 11343 • Fort Wayne, IN 46857
800-242-0489
A refiner of performance fuels and lubricants.

Kowa Tools
13939 Equitable Rd. • Cerritos, CA 90703
562-407-5860 • www.kowatools.com
The best selection of special tools In the motorcycle Industry.

Krause Racing
370 S. Stern Ave. • St. Charles, IL 60174
630-513-1000
www.sidewindersprockets.com
Sidewinder drive products for dirt bikes.

Kustom Kraft
886 Bluff City Blvd. • Elgin, IL 60120
847-697-4343
Cylinder sleeve repair and installation.

L.A. Sleeve
12051 Rivera Rd. • Los Angeles, CA 90670
310-945-7578
A manufacturer and distributor of cylinder sleeves.

LSD Racing
3671 Ben Hill Rd. • Douglasville, GA 30134
770-920-2497
Larry Dukes provides full service and tuning for dirt bikes.

Langcourt Ltd.
2080 McMillen • Auburn, AL 36830
334-887-9633
Repair services for electroplated cylinders.

Lightweight Products
144 North Alta Vista Ave. • Monrovia, CA 91016
818-357-2722
Titanium and aluminum fasteners and axles.

Lockhart Racing
991 Calle Negocio • San Clemente, CA 92672
714-498-9090
Oil coolers and carrier racks for dual-sport bikes.

MCC. Inc.
518 W. St. Charles Rd. • Villa Park, IL 60181
630-782-2010
Chicago area's finest European motorcycle shop.

MMF Racing
12145 Slauson Ave.
Santa Fe Springs, CA 90670
310-693-9096
A manufacturer of aluminum guards for dirt bikes.

MT Racing
7505 Jurupa Ave. Suite C • Riverside, CA 92504
909-353-1253
Importers of Vortex Ignition systems.

MX Tech
4136 W. 6940 N. Rd. • Bourbonnais, IL 60914
815-936-6277 • www.mx-tech.com
A suspension repair and tuning specialist.

Mansson Technologies
Pleasanton, CA • 510-426-1040
Titanium bolts, nuts, washers, and axles.

Megacycle Cams
90 Mitchell Rd. • San Rafael, CA 94903
415-472-3195
Manufacturer of camshafts.

Michael's Cycles
2680 S. Carson Blvd. • Carson City, NV 89701
775-883-6111
A big dirt bike shop in northern Nevada.

Mikuni
8910 Mikuni Ave. • Northridge, CA 91324-3496
West Coast distributor of Mikuni carbs and parts.

Millenium Technologies
1404 Pilgrim Rd. • Plymouth, WI 53073
920-893-5595 • www.mt-llc.com
Cylinder rebuilding with electroplating.

Mossbarger Racing
800-891-1615 • www.mossbargerracing.com
A manufacturer of aftermarket reed valves.

Motion Pro
119 Independence Drive • Menlo Park, CA 94025
415-329-0427 • www.motionpro.com
Manufacturer of special tools for engine repair.

Moto Pro
13605 178th Ave. N.E.
Redmond, WA 98052-2161
800-277-5089
A Race-Tech franchise specializing in enduro bikes.

Motorcycle Mechanics Institute
2844 W. Deer Valley Rd. • Phoenix, AZ 85027
800-528-7995
Technical school that teaches motorcycle repair.

Motorwerks
128 E. Woodruff • Port Washington, WI 53074
414-284-9661
Custom pipe builder.

Moto Worx
74 Garden St. • Feeding Hills, MA 01030
413-786-0141
Specialist in carb modifications.

Mud Creek Engineering
2653 W. Lambs Rd. • Mason, MI 48854
517-676-9534 • hilbert@nscl.nscl.msu.edu
Manufacturer of the RCE crank rebuilding tool referenced In the crankshaft rebuilding chapter.

MX South
561-743-3288 • www.mxsouth.com
Internet mail-order store for motorcycle accessories.

Myler's
8414 McDowell Ct. • West Jordan, UT 84088
800-367-7699
Aluminum radiator repair.

NCY
1315 Las Villas Way • Escondido, CA 92606
619-432-9501
Specializes in Yamaha YZ dirt bikes.

NIKS
12051 Rivera Rd. • Santa Fe Springs, CA 90670
800-487-6457 • www.niksracing.com
NIKS brand connecting rod kits, PRO-X piston kits.

Noleen Racing
16276 Koala Rd. • Adelanto, CA 92301
619-246-5000
Specializing in the tuning of Yamaha YZ dirt bikes.

Northwest Sleeve, Inc.
150-B NE Victory • Gresham, OR 97030
503-666-8430 • www.nwsleeve.com
Repair service for resleeving cylinders.

Onology Engineering Inc.
7917 Silverton Ave. • San Diego, CA 92126
619-578-4688
Manufacturers of aftermarket electrical parts.

Optimum Power Technology
3117 Washington Pike
Bridgeville, PA 15017-1496
412-257-9070 • www.optimum-power.com
Engine management systems for motorcycles.

PC-1 Racing
Box 730 • Orange, CA 92666
Manufacturers of Filter Skins air filter protectors, Plastic Renew, and Pro Vent carb vent kits.

PPS
4065 Lapalma Unit G • Anaheim, CA 92807
714-630-4777
Suspension tuning. Imports Marzocci and Ohlins.

PVL Ignitions
1115 Milan Ave. • Amherst, OH 44001
440-988-4474
Manufacturer of electrical parts like complete ignition systems, internal and external rotor flywheels. www.pentonimports.com

PAX Racing
9724 Nagle Ave. • Arleta, CA 91331
818-897-0373
An aftermarket accessory stockist for 50cc, 60cc, and 80cc bikes.

Penske Racing
Box 301 • Reading, PA 19603
610-375-6180
Manufacturer of shock absorbers.

Performance Engineering
1333 Pine Ave. Suite B • Orlando, FL 32824
407-856-8545 • www.peracing.com
Specializing in engine and suspension tuning, plus aftermarket accessories.

Perma-Flex
614-252-8034
Makes blue silicon molding for port modeling.

Powermist
67 Stickles Pond Rd. • Newton, NJ 07860
201-383-1061
Refiner of specialty fuels for two-stroke racing engines.

Poweroll Inc.
Box 920 • Redmond, OR 97756
541-923-1290
Manufacturer and rebuilder of four-stroke performance kits.

Pro-Action
3611 8th Ave. • Beaver Falls, PA 15010
724-846-9055 • www.pro-action.com
Specialists in suspension repair and tuning services. Over 40 franchises worldwide.

Pro Circuit
2771 Wardlow • Corona, CA 92882
909-738-8050 • www.procircuit.com
Exhaust systems, engine and suspension tuning.

Pro Concept
286 S. Overlook Dr. • San Ramon, CA 94583
510-735-8258
Manufacturer of the Magnum Bottoming System.

Pro Design
11611 Salinaz #C
Garden Grove, CA 92643
714-534-0620
Cylinder heads with interchangeable chambers.

Pro Pilot
25 Squire Terrace • Colts Neck, NJ 07722
732-928-7800 • www.propilotracing.com
An accessory and service shop devoted to dirt bikers.

Pro Source
4 Bonnie Lane • Yorkville, IL 60560
630-553-7002
Yamaha dealer specializing in used and new dirt bikes.

Pro Spec
411 Riverview Dr. • Walnutport, PA 15088
610-760-9568
Aktive reeds; engine and suspension tuning.

ProTec
888-698-8990 • www.protecperformance.com
Speciality parts for dirt bikes.

R&D Racing
11419 Bombardier Ave. • Norwalk, CA 90650
310-864-8218
Exhaust systems, engine and suspension tuning.

RPM
24 Woodland Heights • Wales, MA 01081
413-245-3830
Bearing race repair service.

RPM Motor Sports
1011 San Bernadino Rd. • Covina, CA 91722
626-967-3052
Rick Petersen specializes in big bore engines using crank stroking and overbored plated cylinders.

Race Tech
3227 Producer Way • Pomona, CA 91768
909-594-7755 • www.race-tech.com
Manufacturer of suspension parts and accessories. Has more than 50 franchised service shops in North America.

Race Tools
1356 Buffalo Rd. • Rochester, NY 14624
716-529-3750
Manufacturer of special tools for suspension servicing and tuning.

Radiator Works
17635 Arrow Blvd. • Fontana, CA 92335
800-430-7234
Radiator repair service by mail.

Rev Motorcycles
335 Savannah Dr. • Canton, MI 48187
253-540-1859 • www.revmotorcycles.com
A new American made motorcycle and accessory company. Manufacturer of RCE crank jig.

Ricky Stator
10734 Kenney St. #D • Santee, CA 92071
619-449-3905 • www.rickystator.com
Stator plate rebuilders, mail-order service.

Rick Peterson Motor Sports
1011 San Bernardino Rd. • Covina, CA 91722
818-967-3052
A specialist in over-boring cylinders and
stroking cranks for late model dirt bikes.

Ritter Cycle Racing
11202 Ellis Rd. • St. Jacob, IL 62281
618-644-3211
Engine rebuilding services.

Rocket Rex Racing
10001 Choiceana Ave. • Heperia, CA 92345
619-949-4193
Performance tuning services.

Rossini Racing Products
RD#1 Box 106A • Washington, NJ 07882
908-454-8730
Engine and suspension tuning, large accessory
store for dirt bikes.

SRC
Petersburg, KY
502-732-8675 • www.srcinc.net
Scott and Wade Summers design and
manufacture Innovation products for Honda XRs.

Scott's Performance
2625 Honolulu Ave. • Montrose, CA 91020
818-248-2453 • www.scottsperformance.com
High-performance services for dirt
bike engine and suspension components.
Manufacturer of special tools for cartridge fork
repair. Importer of UNIC steering dampers.

Service Honda
5634 Hohman Ave. • Hammond, IN 46520
219-932-3588 • www.servicehonda.com
Honda mail-order parts and bikes specialists.
Builder of the CR500AF on the cover of this
book.

Shock Therapy
227 N. Brea Blvd. • Brea, CA 92621
714-255-9485
Suspension repair company.

Shoup Enterprises
3172 Glendam Dr. • Grand Junction, CO 81504
970-434-0906
Specialists in rewinding Mitsubishi stator coils.

Sloan's Honda Yamaha
2233 NW Broad St. • Murfreesboro, TN
37129
800-342-1681 ext. 22
A franchised Yamaha and Honda
dealer with a racing support program that
includes discounts on parts,
engine rebuilding, and suspension tuning
services. Ask for Jerry Link.

SoCal/DeCal
1820 Hoffman Ct. • Sycamore, IL 60178
815-899-2349 • www.socaldecal.com
Custom made graphics for racing vehicles and
transports. SoCal brand of riding gear.

Society of Automotive Engineers (SAE)
400 Commonwealth
Warrendale, PA 15096-0001
724-772-7129 • www.sae.org
Books and research papers on engines.

Spectro
Rt. 7 • Brookfield, CT 06804
800-243-8645
Petroleum refiners, offers products ranging
from suspension to premix oils.

Stator Pros
12 First St. • Bridgewater, MA 02324
508-285-9652
Specialists in the repair of electrical
components.

Steahly Products
9950 SE Bullrun Rd. • Corbett, OR 97019
503-695-2417
800-800-2363 (U.S. & Canada)
Manufacturer of thread-on flywheel weights,
other off-road accessories.

Stoughton's Cycle Ranch
4406 W. Washington St.
Indianapolis, IN 46241
317-247-5323
Mail order accessories from a huge retailer
store featuring AXO, Oakley, Pro-Circuit.

Stroker
760-948-2871 • www.strokerspeed.com
Desert racing legend Larry Roseler offers four-
stroke performance products.

Supertrapp
4540 W. 160th • Cleveland, OH 44135
440-265-8400
A manufacturer of aftermarket exhaust systems
for four-stroke dirt bikes.

Sudco
3014 Tanager Ave. • Commerce, CA 90040
800-998-3529
A distributor for Mikuni and Kehin carbs and
parts.

Superior Sleeving
525 Ash St. • Brockton, MA 02401
508-584-7248 • www.wrightmachine.com
Cylinder sleeving specialists.

Suspension By Jake
1732 Border Ave. • Torrence, CA 90501
310-787-7818
Showa suspension repair and tuning specialist.
Stockist and retailer of Showa replacement
parts.

Swain Tech
35 Amin St. • Scottsville, NY 14546
716-889-2786 • www.swaintech.com
A company that applies performance coatings to
engine parts such as pistons, valves, header
pipes.

TM Motorcycles
8468 Loma Plc. • Upland, CA 91786
909-982-6310 • www.twusa.com
U.S. importers of Italian dirt bikes.

TMR
1155 Aviation Dr. • Lake Havasu, AZ 86404
520-453-5061
Engine & suspension tuning services.

TSR
Bellflower, CA
562-804-2530 • www.tsrsoftware.com
Tom Turner Is a two-stroke tuner who
developed computer programs to aid engine
tuners in developing precise changes in engine
components. All the cylinder and head specs
quoted in this book were developed with TSR
software.

Tech Care
7754 M-59 • Waterford, MI 48327
810-666-4651 • www.tech-care.com
A complete dirt bike shop offering parts,
accessories, and suspension and engine
service.

Tech Products
973-686-0012
Solid foam tire inserts for off-road bikes.

Terry Cable
17376 Eucalyptus St. • Hesperia, CA 92345
760-244-9351 • www.terrycable.com
Manufacturer of products for Kawasaki KX
models. Products such as offset triple clamps,
double-pumper fork kits, and KX60 long fork rods,
as well as cables for all dirt bikes.

Throttle Jockey
4728 E. 100 N. • Kokomo, IN 46902
317-457-5784
A manufacturer of graphics, numbers, and
stickers.

Thumper Racing
3441 US Highway 259 • Marshall, TX 75670
800-259-5186 • www.thumperracing.com
A company that offers complete machining
services for four-stroke dirt bike engines.

Too Tech Racing
19333 Sturgess Dr. • Torrance, CA 90505
310-371-3887
Rick Johnson offers suspension repair and
tuning services.

Torque Center
14666 W. National Ave.
New Berlin, WI 53151
414-786-4420
A large retail and mail-order accessories shop
located near Milwaukee.

Trackside Racing
26480 France Ave. • Elko, MN 55020
612-461-2350
A dirt bike accessory and repair shop that
offers custom pipe-building and tuning services.

TUF Racing
1900 Lincoln Hwy. • Dekalb, IL 60115
815-756-3588 • 800-225-5883 •
www.tufracing.com
A mail-order Kawasaki parts and Moose
Off-Road retailer, UFO and Factory Concepts
graphics specialists.

US Chrome
650 Oak Park Ave. • Fondulac, WI 54936-1536
920-922-5066 • www.uschrome.com
Specializing in the repair of cylinders with
electroplating of nickel composite NICOM.

Ultimate Suspension
317 W. Erie • Spring Valley, IL 61362
815-663-1200
Walt Spayer is a suspension tuner who
specializes in working interactively with racers
on revalving.

UNI Filter
1541 S. Harris Ct. • Anaheim, CA 92806
714-939-6300
Manufacturer of foam air filters.

Upstate Cycle
100 Laurens Rd. • Greenville, SC 29607
864-232-7223
A Husky and ATK shop specializing in
performance mods.

VP Engineering
Des Moines, IA 50322
www.dynomation.com
A manufacturer for Hot Rods connecting rod
kits, Pivot Works linkage rebuild kits, and the
publisher of the Dynomation computer design
programs.

Velo Rossa Engineering
406-3 S. Rockford Dr. • Tempe, AZ 85281
602-397-4735
A manufacturer of special tools such as a
tubing vise that works well for drilling
lubrication holes and ports in pistons.

WER
Box 279-A • Great Meadows, NJ 07838
908-637-6385
A manufacturer of steering dampers, specialists
in suspension revalving for enduro racing.

Wheel Works
12787 Nutwood • Garden Grove, CA 92640
714-530-6681
Specialists in rims, spokes, tires, and bearings.

White Brothers
24845 Corbit Place • Yorba Linda, CA 92687
714-692-3404 • www.whitebros.com
A large scale catalog company specializing in
off-road parts and accessories.

Wiseco
7201 Industrial Pkwy. • Mentor, OH 44060
440-951-6600
A manufacturer of forged piston kits for all
motorsports racing vehicles.

Works Connection
6070 Enterprise Drive
Diamond Springs, CA 95619
530-642-9488 • www.worksconnection.com
Skid plates, frame guards, and more.

Works Performance
21045 Osborne St. • Canoga Park, CA 91304
818-701-1010
Handcrafted shock absorbers.

XR's Only
6944 E. Santa Fe Ave. • Hesperia, CA 92345
619-244-2626
A specialist in parts and accessories for Honda
XR motorcycles.

Z Racing
2350 Orangethorpe • Anaheim, CA 92806
714-449-1374
A specialist in tuning and repair of KTM
motorcycles.

United Kingdom

Apico/Vesty UK
Unit 2c Merrow Business Centre • Merrow Lane
Guildford, Surrey GU4 7WA • 01483-450560
Distributors for a line of titanium bolts, frame
guards, RADZ graphics, and drivetrain kits.

Aptec
Southbrook Road • Gloucester GL4 7DN
01452-300800 • www.poetonaptec.co.uk
Cylinder reconditioning specialists.

B&C Express
Station Rd., Potterhanworth,
Lincoln, LN4 2DX
01522 791369
A parts distributor for many products, including
Moto-Air filters and PJ-1 products.

Bert Harkins Racing
Unit 6, Townsend Centre, Oughton Regis,
Dunstable, Beds. LU5 5JP • 01582-472374
Importer for Acerbis plastic products and Scott
goggles.

Bill Brown
High St. • Whitehaven, Cumbria CA28 7PY
01846-692697
Importer for Maico motorcycles and the
distributor for Wulfsport riding gear.

Bryan Goss
8 Yeo Valley Business Centre • Newton Road
Stoford, Yeovil BA22 9US • 01935-72424
A large scale trade-only parts and accessory
distributor.

CDI's 'R' Us
Frances House, 11-15 Frances Ave.
Wallisdown, Bournemouth, BH11-8NX
01202-576699
Specializing in the diagnostic and repair of
ignition components.

CGH Imports Ltd.
88 Mosley St.
Burton - Upon - Trent, Staffordshire DE14 1DT
01283-500450
Importers for Pro-Circuit & Hinson Racing
products.

Corby Kawasaki
Courier Rd. Phoenix Pkwy. • Corby, Northants
NN17 5BA • 01536-401010
Mail-order Kawasaki parts.

Cradley Kawasaki
St. Annes Rd., Cradley Heath • W. Midlands
01384 633455
Mail-order Kawasaki parts.

CPK Moto
Gladiator Way, Glebe Farm Estates
Rugby, CV21 1PX • 01788 540606
*A distributor for Pirelli tires, Regina chain, and
Vemar helmets.*

Dave Clark Racing
Heath House, New Longton • Lancs. PR4 4YS
01772-612118
Importer of Husaberg motorcycles.

Dep Sport
Buckland Hill • Maidstone, Kent ME16 0SQ
01622-765353
*A manufacturer of exhaust systems, bike
stands, and various hardware for dirt bikes.
Also offers a barrel tuning service.*

Dirt Wheels
London Road (A45) Ryton On Dunsmore
Coventry, West Midlands CV8 3FW
01203-301852
*This company specializes in highly modified
KX60 and 80s. They offer custom frame kits,
suspension service, and engine tuning.*

Edmondson Racing
Acorn Unit 2, Ring Road
Chasetown Industrial Estate
Chasetown, Nr Walsall, Staffs
WS7 8JQ • 0543-677088
*Derrick Edmonson offers his expertise in engine
and suspension tuning, and features a powder
coating service for the frames of dirt bikes.*

Elbe Moto-X
524 Stoney Stanton Rd. • Coventry
01203 687049
*Main stockists for Fox, Renthal, D.I.D., Premier,
Arai. Look for their support vehicle at the
British Championships.*

Electrex
Unit 44 Vanalloys Bus. Pk.
Stoke Row, Oxfordshire, RG9 5QB
01491-682369
Stator coil repair.

Eurotek
Ripon Business Park • 16 Campbell Close
Dailamires Lane
Ripon, North Yorkshire HG4 1QY
01765-608209
Importer for MSR riding gear and a KTM dealer.

Falcon Shocks
Unit 5 Ryans Bus. Pk., Stanford Lane
Wareham, Dorset BH20 4DY
01929-554545
Twin shock manufacturer and repair specialist.

Gas Gas
Stable Lane • Off Leek Road
Buxton, Derbyshire SK17 6UG
01298-25460
The importer for Gas Gas motorcycles.

Husky Sport
35 Longshot Lane Industrial Estate
Bracknell, Berkshire RG12 1RL
01344-56860
The importer for Husqvarna motorcycles.

Julian Dobb's Performance Workshop
01623 451334
*This former pro rider and veteran GP mechanic
offers performance tuning services for engine
and suspension components.*

Kais Motorcycles
Punchbowl Garage, Atherton,
Manchester M46 0LT
01942-896366
*Mail-order parts and Ohlins service. KTM,
Suzuki, Gas Gas, RTX, TM dealer.*

MD Racing
Unit 3-6, 10 Armoury Rd.
Lufton Trading Est., Yeovil
Somerset BA22 8RL • 01935-29646
*Importer for FMF exhaust systems and CEET
covers and graphics.*

Merlin Books
PO Box 153 Horsham, • Sussex RH12 2YG
01403 257626 • merlinbooks@dial.pipex.com
www.merlinbooks.co.uk
*Free catalog featuring technical information
products like books and videos on all
motorcycles.*

MH Racing Services
Unit C1 Fiveways Industrial Estate
Westwells Rd., Hawthorn • Wilts. SN13 9RG
01225-811583 • mhracing@dial.pipex.com
*This former GP mechanic specializes in Ohlins,
WP, Showa, and Kayaba suspension service.
Importer for Messico and Race-Tech. Specialty
services such as barrel tuning, crank and
engine rebuilding/ blueprinting, and titanium
nitriding for fork tubes.*

Mick Berrill
1-3 Henry St. • Northampton, NN1 4JD
01604-36760
Mail-order accessories.

Mito UK
105 North Rd. • Parkstone, Poole
01202 741580
*A specialty product importer for Fresco exhaust
systems, Tecnosel seats and stickers, and Pro-
Grip.*

MXB
Wonastow
West Industrial Estate • Monmouth, Gwent,
South Wales NP5 3AH • 0600-772211
*Specializing in reconditioned salvage parts for
dirt bikes.*

Moto Cross Services
148-150 Preston Road • Yeovil, Somerset
01935-26481
*Stocks of accessories from America and
Europe.*

Motocross World
19 Arches Business Centre
Mill Road, Rugby CV21 1QW • 01788-535207
*This company specializes in Honda CR
performance kits.*

Moto Vision
PO Box 257 • Horsham, West Sussex
01403-257984
*A video chronicle of the sport of motocross and
stockist of the GP yearbook MX The Book.*

Moto-X Rivara
29 Hero Walk • Rochester, Kent ME1 2UZ
01634-839764
*Parts and accessory stockist for auto 50cc
bikes.*

Moto-Extreme
High Street, Warmly • Bristol, Avon
01179-600627
*A stockist of accessories and tools for dirt
bikes.*

Multitek Sports
Lancaster Way, Earls Colne Ind. Pk.
Colchester, Essex CO6 2NS • 01787-223228
Importers for SoCal sports wear.

Off-Road Only
Crossgates, Llandrindod, Wells
Powys. LD1 6RB • 01597-851273
Mail-order accessories.

Phil Ayliff Products LTD.
25 Alliance Close • Nuneaton, CV11 6SD
01203-641247
Trade distributor for Dunlopads.

Plymouth Off-Road
36-38 Molesworth Rd.
Plymouth, Devon, PL1 5NA
01752-606888
*Importer for JD Performance pipes for KTM
LC4. Rally bike preparation specialist. KTM and
TM dealer.*

PM Tuning
7 Beech Grove, Hestbank Lane • Nr. Lancaster
Lancs. LA2 6JH • 0374-160266
*Specialists in cylinder repair and tuning. Also
operates a Dynojet dynomometer testing
center.*

Proline Racing Products
Unit 2 The Cottage
Ullingswick, Hereford HR1 3JG
01432-820179
*The trade distributor for MXA seat covers, seat
foam, and graphics.*

Pro-Racing
15 Gresley Close Drayton Fields
Daventry, Northants NN1 5RZ
01327-301322
*A full service mail-order shop specializing in
engine and suspension tuning services. Also
stocks accessories like lighting kits, factory pipes,
and Denicol petroleum products.*

Pro-Tech
4 Greenslate Ave., Apply Bridge
Nr. Wigan, Lancs. WN6 9LG • 01257-254760
Suspension tuning and repair services.

Putoline
Unit 4, Arena Bus. Pk., Roman Bank
Bourne, Lincs. PE10 9LG • 01778-394909

Race Spec
Yauncos Cottage Tillers Green
Dymock, Gloucestershire GL 18 2AP
01281-890250
*GP racing veteran Dave Watson operates this
shop with services ranging from riding lessons
to suspension service for motorcycles and push
bikes, engine tuning services and accessories,
and the importer for Marzocci forks.*

Ray Hockey Motorcycles
The Old Smithy, Lianvapley
Abergavenny, Gwent NP7 8SN
01600-85535
*A Yamaha dealer and mail-order accessory
specialist.*

Ron Humphreys
12 Eden Way Pages Industrial Park
Leighton Buzzard, Bedfordshire LU7 8TP
01525-384829
*A Honda dealer and mail-order accessory
specialist.*

Rsr Sport
The Mill Queen Street • Barnard Castle
Co. Durham DL12 8EG • 01833-631524
Manufacturers of high-quality riding gear.

RTX
Pinewood Lodge • High St.
South Ferriby, South Humberside DN18 5HY
01469-541983
*Manufacturers of inexpensive dirt bikes and
importers of Russian made motorcycle
products.*

Sammy Miller
Gore Road • New Milton, Hampshire BH25 6TF
01425-616446
*A specialist in vintage racing motorcycles;
bikes, parts, and rebuilding services.*

Serval Marketing
Icon House, Iceni Ct., Ickfield Way,
Letchworth, Herts. SG6 1TN
Trade distributor or AXO and Boyesen products.

Silkolene
Derby Rd., Belper • Derby DE56 1WF
*Manufacturer and distributor of petroleum
products.*

Stan Stephens
6 Portobello Parade
West Kingsdown, Kent TN15 6JP
01474-853540
*An engine rebuilding and tuning specialist that
also imports products for all forms of
motorcycles from trials to sidecar and road
race.*

Sylvesters Yamaha
Spring Lane Mills, Woodhead Rd.
Holmfirth, Huddersfield • 01484-683665
Yamaha dealer offering mail-order parts service.

Tallon Engineering
44 Lynx Trading Estate
Yeovil, Somerset BA20 2NZ • 01935-71508
*A manufacturer of high-quality wheel and drive-
train products.*

Taylor's Racing
23-25 Station Hill Rd.
Chippenham, Wilts. SN15 a1EG
01249-444193
*A motorcycle shop specializing in Suzuki and
Honda parts and Feroce riding gear.*

Terry Rudd Motorcycles
Fen Road Holbeach
Spalding, Lincs. PE12 8QD
01406-422430
Honda dealer specializing in custom-built CRs.

Trick Racing
Toftwood, Stoke, Poges, • Bucks
01753-645087
*Importer for Terry Products triple clamps and
Double-Pumper fork kit.*

Walker Engineering
PO Box 100, Halifax • West Yorkshire
01422-345568
Motorcycle trailers and racks.

Watkins Radiators
80 Woodruff Close, Robinswood
Gloucester GL4 6YN • 01452-527135
Radiator repair services.

West Country Windings
Unit 71, City Bus. Pk.
Somerset Plc., Stoke, Plymouth
01752-560906
Stator plate rewinding service.